ALSO BY THE FALL RIVER HISTORICAL SOCIETY PRESS

American Textile Colossus:
The Story of Fall River, Massachusetts,
its Cotton Manufacturing Industry, and its People
by Jay J. Lambert (2020)

Main Street in the Eighteen Seventies and Eighties &
A Businessman's Reminiscences of Fifty Years
by Thomas Richmond Burrell
(Discourses in History Series, Number 2) (2019)

Granite, Grit, and Grace: An Exploration of the
Fascinating Side Streets of Fall River's History
by William A. Moniz (2017)

Anti-Slavery Days in Fall River and the Underground Railroad
by Edward Stowe Adams
(Discourses in History Series, Number 1) (2017)

Women at Work: an Oral History of Working Class Women
in Fall River, Massachusetts, 1920-1970 (2017)

Parallel Lives:
A Social History of Lizzie A. Borden and Her Fall River
by Michael Martins and Dennis A. Binette (2011)

The Commonwealth of Massachusetts vs. Lizzie A. Borden:
The Knowlton Papers, 1892-1893 (1994)

The Commonwealth of Massachusetts
vs.
Lizzie A. Borden

The Knowlton Papers
1892 - 1893

Hosea Morrill Knowlton, circa 1901.
J.E. Purdy, Boston. Prints and Photographs, Library of Congress.

The Commonwealth of Massachusetts vs. Lizzie A. Borden

The Knowlton Papers
1892 - 1893

A collection of previously unpublished letters and documents from the files of Prosecuting Attorney Hosea Morrill Knowlton.

Michael Martins
Dennis A. Binette
Editors

FALL RIVER HISTORICAL SOCIETY PRESS

Fall River Historical Society Press
451 Rock Street
Fall River, MA, 02720
fallriverhistorical.org
(508) 679-1071

All rights reserved. *No part of this book may be used or reproduced in any manner whatsoever, scanned, or distributed in any printed or electronic form without written permission from the publisher, except in the case of brief quotations embodied in critical articles and reviews.*

For information, write us at Fall River Historical Society, 451 Rock Street, Fall River, MA, 02720.

ISBN-10: 0-964-1248-8-2
ISBN-13: 978-0-9641248-8-2

Printed in the United States of America on acid-free paper.

Book and cover design by Stefani Koorey, PearTree Press, Westport, MA and Charles S. Medeiros, Media Concepts Corporation, Assonet, MA.

Scanning services provided by Harold Widdows.

Copyright © 2020, 1994 by the Fall River Historical Society Press

Printed in the United States of America

About the Society

Founded in 1921, the Fall River Historical Society (FRHS), the oldest cultural institution in Fall River, Massachusetts, is dedicated to preserving the history of Fall River and sharing it with the public.

We maintain significant collections of costumes and accessories, decorative arts, furniture, ephemera, photographs, paintings, drawings, sculpture, and manuscripts. We also have distinguished maritime and Fall River textile industry collections.

The museum is housed in a French Second Empire mansion that was once a station on the Underground Railroad. Listed on the National Register of Historic Places, the structure features a magnificent period interior, while our beautiful grounds with Victorian gardens provide a memorable venue for functions such as weddings and cocktail parties and for special events.

Our exhibits include the world's largest collection of artifacts pertaining to the life and trial of Lizzie Borden, and the FRHS curators are recognized as leading Borden case authorities.

Our distinctions also include The Charlton Library of Fall River History, a first-rate Museum Shop & Boutique, our annual Holiday Open House, and Easton Tea Room, a popular spot for social events and meetings.

To promote public understanding of Fall River history, we stage exhibits, host lecture series, and partner with the city and other organizations to present events for the benefit of the community. We are a leading provider of cultural and family-friendly events such as plays, concerts, and festivals.

The FRHS operates Fall River Historical Society Press, dedicated to publishing works on a wide range of historical topics, with all proceeds benefiting the organization.

This volume was the first publication of the Fall River Historical Society.

The publication of this volume would not have been possible without the generosity of the following benefactors:

Janice E.G. C. Bonner
Ruth P. Brown
Neilson Caplain
J. Thomas Cottrell, Jr.
Elizabeth Brayton Dawson
Elizabeth Wells Denning
Dr. and Mrs. Paul P. Dunn
Fall River Gas Company
Edmund Farinha
Friends of the Fall River Day Picnic
of Southern California
Amanda Peirce Macy Gelpke
Virginia Harrison
Family of the late
Matthew Frank Lizak
Dr. and Mrs. Ira H. Rex, Jr.
Sanford W. Udis, M.D.
Betty M. Welch
An Anonymous Friend

Table of Contents

PREFACE	xiii
ACKNOWLEDGMENTS.	xv
LIST OF ILLUSTRATIONS.	xix

THE COLLECTION
    1892 - DATED DOCUMENTS.   003
    1892 - UNDATED DOCUMENTS.   125
    1893 - DATED DOCUMENTS   145
    1893 - UNDATED DOCUMENTS.   337

APPENDICES
    APPENDIX A
    Knowlton's notes on inquest testimony   369
    APPENDIX B
    Knowlton's notes on trial testimony   371
    APPENDIX C
    Index of Correspondents   387

GLOSSARIES
    GLOSSARY A
    Profiles of textual references   405
    GLOSSARY B
    Profiles of correspondents   473

INDEX   531

Preface

On June 20, 1893, a verdict of "Not guilty" brought the case of Commonwealth of Massachusetts vs. Lizzie A Borden to a close, thus ending a trial which had thrust its participants into worldwide media attention. In 1892, Miss Lizzie Andrew Borden was accused of the brutal August 4 murders of her father, Andrew Jackson Borden, and her step mother, Abby Durfee (Gray) Borden. Vindicated by due process of the charges brought against her, Miss Borden returned to Fall River, Massachusetts, only to face the life sentence inflicted upon her by her contemporaries, that of being ostracized. Prosecuting attorney Hosea Morrill Knowlton gladly relinquished his position in the public eye, proceeding with a career which was to bring him numerous successes in the final decade of his life. It is interesting to note that, with the plethora of paperwork which can accumulate in a lifetime, the only file retained by Attorney Knowlton was that of his most famous case, a case which was not ruled in his favor.

In August of 1989, Frank W. Knowlton, Jr. presented the Fall River Historical Society with his grandfather's collection of documents relative to the Borden case, preserved by his family through three generations. A cursory glance at the papers revealed their importance and it was decided by the Board of Directors of the Historical Society that they merited publication.

That which initially appeared to be a simple task has ultimately required months of painstaking reading and scrutinizing of these faded, brittle communications. In order to preserve the integrity of the collection, all of the documents were to be transcribed in their original form, despite errors in content, spelling and punctuation. One error of note is the age of Mrs. Andrew J. Borden, listed on her autopsy report as 54 years at the time of her death when, in actuality, she was 64 years old. The wide spectrum of literary skills displayed provides us with insight into each author's character and allows them all to speak to us in their own words after over a century of silence.

The documents were arranged chronologically, and each was assigned a sequence number, **HK001** through **HK346**. Undated correspondence was judged by content to have been written in 1892 or 1893 and was arranged accordingly. Enclosures have been included when extant but unfortunately all have not survived. The letter numbers have aided in building the index to this volume, which has a format customized to suit the needs of the collection, referencing both letter and page number.

Two intriguing elements have been included as Appendices A and B of this volume. They are the personal notes of Attorney Knowlton, made upon his review of testimony pertinent to the Borden inquest and preliminary trial. It is assumed that these notes were made in preparing his strategy for the trial in June of 1893. The numbers appearing to the right of these brief comments reference the page numbers of the original transcripts of testimony provided by Miss Borden at the inquest and several of the witnesses at the trial. When read in conjunction with the testimonies, they provide tremendous insight into Attorney Knowlton's views on the case.

Following the lengthy process of transcription, there were times when some words still remained indecipherable. This is attributed in some cases to the flowing script of the day and, in others, to the varying levels of the authors' ability to communicate in writing. For each occurrence of this sort, the symbol [?] is used once for each missing word. In instances where handwritten comments appeared in typed or printed documents, italics have been used to distinguish these words within the text.

To further enhance the collection's usefulness as a research tool, two extensive glossaries have been compiled. Containing biographical and historical information pertinent to the documents, they provide another dimension to the collection. The first glossaries of their kind appearing in any publication on this case, they present those who plan further research with a foundation on which to begin.

Through extensive research, individuals and businesses mentioned in the text as well as those who corresponded with Attorney Knowlton have been profiled. For example, Miss Belle Ingalls, who penned a thirteen-page letter headed "Confidential," was found to be Maybelle Ingalls Lovejoy, an elocutionist and entertainer from Haverhill, Massachusetts. Research has made evident the vast cross-section of the populace whose attention was riveted on the events surrounding the Borden crime and its aftermath.

Photographs accompanying the text are from the collection of the Fall River Historical Society. Newspaper illustrations are taken from a scrapbook of clippings about the case compiled by Attorney Knowlton also contained in the Society's archive.

Presented here is a volume comprised of original documents pertaining to the Borden case. It is hoped that this collection, the legacy of Attorney Hosea Morrill Knowlton, will intrigue and fascinate the reader.

The Editors

Acknowledgments

The Board of Directors of the Fall River Historical Society wishes to express its gratitude to Frank W. Knowlton, Jr. for the gift of his grandfather's papers to the Society's permanent collection.

The publication of this collection would not have been possible without the assistance of many people. The Editors wish here to acknowledge the contributions of the following: J. Thomas Cottrell, Jr., for the foresight and vision which led to the final publication of this volume; Barbara M. Ashton, Neilson Caplain and Jeannette Denning, for their work transcribing and assisting in the editing of this collection; Deborah L. Collins, for organizing and transcribing the collection upon its donation to the Society.

Thanks to the following for their helpful assistance: John E. Bahret, Joan Barney, Joan Bedard, Timothy R. Belt, Thomas Bennett, Elizabeth Bernier, Mary L. Billington, Claudette L. Binette, Edward Bolster, Janice E. G. C. Bonner, Elaine Borgino, Claire D. Brault, Kevin M. Brault, Florence C. Brigham, Joyce Ball Brown, Henry R. Burbank, Jane Emack Cambra, Barbara Carroll, William Chestnut, Kathleen Collura, Lisa A. Compton, Marion Conway, Cecilia Coroa, Betty Costa, Paula Costa, Denise Coughlin, Paul Cyr, Mrs. Charles L. Davis, Marion Delaney, Raymond D. DeMello, Jr., Elizabeth Wells Denning, Anna S. Duphiney, Mary Durda, Dr. John G. Erhardt, Muriel Emerson, Marion Flanigan, Georgina J. Flannery, Robert A. Flynn, Alma Foley, Tina V. Furtado, Nancy Gaudette, Ellen K. Gamache, Bridget Gilleney, John E. Grant, Ann W. Grayson, Robert Hanson, Janice Higgins, Debra Hill, Robert Horda, Ann-Marie Klegraefe, Carol Lazzara, Donna Lee, Daniel LeLievre, Dan Lombardo, Sheila Maden, Randall Mason, James McCarthy, Barbara A. McDonald, Chuck Medeiros, Constance C. Mendes, Walter J. Mitchell, Lila S. Parrish, Beverly Pelletier, Margaret Perry, Jessica Peters, Helen Pierce, Robert Poulin, Pamela Raskin, Leonard Rebello, Mary Reynolds, David Roseberry, Loline Sammons, Kathleen Sampson, Louise T. Scroggins, Kenneth J. Souza, Barbara Smith, Paul Stapley. Joseph Stegal, Edward R. Thibault, Jr., Doris Thibeault, Charles Thorp, Miriam Touba, Hazel Varella, Betty M. Welch, G. Barry Whitcomb, Bruce D. White, Richard J. Wolfe, Todd Woodworth, Thomas I. Worrall, George Yelle.

Thanks to the following for allowing us access to private family documents: Florence C. Brigham, Jean Briscoe, Natalie B. Choate, Esq., Edith

Clifford, Donald Dolan, E. Otis Dyer, Dana K. Hilliard, Gen. William A. Knowlton, Janice K. von Kameake Kotch, Elaine C. Massena, Helen Moriarty, Brian Smith, Elizabeth Weaver, and all those who wish to remain anonymous.

For assisting us in our research, our thanks to the reference personnel in the following archives: **in Maine**, Maine State Archives; **in Massachusetts**, McLean Hospital Archives in Belmont, First Church of Christ, Scientist, in Boston, Danvers Archival Center, Immigrant City Archives in Lawrence, The Essex Institute in Salem; **in New Hampshire**, State of New Hampshire Bureau of Vital Statistics; **in Vermont**, State of Vermont Department of Vital Statistics; **in England**, the Selden Society in London.

Our thanks to the reference personnel in the following libraries: **in Arkansas**, Van Buren Public Library; **in Colorado**, Montrose Public Library; **in Maine**, Augusta Public Library, Skidompha Public Library in Damariscotta, Cary Library in Houlton, Portland Public Library, State of Maine Law and Legislative Reference Library, Turner Memorial Library in Presque Isle; **in Massachusetts**, Dyer Memorial Library in Abington, Jones Library in Amherst, Robbins Library in Arlington, Attleboro Public Library, Sturgis Library in Barnstable, Beverly Public Library, Thayer Public Library in Braintree, Bridgewater Public Library, Brockton Public Library, Public Library of Brookline, Cambridge Public Library, Francis A Countaway Library of Medicine in Cambridge, Pusey Library in Cambridge, Canton Public Library, Chelsea Public Library, Concord Free Library, Danvers Public Library, Peabody Institute Library in Danvers, Easton Public Library, Parlin Memorial Library in Everett, Millicent Library in Fairhaven, Fall River Public Library, Fitchburg Public Library, Framingham Public Library, Franklin Public Library, Levi Heywood Memorial Library in Gardner, Grafton Public Library, Mason Library in Great Barrington, Haverhill Public Library, Hingham Public Library, Hyannis Public Library, Lancaster Town Library, Lawrence Public Library, Pollard Memorial Library in Lowell, Lynn Public Library, Malden Public Library, Mattapoisett Free Public Library, Melrose Public Library, Middleboro Public Library, Milton Public Library, Nahant Public Library, Natick Public Library, New Bedford Free Public Library, Newton Free Public Library, Norfolk Public Library, North Adams Public Library, Stevens Memorial Library in North Andover, North Attleboro Public Library, Berkshire Athanaeum in Pittsfield, Pittsfield Public Library, Plymouth Public Library, Somerset Public Library, Somerville Public Library, Southborough Public Library, Springfield Public Library, Swansea Free Public Library, Taunton Public Library, Lucius Beebe Memorial Library in Wakefield, Wellesley Free Library, Winchester Public Library, Worcester Public Library, Yarmouthport Public Library; **in Michigan**, Jackson Public Library; **in Missouri**, DeSoto Public Library; **in Montana**, Anaconda Public Library, Butte

Acknowledgments

Public Library; **in New Hampshire**, New Hampshire State Library, Littleton Public Library, Nashua Public Library, Wilton Public Library; **in New Jersey**, Bridgeton Public Library, Newark Public Library's New Jersey Division; **in New York**, Albany Public Library, Richmond Memorial Library in Batavia, New York State Library, Buffalo Public Library, Catskill Free Library, Steele Memorial Library in Elmira, Basloe Library in Herkimer, Newburgh Free Library, Troy Public Library; **in Ohio**, Toledo-Lucus County Public Library, Carnegie Library in Pittsburg; **in Rhode Island**, Cranston Public Library, Redwood Library in Newport, Pawtucket Public Library, Providence Public Library, Smithfield Public Library, Champlin Memorial Library in West Warwick; **in Vermont**, Goodrich Memorial Library in Newport; **in England**, The Library in Bridgewater, Somerset, the Local History Library in Castle Green, Taunton and the Lancashire County Council Library Department in Burnley; **in Scotland**, Glasgow City Council, Library Department.

Our thanks to the following historical societies and museums: **in Colorado**, State Historical Society of Colorado; **in Connecticut**, Stowe-Day Foundation in Hartford, New Haven Colony Historical Society; **in Illinois**, Vermillion County Museum Society in Danville; **in Maine**, Maine Historical Society in Portland; **in Massachusetts**, Amherst Historical Society, Acton Historical Society, Andover Historical Society, Brookline Historical Society, Cambridge Historical Commission, Cambridge Historical Society, Canton Historical Society, Dedham Historical Society, Haverhill Historical Society, Lynn Historical Society and Museum, Milton Historical Society, the Rotch: Jones-Duff House and Garden Museum in New Bedford, Jackson Homestead in Newton, North Andover Historical Society, Pilgrim Hall Museum in Plymouth, Connecticut Valley Historical Museum in Springfield, Old Colony Historical Society in Taunton, Worcester Historical Museum; **in Missouri**, State Historical Society of Missouri in Columbia; **in New Hampshire**, Wilton Historical Society; **in New Jersey**, Cumberland County Historical Society in Greewich, New Jersey Historical Society in Newark; **in New York**, Albany Institute of History and Art, Genesee County Historical Society in Batavia, Holland Land Office in Batavia, Buffalo and Erie County Historical Society, Chemung County Historical Society in Elmira, Herkimer County Historical Society, New York Historical Society, Rensselaer County Historical Society in Troy; **in Pennsylvania**, Wayne County Historical Society in Honesdale.

We are also grateful to the following offices and organizations for their assistance: the staffs of the City Clerk's offices in Fall River and New Bedford, Massachusetts; the Dietrich-Mothershead Funeral Home, Inc. in DeSoto, Missouri; First Congregational Church in Jackson, Michigan; Bennett Funeral Home in Toledo, Ohio.

Illustrations

Hosea Morrill Knowlton	Frontispiece
Lizzie Andrew Borden	004
Andrew Jackson Borden, postmortem examination	013
Abby Durfee (Gray) Borden, postmortem view #1	017
Abby Durfee (Gray) Borden, postmortem view #2	019
"Juggling with a woman's life"	025
Edward Stickney Wood	047
View of the Borden house	053
View of the Borden well	053
William Dummer Northend	077
Andrew Jackson Jennings	097
Southard Harrison Miller	103
Floor plan of the Borden cellar	133
View of Second Street, looking South	149
View of Second Street, looking North	149
Albert Mason	165
John Wilkes Hammond	169
Frederick Bradford Hart	187
Frank Winthrop Draper	207
David Williams Cheever	207
Jurors' box diagram	218
Albert Enoch Pillsbury	223
Mary Ashton (Rice) Livermore	253
Herbert Parker	269
Charles Francis Choate, Jr.	281
George Dexter Robinson	287
Hosea Kingman	303
"Knowlton summing up the evidence"	317
William Henry Moody	349
"The most horrible of all crimes . . . a parricide."	360
Letter HK345	361

The Collection

1892 Dated Documents

Lizzie Andrew Borden, circa 1894.
Photograph by Pach Brothers, New York, New York.

HK001
Letter, handwritten in lead.

Providence Aug 9th 1892

Attorney Knowlton

It appears that you are somewhat dazed in regard to the Borden murder but to me it is one of the plainest cases I ever read of, and if the parties had been poor they would have been dealt with same as other poor criminals. The woman has manifested guilt from the first. Her object was money alone if you arrest three parties at the home you will soon solve the mystery. The servant girl is satisfied who did but expects pay for silence, first you ask her privately what kind of dress Lizzie had on in the morning and if she changed it up to the time of calling her also if she had on apron then ask Lizzie where they are. This large apron was what concealed the axe when she came downstairs after killing the mother, you will find apron, dress and towel burried either in cellar or burrid under floor in Barn, I should say east cor. of Barn, placed there from outside that is why you saw no tracks. I get this from a dream I had sundy night, why you found so little blood, it was wiped up with cloths which are hid on premesis, unless she has hiard someone to take them away. I am of the opinion of the Pastor which said the murder must be a fiend incarnate and from Lizzie's face I read that she is deep as the bottomless pit and subtle as hell void of soul or feeling all self. I think the public opinion of near all is that she is the guilty one and will slip you if you give her the chance. You will get evidence enough after her arrest. neighbors dont care to tell what they think until she is in safe keeping but they not in her favor. George B. Fisk can enlighten you on her hatred of Mrs Borden.
I write this as a duty to the Public safety.
Shall expect this to be strictly confidential.

In Haste

HK002
Letter, typewritten.

ATTORNEY GENERAL'S DEPARTMENT, COMMONWEALTH BUILDING.
Boston Aug. 10, 1892

My Dear Doctor:-

If Medical Examiner Dolan of Fall River sends for you, I earnestly hope you will respond. The case is most important, and while he is a bright and competent man, your experience will be of great value, and I wish to leave no stone unturned.

Very truly yours,
Attorney General.

Drs. Harris & Draper.

HK003
Postal card, handwritten in ink.

Brooklyn, N. Y., Aug, 10,'92

Dear Sir:-

A lately published detective story, a novel entitled <u>The Catherwood Mystery</u>, by Albert P. Southwick, bears a wonderful resemblance to the conditions surrounding the Borden tragedy of your city.

Respectfully, B.

HK004
Letter, handwritten in ink.

Lynn Aug. 10, 1892

Mr. Knowlton Dear Sir,

I don't know as what I am about to say to you will be of any use to you as I am a spiritualist and believe in the communications of the dead. I get it there is a closet at the end of the sopha upon which Mr. Borden lay and in that closet was a man secreted at the time Mr. Borden lay down upon the sopha immediately upon Mrs. Borden going out he came out and commited the murderious act he went out by the end of the barn and cleaned the hachet and threw it into the celler the hachet was bretty broad blade claw hammer head..

I don't think a western life as cowboy and farmer had the tendency to make Mr. Morse so very tender hearted as Mr. Davis would like you all to believe I think there was an old animosity an old grudge of the past to be settled and he settled it.

Yours most respectfully,
Delia Wilson

P.S. I do not know any of the parties involved in this tragidy.

There is a man here by the name of Willis Edwards 9 Smith St that could tell you every detail even to the names.

HK005
Letter, handwritten in ink.

Worcester, Mass.
535 Main St.
August 10th 1-92

To The District-Attorneys -General of Fall River, Mass.
Mr. Pillsbury and Knowlton
Dear Sirs-
I am A Business Medium located in this City since 1882. I have met during the last 10 years many People in trouble about various things and have done them I trust a good deal of good, so it seemed to me from the Way They Talked. Now I frequently have some very good visions. In thinking recently about The Mr and Mrs Borden Murder that has startled the entire Community & World, I talked the Matter over to some extent on Tuesday afternoon The 9th Inst. to my Wife Who has the name of an Excellent Clairvoyant or Spiritual Seer. After thinking It over and over Who could have been Guilty of such a Terrible Crime and the True Motive I laid myself down on the Bed to take a rest and soon fell fast asleep I dreamed or saw in a vision as They are Wont to call it sometimes. I will now try and relate what I saw. Was taken in the spirit to a House it seemed to be in Fallriver went into a nice Square Room & met a lady that I had never seen before. She was a thin faced woman average size I talked with Her. While Talking a Door opened & I saw a man

with a Hatchet raised. When I looked again the Door closed partly but I could distinctly see the man and would know Him right off should I ever see Him again. The next thing I see was the Dress of the lady. In the Room she had on it seemed a Print Dress with Dark figures on it the features of the lady was grivious sort of long instead of fat face with Dark Eyes- the voice said to me this woman was Murdered first the Man last with Hatchet & knife The voice still further said to me come with Me I followed to the West side of the House. She took me to a Place like A Henery Coop. I looked in and saw in one corner of the Coop A Box of iron sort of Pig iron in another corner of it was something like a Mattress half filled with Hair on one side of the Mattress She drew out a long <u>rusty knife</u> with long round handle bound with brass wire. The knife was an unusual ugly looking - the brass on it run length wise on the handle - still further a voice said to me "Oh" this is some of my Daughters plotting with Uncle Morse & the strange man "Oh" My Daughter did this. Lizzie put her fist to my Mouth When I tried hard to call some one it now seems to me that after having such a wonderful Experience Spiritually as the above account that it may lead to some clue of the Murder. I give the facts to you Gentlemen as I have relived them. Some will say "Oh" it is only a dream. Well even so consider the Matter and please look in the very peculiar place where I was taken and if there is anything found like What has been described then it will no doubt be the means of hunting up the Guilty Parties the Intelligences say that 3 three Persons know who committed the Double Murder and that the Mayor of the City of Fall River should at once offer a Reward of one thousand Dollars, independent of the one offered by the sisters Emma & Lizzie Borden. Should you Gentlemen think at any time that My presence in Fall River would aid you and the Officers I will come at once and do all that I possibly can for you as a Medium to unravel this great Mystery I am yours Most Respectfully,

    J. Burns Strand
Trance Medium and Physician

P.S. The Voice says to me now in closeing this Missive 'Arrest Morse Lizzie and the Man at West Port

J B S

HK006
Letter, handwritten in ink.

Boston Aug. 10th/92.

My Dear Sir:
    In reading very carefully the details in connection with the mysterious "Borden Murder" I have remarked the absence of any allusion to what has become of the <u>piece</u> of <u>lead</u>, or the <u>pieces</u> cut from it that Miss Borden says she went into the Barn to prepare-

-Anon-

HK007
Letter, handwritten in ink.

F. W. DRAPER, M. D.
304 MARLBOROUGH STREET,
BOSTON
August 11, 1892

Hon. A. E. Pillsbury
    Attorney General,
        Dear Sir:-
           I esteem it a great compliment to be considered of use in connection with the Fall River affair and it will give me much pleasure to be of any assistance to the State in the matter. I am going to Fall River this morning to assist Dr. Dolan in the full autopsy of the two bodies and for such further consultation as may appear to be necessary.

Yours very truly,
F. W. Draper

HK008
Report, typewritten, with comments handwritten in ink.

Fall River, Mass. Aug. 11 1892
RECORD OF AUTOPSY HELD AT OAK GROVE CEMETERY
ON BODY OF ANDREW J. BORDEN.

Autopsy performed by W. A. Dolan, medical examiner, assisted by F. W. Draper. Witnesses F. W. Draper of Boston and John H. Leary of Fall River. Clerk D. E. Cone of Fall River. Time of Autopsy 11.15 A. M. August 11, 1892, one week after death.

Body that of a man well nourished. Age 70 years. 5 feet 11 inches in height. No stiffness of body on account of decomposition which was far advanced. Inguinal hernia on right side. Abdomen had already been opened. Artificial teeth in upper jaw. There were no marks of violence on body, but on left side of head and face there were numerous incised wounds, and one contused wound penetrating into brain.

The wounds beginning at the nose and to the left were as follows:-

1. Incised wound 4 inches long, beginning at lower border of left nasal bone and reaching to lower edge of lower jaw, cutting through nose, upper lip, lower lip, and slightly into bone of upper and lower jaw.

2. Began at internal angle of eye and extended to 1- 3/8 inches of lower edge of jaw, being 4-1/2 inches in length, cutting through the tissues and into the bone.

3. Began at lower border of lower eyelid cutting through the tissues and into the cheek bone, 2 inches long and 1-3/8 inches deep.

4. Began 2 inches above upper eyelid 1/2 inch external to wound number 3, thence downward and outward through middle of left eyebrow through the eyeball cutting it completely in halves, and excising a piece of the skull 1-1/2 inches in length by 1/2 inch in width. Length of wound 4-1/2 inches.

5. Began on level of same wound Superficial scalp wound downward and outward 2 inches long.

6. Parallel with this 1/4 inch long, downward and outward.

7. Began 1/2 inch below number 5, 3 inches in length downward and outward, penetrating cavity of the skull. (*On top of skull was a transverse fracture 4-1/2 inches in length.*)

8. Began directly above number 7 and one inch in length downward and outward.

9. Directly posterior to number 8 beginning at ear and extending 4 inches long 2 inches in width crushing bone and carrying bone into brain. Also crushing from without in.

10. Directly behind this and above it a wound running downward and backward 2 inches long superficially. The general direction of all these wounds is parallel to each other.

<u>HEAD</u>. Right half of top of skull removed. Brain found to be completely decomposed, and in fluid condition.

<u>CHEST</u>. Chest and abdomen opened by one incision extending from neck to pubis. Right lung glued to ribs in front. Left lung normal. Heart normal.

<u>ABDOMEN</u>. Spleen normal, kidney normal, liver and bladder normal. Stomach and portion of liver had been removed. Lower part of large bowel filled with solid formed faeces. Faeces also in lower part of small bowel.

W. A. Dolan, Med. Ex.
D. E. Cone, Clerk

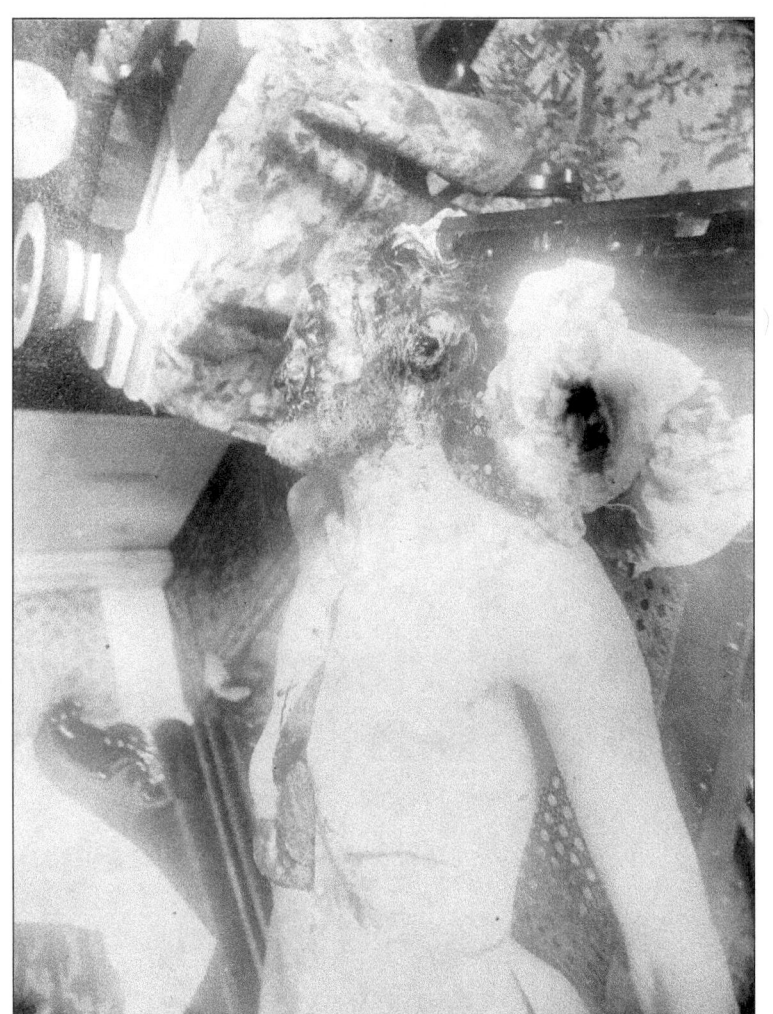

Postmortem examination of the corpse of Andrew Jackson Borden, August 4, 1892, conducted in the sitting room of the victim's Second Street residence. The sofa on which he was murdered can be seen in the background.
Photograph by James A. Walsh, Fall River, Massachusetts.

HK009
Report, typewritten, with comments handwritten in ink.

Fall River, Mass. Aug. 11 1892.
RECORD OF AUTOPSY ON BODY OF ABBIE D. BORDEN, AGE 54 YEARS THURSDAY, AUG. 11, 1892 AT 12- 35 P. M. ONE WEEK AFTER DEATH.

The autopsy was performed by W. A. Dolan, medical examiner, assisted by Dr. F. W. Draper, and was witnessed by F. W. Draper of Boston, and J. H. Leary of Fall River. Clerk of autopsy D. E. Cone of Fall River.

Body that of a female, *54 years of age*, very well nourished and very fleshy. 5 feet, 3 inches in height. No stiffness of body owing to decomposition, which was far advanced. Abdomen had already been opened. Artificial teeth in upper jaw. No marks of violence on front of body. On back of body was

1 an incised wound 2-1/2 inches in length and 2-1/2 inches in depth. The lower angle of the wound was over the spine and 4 inches below the junction of neck with body and extending thence upward and outward to the left. On the forehead and bridge of nose were 3 contused wounds. Those on forehead being oval, lengthwise with body.

2 The contusion on bridge of nose was 1 inch in length by 1/2 inch in width.

3. On the forehead one was 1 inch above left eyebrow, 1-1/4 inches long by 3/8 inch in width, and the other 1-1/4 inches above eyebrow and 1-1/2 inches long by 1/4 inch wide.

On the head there were 18 distinct wounds incised and crushing, and all but 4 were on the right side; counting from left to right with the face downwards the wounds were as follows:-

1 Was a glancing scalp wound 2 inches in length by 1-1/2 inches in width, situated 3 inches above left ear-hole, cut from above downwards and did not penetrate the brain *skull*

2 Was exactly on top of the skull 1 inch long penetrating into but not through the brain *skull*

3 Was parallel to number 2, 1-1/2 inches long, and penetrating through the brain *skull*

4 Was 2-1/4 inches above occipital protuberance and 1-1/2 inches long.

5 Was parallel to number 4 and 1-1/2 inches long.

6 Was just above and parallel to number 5 and 1-1/4 inches long.

(*On top of skull was a transverse fracture two inches in length the continuation of a penetrating wound.*)

7 Was 2 inches long and 2 inches behind ear-hole crushing and carrying bone into brain.

All the wounds of the head following number 7 though incised, crushed through into brain.

8 Was 2-1/2 inches long.
9 " 2-3/4 " "
10 " 1-3/4 " "
11 "1/2 " "
12 "2-1/4 " "
13 " 1-3/4 "
14 "2-1/2 " "
15 reached from middle line of head towards the ear 5 inches long.
16 Was 1 inch long.
17. "1/2" "
18. "3-1/2""

Those wounds on the right side were parallel, the direction being mostly from in front backwards.

HEAD. There was a hole in right side of the skull 4-1/2 by 5-1/4 inches, through which the brain evacuated in a fluid condition, being entirely decomposed.

CHEST. The chest and abdomen were opened by one incision from chin to pubis. Lungs bound down behind but normal. Heart normal.

ABDOMEN. Stomach and part of bowel had been removed. Spleen, pancreas, kidneys, liver, bladder and intestines were normal. Womb was the seat of a small fibroid tumor on anterior surface. Fallopian tubes and ovaries normal. Lower bowel empty. Upper portion of small bowel contained undigested food.

W. A. Dolan, Med. Ex.
D. E. Cone, Clerk

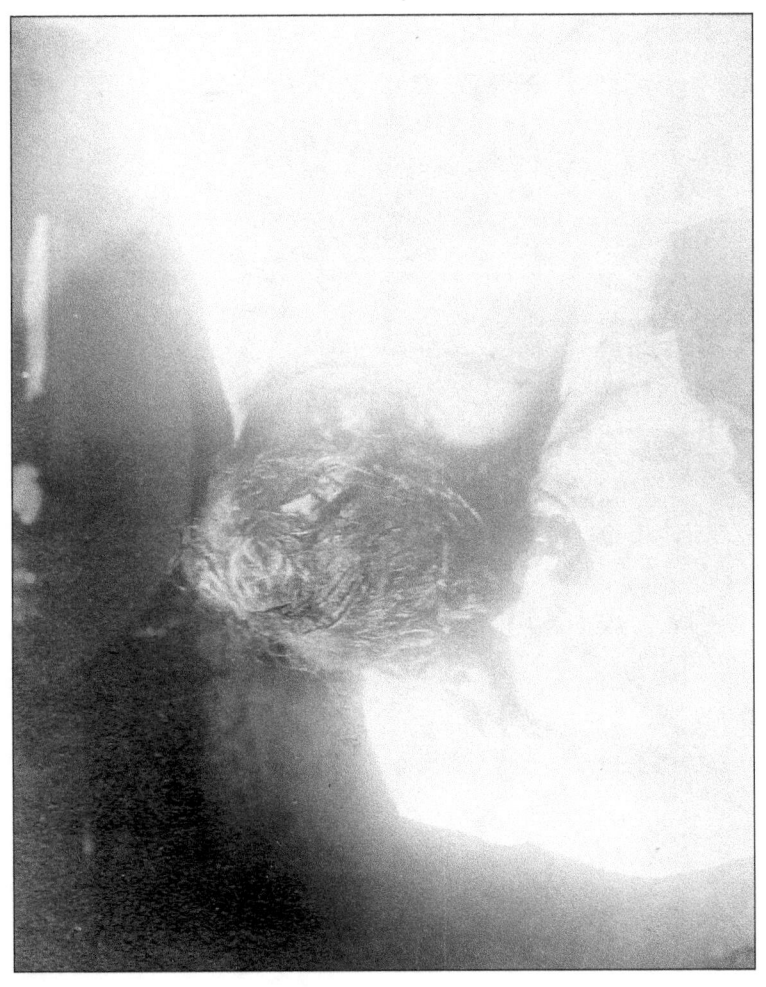

Trial Exhibit #18: Postmortem examination of the corpse of Abby Durfee (Gray) Borden, August 4, 1892. *Photograph by James A. Walsh, Fall River, Massachusetts.*

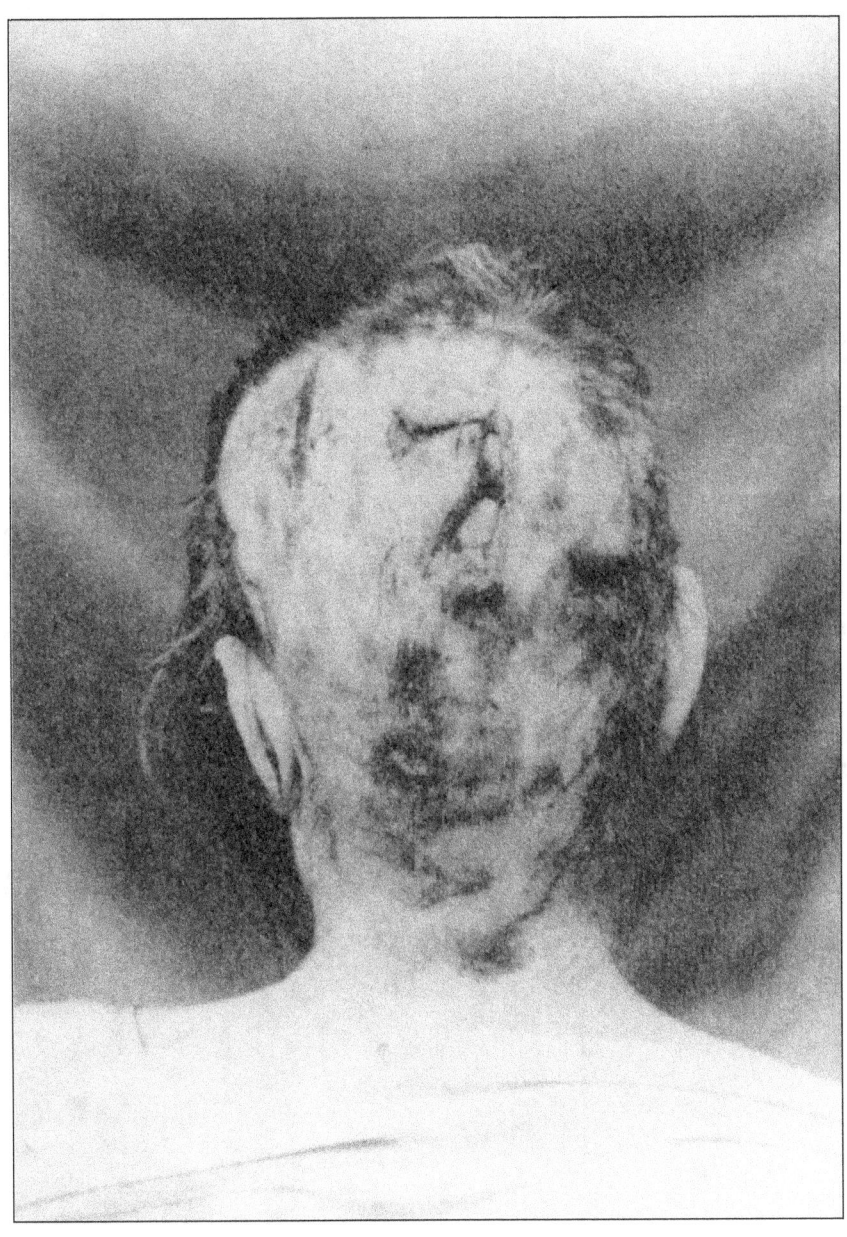

View of the wounds upon the head of Mrs. Borden.
Photograph by James A. Walsh, Fall River, Massachusetts.

HK010
Letter, handwritten in ink.

Newport R.I. Aug 11, 1892

District Attorney Knowlton,
Sir! I have for some time intended to write to you about this so called mysterious murder case, having been for some years connected with secret Police in my native land Holland and a wide traveling experience with an intuitive faculty to detect crime and criminals.
1. This seems to me a plain case and to aid your knowledge I would suggest to ask Lizzie Borden the simple question "Where those leads are now which she cut in the barn in the 20 minutes or a half hour she states, was doing this." I think she will flinch.____
2. The crime is committed not with an ax as stated but with a hot ironing iron, in my opinion because this allone would prevent much blood to flow as heat closes the capilary blood vessels.____
No tramp, robber or maniac theory need be Thought of and not even a man could do such cool <u>premeditated</u> murder, in my opinion Remember that you have to deal with one who has studied her part probably for years, and can laugh and cry with the same face and at the same time, the object of her crime makes her laugh and the necessary crime she had to commit to cover up her deed makes her weep. This is simple a private opinion for you only and not for publication. Of course I am not sure- But I close with informing you that if Lizzie Borden during examination or when she knows that she is watched lifts her upper eyelids high up, so that the full dark part of the eye up to the margin of the white appears that is a good sign and if the white shows on the upper part of the dark she is capable of doing such crimes. Hoping by this opinion to have helped the hands of justice, to in a certain measure counteract the sickly sentiment surrounding this heineous crime
I remain
Yours truly
J. Van Elderen M.D.

251 spring street.

HK011
Letter, handwritten in ink.

PARK SQUARE HOTEL,
OPPOSITE PROVIDENCE DEPOT,
BOSTON.

Boston, Mass., August 11th 1892

District Attorney H M Knowlton. My Dear Sir.
Have you seen this in last Saturdays evening Globe. I think it the strongest proof of guilt. It may be you have not seen it. I ought to have sent it before. Please let me know if it is true and has been considered by the inquest.
Prof Gardner.
No. 11 Bosworth Street Boston Mass
Care of Rev. Elijah Cutlar.

Please send reply to the above address
Prof Gardner.

HK012
Letter, handwritten in ink.

HOTEL KENMORE

Albany N.Y. Aug 12 1892

District Atty. Knowlton
Fall River, Mass.

Dear Sir:-
Feeling quite safe from all possible arrest, I write you This information regarding the Fall River Mystery. The Killing of old man Bordon and his wife was not perportrated by any immediate member of his family as is generally supposed. But They were put out of the way By an illigitimate Son whom Bordon refused to recognize after the Mother of his off-spring died a number of years ago in a certain Mass. Insane Asylum of a Broken heart. That son is now twenty five years of age. He was not known to any member of the family save the old man and woman. When that sons Mother was sent to the asylum

through Bordon, the Son was put in a New York Orphan Asylum. When he was subsequently bound out to a farmer. When he reached his age he left the farmer and went to Bordon and demanded recognition and some sort of an understanding. We mutually agreed to a certain contract part orally & part written. What the contract was does not matter here more than to say - He was to be educated at his, Bordons expense. Allowed a certain sum of money a year and when completed course preparatory to College was to be paid a final sum of $5,000 to commence life with and then they were quits. Through the influence of his Wife who disliked the said son because he once insulted her when she made a stinging remark regarding that sons mother in his presence was persuaded to renounce his obligations & promises after he had partly filled them. The son repeatedly thereafter tried to induce Bordon to carry out his agreement as he was abundantly able to do so. He wouldn't listen. So to make a long story short the son Brooded over his and his mothers past troubles and resolved upon Vengeance, with the result known to all. One point More Lizzie Bordon my half sister may have heard of me and it is to shield her fathers infamy and good name that she is taking the course she has so nobly with stood. The girl is entirely innocent and it is only that justice may be done her that I write this otherwise I would not have written this for I fairly hate the Bordon name.

The instrument the deed was done with was a Lathers Hatchet and was droped over board from a Fall River steamer at the Dock. Entrance to the House was gained by a front window afterwards fastened egress by side window. The time of Revenge about 11:45 I think.

And the illigitimate who took the revenge is the Writer of this confession. No use to track me for it will be an utter impossibilty to do so. At the hour this letter is mailed I shall take a train for hundreds of miles away.

Yours Truly
Phillip Gordon Reed

HK013
Letter, handwritten in ink.

Mass. August 13th, 1892

District Attorney Knowlton:-

The writer after having followed the case of Miss Lizzie Borden, wishes to tell your Hon. self what she thinks of such methods as have been pursued for a week by you and your assistants, who, supposed to be unprejudiced and just men of the law depart. have shown yourselves unworthy of your position. The rights of a noble woman have been trampled upon by you and your bloodhounds who, having run your suspicions to their end, are gloating over their object. You and the Police Officers have been prejudiced against this young lady from the first. Any clews which have been known to reflect upon anyone outside the family you have slighted, when if half the effort put forth upon the defenceless girl had been expended upon them you might have discovered the author of that atrocious deed, for he is no doubt, while you are gloating over your prey, still at liberty and making mockery of you and your bungling methods. When an innocent young lady, whose character and virtue are as much above yours as the light and sky of day are above the darkness, can be arrested, her rights trampled upon, to satisfy the ungrounded suspicions and prejudices of a lot of heartless wretches like yourself and your tools, it is time for the people to take their lives and rights in hand and preserve them. In today's paper I see it stated upon strong grounds that the axe or hatchet had probably been discovered, with wich the deed had been done, and at the same time that a clairvoyant had stated that the weapon used was a long- handled carving knife, which was found according to her directions and that the arrest naturally followed. This is in keeping with the rest of your actions upon which you found your suspicions warranting the arrest, as you think, of this innocent young lady. Any man, it would seem, would not make such silly statements as have been by your eminence, who, all to guard the rights of the people and do justice has trampled upon them. The writer wishes to make a few comments upon the suspicions of your eminence. First, there was Mr. Morse shadowed by your tools the police, strongly suspected any way and perhaps an accomplice. But what do we see? This man after having been suspected and shadowed by your tools the police completely cleared of suspicions. Why not Miss Borden as well? If the suspicion is to be cleared from one why not from the other? Simply because, being alone at this time, she has no one to swear as to whereabouts. Why didn't you arrest this Bridget Sullivan who was alone in the house part of the time instead of holding her to help throw suspicion upon a defenceless and innocent young girl. Your statements as to why Miss Lizzie should have remained indoors on a warm day instead of being in the barn are the silliest trash ever uttered by a man with reason and are only more of your manufactured proofs to uphold your ground- less suspicions. If this terrible crime was committed by this virtuous girl, why should she have nerve enough to commit it, and go out and return, but when returned and seeing the corpse, why did she experience a shock to her nerves sufficient to incapacitate her for a day or two? There is no doubt that a great injustice has been done and that if you have your way and say, a judicial murder will be committed. The perpetrator of this atrocious crime, as has been said in the hearing of the writer even, was probably secreted in the house. That

"JUGGLING WITH A WOMAN'S LIFE."
Brave (?) Fall River Police in Their Great Hatchet Throwing Feat to Convict Lizzie Borden of Murder.

a Good (or bad) fortune favored his attempt. That in the hurry and excitement of the discovery he escaped and is now perhaps hundreds of miles away. Taking a young and defenceless lady into a room and subjecting her to a severe examination without friends and council is only another of your unjust methods to uphold your groundless suspicions, and if she had not been innocent and of a grit equal to your own she would have been insane ere this.

As the writer is in a hurry, she will give you some more illustrations of your methods and prejudice. Yours etc.

HK014
Letter, handwritten in ink.

"THE QUEENS"
M. Caw & Winnett
Proprietors
Toronto 15 Aug. 189

Dear Hosea:

I read in a local paper a yarn about the Jefferson Borden mutineers as the authors of the murder, etc. This is all [?]. C. J. Field and I defended (and acquitted) one of them, John Glen, an Englishman, who was shot in the fracas, afterward pleaded guilty to mutiny, was given 10 yrs in state prison by Judge Lovell, served it out, and when I last heard of him was harness making in St. Paul, a permanent cripple. There were but two others, Miller, a Russian Finn, and Smith, a Yankee, originally from Rockland Me. They were convicted & sentenced to death by Judge Clifford, but some Maine friends of Smith got hold of Blaine and the Sentences were commuted by Prest. Grant to imp. for life at Thomaston Me. I have never heard of their pardon though it has been attempted. But neither Thos. J. nor any other Borden had any connection whatever with the case. The Schooner belonged to the master Mr. Patterson, who with his wife were the principle witnesses. The men complained bitterly of his treatment and would undoubtedly have "Stuck Billy Patterson," if they ever had a chance - and he is the man described by the papers. Doubtless this is all unnecessary, but seeing the story going, and happening to know the facts, I send it in. Have the <u>ashes</u> been carefully examined, for traces of burned clothing etc..? I meant to suggest when I saw you that every particle of ashes in the house or on the premises be carefully sifted. Even a button found might be very important and it may not yet be too late if not already done.

So far as I can judge from the papers, everything seems to have gone rightly since you came in. Of course she must be held, and we can confer further before the grand jury comes on.

                              Yours truly
                              A. E. Pillsbury.

HK015
Letter, typewritten.

COMMONWEALTH OF MASSACHUSETTS, OFFICE OF THE DISTRICT ATTORNEY FOR THE SOUTHERN DISTRICT

                              New Bedford, Aug. 15, 1892

Rufus B. Hilliard, City Marshall,
    Dear Sir:-
        In the mass of rubbish the enclosed has a very remarkable look. Please keep it in strict confidence and see what you can find about it. Don't trust the reading of it outside of those whom you have entire confidence in, for if there is any truth in it the other side will get a similar letter, if not, they are not likely to.
    What is the fact about Medley being the first man in the barn?

                              Yours truly,
                                H. M. Knowlton

HK016
Letter, handwritten in ink.

ANDREW J. JENNINGS, COUNSELOR AT LAW, SECTION G, GRANITE BLOCK
Fall River, Mass. Aug. 18 1892

H. M. Knowlton Esq.
    District Attorney
    You are hereby notified to produce and have at the trial of the complaint for murder against Lizzie A. Borden at the 2nd Dist. Court of Bristol on Monday next, the dress, skirt, shoes stockings and any other article of clothing claimed to have been worn by said Lizzie also any articles of clothing

claimed to have been worn by the persons killed together with all portions of the bodies now in your possession or under your control including the hair also pictures of the wood work and furniture of the house of said deceased now in your possession or under your control also any and all axes, hatchets and other similar instruments taken from the house of the deceased in your possession or under your control and generally to produce and have with you then and there any and all instruments and articles which have come into your possession or under your control which were taken from the house barn or premises where Andrew J. Borden was Killed.

         Andrew J. Jennings
         Atty. for Lizzie A. Borden

HK017
Letter, handwritten in ink.

         Boston Aug. 19, 1892

H. M. Knowlton Esq.
  Dear Sir,
  Enclosed please find something for your consideration. The rascally reporters and cheap detectives (??) are bound to fix the crime on a woman. It is a shameful thing all round and the decent people hope you will not be misled by those wretches.

         Yours
         Geo. Franklin.

HK018
Letter, handwritten in ink.

         Boston Aug 19th

Dist. Atty Knowlton
  Sir
your Coz spread out to get Miss Lizzie Borden to testify at inquest reminds me of a circumstance here I saw the Patrol Wagon taking some nice Looking young ladies and asking what it meant. Was told that some slick Police had put on citizens cloths & with a wink & smile had cozed these young

ladies and arrested them as night walkers. I do not believe such dishonest underhanded practice honest. the case is similar at fall river only a thousand times worse in your underhanded treatment with Miss Borden. As rumor has it someone must be arrested & some one convicted. The News has it about right.

HK019
Letter, handwritten in ink.

HARVARD MEDICAL SCHOOL.
CHEMICAL LABORATORY
Pocasset, Aug. 23d 1892

My dear Mr. Knowlton:

I rec'd your letter this P.M. on my return from Boston. I much prefer to go to Fall River on Saturday if I can testify so as to get home Sat. night.

I have completed today a very careful analysis of both stomachs for Prussic acid but none is present. Had death been due to that poison I should have found it, because the stomachs have been tightly enclosed in glass bottles, moreover I see no reason for suspecting that Mr. or Mrs. Borden were dead before the blows were inflicted on their heads.

Mrs. Borden's stomach contained nearly 11 ounces of nearly solid food consisting chiefly of meat & bread partly in solid lumps. There was also considerable fat (broth & Butter) and some vegetable pulp cells (potato or fruit, such as apple) and a few shreds of vegetable tissue (possibly vegetables in the broth or apple skin)- I saw one large flake which looked like the skin of a red apple.

The quantity of bread & meat shows that digestion was in the early stage at the time of death -

Mr. Borden's stomach contained about 8 ounces of very liquid contents (almost all water) with but little solid matter which consisted chiefly of vegetable pulp cells & some fat - There were only very few fibers of meat & few starch granules (bread) remaining in the stomach. If possible it would be well to ascertain whether he ate an apple while up town or not -There were also a number of small flakes of vegetable cells like those of an apple or pear skin in his stomach - The small quantity of solid food in his stomach shows digestion in his case was far advanced - say 3 to 4 hours if digestion went on normally. The stomachs of both Mr. & Mrs. Borden were perfectly healthy in appearance and showed no evidence of the action of any poison - The stomachs were neither congested nor irritated, so that I do not consider it necessary for the purpose of your preliminary hearing to make an analysis to prove the absence of ordinary poisons -Prussic acid is the only ordinary poison which would kill immediately within 15 minutes & leave no marks (either congestion or irritation) except in very rare cases & under rare circumstances. If an indictment should be found, it will then be time enough to prove the absence of the other poisons. Such an analysis would require 2 or 3 weeks steady work.

 I will come to Fall River on Saturday reaching there at 10, 11 A.M. unless I hear from you to come Friday or Monday.

 I would like to know the exact ingredients of the mutton broth which they had for breakfast.

Very sincerely yours
Edward S. Wood.

Hon. H. M. Knowlton

HK020
Letter, handwritten in ink.

Van Buren. 8/23 92

Mr. Knowlton
 District Attorney
  Fall River Mass.
   Dear Sir,
For the past twenty years I have been a constant reader of the St. Louis Globe Democrat. Our great religous daily and Exponent of Republicanism of the West and South, west. by chance I noticed an artical where Mr. & Mrs. Borden had been murdered and as my mother's maiden name was Clorisa Borden. I became more and more Interested and you may Judge my surprise and astonishment when I seen your name as, Prosicuting Attorney as my Fathers name was Jas. M. Knowlton. My Father was born in Lowell, Mass. in the year 1811 died at Carlyle, Ills. Aug 11 1855 He had several Brothers George, William, John, and Moltyn. My Grand Mother on my Fathers side Madin name was Ann Fuller. her husband my Grand Father was Major of Continental Troops and Fell at the Battle of Bunker Hill My mother is now 82 years of age and is living at Salem, Ills Marion Co. with my neice my sisters Daughter Sister Died last spring and mother will allways remain at Salem to be near Nellies Tomb My Grandmother on my mothers side was a Freeborn. Poor Lizzie Borden if she is guilty she must be insane. it is the first time I Ever heard of a Borden be accused of crime or a Knowlton eather for that matter. I

am also verry sorry That It is indeed nessesary as a duty to prosicute the poor girl I wish you to send me some papers published in your City Giving the Court proseedings as published When I have read It I can send it to mother. As she is verry much Interested on account of names. of Corse my whole sympathy is with poor Miss Borden and I do trust she is not guilty and will so prove her self Inocant You will pls pardon me for occupying so much of your Valuable time and have the paper sent me daily during the Trial and oblige

         Yours Truly

          Jos. D. Knowlton
          Conductor
          St. Louis Iron Mountain
VanBuren   R.R.
 Ark.

HK021

Telegram, handwritten in lead.

THE WESTERN UNION TELEGRAPH COMPANY.

        Aug 23 1892

New Bedford Mass
Hon EA Pillsbury
Meet me Boston Wednesday without fail Very Important
Answer

       H. M. Knowlton

HK022

Telegram, handwritten in ink.

THE WESTERN UNION TELEGRAPH COMPANY.

        Aug 24, 1892

Boston, Mass. To: Hon. A. E. Pillsbury
  c/o Auderhill Newbury
Need not come disregard all other telegrams
       H. M. Knowlton

HK023
Document, typewritten, with notations handwritten in ink.

Rufus B. Hilliard
       City Marshal
              Fall River.

Dear Sir.

    I herein enclose the statement of Bridget Sullivan made to me at her boarding place in Fall River on the 19th of Aug. 1892. between 8 and 9 o'clock in the morning, after stating to her that I was from Tiverton, RI. and related to poor Mrs. Borden that I wished to hear her story myself therefore I called upon her personally for that reason after talking with her for about two hours I elicited the following.

    <u>That Mr. & Mrs. Borden had been very sick all night</u>. Mrs. Borden asked Bridget if she had heard them vomiting said some one had been trying to poison them and that she was going to see Dr. Bowen but she knew they would not like it? also asked Bridget if she (Bridget) had eaten the same food she answered yes all but the Bakers bread Mrs. Borden burned the bread then herself in the stove. Bridget ate her breakfast was taken sick went into the yard and vomited it all up.

    Bridget denied telling the O'Neil girl that Lizzie sent her upstairs to clean windows, Mrs. Borden told Bridget to clean the windows herself, and she did so with a brush, she saw Mr. Baker and a Mrs. Kellys girl, while doing so- that was the last she ever heard Mrs. Borden say, and the last she ever saw of her. Mrs. Borden had been talking about Mr. Morse all the week long saying "now he is here I suppose we will have him on our hands all summer, I dont see why he dont get married and go away" Bridget also said that she thought if he had not come there the poor old lady would be alive today, as it was his being there that took her to that part of the house, she never went there as she knew well she was not wanted, the bed was found made even to the shams and Bridget supposed the old lady had made it as she was found dead in his room. Bridget was positive Lizzie was ironing when she went upstairs, Lizzie told <u>Bridget that morning that there was a special sale of ginghams at Sargents Dry Goods Store that they were selling the gingham for 8 cts. per yard and asked Bridget why she did not go down Bridget said she would get there before they were all gone.</u>

    I asked Bridget why the news papers said so much about the fire she said Oh there was <u>no clothes or rags found she might have burned</u> them all up -Bridget then referred to the fact that Mrs. Borden always spoke about anything she was going to do or anything that happened about the house if she was only going out for a yeast cake she would tell Bridget that she was going for it so in answer to the question if Mrs. Borden received a note said no she did not beleive Mrs. Borden did as she was sure she would have spoken to her about it also the front door had not been opened by Bridget until the old gentleman returned) (meaning Mr. Borden then the front door was fastened in such a way that Mr. Borden could not open it with his key and when Bridget tried to let him in she could not open it at first and she said "Oh shaw" as soon as she spoke she heard Lizzie laugh from upstairs and looked up and saw her on the landing: Mr. Borden came in and went into the sitting room he did not ask for Mrs. Borden as was his usual habit. Bridget felt sick at her stomach & had a bad headache after she finished the windows she went upstairs, because she was sick and laid down accross the foot of her own bed, she did not go to sleep but heard the clock strike eleven got up and looked at her own clock thought it would soon be time to go down stairs to get the regular noon meal it did not seem but a few minutes, when Miss Lizzie called Maggie come down father is dead go for Dr. Bowen) (Bridget was called Maggie) Bridget was so frightened she did not look at Mr. Borden but ran out for the Dr. then Bridget asked where is Mrs. Borden Lizzie said she went out, go up to Mrs. Churchill's house I think you will find her there Bridget went and came back with Mrs. Churchill together they went over the house and upstairs in Morse's room they found her Mrs. Borden dead Bridget said she was the first one to find poor Mrs. Borden dead and she was so awfully frightened she put her arms around Mrs. Churchill and cried. <u>Miss Lizzie was quite cool not nervous</u> Dr. Bowen came running out from the old gentlemen all excited with the tears coming down his cheeks saying Oh he is murdered murdered_____

 I asked Bridget how it could happen that Mrs. Borden was killed right in her own house and no one hear her cry out although Lizzie was so near Bridget answer was "that is just what I said to Miss Lizzie and she said oh I heard her groan then Bridget added I told that up to the Court to the Judge.

 Bridget said it was <u>her</u> habit to fasten the cellar door after washing and if it was open some one opened it. When she started to clean the windows Lizzie was going to hook the back door but Bridget said she would be at work right there that she could see to it.

 Bridget spoke of where she had worked in Fall River at Mrs. Reads & Remington.

 She said she came from Newport about three years ago" was there to visit three weeks before and stayed all night that when she got out of this she was going back to Newport.

 Bridget further stated that Mrs. Borden was always very kind and good to her & would talk to her tell her what she was going to do, the girls particularly <u>Miss Lizzie</u> was very different always keeping to themselves, and no one ever was <u>allowed</u> to go to Miss Lizzies room she took care of it herself.

Bridget often said it was too bad Mrs. Borden was their stepmother she was too good for them and they did not like her.

I asked Bridget if they quarelled she said she would not want to say anthing about that of course they would not quarel in front of me. I pressed her upon this subject but she evidently did not want to talk about it.

She further stated that she made up her mind three times to leave their and gave in her notice but Mrs. Borden coaxed her to stay and once raised her wages Mrs. Borden was so good that Bridget stayed but was intending to leave? she gave as her reason that while the work was not hard the place was not pleasant for any girl on account of the odd habits of the family she said things were not very pleasant in the house, I asked how it was, well the girls kept so much to themselves their was no love for their stepmother.

The above report is in substance the result of the two hours of conversation.

Mrs. Nellie S. Mc'Henry

Provo Aug. 25/92

(Note: "Statement of Bridget Sullivan to Nellie S. McHenry" handwritten in ink on reverse side of document.)

HK024

Telegram, handwritten in ink.

THE WESTERN UNION TELEGRAPH COMPANY.

Boston 8/25
To: A.E. Pillsbury

> Newbury need not come.
> C. N. Harris

HK025

Letter, handwritten in lead.

Hon. A. E. Pillsbury:

My Dear Sir:- If, as now looks more than likely, this preliminary hearing runs over to next week, I should be pleased to meet you Sunday and talk the matter over with you; although it is not of sufficient vital importance to break up a vacation (Alas! the word "vacation" makes me tired. Mine is killed with the Bordens) If I find it is going over, I will telegraph you. Then if you would like to make an appointment in Boston I will come up whenever you say. To make sure of reaching me, telegraph both to New Bedford and Marion.

It is a singular case and must be very carefully. managed.

Yours,
H. M. Knowlton

Aug 26, 1892
Fall River.

HK026
Note, handwritten in ink.

City Mills 8/26-92

Dist. Atty. Knowlton
Dear Sir,
    Are you in want or, can I give you assistance in obtaining further evidence in the Borden case?

Yours
Henry [?] , J.P.
City Mills, Mass.

HK027
Letter, handwritten in ink.

Boston Mass. Aug. 26/92

Dist. Attorney Knowlton
        Fall River Mass.

    Dear Sir you are fooling your time away trying to place the Deed of the Borden Family upon the young Lady Miss Lizzie Borden as I can Satisfy you if you Could only get hold of me that she is not quilty the Peddler Robesky speeks the truth I did purchase the several articals of him, and took his advice and walked to New Bedford then took the train for Boston Where I have been ever since. No power Will Ever hang me for the Deed for I Shall Blow

My Brains out, but before I do I shall Clear Miss Borden in some way, Without Showing the Fall River Police that thay are in any way Smart. I had a motive an I Swore that I Should kill the Bordens and kill I have <u>but</u> I hope no Innocent person will suffer for my Crime. I could tell you all the particulars if I could have my revolver at my head to not give you a Chance to hang me I slept in the Barn the night before. after the deed I jumped the fence and flew down to the Pond, and Washed my face and hands the police will find my coat and pants buried about 10 feet out in the Pond also my old Black Slouch Hat, is all covered up by 3 large stones, don t fail to hunt for the Same. As I speek truthful for this once, if never again. please try to Convince all people that poor Lizzie is <u>Innocent</u> for God Knows she is and so do I Murder will out, but I will kill Myself before any of you get hold of me. poor girl poor girl She is all I care for. I have a good mind to give Myself up, but know I will Clear the Girl before she will suffer more then she does now.

I live at # North St. ever since. Whiskey done the deed not me.

HK028
Letter, handwritten in lead, accompanied by printed business card of author.

GENERAL CLAIM AGENCY,
OFFICE OF A. E. ALLEN,
~~240 WASHINGTON ST,~~

ASSOCIATED OFFICES:
NEW YORK
AND
WASHINGTON, D. C.   Boston, Aug 26 1892

H. M. Knowlton Esq.
Dr Sir

I have been in Fall River for a week past. Came home because I was ill. Saw Detective McHenry & gave him my theory as to the Borden murder. I was with Genl. Marston until his death and he consulted with me very often and had a high opinion of my qualities in this line. Now Mr McHenry can give you my theory as I gave it to him but on study I have thought perhaps the murder of the old man was <u>not</u> premeditated but the party trying make an exit was seen by Mr Borden when he must in self preservation Kill to escape and this would change the case in many ways. Mr McHenry boards at the Wilbur House. He can tell you my idea and may perhaps hand you this if I do not find Mr Geo. F. Tucker at the train tonight. I am sick and have to write hastily & with pencil but Mr Tucker or Mr Cobb can post you as to what Mr Marston thought of me in this line. If you desire I can go to you at any time.

Yours & C
A. E. Allen

HK029
Letter, handwritten in ink.

Lancaster Pennsylvania
August 27/92

Mr. Knowlton
District Attorney
Fall River
Dear Sir

Do your Duty <u>without</u> fear. The whole world thinks Elizabeth Borden <u>murdered</u> her poor old Father and Step Mother. Elizabeth Borden chopped up those <u>two</u> poor old people, all for <u>money</u>, and <u>spite</u>, and <u>Hate</u>. She is a <u>Double Murderer</u>. Elizabeth Borden should be <u>hung twice</u>. She committed <u>Two</u> murders, and <u>chopped up</u> her poor old Father and his Wife in <u>cold</u> blood - She is a wicked wretch, a vile <u>cruel</u> murderer. She is a child of the Devil. Do <u>not</u> let her off. She will "<u>chop up</u>" some one else if you let her off. Do your Duty and Hang her <u>twice</u>. Elizabeth Borden committed Two murders. the Jezabel Mrs. Serratt was hung - she did not commit murder only harbored the Lincoln murderer.

No Person chopped up old Mr. Borden and wife but Elizabeth Borden. The Laws of this Country demand for her Capital punishment. Tis time for you District Attorneys to do your duty, and then we would have fewer murders and less crime. All a wicked person has to do is to kill the persons they <u>Hate</u>. Chop them up with an Axe, and pay some unprincipaled Lawyer to get them off, either for innocence or Insanity. Elizabeth Borden is not Insane - She is a strong minded cruel Devil.

The whole Country demands Elizabeth Borden be brought to justice and punished for her Crimes <u>Two Cold Blooded Murders</u>. Whose Life is safe? Oh horrors!!! how well She had planned these murders, how steathelly Elizabeth came behind those two poor old People, Oh Horrors; how Elizabeth chopped and hacked them to Death. <u>No</u> Mercy for <u>her victims</u>, and her Father too. No mercy in Elizabeth Borden's soul - Treat her as she treated them. She is <u>Not</u> Insane as her whole conduct has shown since.

HK030
Letter, handwritten in ink.

69 Newbury St. Boston
    Aug. 27, 1892

My dear Mr. Pillsbury,
    I have received your letter of today.
    I do not think that the indications of insanity which you mention, are sufficiently strong or tangible enough to enable me to express an opinion.

                      Yours very truly
                        George F. Jelly

HK031
Letter, handwritten in ink.

            T. J. MACKEY,
        COUNSELLOR AT LAW,
             287 BROADWAY,

C O N F I D E N T I A L
                        New York, Aug. 28th 1892

    Dear Sir:
    As I seek only to advance the ends of justice, I beg that you will par- don my intrusiveness, in venturing to suggest certain lines of investigation, which, I believe, have not been entered upon in the Borden case, which you are so <u>ably</u> conducting.
1st. An examination of ashes removed from cooking stove, or range in kitchen, to discover fragments of burnt clothing or buttons, or hooks and eyes.
My theory is, that the accused engaged in ironing on the morning of murder in order to keep up a good fire, that she might burn such articles of her clothing as should be spattered with the blood of her intended victims.
2d. Investigate as to blouses or jackets, and <u>aprons</u>, owned by accused at date of murder, and have them accounted for.
Theory = That accused prepared for the butchery carefully, and wore a blouse and <u>long apron</u> to protect her dress from tell-tale blood-spots.

3rd. Have furnace and flues of chimneys, searched to discover clothing with blood stains. Also examine under flooring of kitchen. Note all loose flooring and search under it, not only for clothing but for <u>letters</u> concealed by accused.

4th. Ascertain whether any books on medicine referring to <u>poisons</u>, or on <u>anatomy</u> were in the house and if accused read them or ever borrowed such works. Notice if marked for reference.

5th. Investigate ~~the circumstances of~~ the <u>alleged</u> burglary of July 1891, as to the hour at which it occurred, and all the circumstances. It may be shown that the evidence points to a member of the family as the guilty party, who as confederate of the accused (L.B.) was even then building up a defence in view of premeditated murder, by causing it to appear that perhaps the same criminal who committed the burglary unseen when Emma B. and B. S. were around the house, also entered in like manner and committed the murders.

6th. If accused went to Paris while on her European tour ascertain if she visited the Morgue.

Theory = That she has always exhibited a want of feminine sensibility, and such visit would be evidence of this.

7th. Inquire as to her bodily strength as indicated in house work etc. This must be known to Bridget S.

8th. Where was the hatchet usually Kept? Was accused ever known to use it?

9th. If she had correspondents secure some of her letters.

Theory - Her letters will show her temper towards Mrs. B. and her unfilial spirit as to her father.

I would state, that I have had a large experience with crime, as presiding Judge for 14 years in the Courts of Common Pleas and General Sessions in South Carolina. While in Paris in May 1890, I traced out through the same inductive method that I apply to the Borden case, the murderer of Marie Gagnol. It was a mysterious case, that baffled the French detective service. The victim was found dead on the floor of her bedroom, with 18 wounds in her head, inflicted, apparently, with a hatchet. The police arrested a man of whose guilt they were satisfied. I pronounced the deed as the act of a woman living in the same house with the deceased, and bearing a spotless reputation. I finally brought the circumstances so strongly to bear against her that she was arrested, and after conviction confessed her guilt. When the telegraph announced the murder of Mrs. and Mr. B. I at once stated from <u>certain indicia</u> that the deed was done by a woman. I can cite a long line of cases from Beatrice Cenci down where children have slain their parents. As to the "laughing" by accused at the exclamation of B.S. on admitting Mr. B. there is no proof that she heard that exclamation. The proof is only that Bridget heard the "laugh" which may have been hysterical, or in exultation over the success of her plan of murder as to Mrs. B. and the prospect of executing it fully at once, through the early return of her father to the house of death, which she could not have anticipated.

I beg that you will regard this letter as strictly <u>confidential</u>, and <u>freely</u> command my services. I would add that I have no doubt that counsel for the defence will, as a last resort, set up the plea of insanity for their client.

                                      I am, dear Sir,

Dist. Attorney Knowlton   Yours Truly,
   Fall River, Mass.   T. J .Mackey.

P.S. The strictures of a portion of the press on the prosecution in the Borden case, fatigue the indignation of every intelligent reader who impartially weighs the proved facts. I enclose an extract from the "New York Press" of to-day, in which the Editor argues, that as Bridget S. was about the house and did not know that the murders were being commit- ted, it is reasonable to assume, that neither did Lizzie Borden know any- thing of their commission. The sapient writer might as well argue that as it is clear that Bridget Sullivan did not commit the murders it must follow that Lizzie Borden did not commit them. I am writing a work on 'The Law of Circumstantial Evidence", in which I shall have a chapter entitled - "Newspaper Trials of Criminal Cases". I regard this case against the accused as meeting every requirement of the most severe judicial test.
                                                T.J.M.

HK032
Letter, typewritten.

ATTORNEY GENERAL'S DEPARTMENT, COMMONWEALTH BUILDING,
Boston, Aug. 29, 1892.

Dear Knowlton:-
            I regret that your letter was not delivered until this morning. I was here all day Saturday and Sunday forenoon, and could have been, as I shall be at any time, at your service.

   I think of nothing in particular to suggest since I saw you. I have a line from Dr. Jelly this morning, to whom i wrote, saying that he has no such knowledge of the case yet as enables him to see any insanity in it.

If you wish to see me at any time this week give me as much notice as possible, as I shall have to be out of town once or twice during the week.

Yours truly,
Attorney General.

Hon. Hosea M. Knowlton,
    District Court House.

HK033
Letter, handwritten in ink.

Prov. Aug.29-92

District Atty. Knowlton

Dear Sir:
    I have just seen for the first time the floor plan of the "Borden House". It is evident that Bridget Sullivan is in complicity perhaps under a promise of a small fortune, for a fall like that of Mrs. Borden could not but be heard by anyone, in, or very near the building If Bridget had been arrested on the spot and handled by detectives who understood their business the truth would have been "out".

A. G. Williams

HK034
Letter, handwritten in ink.

HOSEA MORRILL KNOWLTON,
NEW BEDFORD, MASS.

My Dear Mr. Att. Genl.

    The pencilled letter requesting a Sunday interview was written <u>before</u> I got your telegram from Plymouth & its subsequent arrangements for an interview Friday night. I intended to tell you so, but it escaped me.

    What do you think about reading Lizzie's inquest testimony? Telegraph me. I confess I am inclined to use it. I can't well get the "Sinker" story in any other way; for it was to Hilliard & Coughlin that she made that statement: and I don't want to put them on now.

I don't believe we will be playing into their hands very much: ~~and~~ for the story she told was evidently prepared with care & she will stick to it. It is her manner and the trace's of ill-feeling between her and her step-mother that crop out, that make it bad for her; as well as the numerous contradictions.

Telegraph me your opinion as soon as you can. I shall reach it tomorrow noon, probably. I have put in a good deal of my case. Have not put in the Medley barn-dust story, nor anything about bad state of feeling. The case looks strong as it stands.

Of course, Wood is going to stiffen up the defense: for it is expected he will swear to blood & hairs.

Yours in haste
H M Knowlton

Monday evening
Aug 29 1892

HK035

Letter, handwritten in ink.

District Attorney Knowlton.
        Fall River, Mass.
Dear Sir:

After a very careful perusal of the testimony of Bridget Sullivan in the Borden tragedy I have come to the following conclusions. - first:
That the murders were premiditated and planned carefully for some time previously. Second: that a garment to cover the entire person of the murderer preventing a possibility of blood stains on his clothes and composed of black calico or some other dark but light in texture material, making a very small parcel when folded up, had been provided for the occasion. Third. That the murderer - a man presumably - had been in the house overnight having accompanied Lizzy Borden noiselessly at the time Mr. Morse had heard her going up stairs.
Fourth That the substance that had caused the sickness of the family was given in the food designedly to compel the old people to lay down, in which position they could make no resistance and could be taken completely unaware.
Fifth: that Lizzy Borden did not actually commit the murders but stood by and kept watch at a safe distance to avoid any blood stains.

Sixth: that the laughing of Lizzy Borden, as told by Bridget, was caused by the ridiculous appearance of the murderer covered with the disguise mentioned. Seventh: that had not Bridget Sullivan gone up stairs so opportunly her life would also have been sacrificed.

Eight: that the murderer, after the killing of Mr Borden had calmly divested himself of his disguise and folding it up neatly, assisted no doubt by Miss Lizzy, had placed it inside his vest, and that the axe or small hatchet used had been placed inside the breast of his coat - the handle run through loop on which the head rested.

Ninth: that the murderer was inside the door of the room where Lizzy Borden stood when she so coolly called Bridget Sullivan and sent her for a doctor. Tenth: that the murderer took his departure just then right in the tracks of Bridget Sullivan who I feel sure was too much confused to take much notice. Eleventh: That the axes found in the cellar after the murder, which Bridget during her stay there had never before seen, played no part in the tragedy but were merely put there for a blind. Twelfth: that the murderer is now in Fall River probably attending the daily court proceedings feeling satisfied that detection is impossible if Lizzy Borden will not break down and confess. Lastly: that the murderer is an old time acquaintance of Miss Borden's to whom she has no doubt promised her person and all the wealth to come to her by the death of her parents as a reward for his share in the transaction and that a rigid and careful scrutiny of her male acquaintances of late years may possibly lead to the de his detection.

       Respectfully
       John J. Clancy
528 Market St. Newark, N. J.

                Aug 29/92

HK036
Note, handwritten in ink.

            Springfield
            Aug. 30 '92

Attorney for the Commonwealth

  Dear Sir,

    Have you thought that a smoothing iron might have been the weapon used on the heads of the Borden's?

HK037
Letter, handwritten in ink.

New York Aug 30th 1892

District Attorney Knowlton
Dear Sir !

    If the Borden family are anxious to clear the name of Lizzie Borden why dont they offer a reward for the party who delivered a note to Mrs. Borden the day she was murdered? Why was she so attentive to her father when he came home that morning? She assisted him to take off his coat and made him comfortable before she left him for a nap. This was some- thing new for her to do. Bridget certainly "knows what dresses Lizzie wore at home. By looking over those dresses she could soon ascertain which one is missing. Lizzie after telling her father her mother was out she (the mother) had received a note from a friend saying she was sick and please to call. That was sufficent for the father not to enquire any further. Did Bridget see Mrs. Borden going out? The party who sent the note would certainly come forward and say so. Did Lizzie tell Bridget before the murders that her mother was out. How did Lizzie know the contents of that note? as she had not spoken to her mother that morning. Every one is watching the case very carefully because she is a woman brought up refined and educated and it seems impossible for her to exhibit so little feeling at the sight of two murdered persons and one a father, such a sight would drive a sensitive woman insane, she would be frantic at the first sight instead of which she remained alone while Bridget was going for the Doctor. It is the most terrible case which has ever come before the public and everyone is deeply interested to learn the innocence or guilt of Lizzie Borden.

Views of New York
Ladies

HK038
Letter, typewritten.

ATTORNEY GENERAL'S DEPARTMENT,
COMMONWEALTH BUILDING,
Boston, Aug. 30, 1892.

Dear Mr. Attorney:-

    If you learn that Lizzie is sure to testify, please let me know it in advance, I should be strongly tempted, if sufficiently at leisure, to look in and see how she appears.

I have read Lizzie's evidence carefully, and agree with you that it is better to put it in than to call her. If I knew she was to be called by the defence, I should incline to withold it, and put it in afterward for contra- diction, if any contradictions appeared; and if not, let it stand upon her evidence as they themselv put it forward.

I think the general impression is gaining that "it is a serious matter for Lizzie; but I have no doubt that when Wood testifies, and it appears that no weapon is found, and no blood on or about Lizzie's clothing, there will be a recoil again. Still, I think the public and the press have about come to the conclusion that she will be held for the grand jury, and that she ought to be.

I still favor holding back all that can be prudently held back especially as I now think that what you have absolutely determined to put in will make the case about as strong to the public, as if everything went in.

Your letter of last evening just received while dictating this.

Very truly yours,
Attorney General.

Hon. H. M. Knowlton,
    District Court Room,
        Fall River,

HK039
Letter, handwritten in ink.

Boston Aug. 30/92
F. River Mass.

Dis Atty Knowlton -

D.Sir

I want to place my idea in regard to the Borden murder in your hands. You are at liberty of course to act as you please regarding it. I have always thought that none of the cellar axes took any part in the murder. Prof Wood confirms that idea - I cannot think but that you hold in custody the right party. I think time was taken to do the job and that an overdress and axe were disposed of after being used, perhaps placed in the privy that was in use. (as no water-closet was in the house) or they could have been hidden or burried about the place in the time she had after the murder, as she was alone, long enough.

Yours truly,
Detective Daniel

Edward Stickney Wood, circa 1900.

HK040
Letter, handwritten in ink.

78 West 46th
N.Y. City
August 31 .92

District Attorney
   Mr. Knowlton
Dear Sir,

    There can be no doubt in the minds of people whose profession is to discover the cause of crime (murders in particular) and the criminals, But that the woman Lizzie Borden is the guilty party, & murderer of her father and stepmother. <u>In my own opinion</u> the <u>woman wore a dress or wrap for the occasion</u> which would require but a few moments to destroy, gloves also. If newspaper accounts are to be relied upon (of course I mean the nonsensational). The woman is without sympathy or feeling and of that strong determined deep planning nature characteristic of persons who commit such crimes.

    Respectfully Surgeon E. T Osbaldeston
       formerly Governor of
         Parematta Convict Prison

HK041
Letter, handwritten in ink.

Hon. Hosea Knowlton:
        Dist. Atty. etc.

    Since the papers suggest this morning that "the tide has turned in favor of Lizzie Borden" from the fact that "no blood was found upon the hatchet", why does no one think that the instrument used might be a flat-iron? And does not every New England woman wear an apron at her work / usually large / which may have been immediately burned?

    Flat-irons have been deadly instruments before now, and are easily cleaned: one wipe of a wet cloth would cleanse it of any quantity of blood, and cloth and apron or "wrapper" even could easily be burned in an "ironing" fire.

    The writer burned <u>a very large thick sheet and two towels</u> (during typhoid fever) in a ordinary range in a very few minutes and knows how easily it can be done.

Don't take this letter as coming from "a crank" but from a woman who has studied "possibilities", and has also seen a wound inflicted by a flat iron (in a criminal case) and knows its edge can "cut clean "!
one who bids you "Godspeed" in the cause of Justice!
Anonymous
Boston, Aug. 31, '92

HK042
Letter, handwritten in ink.

Mr. Knowlton Dist Atty Fall River Mass

Dear Sir
          Please do not consider it impertinent for <u>me</u> to call your attention (If it has not been done) to a few points I think is rather <u>singular</u> & suggestive. (ie) If the reports of the trial as read in the papers are true. In regard to Dr Bowen. Why did he refuse to let the Dept Marshal in Lizzies room when he tried to gain admittance. And he Dr Bowen being in the room with Lizzie kept the door closed and saying to the Marshal "<u>wait a few minutes</u>." Now <u>why</u> should <u>Dr Bowen</u> want the Dept Marshal to wait a few minutes if every thing was O.K! Wasnt Lizzie <u>changing her clothes</u>! and wasnt an axe or hatchet in her room? and after Dr B had asked her some questions <u>which he states he did</u>, didn t he Dr B think she (Lizzie) done the foul deed and went to her room to help conceal it. Didn t he help to conceal a hatchet or axe! Why should Mrs Dr Bowen feel so effected? Didn t she know something about the mystry that caused her to feel faint as the crisis was approaching I can t help thinking Dr Bowen knows more than he is willing to state in this matter for if every thing had been all right he would not been in that room of Lizzie's on a secret mission as it must of been or he wouldn t objected to anyone. An officer of the Law especially to enter at any time

Hoping you will take no offense at these few remarks I am Respect a lover of justice.
8-31-/ ,92
Please do not consider this from a <u>crank</u>.

HK043
Letter, handwritten in ink.

Providence Aug 31/92

Mr. Knowlton,
    Dear Sir:
        People generally believe that Miss Lizzie either did the deed herself or had a helper which she hired and secreted until he had an opportunity to get away. He could have been secreted easily. perhaps under the barn floor It is the opinion of the writer that she did the whole job. She would naturally put a wrapper or dress on that could be taken off quickly, so with shoes and stockings and she would not allow her hair to be or remain disarranged. Her head and face could have been protected. All that could have easily done. It was stated that paper or rags had been burned in the stove. She could easily have hid the hatchet where it could not be found. Probably there is a hole in the chimney where she could easily have put the hatchet that would have dropped down where it could not be got at. She could have hid the hatchet easily enough and clothes might also have been put into the chimney. Probably she had been planning it for a long time and had every move well provided for, and she had ample time to do it all. Her appearance proves her guilt.
        Yours etc.
        Justice.

HK044
Letter, handwritten in ink.

ARTISTIC JOB PRINTING,   **ELECTRIC POWER PRINT,**
ALSO DIRECTORIES,   **VERY LOWEST RATES,**
BOOKS, ETC.   **38 THIRD ST.**

HENRY D. MORRIS,

Newburgh, N.Y., Aug 31, 1892
Mr. Knowlton
    Please ascertain by examination of skulls whether the blows fell <u>perpendicular</u>, <u>as women strike</u> - or <u>slanting blows</u> as <u>a man would strike</u> A man would strike with one hand - a woman with one or both, and perpendicular.
        Yours
        H. D. Morris

HK045
Letter, handwritten in ink.

LINCOLN HOUSE   **TOWERS HOTEL**
WORCESTER   **FALMOUTH HEIGHTS, MASS.**
GEO. TOWER, PROPRIETOR

Worcester, Mass., Aug. 31, 1892

Mr. Knowlton
    Dear Sir:
Has it occurred to the prosecution in the Borden case that the murderer could have prepared him or herself against the danger of tell tale blood spots on clothing, by wearing a <u>waterproof cloak</u>.
Would it not be well to find out how many such garments were in the Borden household at the time of the murder and if there is one or more missing?
    A garment of that kind would be covered with blood, while the clothing underneath it would be entirely protected.

Yours truly
W. S. Jones

HK046
Letter, handwritten in ink.

Grafton Aug 1st/92

Mr. Knowlton Dist Atty.
    Dear Sir:
        Do I understand that there is an open well on the "Borden" estate near the barn? if so, would not that be a good place to look for evidence? The "Billings" murder that happened some twelve years ago at Saratoga N.Y. is what suggests the above to me.

Yours truly
T. T. von Kameake
Box 192 Grafton Mass

(Note: The content of this letter indicates that author's date of "Aug 1st/92" is incorrect.)

1892 Dated Documents

Trial Exhibit #28: "Borden house, rear view, looking West," 1893.
Photograph by James A. Walsh, Fall River, Massachusetts.

Trial Exhibit #41: "The old well, Mrs. Churchill's house and Borden barn," 1893.
Photograph by James A. Walsh, Fall River, Massachusetts.

HK047

Letter, handwritten in ink, accompanied by newspaper clipping.

Boston Sept. 1st 1892
Dear Sir
reading Dr. Drapers testamony where he says that a new axe that has not been ground round the corners could have caused the wound an old one I do not think could have reading that testomony strikes me that you overlooked one thing. Lizzie was ironing at the time and as there has been no axe found why not look after some of those flat irons some of those are sharp enough to kill a horse if new and struck with force hopeing that this will bring reward and lead to discovery of the murderer I remain yours

                                            T Austin

P.S. as the axe has not been found whats the matter with trying these flat irons.

                Boston P O

Clipping:

DR. DRAPER'S TESTIMONY
In His Opinion Cut No.9 on Mr. Borden
Was the Fatal One.

Dr. Draper, medical examiner of Boston, testified: "I came to Fall River on the Thursday following the murders at the request of Attorney-General Pillsbury. I was present at an autopsy that day at Oak Grove cemetery, held by Medical Examiner Dolan, Dr. Leary and Dr. Cone.

"I took notes of the autopsy. On Mr. Borden I found all the injuries in a group on the left side of the head. In my opinion they were made by some sharp edged instrument of consider- able weight. I should think a hatchet would be adequate to cause the injuries I saw. A chisel of sufficiently broad blade could have done it, but a hatchet was first suggested by the injuries.

"A new axe that has not been ground round at the corners could have caused the wounds. An old one I do not think could have.

"The wound beginning at the angle of the nose was not necessarily fatal. The one beginning at the eye and extending four inches in length and down to the jaw was not necessarily fatal.

"The wound, four and three-quarters inches long, starting from the eyebrow, cutting the eyeball and extending down through the cheekbone, was not necessarily fatal."

Witness described the first wounds on the face, and said none were necessarily fatal. He said: "No. 9, a cut four inches long, extending from the ear to the left temple, crushed into the skull. The edges were parted two inches, and the wound was probably fatal. I should say that the wounds on the left temple were the cause of death.

"The wound bisecting the eye was bevelled, as also was the one in front of the ear. The skull was of average thickness. At its thickest point it was three-eights of an inch.

"I did not find any wound over the temple or side of the head, caused by any crushing blow of the blunt end of the hatchet.

"I have made experiments in regard to this case. I pricked my finger with a sharp needle, and threw the blood so that it would strike a piece of white paper at an acute angle from upward down.

"Assuming that blood is thrown from an instrument from upward down against any perpendicular surface, the spot would be pear shaped with the stem end down. If thrown up the stem end would be farther from the floor. When there is a skipping of blood beyond the pear shaped spot it indicates considerable force. I have not seen the Borden house."

"I am not prepared to give any opinion as to where the assailant stood in delivering the blows. I should prefer to study the matter more.

"All the wounds remained distinct, those cutting the flesh being separated from those entering the bone, there not being a general crushing.

"I observed the hair on both bodies, and saw no evidences of any cutting of the hair. I am unable to say how much force was used to cause these blows.

"I do not know what causes coagulation of blood. Within very narrow limits the opinion of the time of death by coagulation of blood that has flowed from a wound or found near it, I should say that it would not be safe to form any opinion after 15 minutes."

This demolishes any opinion as to the time of death of either of the victims, as by Dr. Draper's testimony after 15 minutes has elapsed it is impossible to tell how long the person has been dead. This places it beyond determination by medical means when Mrs. Borden died. Dr. Draper in reply to a question said: "I would not want to determine within an hour the actual time of a person's death by the condition of the contents of the stomach as determined by a chemical analysis. A different standard of estimates are employed, and in a degree any opinion must be conjecture.

"Blood from an artery spurts in jets, following the action of the heart, and there would be a trail of blood from such spurts from the object to the subject, from its end to its source.

"I made notes on the body of Mrs. Borden. From appearance at the autopsy I saw no injuries on her that would not have been caused by any sharp-edge instrument. I think the blow on the back was a miss blow, one that was not intended to go there."

Cross-examined-"I received a telephone despatch from Dr. Dolan, and also a letter from the attorney-general, both asking me to come to Fall River."

A recess was taken until 2 o'clock.

HK048

Letter, handwritten in ink.

New York Sept. 1st 1892

Mr. Knowlton, Dist. Atty.
        Fall River
                Mass.

Dear Sir-

    I beg leave to submit to you some points about the Borden case. First and been established in my mind the Borden girl is guilty - without the slightest doubt. You have perhaps failed to discover the previous Domestic life of her - I mean have you investigated her antecedents Strictly, minutiously? if not, you have failed an important fact. Have you taken any cognizance of the fact that nobody has seen either Mr. or Mrs. Borden out of the house the day of the murder? Have you directed your thoughts towards the influence of prussic acid - where you could have found that after three hours the poisoned person is dead - no trace of that poison can be found only the foremost chemist being able with hard work to do so? Whats the matter with that black blood found by the policeman the very hour both were killed? black blood is only found after death by prussic acid, and only during the <u>two</u> hours following death? Did you investigate the fact that the girl could have do the murder indeed the butchering after her parents where already killed by poison, and fearing that her planned murder theorie of being done by outsiders could possibly not be tenable in case only poisoning was found - led her to commit the butcherie - which reasonably could not have soiled her garments with blood and only one shoe was found with spots resembling blood? Have you positive proof that Pf. Wood is as reliable as gold and incorruptible? anyway he is not much of an expert. Now permit me to say that if no objections of any kind lead you or impeach you or any of your <u>trusted</u> subordinates to perform the imposed duty I would perform another and perhaps two more searchings in the house -search <u>everywhere</u>, sound walls - closets - look for fresh dug spots in the yard, cellar etc. and do not let you misguide by that shrewd woman - she fears only you - and your searching and inquiring -nobody else, perhaps there can be some other druggist who furnished the poison - not in F. R. - but in some other near by place - all you can do as I previously state is to be absolutely aware of everything, small or large - the girl has done previously - in fact you must go as far back as one year or 18 months - but there lies the key

      Most respectfully yours
      Hamilton Storrey

HK049
Letter, handwritten in ink.

      Peabody Mass
      Sept 1st, 1892

Mr Adams
Dear Sir who do you supose would Enter the Borden house at 9 and kill Mrs Borden then in 2 or 3 hours Enter again and kill the Husband and Lie about house all the time and the Servant girl I See dr Woods anilies Saying that Mrs Bordens food in her Stomach was Eaten 2 or more hours before death and Mr Bordens 3 or more and She died 2 hours before him and at his Death when Discovered his watch and money was on his per- son. No murderer would of left it there (no Sir) and no One was in the house but its Ocupents and about the Robery 2 or 3 years ago no one Could Enter and go up Stairs without being Detectted at it reads in Court and no One Ever Ransactted the draws up Stairs but Lizzie Borden She done it to Sceare her Parrents as She then hatted her Mother in law. This Liz Borden is one Cunning Brass faced Hyprecate it seem a great many Strange faces are Seen, pale faced, and Bloody fingers, I arsk you does it Look like tramp Murder or any man Murder no Sir it does not, Liz was Ironing She pretended to be to have a fire to burn up her dress or her Bloody Apron She had on at the time now you See how She has con- tradectted her Statements in Examination Cant you See it She pretended She was in the Barn what was She Laufghing about on the Stairs when Bridget was trying to unbolt the Door how did the Murderer Enter in 15 or 20 Minutes and kill the Old man he must of been an Expert Murderer with money Enoufgh and Watches too and the Old Lady was in up Stairs doing her Choirs no note no Message Boy or man or girl has Ever been hear of nor never will but a host of Pale faced and all Sorts of People has been Seen Standing around but who was it that done the Damnable Work, it was none Other than Lizzie Borden. it all Came right Back to the Borden house She was qite Contented She did not mourn

She was the Sole Ocupent of the room where her farther was found that of Course She Says She heard her farther groan why dident Bridget hear him or Mrs Churchell as weel Lizzie pretended to hear him way off in the Barn, then why dident She or Bridgett See the one man who done it Mr Adams Cant you see through it all I am 77 years Old   I can See

---

HK050
Letter, handwritten in lead.

Sept. 1st.

Is it not now about time to look up the Chinaman whom Lizzie Borden is said to have had so much interest in as a pupil? If Lizzie had a hand in the murders it is pretty clear another hand committed the deed, & an Effeminate one.

HK51
Letter, typewritten.

COMMONWEALTH OF MASSACHUSETTS,
OFFICE OF THE DISTRICT ATTORNEY
FOR THE SOUTHERN DISTRICT.

New Bedford, Mass., Sept. 2, 1892

Hon. A. E. Pillsbury,
    Dear Sir,
        Do you think it best to have the evidence all typewritten? I have assumed that you desired it. It seems to me it better be done so that you can read it over and form a more accurate judgment of the whole matter.

    If you see Wood give him a little caution about disclosing anything, particularly with reference to the broken hatchet. Some of my Fall River friends have a feeling that Adams and he are too thick. This is partly caused by Wood's frankness in saying that he was a special friend of Adams, and was also his client.

    What do you think of a circular like the enclosed sent to the grand jury both as a matter of practical politics and as to its possible effect in case the matter should ever come to trial?
        Yours truly,

H. M. Knowlton.
per M. H.

HK052
Postal card, handwritten in ink, with partially legible postmark "MASS SEPT 2, 3 PM."

Could it not have been with a flat iron that Mr & Mrs Borden were killed.

HK053
Letter, handwritten in ink.

Dear Sir,

    I asked myself how I could commit a murder with a weapon that most certainly cause the blood to fly in all directions, and yet keep myself unspotted. This is the answer:--- I should put on a gossamer, (rubber cloak) and after the deed just sponge it off, with water prepared for the purpose, and hang it up in its place, or dispose of it in some way fixed upon in my mind beforehand.
    I would suggest to you that all or any gossamers in that house be examined, and if any are missing trace them. That one tiny spot of blood might have spattered in between the buttons. The weapon is probably hidden in some prepared place; it may be wrapped up in old clothes or rags, or buried in the garden among vegetables or flowers.
    If these suggestions prove of any value, I shall expect to be suitably rewarded.

                            Dorcas Bell

                            Brooklyn P.O. N.Y.

9-2-'92

HK054
Letter, typewritten.

ATTORNEY GENERAL'S DEPARTMENT,
COMMONWEALTH BUILDING,
Boston, Sept. 3, 1892.

Dear Knowlton:-

The circular is good in form and substance, and they ought to act upon the contents without being asked to; but I should not send it out unless confident that it could and would be kept absolutely confidential, partly for the reason that if this case is ever tried, we may have to call the attention of the court to some newspaper performances calculated to prejudice the public mind; and in that occasion this circular might be complained of, though I don't think it could justly.

I don't think the evidence need be written out at present, unless you wish to take my judgment on the question whether to present the case to the grand jury at all; and in my view that question cannot be determined until the time comes, as, in the meantime, all sorts of things may happen. I had supposed that you would at least present the case to the grand jury, unless something very important happens; but there will be time and opportunity to confer orally about this.

I have cautioned Wood several times, and am afraid he rather resents it. But they all leak to their intimate friends, even Draper, the most cautious man ever I knew, who, as I learned from Adams, on the way up Thursday, had talked the matter over fully with him before he was put upon the stand; having been sent for by Adams to be used by him for the defence the same night that Dr. Dolan's message was sent.

I hear considerable said of the burglar theory, evidently based on a former alleged burglary of the Borden house, of which I had not heard before, namely:- that this same burglar, probably a professional, or per- haps some other, entered the house to rob the old man or rob the safe, and was compelled to kill to escape without detection, etc; and some people think Bridget was in the former burglary, and in this affair too as a confederate to the burglar. Of course this is very thin, but it is the only theory I have heard suggested which is capable of belief for a moment; and this doubtless is believed by some. There is also some quiet talk about the Catholic element in the case, of which I had never heard until yesterday.

I am not at all satisfied that any such search has been made for the weapon as absolutely to exclude the presence of it somewhere on the premises. But to make an absolutely thorough search for it might involve the total destruction of the buildings; and this, doubtless, is not worth while, especially as the weapon when found cannot *absolutely* settle the identify of the murderer.

   Yours truly,

      Attorney General

Hon. H. M. Knowlton,
  Dew Bedford, Mass.

HK055
Letter, handwritten in ink.

      Lowell Sept. 3/92

H. M. Knowlton Esq.
  Dear Sir -

    A suggestion may not be amis-
There have been found <u>Hatchets</u> enough to to murder hundreds of people, but it does not appear as yet, that they have been used for that purpose.- Now what was there to hinder the use of a <u>Flat Iron</u>?

     Respectfully,

       H._____

HK056
Letter, handwritten in ink.

     Athol Centre,
    Mass. Sep. 3/92

District Atty. Knowlton
  Fall River, Mass.
    Dear Sir:

      In the matter of the "Borden" case, I beg leave to suggest, that in as much as "Morse" was to dine with the Bordens on the day of the murders, it is surprising, that no preparation for dinner, which was to be at 12M. appears to have been made. Bridget, it seems from the evidence, received her orders from Mrs. B. - now, Mrs. B. being absent according to representations of Lizzie - why did not Lizzie see to it that Bridget should be in the kitchen preparing the dinner instead of being in her room at 11o'c.

and after. If it is argued that Lizzie would not take upon herself the giving of instructions in the absence of her mother - then why did she request one of the parties present after her announcing the murder of her father, to go up stairs & see if her mother also might not have been murdered showing that she knew her mother was upstairs - As nothing appears in the evidence in regard to preparation for dinner & when too an invited guest was expected I have taken the liberty of for- warding you this communication.

      Respectfully Your's,
      P.O. Box 191
      Athol Centre, Mass.

HK057
Letter, handwritten in lead.

      Boston, Mass. Sept 4th, 1892

Sir- In my vision I see the blood stained effects of the merderer of Mr. & Mrs. Borden, of Fall River, Mass. under the the floor - a board of the floor of a lower room that appears to be covered by a carpet.

 As my visions are inspirational it my do well to give it a trial.
      Yours Respectfully,
      My name Shall be faouth
       coming in the event of
        your success.

HK058
Letter, handwritten in ink.

      Lowell Sept 4, 92.

Mr. District Attorney.
 Dear Sir.-
   If a new Inquest is to be held in the Borden case, why not offer those <u>Trunk-less skulls</u> for the damning evidence to convict the heartless paracide; - they will certainly show. indentations that nothing but a Flat Iron could produce.

 When this new evidence is established, then many things that were brought at the hearing last week will be accounted for.-

 I do hope <u>you</u> will succeed in unveiling this horrible crime.

No one knows that I write to you about it, and I shall not mention it to anyone.- I am only anxious that the truth may be brought out,- that <u>you</u> may be instrumental in in doing it - and that Gold may not be powerful enough to sheild the murderess.-

Respectfully H.

Box 296

HK059
Letter, handwritten in ink.

160 West Brookline St.
Boston, Sept. 4th/92

District Attorney Knowlton,
Dear Sir:
 Begging your pardon if unwelcome, a woman who has closely followed the government's side in the "Borden case," hereby ventures to direct its attention to what seems to her a very strong point of negative evidence, - one that no human being of intelligence can help feeling the force of- namely: Self preservation being the first law of nature, why was Lizzie Borden not <u>afraid</u> that the assassin of <u>her</u> father would attack her when she stood inside of that screen door, awaiting Bridget's return from the places to which she had sent her - <u>alone</u> in that house where, she was convinced, that horrible treatment of her father had but <u>just</u> taken place - thinking, as she declares, to explain her saying it to Mrs. Churchill, "Mrs. Borden may be killed, too." - would not every woman in the world, unless confident of ability to control the assailant, have rushed from that house, instinctively, in fear for their own safety?

Mary A. Maxwell

HK060
Letter, handwritten in ink.

(This comm'n requires none of the Dist. Atty's valuable time in the way of response.)

Norton, Bristol Co., Mass.,
Sept 4,'92

Hon. H. M. Knowlton:

    My Dear Sir:

<u>Many</u> thanks to you for your serious and straightforward handl'g of the great great Crime. Your address showed excellent adaptation, alike in its forthputting and in its prudential reserves. (1) Now, judging by the houses in which, thro' a long life, I myself have lived, there are very few in which <u>a board may not</u> be easily lifted from <u>one part of the floor or another</u> of the various rooms, affording ample receptacles for clothing or implements, etc. to be thrust in.
(2) Almost every house has rooms or a room, where some inches' communication is open between the mortar or <u>inside</u> walls and the <u>outer</u> one, or that of the rooms adjoining, especially where an apartment or attic is unfinished, or the space inclosing the chimney, & etc.; <u>ample</u> for deposits; yes.
(3) It does not appear that any boards, indoors or out, have been turned over by the officers, - nor the wells, drains, sewers, flues, privies, funnels etc., sounded, dragged or searched, as yet, - ovens, drafts, ash holes, etc., & steps.
(4) It would be known by Bridget & others whether L. B. had a gossamer, or water-proof, which is or is not now on hand, or to be found.
(5) If Mrs. B. *was* absent from home that forenoon, is it <u>possible</u> that none of her hundreds of friends in F.R. saw or spoke with her? (This, my dear sir, is <u>pivotal</u>.)
(6) If it was an outside assassin (absurd) he would have made <u>instant</u> & nearby disposition of the all-bloody weapon, - concealment no object.
(7) As to <u>burning</u> the house, this would be no <u>financial</u> loss to anyone, as nobody could ever be induced to occupy or use it; e.g., the Surdell and Nathan houses in N.Y., etc. But burning would <u>also</u> destroy the clothing (a gossamer or water-proof is easily worn so as to cover the ankles, etc.), and would obliterate the blood on the weapon, with which it must at this moment be thoroughly caked, somewhere.

Yours most truly,
<u>and respectfully</u>,
(Rev.) Richard M. Devens.

In preparing my volume, "One Hundred Great and Memorable Events of Perpetual Interest in the History of the United States: 1776-1876", I was made sadly familiar with the tactics and finesse characterizing the Great Crimes of the century - White, Avery, Burdell, Parkman, Booth, etc. etc.

HK061
Letter, handwritten in ink.

District Atty. Knowlton
    Dear Sir -
        I read with deep interest your powerful argument in the Borden Case. You say "we have not yet found the instrument with which it was done" - From what I have read I think the terrible deed was done with a <u>chopping</u> knife such as is used in every kitchen by every cook. Please investigate -& dont mention this -
                              Attentive Reader
9-5-92

HK062
Letter, handwritten in ink, enclosed in holograph envelope.

September 5th /92
Scotland -Mass - United States -
To
    District Attorney Knowlton &c &c
    New Bedford -
        Dear Sir
            I wish you to read this letter - and give it your best attention -
In the first place let me say that during a long life of many experiences - and many of them most bitter and painful - I have always found that when I did not obey my instincts & intuitions I have had cause to suffer for it - They <u>have been</u> my safeguards all through life - and a kind Providence has given them to me -
    I am impelled to write to you - and forced on by those instincts - <u>quite contrary</u> to my own desire or wish - for I have a natural repugnance to mix myself in the matter I wish to speak of - In the first place let me assure you that I am no "<u>crank</u>" - but the daughter of an English Chief Justice - whose name has been known in almost every household in the British Islands - as

well as in the British Provinces - who has filled most important offices - the first ones signed by "King William" the Fourth - His last ones by Her Most Gracious Majesty Queen Victoria -

He has been Judge of Probate - Judge in Chancery &c &c -and been twice a member of the Legislature - and has written most valuable Law books - used in every Court in the Dominion of Canada - whose Judgments have never been appealed against but in one instance when it was taken to the Privy Councel in England when his Judgment was con- firmed

You will most naturally ask - what has all this to do with me - or the matter you wish to speak of - only this - to shew you that the daughter of such a man would be likely to have common sense - if no other kind - especially when I tell you that all my life I have taken a deep interest in all law matters - indeed have had occasion to do so for I am one of those unfortunate women who was born with not one but two silver spoons in their mouth - and the consequence has been that my whole married life has been imbittered by it - <u>by outsiders</u> -

In all Gods fair creation there does not - nor has lived - one so hounded almost to death on account of it - since especially the death of my beloved father whose advice and counsel were ever at my service - He died full of years, two months short of 96 - and in possession of all his mental faculties -

Now to the matter I wish to call your <u>earnest</u> attention to - I will promise to be as brief as I can knowing you are - and must be - particularly engaged at present - so will not encroach on valuable moments -

When I first read about the "Borden" murder I did not pay much attention to it - thinking it but one of the common murders of the day - and not having a morbid taste in such horrors - but when I could not avoid hearing the talk about it - in the streets - stores - cars &c &c I began to read up and take an interest in it - I am <u>perfectly ignorant</u> of all the parties concerned in it - and must confess to my ignorance of the geography - or rather I should say - of the different localities in the seperate States - So I may be mistaken in my conclusions about who the murderer - I think - was - if the distance from - or between - Fall River and Fair Haven was too great to be gone over between Wednesday night - and Thursday afternoon -

After reading the papers day by day - those of them I got - for I am sorry to say I've missed some - my first impression was - <u>and now again is</u> - that "<u>Emma</u>" was the guilty party - But you say she was away therefore could not do it -You know better than myself whether she could bridge the distance in the time –

Remember she was in the house of an old,couple who would be likely to retire early - or she - "Emma" could have made an excuse for so doing on the plea of having to go out early in the morning to visit friends or shop &c &c and not being suspected she would not be watched by the old couple - but would get home in the afternoon unsuspected - and not having visited any friends in the meantime they would not enquire for her thinking - if they knew of it - that she was at the old couple's -

As I say my first impression was that it was "Emma" not "Lizzie" - nor "Morse" nor "Bridget" I never for one moment - nor do I believe it now - that it was either a Thief -maniac - or outsider - It seems incredible to think it - and as for the supposition that it was <u>two maniacs</u> that is simply absurd - No two maniacs could plan and hold together so long as to do it- it is most unreasonable to think it - At same time it may be possible there were two engaged in the horrible butchery - or a knowledge of it by "Lizzie" and her endeavour to screen her sister -

Let us go over the whole matter & recapitulate - Here are two aged people - two daughters - the eldest one about thirteen or fourteen -when her father marries the second time - therefore well able to remember her own mother whom she may have loved very much and who before the second marriage may have been looking forward to be the mistress of her fathers house - a much more reticent secretive girl than her sister seems to be - and most likely to be at the age she was when her father again married - most rebellious and uncontrollable - and not liking to be kept in her place - Her power seemed gone of ruling which at that age may have been more than <u>money</u> -

The youngest sister twelve years younger - therefore too young to know much difference in her treatment - And can you say that "Emma" did not foster in that young mind a hatred of the stepmother had she loved the stepmother she would have encouraged a love for her in the mind of her young sister - an elder sister can do so much - They do not appear to have been harshly treated - only not given those pleasures and that society natural to their age - And in judging the parents we must not forget their bringing up - and at their time of life - when first married - they set a higher value on money than we do now - And at that period what we now call the common necessaries of life were hardly known - and were considered the luxuries - and only for very rich people - They were of a frugal turn of mind and I think saving for the future benefit of their children - As I said my first impression was that "Emma" was guilty - for these reasons - I asked myself as you all have asked - who was to be the greatest gainer? Why "Emma" - As the eldest she would naturally be the executrix of her fathers estate - and I see by the papers she is - She has the sole control of it - besides her portion she will receive a large commission - most likely ten percent - Power is what she loves the most -

Now "Lizzie" has always shown a more open disposition and has spoken out more plainly in the family - urged no doubt by her sister in the back ground - has religious convictions - though I have lived too long not to know they can be made a cloak of - but never for <u>one moment</u> would I doubt that true religion exists - but there are many "Mr. Hydes" and "Jeykells" in the world - After reading up the case I began to doubt the correction of my suspicion - and suspected "Lizzie" - <u>never</u> "Bridget" unless she was bought over for or with the promise of a large sum - or she may have come upon the ghastly scene and then bought over -

As I have said I began to suspect "Lizzie" until one day in Court when as "Mrs Chagnon" was testifying about the noise in the back part of their house "Lizzie" turns with a happy face and put her arm around "Emma" - Then my first impression returned - for why did <u>she</u> do that - would it not have been more natural for "Emma" to have put <u>her</u> arm around Lizzie - was it not to reassure "Emma" that suspicion would be pointed elsewhere - And knowing that she "Lizzie" was innocent her stolid cool - demeanour can be accounted for - for as long as "Emma" is not suspected she "Lizzie" <u>never</u> can be convicted - unless the State has more undoubted testimony to bring in than it has as yet brought forward - Her apparent indifference I can account for in no other way - she is no more insane than I am - and I think it a great pity that the Courts would think a little more about the poor victims than they seem to do about releasing the prisoners on the plea of insanity -

If "Bridget" had a key to let herself in - "Emma" had a better right to one - and could have got in and secreted herself - As for the dog - he may be old & lazy - but not too much so to utter a growl - though the young woman next door may have been in too great a tremor to have heard - on the other hand had it been "Emma" he may have recognized her - and taken no notice though he may have given a sniff to an old friend who may have often patted him - and in that case he may have laid down again - Now to "Dr. Handy's" evidence - and I am more inclined to believe his statement about the person he saw - A "Dr." would know every one of his sick visits - and the time of each - At same time it may have been that <u>two persons</u> passed the house that morning of <u>very pale</u> countenance - and he the young workman to have gone bye when he said earlier than "Dr. Handy" places him - for if he came off from a drunken spree he might not remember the time - if he was going to work it would have been early -

Now I want you to pay attention to what "Dr. Handy" says - The mans whole appearance and walk was <u>most peculiar</u> - That he had a <u>very full white forehead</u> - To see that his hat or cap must have been well off his forehead - Now in such extreme heat - as we were then having - was that not rather strange? Would he not have been more inclined to shade his face - <u>unless</u>

he had something concealed in his hat - a "hatchet" without a handle - the latter could easily have been burnt - Again - if it were "Emma" disguised in man's apparel would not her walk be peculiar - especially if she were agitated - and knowing the "Dr." also and fearing to be recognized would turn aside in walking - and not accustomed to the clothes she would feel very strange in them - If it were "Emma" could she not have left Fair Haven in her own clothes gone into some wood and hid them - then returned and made away with the others - But you say she must have had them bloody - Suppose she did the deed in Pyjamma's and then put the mens clothes over them when they could answer for <u>under flannels</u> - or she might have done the deed in her own clothes and then burnt them - and then left in mens clothes -

I wish to say this - that while "Dr. Handy" thought it his duty to tell what he saw I have a suspicion that he did not tell you he recognized "Emma" for it was not his duty - he <u>might think</u> - to betray his old friend's daughter -though clearly so to put you on the trail - And I believe had he been asked to look around the Court - you watching him at same time - his eye would have involuntary have turned to "Emma" and said -his eye - Yes I recognize someone like the young man - A "Dr.'s" eye would natural- ly see something strange in the figure of the young man -at least if he was posing as such – If "Emma" - either in man's or womans clothes he or she would feel awkward in climbing a fence and therefore would be likely to make a slight noise -
And then again "Mrs. Manley" saw a young man - smaller than "Mr. Morse" a woman is always smaller in mens clothing - as men are taller in womens -

Supposing for the moment that "Emma" is the guilty one then her remark to "Lizzie" or rather the latters to "Emma" - "You have given me away" can be explained - It meant this - Here am I under the odium of this thing and knowing they cannot convict me - being innocent and trying to save you - yet you go and tell the lawyers what you should not She resents it and takes no notice of her sister in Court in consequence - while her sister is very pale - And "Emma" is <u>not</u> with her sister when she is committed for trial at the Supreme Court - was not her place near her sister? - All through "Lizzie" has shown a much nobler nature if there is any nobility in either - If "Emma" is guilty than most certainly her sister has nobility of character -

I have told you my impressions and I think it worth while to ascertain what "Emma's" movements where on the day before & on the day of the murder -

It was somebodys suggestion that "Emma" should not be telegraphed to "<u>for fear</u>" the old couple she was with might be shocked to death Might it not have been that they wished "Emma" to be safe at home with the old couple before the news arrived - Another strange thing Why did "Emma" burn the letter received from "Lizzie" about the man seen about the place? - what was the necessity for so doing? - yet she could show it around among her friends in Fair Haven - Once more - might it not have been "Emma" who tried to buy prussic acid and the sisters being so much alike to <u>strangers</u> the difference in their appearance could not be observed? -

Think over all these impressions of mine - but will you please keep them to yourself - it would be most painful to me - and very horrible - did my name appear as that of one hinting to you that "Emma" was most like- ly to be the guilty one -

I am living a quiet life in this Country village near Bridgewater - and at my age would feel most keenly were I pointed out as the one who wrote to you - especially if it got into the papers - Neither my husband or son knows of my writing this - As I said before <u>I am impelled</u> to do so - I believe you are one who <u>has</u> - and <u>will</u> do all you can in this case to solve what appears at the present - a great mystery - If you should deem this of sufficient importance to investigate you <u>must</u> impress it on all who under- take to do so the utmost necessity there is for prudence so as not to give the defence an inkling of it - Some lady friend could make the acquaintance of the old couple - you have [?] before you to make all enquiries - In the end you may be proved quite right and "Lizzie" may be the one who committed the horrible deed - may it not have been "Emma" who laughed on the stairs - If it was "Emma" I have not the slightest doubt but what "Lizzie" knew who was the one if she herself had no hand in it - and so went into the barn to give "Emma" a chance to get out of the house -

But I will say no more - review the whole case and see what "Emma's" conduct was from the very first - I promised to be brief - You will say "brevity has not been the soul of wit" in my case - You will please excuse this ill-writ- ten letter - I'm not so smart with my pen as I was - Please do <u>not</u> answer this - unless I have put you on the right track and you have the right clue - even then the papers will tell me so - but do as you like only you <u>must</u> keep my name from every one -

Trusting you will beat all your opponents and come out with flying col- ors and justice be done to all - And though in the words of one of your States- man - let the "<u>millions</u> be for the defence yet <u>yours</u> the words -"not one cent for tribute" for the wrong

I remain
most respectfully
"Mrs. H. F. Worrall"

HK063
Letter, handwritten in ink.

COMMONWEALTH OF MASSACHUSETTS, DISTRICT ATTORNEY'S OFFICE, EASTERN DISTRICT.

Dear Mr. Knowlton:

A scientific friend was talking with me concerning the Borden case. Suggested in detail a possible use of a search light and prism by which the spaces in the walls could be explored from attic to cellar. Unluckily I said this idea might be of use to you and I soon found myself forced to offer to communicate the idea to you.

Now, having done it, I leave the matter without comment, expecting neither acknowlegment nor other reply.

I read with intense interest every word of your close and have admired the manner in which you have borne the very unwelcome responsibilities which have been yours.

Very truly yours
Alden P. White

Salem Sept. 6, 92

HK064
Postal card, handwritten in ink.

One thing is sure and that is that you will never be <u>District Attorney</u> again.
The people of Bristol Co will attend to that next Nov.
After the mean underhanded part you have taken in the Borden case you deserve to be <u>kicked out</u>

Respectfully yours
Voter.

Sept. 7 1892

HK065
Letter, handwritten in ink.

                                                                                Fall River

                                                                               Sept. 8,'92

H.M. Knowlton Esq.

Dear Sir, -

    Not knowing Marshal Hilliard's whereabouts, I forward this to you.

    The F. R. Daily Globe has another story of a letter sent by Lizzie Borden to her friends at Marion. They claim, that without any introduction to or comment upon, the following sentence appears: "When I come I will chop all the wood, for I have a new sharper ax."
    To this I would not pay much attention, but my informant told me he thought the Globe could and would produce the letter.
    Tomorrow or in a few days a representative of the F.R. Globe is to call on you and state the facts of the above. Possibly Mr. Thurston or Mr. Porter.

                                                              Yours etc.
                                                    Officer Phil Harrington

---

HK066
Letter, handwritten in ink.

Dear Sir,
    It is just possible it has not occurred to the detectives to search the airchambers around and beneath the oven in the stove, for the weapon with which the Bordens were killed. The sides are easily traversed, and there is always a slide in the bottom of the oven which is removed to clean it out. It is a fine hiding place, and just at hand.

                                                         Dorcas Bell
                                                         Blyn.

9-8-92.

HK067
Letter, typewritten, with enclosure handwritten in ink.

**COMMONWEALTH OF MASSACHUSETTS,
OFFICE OF THE DISTRICT ATTORNEY
FOR THE SOUTHERN DISTRICT.**

New Bedford, Mass., Sept. 9, 1892.

Hon. A. E. Pillsbury,
    Dear Sir,
        The enclosed reports gives all the facts the police had in regard to the burglary. It certainly lends some additional mystery to the case. Please keep it among the papers.
        If you see Wood ask him if he thinks there would be any use in now examining a gossamer which was found in the closet with no apparent stains upon it, whether it could be easily cleaned so that blood could not be found anywhere upon it.
        What has become of the fifth hatchet?

                Yours truly,

                H. M. Knowlton,
                    per M. E.

Enclosure:

On or about the 24 of June 1891 I Was called into City Marshal's office. "Marshal Hilliard said "Mr Desmond, Mr Borden says his house has been robbed. You go with him, and see what there is to it." Mr Borden and myself left the office and went direct to Mr Borden's house Second St. I found there Mrs Borden, Emma Borden Lizzie Borden & Bridget Sullivan.
On 2nd floor in a small room on north side of house I found Mr Borden's desk. It had been broken open. Mr Borden said "$80.00 in money and 25 to 30 dollars in gold, and a large number of H car tickets had been taken. The tickets bore name or signature of Frank Brightman." Brightman was a former treasurer of Globe St. railroad co. Mrs. Borden said "her gold watch & chain, ladies chain, with slide & tassel attached, some other small trinkets of jewelry, and a red Russia leather pocket-book containing a lock of hair had been taken. I prize the watch very much, and I wish & hope that you can get it; but I have a feeling that you never will." Nothing but the property of Mr & Mrs Borden reported as missing.

The family was at a loss to see how any person could get in, and out without somebody seeing them. Lizzie Borden said "the cellar door was open, and someone might have come in that way." I visited all the adjoining houses, including the Mrs Churchills house on the north, Dr Kelly's house on the south, Dr Gibbs house & Dr Chagnon's house on the east, and made a thorough search of the neighborhood to find some person who might have seen someone going, or coming from Mr Borden's house; but I failed to find any trace.

I did get a 6 or 8 penny nail which "Lizzie Borden said she found in the Key hole of door," leading to a sleeping room on 2nd floor, east end of building. So far as I know this robbery has never been solved.

P.S. Mr Borden told me three times within two weeks after the robbery in these words "I am afraid the police will not be able to find the real thief."

(Note: "Capt. Desmonde" and "Robbery Case" handwritten in lead and ink respectively on reverse side of document.)

HK068
Letter, handwritten in ink.

Salem Sept 12, 1892

Dear Sir

Bovey, James G., as I remember the name, was committed by the Somerville Police Court on complaints for murder, I think some nearly 20 years ago. Frain was Atty. Genl. I made application for Bail. It was heard at Boston before either Colt or Ames & the prisoner released on bail.

Yours truly
W. D. Northend

To
Hon. A. E. Pillsbury
    Atty. Genl.

HK069
Letter, handwritten in ink.

HOSEA MORRILL KNOWLTON, NEW BEDFORD, MASS.

My Dear Pillsbury;-

 I have sent for the Sunday Herald. I know nothing of the author- ship: & I guess you can learn about it from the Boston fellows, more easily than I can. I neither wrote that nor any other word or line that has been printed, nor suggessted or inspired anything that has been written.

 I have noticed that the New York papers, the Herald particularly, thought more of the Gov't case than the Boston papers did. It may have been an ~~coincidence~~ accident or it may have been the result of the bribery you said would be done, that the Boston Herald & Globe, which purported to give my argument stenographically, almost entirely omitted that part of it which dwelt upon the attempt to purchase the poison.

 It is doubtless true that Lizzie Borden wrote to her Marion friends the day before the murder that she should be over Monday: and would chop all their wood for them for she had been looking at the axes in the cellar and she had found one as sharp as a razor.

 If this is so, it means insanity.

    Yours
     H. M. Knowlton

Sept. 12, 1892

HK070
Letter, handwritten in ink.

       Toledo Ohio
       #526 Front St.
       Sep 13 '92

District Attorney Knowlton
  Fall River
    Mass.

Dear Sir-

 Have been reading with some interest the Borden murder case and a suggestion occurred to me which I have not seen spoken of in the paper- & which would explain some mysteries connected with the case. From the

William Dummer Northend, circa 1895.

description of the case the thought came to me that the murderer of the Bordens used chloroform to facilitate the murder of the aged couple. This theory seems feasible from the following points:
1. It explains the difference of 1-1/2 hours between the deaths of the victims as the murderer after catching one of the victims asleep & finishing her would perhaps have to wait some time to catch the other sleeping.
2. This accounts for no noise being heard.
3. It would account largely for the bloodless clothes.
4. It accounts for the slumbering position in which the old couple were found, the old man especially in his usual place on the sofa in his usual position.
5. It accounts for so many slashes on the victims inflicted by the murderer as under the anaesthetic it would be difficult to tell when life had ceased. Thus the murderer would make many slashes or cuts to make death sure.

Mr. Johnson a legal friend of mine suggested to me that I acquaint you with this theory. Should it prove of any benefit to you I should be pleased to know it.

Respectfully Yours,
Dr. M. M. Park
Dentist

Address me at
  #526 Front St. Toledo Ohio

P.S. I might add if such were the case post mortem examination of the stomach would develop nothing.
  Yours M. M. P.

HK071

Newspaper clippings affixed to paper with comments handwritten in ink.

Boston letter to Hingham Journal
Sept 2, 1892

> The judges who will try this perplexing prosecution at Taunton, no matter who is brought before them, will have no enviable task, for the Massachusetts bench has the credit of being <u>throroughly conscientious</u>, and such minds enter upon an ordeal like this to come with dread. The examination before the judge of a petty court is making but slow progress, but it seems to whet the edge of gossipers' chinning as every little incident

mentioned in evidence tends to the point of crimination. Yet this is likely to turn out as did the double tragedy in Warwick, R.I., in William and Mary's reign, when two girls named Baudin were hanged for murdering their parents for money, the dead and mutilated bodies having been discovered in the house in the morning by the daughters. The elder Baudins had attended a celebration in Providence and the girls, alter waiting impatiently for their return, retired late, only to be dumbfounded on awaking to find their parents at home and murdered. Despite their protestations of innocense they were crudely amd cruelly hanged to a tree in front of their home. Their skeletons were still dangling from the limb of that tree when Jabob Dummer confessed on his dying bed that he and John Martin had killed the Baudins on the road from Providence. They had been put in the stocks by Baudin for drinking health to King James and death to William of Orange, and they had determined to be revenged. They had brought the bodies to the home to make it appear that the murder had been committed there, although they had no thought of fixing it upon the girls. Dummer witnessed the execution, and said that at one moment he was on the point of confessing all. The testimony of Professor Wood on Tuesday that there was no blood on hatchets, axes, or clothing in the Borden case reduces the probability of the guilt of Lizzie Borden down to the minimum, and the time lapsing between the entrance of Mr. Borden to the house and that of the alarm given by Lizzie counters all surmises of a complete change of raiment on her part in the interim.

Friends of Justice, Attention.

At the hearing of the Legislative Committee in New Bedford, Mass. on revision of the judicial system of the Commonwealth, Hon. Alanson Borden, Justice of the Third Bristol District Court in Bristol Co., suggested the advisability of having an attorney appear in the interests of the government before district courts. Also he advocates warrants being issued from some other than the district judge, and said his own court experience supports him in his opinion. Issuing warrants and then hearing a case is necessarily liable to bias a justice in his decision on the bench. As an example of this, Judge Borden cited the recent case of Judge Blaisdell of Fall River presiding at the Borden ,inquest and then sitting on the case of Lizzie Borden.

"HAS DONE HUMANITY GOOD SERVICE"

"The Boston Journal has done humanity good service in fearlessly championing Miss Borden's interests and in denouncing what we believe will eventually prove to have been one of the most scandalous decisions ever rendered by a New England Justice." (The Journal, Moosup, Conn.)

Sept. 14 –92

William B. Gale, Esq., in speaking of the trial of Lizzie Borden says: "There were no grounds at all for holding her. Mere guess-work and nonsense."

Concord Enterprise Sept. 9-1892

HK072
Letter, handwritten in ink.

Powderhorn, Colo., Sept. 20, '92

District Attorney Knowlton:
                  Dear Sir:

                  In reference to the Borden murder case, will you kindly accept a suggestion from one whose remoteness from the scene, and .lack of acquaintanceship with any of the parties involved, may, per- haps, exempt him from the charge of being unduly biased on either side. Being in receipt of several Boston papers, from a close scouring of all that has been adduced in evidence, I have not seen that Bridget Sullivan as been inquires of as to the particular circumstances of her ascending to the attic to lie down - at that time of day, when most domestics are busying themselves with prepara-tions for the noon meal; and, it would appear, that Mr. Borden was a man of old-fashioned habits, which would involve dining at home, and at noon. It would hardly seem that a servant of aver- age constitution and physical ability, would feel the necessity for retiring at that time of day, to secure the very brief rest that under the circumstances would be possible - <u>unless she was prompted there to.</u>

Now, Miss Lizzie Borden, for a daughter who had a long-standing griev-ance against her parents, and of so deep a nature as practically to make two families of a family circle of but four members, involving separate meals - was, from her own statement, remarkably effusive in her kindness to her father that day, preparing his lounge and adjusting his pillow, with an officious care and solicitude that many fonder and more filial daughters might perhaps have over-looked. Such was the kindness of Jael to Sisera, when she prepared him a couch, invited him to rest on it, spread a mantle over him - and them smate him on the temple with a hammer. Through the medium of her Sunday school lessons, did the act of the one woman furnish the example to the other?

Now was the opportunity, if ever. The impulse that impelled the act, was not new -not even recent. It had been meditated and brooded upon for years. It may have had its inception at or about the time that the oppressing thought come over the alleged murderess that she was being deprived of her birth-right - the right to live upon the same plane of social equality with others of her age and sex, whose expectations were no better than hers. She could not do this, or did not feel that she could, upon the allowance which her father considered reasonable, and so she did not mingle in society at all - except to attend a few sociable church gatherings, this church joining, and whole church business, being in my opinion - a part of the long meditated scheme that ended as it did end. For, as appears, there was no season of special religious interest when she united with the church, and she was not swept into its fold on a wave of emotion, as many, if not most women are, who do join. The leading for some years, of a lowly, humble, Christian life, would be a potent factor in dis- arming all suspicion. To say that this girl could not have committed the deed, because such an act by such a one is inconceivable, is fatuous. Such things have been, and will yet be. We should not have had the <u>word</u> paracide, if there had not been the act.

Brief as the time was, for the commission of the act, another opportunity when circumstances so nearly favored was not likely to occur. again. The poison had failed of its perfect work. (The failure to find the poison after so long a time, is by no means proof positive that it had not been there) The presence of the cousin Morse, in the household, which would seem to be a hindrance to the plan, actually proved to be an aid to it, for it involved the presence of the mother in the guest-chamber at just the desired time. The sister was away, and but just one person - the servant- remained to be a possible surviving witness; and she, right in this remark- able juxtaposition of circumstances, that the opportunity might not suffer the last needed connecting link, must needs go to bed. May not the kind- ness that was lavished on the victim in adjusting his couch, not wholly have spent itself there, but have extended also, to this sole possible witness through a suggestion that she go and lie down and rest herself, after her window washing?

So far as can be judged merely through the press reports, Bridget seems hardly to be a "willing witness." She has no information of value to <u>volunteer</u>, and what is learned from her is extracted from her. I believe she could tell more, "an' she would." She evidently knows enough of Miss Lizzie, at least, to be afraid of her. They had free intercourse for days between the crime and the arrest; and if any injunctions could be made to serve, about keeping silent on certain points, they were doubtless given.

It is to be hoped that the Grand Jury will examine into the point as to whether Bridget was in the habit of taking forenoon naps; if she had ever before done so; what suggested the taking one on this occasion; whether she acted upon her own motive, or whether the suggestion was from Lizzie Borden?

Again it does not appear from all I have seen, that Bridget was inquired of to ascertain if Lizzie had any wrapper, overskirt, apron, or other outer garment besides what was found in the search. Bridget would be likely to know, if there was such a one; and if there was, can there be any doubt that that hot ironing stove was its final receptacle? Was Thursday their regular ironing day? or was the one occasion specially devised to fit the other? It is not usual to postpone ironing so late after the regulation washing-day - Monday.

The press, or at least the reporters, dwell much on the assumed fact that no <u>motive</u> has been shown for the deed, so far as concerns the accused. Enmity is proved, and if long-abiding enmity of years does not constitute sufficient motive, hundreds of convicted felons should have gone free. More than this, remains the fact in this case, remains that the share of the estate which otherwise would accrue to the hated step-moth- er, would go to the two surviving heirs, who would come immediately into possession of all the property. The prospect otherwise was that the robust man would survive ten, perhaps 20 years yet, and she herself would grow gray in waiting for that time when she could spend, entertain, and be an equal among equals. .

I trust you will pardon this intrusion by one, who, beginning and spending most of his days as a Massachusetts citizen, and hoping still to end them as one, still feels the keenest interest in everything of moment that transpires within her borders; an interest that is not likely to diminish in intensity from the fact of 20 years of reporting, journalistic labor and magazine editing experience in Boston and New York City. I was not so fortunate as to read your speech in summing up the evidence, it being contained in a later edition of the Sept. 2d issue of the paper I rec'd. <u>That</u> may have taken up these points, but, they not appearing in the evidence, I assumed you confined your remarks to a review of that evidence.

Excuse my rather indefinite address within, and on the super-scription. I have gone over the newspapers to ascertain your initials, but unsuccessfully.

I remain,
Very respectfully yours,
A. A. Foster

HK073
Letter, typewritten.

Sept. 20, 1892

My Dear Knowlton:-

Jennings spent the afternoon with me Friday on the question of bail, but I think I have quieted him so that no application will be made. As soon as any further inquiry which may now be going on is completed, I hope you will take advantage of your first visit to Boston to talk things over. It is an important matter, and I feel, as you doubtless do, that we ought to determine our course as early as may be.

How do you feel about bringing on the McDougall case? If you prefer to let it rest until we determine our case in the other, it shall be done; but I have to begin very soon to layout the season campaign with the Chief Justice, and want to know as nearly as possible what is to be done. Perhaps when you next meet Cummings, if he has returned, you can get his view as to having the pleas disposed of at the time of the trial; and also as to the time of the trial, though as to that, of course, we shall consult our own convenience, chiefly. Have you any idea that he will plead to second degree? I hardly see how he can expect to escape conviction, if our view of the the effect of the former conviction is correct.

I have a letter from Mr. Pratt, saying that an agreed statement of facts is to be submitted to the court in the Menhaden seizure cases. Do you know anything about them? If so, I should be glad to have you make any suggestions that occur to you.

    Very truly yours,

       Attorney General.

Hon. H. M. Knowlton,

HK074
Letter, typewritten.

LAW OFFICES
20 PEMBERTON SQ.
MELVIN O. ADAMS

Boston, September 21st, 1892

Hon. A. E. Pillsbury,
  Attorney General, Commonwealth Building, Boston.
Dear Albert,-
  You remember, some days ago, you suggested having a conference with Mr. Knowlton, Mr. Jennings, and myself about <u>the</u> case.
  Have you abandoned that project and, if not, when do you propose

to have it? I am trying hard to get away and I wish this could be brought about, if it is to be done, before I go.

Very truly yours as ever.

M O A

HK075
Letter, typewritten.

Sept. 22, 1892.

Bro. Adams:-

It did not and does not appear to me worth while to confer as suggested, until inquiry is practically completed, so that we may know substantially all which the case presents, or is likely to present, and I am only waiting to hear from Mr. Knowlton on this point. I still intend to confer with you, if you are willing, as soon as the time seems ripe. Meantime let me congratulate you that you did not participate last evening in the stump speeches on the case at Watertown. The papers do not say whether the meeting voted on the subject, if it did, we ought to be notified and govern ourselves accordingly; but this is too serious a subject for jokes, or even for sarcasm.

I see that the Chapman cases are on the Cambridge trial list, and I suppose we must stand on our guard, at least. Why don't you try your hand on seeing Gale? Possibly you could worm more out of him than I have been able to do, as you have very worming (though not wormy) ways.

Yours truly,

Attorney General.

HK076
Letter, typewritten.

Sept. 22, 1892

Mrs. Susan S. Fessenden,
    President Mass. Women's Christian Temperance Union,
        Dear Madam:-

I have received your request to have Lizzie A. Borden admitted to bail with full appreciation of your feelings, and of all the suggestions which you make in support of the request, all of which, however, with many other circumstances, have already been carefully considered. I cannot properly make any further reply than to ask that you will give the prosecuting officers credit for some knowledge of the circumstances of the case, and of their own duty; and that you will extend to them the consideration which is due to public servants who are trying faithfully and conscientiously to discharge their duty without fear or favor.

        Very respectfully, your obedient servant,
171 Tremont st.

HK077
Letter, typewritten.

                Sept. 22, 1892

My Dear Doctor:-

        From such general knowledge as you have of the Borden case, have you observed in it any indications of insanity? I should be glad to talk with you a moment concerning it, if you can look in when passing this way. There are some indications in the mechanical aspects of the case that it was the work of a maniac, and I am not sure but that we must explore somewhat in that direction.

        Very truly yours,
            Attorney General.

Dr. Edward Cowles,
    McLean Asylum for the Insane,

HK078
Letter, handwritten in ink.

MC LEAN ASYLUM,
SOMERVILLE, MASS.

                Hanover, N.H.
                Sept. 24, 1892

My Dear Sir:-
    In yours of the 22d inst., forwarded to me here from Somerville, I have your question whether from such general knowledge as I have of the Borden case, I have observed in it any indications of insanity?

I shall be absent from home until about the 5th of October, and I can not call at your office till after that time, but I will then do so should you still wish it.

I will say now, however, that my inferences have been <u>against</u> a theory of insanity in the person charged with the crime, from anything I have so far read concerning <u>her conduct</u> before or after the event. As to "the mechanical aspects of the case", I have not knowledge enough of them to have attempted any inference.

I would willingly talk with you concerning this matter;- I will find time enough for that, altho' an extraordinary winter's work is to begin immediately upon my return.

Very Truly Yours
Edward Cowles

Hon. A.E. Pillsbury
    Attorney General.

HK079
Letter, handwritten in ink.

Dedham, Mass. Sep. 26/92

Dist. Attor. Knowlton,
    Dear Sir,
        From the evidence so far rendered in the Borden case I can come to no other conclusion than that Lizzie B. is guilty, and I am thankful that you and the Judge are evidently determined to do your duty, and I trust you will not be turned aside from your course by morbid sympathy for criminals, of which there is so much afloat.

I have thought about the hatchet which you have been hunting for. Is there an <u>old-fashioned privy</u> belonging to the house? If so you may find it there.

My advice is to have it thoroughly cleaned out, and closely watched while the process is going on.

    Your's, in the cause of Justice,
    E Whitefield.

HK080
Letter, handwritten in ink.

September 1892

Dear Sir. I have read about all acts of the Borden Murder - I have never been in that county - do not claim to know any of the parties concerned, but I like every body have an idea regarding the Murder - My theory is that when Lizy went to the barn she went to bury the Hatchet or hide it If I had anything to do with the case I should certainly thoroughly investigate & see under the Barn & in every part of the yard & see if the ground had been dug in It would be a Shame if Such a murder could be commit- ed at Such time & place & never be detected - there seems to be no case of robery but a future object For the sake of Humanity I hope you may Succeed in establishing justice - Sometimes circumstantial evidence is so conclusive that a doubt dont exist -
            Success-

HK081
Letter, handwritten in ink.

Yarmouth, N.S.
Oct. 5th/92

Mr. Knowlton,
            Why not have the chimneys in the Borden house examined. Might not the weapon with which the murders were committed have been dropped through a stovepipe hole into the bottom of the chimney?
            A suggestion

HK082
Telegram, handwritten in ink.

THE WESTERN UNION TELEGRAPH COMPANY.

10/7 1892

New Bedford Ms
Hon A.E. Pillsbury   Atty Genl
                    Boston
Will meet you Saturday morning at half past ten-

                              HM Knowlton

HK083
Telegram, handwritten in ink.

THE WESTERN UNION TELEGRAPH COMPANY.

Barnstable, Mass.   11 Oct 11 1892
Hon. A. E. Pillsbury
           Attorney General
                    Boston
Will come to your house tonight tuesday

                              H. M. Knowlton

HK084
Telegram, handwritten in ink.

THE WESTERN UNION TELEGRAPH COMPANY.

Fall River ms11   10/11 1892
A. E. Pillsbury Esq Atty Genl
Mr Vernon St   Boston
Will come on three forty train
meet you at office at six tonight -

                              Andrew J Jennings

HK085
Letter, handwritten in ink.

LeRoy Fales, President.
E. L. Slocum, Treas. and Gen'l Man.
RHODE ISLAND TIME REGISTER CO.
Manufacturers of and Contractors for the
Setting up of Automatic Time Registers.
Auxiliary Fire Alarm, Electric Dials, Electric or Signal
Gongs, and other Electric Devices.
Providence, R. I.

Oct 12th 1892

Dist. Attorney Knowlton,
    Dear Sir
if you will have the stove, or kitchen range broken up 1 think you will fiend in its flues the blade of the hatchet used by Miss Borden to murder her Father and mother. it will be remmered that on that morning that she had a hot fire ironing. the hatchet (I think) was put into the range. the handle burnt off and out. and the blade poked over the oven into the flues, (break it up and see) hopeing you will fiend the blade. (the missing link)
                I am   Yours truly
                              E. L. Slocum.

HK086
Telegram, typewritten.

TELEGRAM

Fr 42 BN:C 12paid   234 Devonshire Street,
Boston
Fall River, Mass. Oct 13th-92
A. E. Pillsbury Esq.,
      Globe Building,
            Boston, Mass.
Would like to see you at your Vernon office at eight tonight.
                                            Andrew J. Jennings

HK087
Letter, typewritten.

ATTORNEY GENERAL'S DEPARTMENT, COMMONWEALTH BUILDING.
Boston, Oct. 13, 1892.

My Dear Knowlton:-

    An additional reason for putting out some authoritative statement as to the McHenry business, or for publishing the fact that Trickey was engaged in the attempt to commit an offence for which war- rants are out against him, and that he has fled, is in the fact that the news- papers are giving the public an entirely erroneous idea as to the whole episode, namely:- that Trickey was a guileless, even if somewhat too enter- prising, newspaper man, but has been fooled and swindled by a rascal, who cared nothing for the results to Lizzie Borden, or to justice, if he could get two or three hundred dollars for himself. This is illustrated by two or three slips from last night's Record, which I enclose. The public mind ought not to beallowed to settle upon such a belief. Still I am reluctant, as always, to have anything in partic- ular said by authority. Write me your notion of this also.

                        Yours truly,

Hon. H. M. Knowlton.

HK088
Letter, handwritten in ink, enclosed in holograph envelope.

<u>Personal.</u>

              Norton, "in our county of Bristol", etc.
                        Oct. 13, '92

My Dear Sir:

    Assuming, as I may justly, the righteousness of your position in the Bor- den case, let me say, briefly, that the discovery of the weapon - (seeing that the involved parties were in free possession of the whole premises a full week before any arrest, & thus able to clean and cover every track) -is to the last degree a dubious task. It may be lodged between the ceilings or partitions of the walls or floors, somewhere, & most likely is.

There is one <u>accessus criminis</u>. however; in the act, which you can almost certainly trace. The deed was done with the person fully protected from blood, viz., by a water-proof, or weather-proof, of female wear. Of these, rarely, if ever, does a woman possess more than one, or two, and, in this case, Bridget's knowledge, as well as that of other persons, would be instant and lucid. If the accused had <u>one</u>, let it be brought forward; if <u>two</u>, and one be now missing, the fact would be most weighty.

  Yours, most truly.
  Rev. Rich' d M. Devens.

HK089
Letter, handwritten in ink.

My Dear Pillsbury:-

  This is at hand when the stenographer is not, and a letter the size of a grass-hopper is a burden. - I see no harm in having a complaint for libel against T.; but I still think we cant afford to champion McHenry. If it was a mess of our cooking I should say stand by him at all cost: but it is his own funeral. He is right: but he can never made the public think he is ; and if we try to make the public think so, it will only end in the said p. thinking we were responsible for his performance.

           Yours
           H.M. Knowlton

Oct. '14, 1892
If you see Mr. Trickey has fled, that fact need not be hid, but further I wouldn't go, yet

---

HK090
Letter, typewritten.

ATTORNEY GENERAL'S DEPARTMENT,
COMMONWEALTH BUILDING,
        Boston Nov. 1, 1892.

Bro. Hurd:-

  Are you preparing indictments against Trickey? I should like them ready for use, in each county, before the next grand jury, which comes in, I believe, next Monday in each case.

I think each indictment should include as many counts as the facts call for or warrant, short of including libels against Lizzie in the Suffolk indictment. If expedient or necessary another indictment can be found on these later.

Very truly yours,

Ass't Dist. Att'y Hurd,

HK091
Leaflet, printed.

Supplement to "United States and Russia."

The Fall River Borden murders were accomplished by a large number of persons, some of whom were inside, but many outside of the house. Mrs. Borden's attention had probably been attracted by something in the street, and, with noisy vehicles passing, she did not hear the approaching steps of the assassin. A heavily loaded team, rumbling ice-cart, a wagon with a few bars of iron, or one driven against the edgestone (producing a "grating sound") would deaden the sound of the fall and the axe.

As the daughter was leaving the lower part of the house, the signals were given for the vehicles to again commence their work, and the assassin of the father to leave his hiding-place in the cellar, attic, or elsewhere, perform his fiendish work, and back again, all of which could be done in two or three minutes. When the alarm was given, he or they in the confusion mingled with others, being, perhaps, not unfamiliar faces in that locality, and arranged evidence to implicate the daughter, or throw suspicion from themselves and their cause. Evidently, the mode of death by the axe was an afterthought, the original design being by poison occasioned by the affairs at Marion.

This noble, pure, and innocent girl is the victim of a deep-laid conspiracy, and is in the hands of those who will use every effort to convict her, by malicious stories, manufactured evidence, false witnesses, etc., and she may some time be made insane.

Miss Borden is but one of many: some have suffered punishment for petty crimes, and others have been executed for crimes of which they were guiltless.

From this source came the Nathan murder of New York, in which the son appeared to be the guilty one; the Carleton murder of Watertown, with suspicion of guilt resting on the husband, and many others.

Boston, November 10, 1892.

HK092
Letter, handwritten in ink.

PAGE & OWEN,
ATTORNEYS AND COUNSELLORS AT LAW
19 COLLEGE ST. ROOMS 17, 18 & 25
P.O. BOX 1030
CHARLES H. PAGE. FRANKLIN P. OWEN.

Providence, R.I. Nov. 14, 1892

Hon. H.M. Knowlton
    Atty.
        Dear Sir

Yours this day received - At the request of Mr. Hilliard I desire to state that I told Mr. McHenry that from the appearance of the cut in the newspaper I thought I had seen Miss Borden on the street in this city about a week before the murder. I also said sometime subsequently that I felt quite positive some member of the Borden family had called to see me about the property but I did not know who it was - I never told McHenry that Miss Lizzie Borden had been to my office and I never came to Fall River to the court and I am of the opinion that if any communications were made to me by her they are privileged. I could not tell if she did unless I should first see her.

                Yours Resply
                Franklin P. Owen

HK093
Letter, typewritten, with comments handwritten in ink.

ATTORNEY GENERAL'S DEPARTMENT,
COMMONWEALTH BUILDING,

Boston, Nov. 21, 1892.

Dear Mr. Attorney:-

    As ~~under the Robinson doctrine~~, I see no possible doubt that the whole transaction can be put in evidence in a trial for the killing of either, I incline, on reflection, toward two indictments, if there are to be any. Has it ever occurred to you to put in a count or counts as accessory *before & after*? There is, to be sure, no affirmative evidence, at present, that any other person was concerned, but a great many people believe that she was in it, but that hers was not the hand that did it. I could easily believe this if there were any evidence of it. *Perhaps one indict for killing both & others for killing each will be best of all.*

I write these suggestions now as they occur to me, and as you will have time to think of them. I wish the investigation just begun in the other line to be thoroughly, and, if possible, exhaustive, chiefly for the satisfaction of my own mind, as I doubt as if it develops anything of consequence for any other purpose.

Very truly yours,
Attorney General.

Hon. H. M. Knowlton,

HK094
Telegram, handwritten in ink.

THE WESTERN UNION TELEGRAPH COMPANY.

Nov 21 1892

Taunton MS 21
A E Pillsbury Atty Genl
    Boston

Will Come to Boston tomorrow morning your office ten fifteen

Andrew J. Jennings

HK095
Letter, handwritten in ink.

ANDREW J. JENNINGS,
COUNSELOR AT LAW,
SECTION G. GRANITE BLOCK.
Fall River, Mass., Nov. 22, 1892

Hon A. E. Pillsbury
    Attorney General
        My Dear Pillsbury

Since my talk with you I have been seriously considering your proposition and have come to the conclusion that I cannot consent to unite with you in the examination proposed. I asked Adams opinion on the advisability of the course proposed without expressing any opinion of my own and also on my return home that of Mr Holmes who to a certain extent represents the Borden girls, without informing him that I had consulted Adams. Both came to the same conclusion that in view of all the circumstances we could not do anything which suggested a doubt of her innocence and that the course proposed would not be wise or expedient on our part.

                Sincerely Yours
                Andrew J Jennings

HK096
Letter, typewritten.

HOSEA M. KNOWLTON. ARTHUR E. PERRY.
COUNSELLORS AT LAW.
OFFICE:
38 NORTH WATER STREET.

{Dictated.}

                NEW BEDFORD, MASS., November 22, 1892.

Hon. A. E. Pillsbury,
    Attorney-General.
        Dear Sir:-
            I did not have time to write so fully as I desired about the sanity business. I could do nothing whatever with Jennings. He took exactly the position I feared he would, and seemed to regard it as some sort of surrender if he consented to anything. We can make some investigations into the family matters without him, but it will not be so thorough as it would be if we had his assistance.

    I note your suggestions about form of indictment, which I will adopt if we ever get so far; of which, however, I am far from certain.

        Yours truly,
        H. M. Knowlton

Andrew Jackson Jennings, circa 1890.

HK097
Letter, typewritten.

HOSEA M. KNOWLTON. ARTHUR E. PERRY.
COUNSELLORS AT LAW.
OFFICE:
38 NORTH WATER STREET.

{Dictated.}

NEW BEDFORD, MASS., November 22, 1892.

Hon. A. E. Pillsbury,
    Attorney General.

Dear Sir:- I see no need of account for accessory. If she did not do the killing, but only instigated some one else to, it can hardly be said that she was not so far present as to make her principal, for she was certainly in the house, and in hearing of both murders.

It had occurred to me, however, since I saw you, that the jury should be instructed as to the principles of law relating to principal and accessory; and, if you see no objection, I propose to state to them the law upon that subject.

I have already written you about Jennings, and you have probably seen him before this time.

                Yours Truly,

                H. M. Knowlton

HK098
Notes, handwritten in lead.

Joe Carpenter, about 35.
Stole from Borden & Almy.
Family in F. Riv.

Once in Binghampton, N.Y.
Last known in Holyoke
    Peddling ink &   <u>before</u> murder!

Man shaved him in Fall Riv Monday Aug. 1 -
    (Pete Driscoll, barber.)

Geo. W. Barney is his father in law-
School teacher in F R named Dean knows that Carpenter was in F.R. Aug 4th & left with his wife next day.

HK099
Letter, typewritten.

ATTORNEY GENERAL'S DEPARTMENT, COMMONWEALTH BUILDING,
Boston, Nov. 22, 1892.

My Dear Knowlton:-

Jennings was here to-day, evidently indisposed to consent at first, , but more inclined to before he left, I think. He went away saying that he must see Adams, and that he would let us hear from him as soon as possible.

Jennings tells me a story about one Joe. Carpenter, who had a grudge against Borden, who he says ought to have been looked up. He says Pete Driscoll a Fall River barber shaved Carpenter in Fall River Monday, August 1st. He is a son-in-law of George W. Barney, of Fall River, and is known there as a rather shady character. Have you ever heard of this; or has anything been done about it?

Yours truly,

Attorney General

Hon. H. M. Knowlton,

HK100
Letter, typewritten, with comment handwritten in lead.

ATTORNEY GENERAL'S DEPARTMENT, COMMONWEALTH BUILDING,
Boston, Nov. 23, 1892.

Dear Mr. Attorney:-

You saw the Herald article yesterday morning, of course. This will indicate to you doubtless, as it does to me, not only that the reporter

(Billings, I think, but don't know certain) has lied a good deal, and also that some juror has "leaked" a little. The unavoidable difficulties of this accursed case are such that I am reluctant to add to them, but I think you ought to bring this before the grand jury, and have something done about it. There never was a better opportunity for teaching the officers of the law to hold their tongues, and newspaper reporters to let them alone, and it ought to be availed of. Probably I shall see you in the interval.

Very truly yours,
A. E. Pillsbury,
Attorney General.

Hon. H. M. Knowlton,

Nous sommes d'accord, mais <u>comment</u> ale fairer

(Note: French comment at end of letter is in handwriting of Hosea Monill Knowlton.)

HK101
Letter, typewritten.

ATTORNEY GENERAL'S DEPARTMENT,
COMMONWEALTH BUILDING.

Boston, Nov. 23, 1892.

Dear Mr. Attorney:-

You saw the Herald article yesterday morning, of course. This will indicate to you doubtless, as it does to me, not only that the reporter (Billings, I think, but don't know certain) has lied a good deal, and also that some juror has "leaked" a little. The unavoidable difficulties of this accursed case are such that I am reluctant to add to them, but I think you ought to bring this before the grand jury, and have something done about it. There never was a better opportunity for teaching the officers of the law to hold their tongues, and newspaper reporters to let them alone, and it ought to be availed of. Probably I shall see you in the interval.

Very truly yours,

Attorney General.

Hon. H.M. Knowlton,

(Note: This letter is a carbon copy of the preceding letter.)

HK102
Report, handwritten in ink.

November 24, 1892

H. A. Knowlton
District Atty.
New Bedford, Mass.

Sir,
    I have interviewed the following named persons in reference to the relatives of Lizzie Borden who said as follows:

<u>Capt. James C. Stafford</u> North St. New Bedford.
    I use to know quite well the mother of Lizzie Borden, her name was Sarah Morse. She had a sister and brothers. John now in Fall River, another brother who is a Blacksmith and is now out West. Mrs. Morse the mother of Lizzie Bordon was a very peculiar woman. She had a <u>Very bad temper</u>. She was very strong in her likes and dislikes. I never knew or heard of any of the Morses or Bordons was ever Insane or anything like it. I use to live in Fall River and always knew the Bordens and the Morses. Mrs Gray who lives on this St. may tell you something aboute them, also a Mrs Almy who lives on Franklin St, Fall River.

<u>Mrs. - Holland</u> Daughter of Mrs. Gray Resides on North St. New Bedford. Same house with Mrs. Gray. I never heard my mother say that Lizzie Bordon her mother or any of the Morses is or ever was Insane or anything like it. I always have heard that they were somewhat peculiar and odd. I have heard my mother talk considerable about Bordens and the Morses but never heard her say that any of them were Insane.

<u>Abraham G. Hart</u> Cashier Savings bank Fall River. I have live here most all my life. I never knew much aboute Lizzie Borden or her mother. I never knew much about the brothers of Lizzie Bordens mother. Always known of them. I never heard that any of the Morses or Bordens was ever Insane.

<u>S. H. Miller</u> 93 Second St. Fall River opp. the Bordon House. I have lived in Fall River 64 years. Bordon use to work for me. I know the Bordons and all of the Morses. the father of Lizzies mother was Anthony Morse. I use to know his two brothers. Know the brothers of Mrs. Morse, Lizzies mother. One is

Southard Harrison Miller, circa 1885.
Photograph by Mrs. Edwin F. Gay, Fall River, Massachusetts.

now supposed to be out West. I never knew or never heard that any of the Morses is or was Insane. Know they were somewhat peculiar. Anthony Morse had two brothers George and Gardiner Morse. I was not a witness at the trial. I did not intend to be. I saw Mr. Borden a little while before the murder. Bridget, the Servant girl came running into my house and said both was dead just then a man was passing I called him and told Bridget to tell him what she told me. She did and that man was a witness. I did not want anything to do with it and I did not go near the house.

Rescom Case 199 Second St. Fall River. I have lived in Fall River 57 years and I know all the Bordens and the Morses well. A sister of Mrs. Morse (Lizzies mother, married his cousin, a man named Morse, they now live here in Fall River. I use to know Anthony, father of Lizzies mother. He has a brother now living in Warren Mass. the woman that was murdered use to visit my house often, but she use to keep her affairs to herself pretty well, but I assure you I have my opinion of Lizzie Borden and I hope they will get more evidence. My wife dont know any more than I do aboute the Bordons or Morses. We never heard that anyone of them is or ever was Insane but <u>I think some of them worse than Insane.</u>

Nov. 26.
<u>John S. Brayton</u> Fall River. I have lived here great meny years. I know the Morses Mother of Lizzie Borden was Sarah, her father was Anthony Morse. I think her sister is dead. Anthony Morse was a farmer, after he owned a milk route. I never heard of anyone of them as being Insane or having any streak of Insanity.

<u>D. S. Brigam</u> Ex. City Marshal of Fall River I use to know the Morses never heard of any of them as being Insane, but this girl Lizzie Borden is known by a number of people here to be a woman of a bad disposition if they tell what they know.

<u>Geo. A. Patty</u>, Fall River I did not know much aboute the history of the Morses but never heard that any of them is or was ever Insane but Lizzie is known to be ugly.

<u>Mrs. Geo. W. Whitehead</u> 45 4th St. Fall River   Sister of Mrs. Borden who was murdered never heard that any of the Morses was Insane but ugly. Since the murder people have said if she is guilty she must be Insane.

Mrs. William Almy Franklin St. Fall River Always known the Bordens and the Morses, but for several years I have not known much aboute any of them. Some 30 years ago my husband who is now dead was in company with Mr Bordon. I use to know the brother of Mrs. Morse (Lizzies Mother) also her sister. I think their was 4 brothers. I have never heard that their was ever any Insanity or anything like it among any of the Morses.

Chester W. Green 80 years old lives in Fall River and have for 40 years. I know the Bordens and the Morses but I dont know much aboute. Never heard as any of them was ever Insane or anything like it.

William Carr lived in Fall River for 40 years I know the Bordons better then I know the Morses. The Bordons are peculiar people but I never heard that any of the Bordons or the Morses is or was ever Insane.
                        Respectfully,

                                        Moulton Batchelder .
                                        Dist. Police

HK103
Letter, typewritten.

ATTORNEY GENERAL'S DEPARTMENT, COMMONWEALTH BUILDING,
                        Boston, Nov. 25, 1892.

Dear Mr. Attorney:-
            I send you by this mail another choice production of the Herald, which obviously should go with the other, if anything is to be done about either.
                        Very truly yours,

Hon. H. M. Knowlton,
            New Bedford, Mass.

HK104
Letter, handwritten in ink.

Hon. Albert Pillsbury,

    A lady in Concord desires to thank you for your efforts to sift the evidence in the Borden case. Your appearance before the Grand Jury at Taunton is the <u>greatest possible</u> relief to the public mind. We have been so anxious about Miss Borden for fear certain people might do what they appear to wish to do, <u>convict her</u>. If it were not that you are the control- ling power, the people would rise an take Miss Borden out of jail.
    Very prominent physicians agree that a woman, or they think that a woman could not perform such a double crime without certain physical conditions following and these did not follow with Miss Borden.
    We feel satisfied to leave the case in your hands at present.

Respectfully yours,

Citizen of Concord

Nov. 25. 1892.

HK105
Letter, typewritten.

ATTORNEY GENERAL'S DEPARTMENT,
COMMONWEALTH BUILDING,
Boston, Nov. 28, 1892.

Dear Mr. Attorney:-
    Your French communication was received this morning, but perhaps we disposed of it yesterday. The managing editor of the Herald is John H. Holmes; and Warren T. Billings is the reporter to whom I have heard these articles ascribed. Perhaps they originated in Taunton, in which case the grand jury can begin nearer home. I should be inclined to follow up this Herald matter, even if the grand jury had to be held, or adjourned over for it. I incline to think the best way is for them to make a special presentation of these matters to the court, requesting action.

I return Batchelder's report, which seems to contain nothing.
Yours truly,
Attorney General

Hon. H. M. Knowlton,
New Bedford, Mass.

HK106
Letter, typewritten, with postscript handwritten in ink.

HOSEA M. KNOWLTON.   ARTHUR E. PERRY.
COUNSELLORS AT LAW.
OFFICE:
38 NORTH WATER STREET.

{Dictated.}

NEW BEDFORD, MASS. November 29, 1892.

Hon. A. E. Pillsbury,
            Attorney General.
                        Dear Sir:-
                                    I hand you enclosed a "Standard" containing an extract from the Fall River "Globe." Of course such things are very annoying, particularly when there is no opportunity to strike back, or to deny. The only possible foundation in the story that I can conceive of is on the one hand the persistence with which the reporters, and a portion of the public, have regarded me as being blindly bent upon l prosecution; and, on the other hand, the fact that you addressed the grand jury, which latter fact has probably leaked out through some hot headed partisan of the governments case. These two things added to the unexpected adjournment have furnished a page of rot, which is as dis- agreeable as it is untrue.

I thought you ought to see it and read it. Of course you may well believe that no hint or expression of mine has led to it, for I have entirely agreed with you in the whole matter, excepting as to one matter of policy which you stated to the jury, and as to which I have expressed no dissent, excepting so far as I had to you personally.

Yours truly,
H.M.K

P.S. *Much obliged for citations by telephone. A non-[?] of his child was for denying its legitimacy; but I unexpectedly found he had been once before convicted, of the same offense: so I shut off his wind.*

HK107
Letter, typewritten.

ATTORNEY GENERAL'S DEPARTMENT, COMMONWEALTH BUILDING.
Boston, Nov. 30, 1892.

Dear Mr. Attorney:-

The whole procession of reporters has been here this morning, inquiring about the truth of the statement in this morning's journal. I have seen none of the reporters, and have not even seen the story, but am told that it relates to insanity; and that the statement in general is that you or I, or both, have come to the conclusion that she is insane, and that the case is to be stopped. Perhaps you had better get hold of it, and I shall later. It is, of course, unnecessary to say to you that there is not one atom of foundation in fact for any of these statements. I have given no living man, woman or child the remotest intimation of my view of the case; not even my wife, who knows as little how I regard it as your wife does.

Adams has been in here in quite a state of excitement, saying that he has heard an ugly rumor that he was before the grand jury, and liable to be indicted. I did not ask him the source of it, and said only that I knew nothing about it; and that it was not likely that it would happen without any knowledge of mine. Nothing more was said of consequence.

Very truly, yours,

Attorney General.

HK108
Letter, handwritten.

ATTORNEY GENERAL'S DEPARTMENT, COMMONWEALTH BUILDING,
Boston, Nov. 30, 1892.

Dear Knowlton:-

Yours and the paper just received. It is all in the highest degree damnable, but don't see that we can say anything, unless you choose to deny the statement that that there is any difference between you and me. I should not wish the public to believe there was, especially as it is not true; but of course it is doubtful whether anything had better be denied. I leave it to you to act as you see fit.

Yours truly,

Hon. H. M. Knowlton,
          New Bedford, Mass.

Page 111

HK109
Document, printed, with notation handwritten in ink.

No.

INDICTMENT.
COMMONWEALTH
vs.
LIZZIE ANDREW BORDEN.
MURDER.

Bristol SS.   Sup. Court. Nov. Term, 1892.

Rec'd Dec 6 1892

COMMONWEALTH of MASSACHUSETTS.

BRISTOL SS.   At the Superior Court begun and holden at Taunton within and for said County of Bristol, on the first Monday of November, in the year of our Lord one thousand eight hundred and ninety-two.

The Jurors for the said Commonwealth, on their oath present,- That Lizzie Andrew Borden of Fall River in the County of Bristol, at Fall River in the County of Bristol, on the fourth day of August in the year eighteen hundred and ninety-two, in and upon one Andrew Jackson Borden, feloniously, wilfully and of her malice aforethought, an assault did make, and with a certain weapon, to wit, a sharp cutting instrument, the name and a more particular description of which is to the Jurors unknown, him, the said Andrew Jackson Borden feloniously, wilfully and of her malice aforethought, did strike, cut, beat and bruise, in and upon the head of him, the said Andrew Jackson Borden, giving to him, the said Andrew Jackson Borden, by the said striking cutting, beating and bruising, in and upon the head of him, the said Andrew Jackson Borden, divers, to wit, ten mortal wounds, of which said mortal wounds the said Andrew Jackson Borden then and there instantly died.

And so the Jurors aforesaid, upon their oath aforesaid, do say, that the said Lizzie Andrew Borden, the said Andrew Jackson Borden, in manner and form aforesaid, then and there feloniously, willfully and or her malice aforethought did kill and murder; against the peace of said Commonwealth and contrary to the form of the statute in such case made and provided.

    A true bill.

HENRY A. BODMAN
Foreman of the Grand Jury.

HOSEA M. KNOWLTON
District Attorney

    Bristol ss. On the second day of December, in the year eighteen hundred and ninety-two, this indictment was returned and presented to said Superior Court by the Grand Jury, ordered to be filed, and filed; and it was further ordered by the Court that notice be given to said Lizzie Andrew Borden that said indictment will be entered forthwith upon the docket of the Superior Court in said County.

    Attest:--

SIMEON BORDEN Jr.,
Asst. Clerk.

A true copy
    Attest: Simeon Borden Clerk.

HK110

Document, printed, with notation handwritten in ink.

No. _____

INDICTMENT.

COMMONWEALTH
vs.
LIZZIE ANDREW BORDEN.

MURDER.

Bristol SS.   Sup. Court. Nov. Term, 1892.

Rec'd Dec 6 1892

COMMONWEALTH of MASSACHUSETTS.
BRISTOL SS.   At the Superior Court begun and holden at Taunton within and for said County of Bristol, on the first Monday of November, in the year of our Lord one thousand eight hundred and ninety-two.

The Jurors for the said Commonwealth, on their oath present,- That Lizzie Andrew Borden of Fall River in the County of Bristol, at Fall River in the County of Bristol, on the fourth day of August in the year eighteen hundred and ninety-two, in and upon one Abby Durfee Borden, feloniously, wilfully and of her malice aforethought, an assault did make, and with a certain weapon, to wit, a sharp cutting instrument, the name and a more particular description of which is to the Jurors unknown, her, the said Abby Durfee Borden feloniously, wilfully and of her malice aforethought, did strike, cut, beat and bruise, in and upon the head of her, the said Abby Durfee Borden, giving to her, the said Abby Durfee Borden, by the said striking cutting, beating and bruising, in and upon the head of her, the said Abby Durfee Borden, divers, to wit, twenty mortal wounds, of which said mortal wounds the said Abby Durfee Borden then and there instantly died.

And so the Jurors aforesaid, upon their oath aforesaid, do say, that the said Lizzie Andrew Borden, the said Abby Durfee Borden, in manner and form aforesaid, then and there feloniously, wilfully and or her malice aforethought did kill and murder; against the peace of said Commonwealth and contrary to the form of the statute in such case made and provided.

    A true bill.

HENRY A. BODMAN,
Foreman of the Grand Jury.

HOSEA M. KNOWLTON,
District Attorney

Bristol ss. On the second day of December, in the year eighteen hundred and ninety-two, this indictment was returned and presented to said Superior Court by the Grand Jury, ordered to be filed, and filed; and it was further ordered by the Court that notice be given to said Lizzie Andrew Borden that said indictment will be entered forthwith upon the docket of the Superior Court in said County.

    Attest:--

SIMEON BORDEN Jr.,
Asst. Clerk.

A true copy
    Attest: Simeon Borden Clerk.

HK111
Document, printed, with notation handwritten in ink.

No.

INDICTMENT.

COMMONWEALTH
vs.
LIZZIE ANDREW BORDEN.

MURDER.

Bristol SS.   Sup. Court. Nov. Term, 1892.

Rec'd Dec 6 1892

COMMONWEALTH of MASSACHUSETTS.

BRISTOL SS.   At the Superior Court begun and holden at Taunton within and for said County of Bristol, on the first Monday of November, in the year of our Lord one thousand eight hundred and ninety-two.

The jurors for the said Commonwealth on their oath present, -- That Lizzie Andrew Borden of Fall River in the County of Bristol, at Fall River in the County of Bristol, on the fourth day of August in the year eighteen hundred and ninety-two in and upon one Abby Durfee Borden, feloniously and wilfully and of her malice aforethought an assault did make, and with a certain weapon, to wit, a sharp cutting instrument, the name and a more particular description of which is to the jurors unknown, her, the said Abby Durfee Borden, feloniously, wilfully and of her malice aforethought, did strike, cut, beat and bruise in and upon the head of her, the said Abby Durfee Borden, giving to her, the said Abby Durfee Borden, by the said striking, cutting, beating and bruising in and upon the head of her, the said Abby Durfee Borden, divers to wit, twenty mortal wounds, of which said mortal wounds the said Abby Durfee Borden then and there instantly died.

And so the jurors aforesaid upon their oath aforesaid, do say, that the said Lizzie Andrew Borden, the said Abby Durfee Borden, in manner and form aforesaid, then and there feloniously, wilfully and of her malice aforethought did kill and murder; against the peace of said Commonwealth and contrary to the form of the statute in such case made and provided.

And the jurors for the said Commonwealth on their oaths do further present, -- That Lizzie Andrew Borden, of Fall River in the county of Bristol at Fall River in the county of Bristol, on the fourth day of August in the year eighteen hundred and ninety-two, in and upon one Andrew Jackson Borden feloniously, wilfully and of her malice aforethought, an assault did make, and with a certain weapon, to wit, a sharp cutting instrument, the name and a more particular description of which is to the Jurors unknown, him, the said Andrew Jackson Borden, feloniously, wilfully and of her malice aforethought, did strike, cut, beat and bruise in and upon the head of him, the said Andrew Jackson Borden, giving to him, the said Andrew Jackson Borden, by the said striking, cutting, beating and bruising, in and upon the head of him, the said Andrew Jackson Borden, divers, to wit, ten mortal wounds, of which said mortal wounds the said Andrew Jackson Borden then and there instantly died.

And so the jurors aforesaid, upon their oath aforesaid, do say, that the said Lizzie Andrew Borden, the said Andrew Jackson Borden in manner and form aforesaid, then and there feloniously, wilfully and of her malice aforethought did kill and murder; against the peace of said Commonwealth contrary to the form of the statutes in such case made and provided.

A true bill.

HENRY A. BODMAN,
Foreman of the Grand Jury.

HOSEA M. KNOWLTON,
District Attorney.

Bristol ss. On the second day of December, in the year eighteen hundred and ninety-two, this indictment was returned and presented to said Superior Court by the Grand Jury, ordered to be filed, and filed; and it was further ordered by the Court that notice be given to said Lizzie Andrew Borden that said indictment will be entered forthwith upon the docket of the Superior Court in said County.

Attest:--

SIMEON BORDEN Jr.,
Asst. Clerk.

A true copy
Attest: Simeon Borden Clerk.

HK112
Letter, handwritten in ink.

Brattleboro Vt.Dec1st/92

Hon. Attorney Knowlton
        Taunton
              Dear Sir:
befor you condem Miss Borden Please take that Bridget Sullivan & her Confessor & Put them in Stateprison until they tell what know about that murder & you will get at the real murderer of the two Bordens & tell just how the job was put up & executed & covered up this is the opinion of most of the New England states beware of Jesuits sure
              Res yours
              ABD

HK113
Letter, handwritten in ink, enclosed in holograph envelope.

Fall River Dec 2nd/92

    I have a few words of importance that I think will be of service in Lizzie Borden's Case. on the day of the murder I was coming towards Fall River from the Shove Mill, where I met Doctor Bowen and a young man In a Carriage, driving so fast that I turned around to look after them. I thought at the time that someone was dieing and He was going to see them. I am well acquainted with Him, but I never saw Him look so wild in my life before, it was 15 about minets to eleven. the young man was sitting on the left side of the Doctor. I met them near the Slade School house, the Doctor had hold of the reins with boath hands, driving for dear life. has Doctor Bowen ever been questioned were He was on the morning of the Murder. this is the truth and nothing but the truth.

HK114

Letter, typewritten, with notations handwritten in ink.

HOSEA M. KNOWLTON. ARTHUR E. PERRY
COUNSELLORS AT LAW
OFFICE:
38 NORTH WATER STREET.

{Dictated}

NEW BEDFORD, MASS. December 3, 1892

Hon. A. E. Pillsbury,

Dear Sir: -

A few things you will not read in the newspapers may interest you. We met Thursday morning, and Miss Russell delivered herself of her story: It was on Sunday (not Saturday) the morning after the search, and the first day that Bridget was not in the kitchen. Miss Russell came in about nine o'clock, and Lizzie *stood* sat by the stove and Emma was washing dishes. The whole story is a singular one, and I will go into details when I see you. Mrs. Churchill and Bridget Sullivan also testified briefly.

I then told them what the law was in relation to principals and accessories, following the line of the Knapp case, but warning them that while I gave them this law I did not want them to infer anything in relation to our views as to the case, but only to put before them the law bearing upon all possible aspects. I also took the occasion to say to them that among the many untrue things that have been reported in the paper it might be gratifying to them to know that there was not any difference in regard to the case between you and me, and that you were present by my request.

I then left them at 10:30 A.M. They adjourned for dinner and reached a vote at five o'clock. It was a substantial vote but not unanimous, which is all I know. I do not even know how any man voted. We then agreed to keep the matter to ourselves until the next day, an agreement which I think faithfully kept. Next morning we introduced the evidence, and indicted Trickey.

I showed the newspapers, and called their attention to them, but, after talking the matter over, they decided not to do anything: and perhaps it is well on the whole. They were quite anxious to put in the *a* paper certifying to the impartial way in which we have presented the case, but I told them they better not do that.

I hope to see you soon, but this month I propose to attend to the support of my family. The civil term begins Tuesday, and I must look out for it to the exclusion all of other things.

Yours Truly,
H. M. Knowlton

HK115
Letter, handwritten in ink.

Dec 3/92

My Dear Pillsbury

Mr. Morse wishes to go out West and wants to know if any chance of his being needed this month. As he wishes to go Tuesday – wire or write me so I can get it Monday. I spoke to Knowlton about it & he said he had no objection if he would come back.

A. J. Jennings

HK116
Letter, typewritten.

ATTORNEY GENERAL'S DEPARTMENT
COMMONWEALTH BUILDING

Boston, Dec. 5, 1892.

Bro. Hurd: -

Without actually doubting the truth of this Trickey story, I wish to know the truth; as I knew the alleged deceased pretty well, and know him to be capable of a number of things, unless you have yourself absolute means of knowledge that the story is true, and that it is actually Trickey who was killed. I wish you would take, immediately, the necessary steps to have such inquiry made through the police as will settle the fact. I made the request of you as your office is in charge of the indictment here; and as you know the police and the proper instruments or channels of inquiry so much better than I do.

Very truly yours,
Attorney General.

F. W. Hurd, Esq.

HK117
Letter, typewritten.

ATTORNEY GENERAL'S DEPARTMENT, COMMONWEALTH BUILDING,
Boston, Dec. 5, 1892.

Bro. Jennings:-

    I can make no promise or stipulation, of course, but I should think you might safely rely on what Mr. Knowlton said to you.

    Very truly yours,

Hon. Andrew J. Jennings,

HK118
Letter, typewritten.

HOSEA M. KNOWLTON. ARTHUR E. PERRY.
COUNSELLORS AT LAW.
OFFICE:
38 NORTH WATER STREET,

{Dictated}.

NEW BEDFORD, MASS. December 6, 1892.

Hon. A. E. Pillsbury,

    My Dear Mr. Attorney General:-

    I do not know when I can come down to see you, probably not until Saturday. Of course the future disposition of the Borden case is in your hands entirely; but I will venture a suggestion. I am pretty well occupied every month between now and June with civil business, and if the trial could be assigned for some time in February, or June, I could have some one else take my regular criminal work, and it would not be so expensive for me.

    I write this not knowing whether you are proposing to make any arrangements or not at present.

    Yours Truly,
    H. M. Knowlton
    per C.

HK119

Letter, typewritten.

ATTORNEY GENERAL'S DEPARTMENT, COMMONWEALTH BUILDING,

Boston, Dec. 7, 1892

Dear Mr. Attorney:-
      The subject of your letter depends upon so many considerations, that nothing can be said about it until we can confer. I shall be here Saturday, and all days at present, so far as I know, and shall be glad to see you at any time when you can catch me.

                Very truly yours,
                Attorney General.

Hon. H. M. Knowlton,

HK120

Letter, handwritten in ink.

COMMONWEALTH OF MASSACHUSETTS.
OFFICE of DISTRICT ATTORNEY.
BOSTON.

7th. Dec. 1892.

Dear Mr. Pillsbury,
      After receiving your letter of the 5th. I sent Inspector Dugan, who was acquainted with Trickey, to satisfy himself. He went to the funeral and informs me this morning that there is no doubt that Mr. Trickey is no more.

                Yours very truly
                F. E. Hurd.

P.S. Herewith please find the minutes of testimony
                F.E.H.

HK121
Letter, typewritten.

ANDREW J. JENNINGS,
COUNSELLOR AT LAW
SECTION G, GRANITE BLOCK

December 10, 1892.

Hon. A. E. Pillsbury,
    Attorney General,
        Boston, Mass.

My dear Pillsbury:-

    Cac you give me any idea when the Borden case will be likely to be set down for trial? I do not care to know the day but would like, if possible, to know the month. As I told you my client is very anxious to have the case tried at Taunton as she very much prefers to stay at her present quarters, as she has got accustomed to them, and also on account of the fact that Mrs. Wright is in charge who has been very kind to her and who was a neighbor of her parents for a number of years when she was a little girl.

    She is very urgent in this desire and I trust it can be brought about without seriously interfering with the arrangements of the Government, and if so her request may be granted.

        Truly yours,

            Andrew J. Jennings.
            per J.B.

HK122
Letter, typewritten.

ATTORNEY GENERAL'S DEPARTMENT,
COMMONWEALTH BUILDING.

Boston Dec. 12, 1892

Hon. Andrew J. Jennings.
        My Dear Sir:-

           I am not at present able to give you any information upon the subject of your first inquiry.

As to the place, I don't suppose anybody on the part of the government has so much as thought of it; and of course it will be for the court to determine. At present, I know no reason why it may not be at Taunton as well as anywhere.

Please treat this as personal to yourself. I am not now in position to know or to stipulate anything upon either point.

Very truly yours,
Attorney General

Fall River, Mass.

HK123
Letter, typewritten.

HOSEA M. KNOWLTON. ARTHUR E. PERRY.
COUNSELLORS AT LAW.
Office:
38 NORTH WATER STREET.

{Dictated}.

NEW BEDFORD, MASS., December 27, 1892.

Mrs. A. E. Pillsbury,

Dear Mrs. Pillsbury:- Your letter of the 26th is received. I will see that nothing is done in any case in which I am interested with the Attorney General, until he is so far recovered that we can confer together.

I am very glad to hear of his improvement, and trust that it will be as speedy as you hope. Please give him my regards.

Yours Truly,
H. M. Knowlton
per E.

1892 Undated Documents

HK124
Letter, handwritten in lead.

Any one deliberately planning a murder might have wrapped a newspaper around each arm fastening it at the wrist with a string or rubber band -and pinned another paper as an apron. These would have held perhaps all or most of the blood. These papers could be quickly removed -and might have been perhaps the roll that was seen in the stove nearly burned.

HK125
Letter, typewritten.

Dear Sir:-

I understand that the "Bordens" have an old-fashioned piano; has it been examined? There is usually a vacant place on the left side of the key board, where by removing the paneling a sufficient space could be made to hide several hatchets if need be. The tone of the piano would not be affected:it is sometimes necessary to remove the action first, but if pre- pared beforehand it would take but a few minutes.

There is also a space in the back of a stove, where an axe would go in, and hidden temporarily. not affect the draft in case the fire was kindled.

?.?.??????.

HK126
Letter, handwritten in ink.

<u>Confidential</u>

A theory of the Borden murders by a person who has had some experience with insane persons & criminals.

1<u>st</u>   The motive was money & hatred of a stepmother.
2<u>nd</u> The parties to be benefited were the Borden girls and the girls uncle.
3<u>rd</u> Mrs. Borden was killed first & Mr. Borden was her heir.
4<u>th</u> Mr. Borden was killed last and so the Borden girls were the heirs to all the Borden money.

5th   The uncle is the heir of the Borden girls, if they should die before him (without children) which is very likely at their age.
6th   A fourth of a million of dollars was saved to the Borden girls by the mothers death: by the mothers death before the fathers, and a per cent of a fourth of a million of dollars to some persons, would be a sufficient motive for the committal of a crime, even a murder, or murders.
7th   The murders were committed & by whom? - and
8th   It was done by some member of the household. or by an outside party.
9th   If by a member of the household, it must have been one of two persons. Bridget Sullivan or Lizzie Borden. If by an outsider how did he get in & out of the house & where was he secreted while in the house?
10th   If the murders were committed by an outsider, he must have been let in by an interested party and secreted in a closet or under a bed.
11th   There were five persons in the house, Mr. & Mrs. Borden Mr. Morse, Lizzie Borden & Bridget Sullivan. Mr & Mrs. Borden did not let him in. Then he must have been admitted by one of the other three. He might have been secreted in Mr. Morse s room as Mrs Borden was killed in his room. If so did Mr. Morse let him in?
12th   He was admitted during the night - & perhaps was the party who made the noise in getting over the neighbors fence.
13th
    This man whoever he might have been, was a cool calculating villain, & went about his work in a way to cover his tracks so there would be no possible means of detection.
    The instrument with which the crime was committed was evidently carried about his person, probably in a leather lined pocket, to which pocket it was returned immediately after each of the murders, even before the murderer had changed his position.
14th   If the murderer had have moved one foot or one yard from his murderous position, with his his hands & instrument of death, dripping with, blood, there must have been a perfect windrow of blood drops on the floor or carpet.
15th   No blood drops were found for the instrument was immediately returned to the leather lined pocket. As no bloody finger marks were found on doors or windows, the murders were without doubt committed with gloved hands & the gloves were returned to the leather lined pocket. -
16th   A long outside garment was on hand, ready for the occasion and when buttoned from top to bottom would hide ell all the blood spots on the clothing. And as the cellar door was found open (according to Mr. Morses last testimony) his escape was easy.
17th   It is said Lizzie did'nt see her uncle to speak to him from the time he

came to the house till after the murders. Was not that a part of an arrangement? And was not Mr. Morses leaving the house before 9 o'clock A.M. another part of the arrangement -?

18th   Emma was away and Lizzie did not go on her vacation. Was that another part of the arrangement? -

19th   If the murderer was in the house during a part of the night of Aug the 3rd, Why did he not do the killing while Mr. & Mrs. Borden were in bed & asleep, and escape during the night & darkness? Ans- Because he was afraid one or the other might awake & give an alarm -, and Mr. Morse would not be out of the house & consequently might & would have been suspected, & could not then have proved an alibi -

19th   I wish to repeat once more before leaving this part of the subject that the murderer was let in by an interested party & instructed how to get out by the same party. - Again if they had been killed in bed during the night there would have been a question to be settled, which died first, and the fourth of a million of dollars might have gone to Mrs. Bordens heirs. Now was not that a very <u>particular</u> part of the arrangement? -

20th   It is said the Borden house was the most "uniquely locked house in Fall River" then if the murderer was an outsider <u>he must have been let in by an interested party</u>. Leaving out of the question, as an interested party, Bridget Sullivan, it leaves only two persons who could have done it - Mr. Morse or Lizzie Borden.

21st   Whoever let the murderer into the house perfectly understood Mr. & Mrs. Bordens movements and instructed him in regards to their lying <u>down</u> and <u>rising up</u>, their <u>going out</u> & their <u>coming in</u>.

22nd   Were not the movements of Mr. Morse, Lizzie Borden & Bridget Sullivan that morning a part of the <u>arrangement</u>? But not arranged by Bridget Sullivan but by Mr. Morse & Lizzie Borden! - Every thing was arranged & went on like clockwork. There was no failure in any of the arrangements

23rd
The murderer secreted in the closet with the key in Lizzie Bordens pocket he would not be likely to know when Mr. Borden came into the house or when he was quiet in sleep on the lounge, until some person who knew, went up the stairs & let him understand that the coast was clear and the victim asleep (The same explination will apply to the killing of Mrs. Borden) & the same person who informed him that the coast was clear let him out of the house, after seeing that the <u>outside coast was clear</u>. Perhaps out of the front door and perhaps through the cellar.

24
It has been proved that Lizzie Borden was in the chambers most of the time while Bridget Sullivan was washing the outside windows. Was she there to let

the murderer out of the closet at the right time and to return him to it & lock him in & keep the key in her pocket until her fathers return?---

25th
Did Lizzie Borden kill her father & step mother?

26th
No.-

27th
It was a physical impossibility for her to have done it and to have covered her tracks so completely in the short space of 13 minutes. - Blood Stains are so dificult to remove. She could not have cleansed the instrument of death in 13 minutes, if she had have had a <u>river of water at hand</u>. The blood would have clung to every rough point and would have settled between the handle & blade & clotted there & all of it could not have been removed. She could not have washed it all from her hands. It would have clung about the nails & between the fingers & when dried would have shown. Every surgeon knows how dificult it is to remove all the blood stains from the best & highest polished instruments.

28th
Again if the clothing had been burned or the shoes the oder of burnt cloth, of burnt leather and of burnt blood, would have remained in the house for hours. - I once more repeat it was a physical impossibility for Lizzie Borden, or any other living person, to have committed the murders and cleaned up every thing So there should have been no blood spots on the floor, finger blood marks on the walls doors or windows or other traces of blood discovered or the oder of burned cloth, leather or blood in 13 minutes. -

29   Every thing was carried out of the house by the murderer

30   The one drop of blood on the garment was undoubtedly menstrual blood -

31st   If Mr. Morse had any thing to do with it the men & the horses in Westport woods were there as a <u>part of the arrangement</u>, and the murders planned accordingly

32nd   I have no doubt of the insanity of Lizzie Borden. She is a monomaniac in regard to her step-mother and her fathers money. She may be perfectly sane on all other subjects. The party who <u>executed the murders was not insane</u>.

33rd   Western men who have led irregular lives hold human life cheap. They always go armed and are walking (or rather riding) arsenals. They have leather pockets, in which they carry every kind of a tool as well as firearms - "Mr. & Mrs. Borden were killed with their backs turned to the murderer and the murders were done, and were the result of a deliberate plan and arranged with the utmost care in all its details beforehand." -

34<u>th</u> Mr. Morse came to the Borden house ostensibly to visit his niece with no <u>particular liking</u> for Mr. & Mrs. Borden. Still his niece was in the <u>house & well</u> not sick, did not see him from the time he arrived till after the murders. Was not that a part of the <u>arrangement</u>?

If you should wish to communicate with the writer, Direct to Miss Belle Ingalls, 76 White St. Haverhill Mass.

HK127

Letter, handwritten in ink, with comment handwritten in lead preceding greeting.

(I have just had this brilliant & original suggestion.)

Honorable
E.L. Pillsbury,
    Attorney General:-
      Sir,-

        Perhaps the well in the barn visited by Lizzie Borden about the hour of the murders may contain the hatchet used. Very likely this thought may have occurred to those having the matter in charge, but I have not learned of an intimation of it.

<u>Very respectfully,</u>

HK128

Letter, handwritten in ink.

Dear Sir:

    It has been stated in evidence that the sofa upon which Mr. Borden lay when first discovered after the murder was placed so that the end at head of body was even with door casing of door opening into dining room. Now a <u>left handed</u> person could have used a hatchet effectively, while <u>standing in the dining room</u> as only the left arm would be exposed to the spattering blood. Is L.B. left handed? Why was Mr. Morse permit- ted to remove the catch lock from door of house two or three days after the murder? That lock ought to be in evidence

    A <u>newspaper</u> could have been used to protect the murderer or -ers from blood, and then burned in stove - If left hand was used as before suggested, a paper wrapped around arm would have afforded ample covering.

HK129
Letter, handwritten in ink.

Miss Lizzie Borden evidently did not Kill her father & mother but had some man come in, who brought in his own hatchet and took the same with him after he done the deed. He killed the mother while Bridget was cleaning the windows outside and Lizzie concealed him till Bridget went up to her room, then the man Killed the father and left for parts unknown. Lizzie wanted to get her parents out of the way, so to live in better style, while she was yet not too old.

HK130
Letter, handwritten in ink.

District Atty. Knowlton
Dear Sir,
    There has been a deal said about the impossibility of Lizzie Borden killing her father and mother without without her clothing being stained with blood. Now every woman knows that a gossamer waterproof cloak, such as every owns, would protect the clothing completely and that a fire hot enough for our ironing would reduce it to ashes in less than five minutes. I have heard the subject discussed among women who claim to know.
                      An interested Spectator. J.D.V.

HK131
Letter, handwritten in ink.

A most mysterious murder - double murder! Murders by outsiders are generally from wrath or for theft. No wrathful outside party is known - and such kill in open quarel or waylay with chances to escape undetected - Who would kill the <u>woman</u> from wrath? - kill her an hour more or less before hand, and wait for the husband in broad day light in an inhabited house? - then kill a man and vanish - unseen - unheard! Not for theft for none committed. Both daughters conveniently (?) away - Lizzie reporting Mrs. Borden out on an unknown call - she is in the house when the woman was killed - in the barn loft when he was slain! - object for barn visit trifling - length of visit

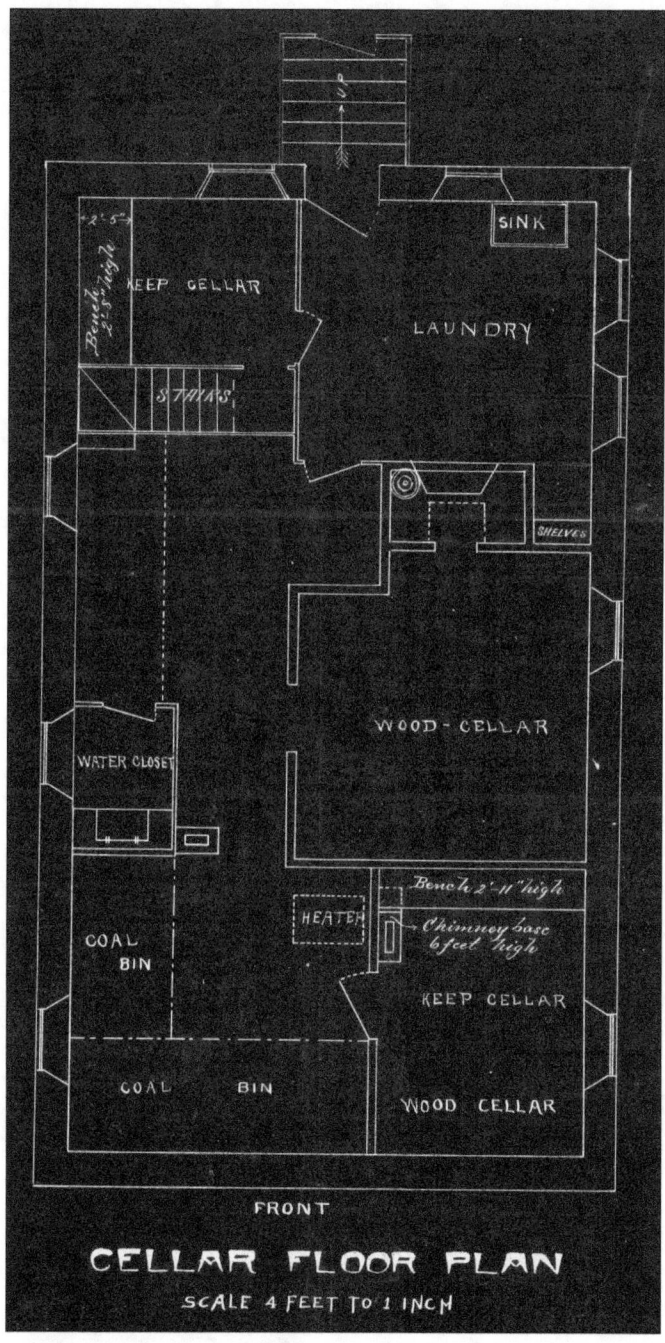

Trial Exhibit #8: cellar of the Borden residence.
Plan drawn by Thomas Kieran, Fall River, Massachusetts.

remarkable - No sudden, frantic scream when she finds her murdered father - no rushing to his side - no examination to find a spark of life - no calling for the mother whom she had heard come in - nor to neighbors! Suggest that mother may have been murdered! Considering all things it is next to impossible that she could or would have committed the murders. They were committed. What motive? Inheritance? Slight. It seems impossible that the murder should be committed - they were. If Lizzie thought to poison them I think she is the murderer - I seems incredible that she knows nothing about it. She at once defends the farm hands - I should hunt up there wheareabout that forenoon - In the Salem case (Murder of White) the murderer was sick abed and had been for days. One hired man sick and away from the other - one sister visiting and away from the other. Who sent the note to Mrs. Borden that morning if note there was? What was that burned paper in the stove? What became of the Providence Journal Mr. Borden was reading - could bloody clothes have been burned? Which way was the wind? Is the visitor all right? Bridget all right? The wood sawer all right? Have cellar and its walls - its bottom - chimney & pipe flues - between walls - under buildings and floors - out of sight spaces for burial - all - all been searched for it seems that an unfound weapon mayor perhaps must exist? A Haverhill clergyman's wife with boy & girl killed 10 Indians as they slept in 1697 - A Western Minister's wife during a protracted meeting waylaid and killed a woman for jealousy with a flat iron - was tried and acquitted and confessed on her death bed. God protect Lizzie if innocent!

HK132
Note, handwritten in ink.

Would like explanation.
When did she get paint on dress? How so? Why burn it at that time of trouble. Women usually use a <u>rag bag</u> for that purpose, not a stove.

HK133
Note, handwritten in ink.

Do you not think that <u>Dalton</u> the Murderer of Haskell may have committed the Borden Murders. He was seen in Fall River.

E.L.

HK134
Letter, handwritten in ink.

The skull cannot be crushed by a sharp blade -
The scalp is notorious for opening like a gash as if made by an ax or hatchet, when a blow from a billet, or a fall on stone or timber, as is well known, has caused the cut. No one unless an adept could have given as many blows on the head as appears in the evidence, in quick succession, without having some, if not many of them, glide off and strike that on which the head lay, cutting or marking or causing a blood mark showing the line of the edge.

A flat-iron would do all the bloody work in the hand of a woman. It could easily be washed clean in hot water & replaced on the hot stove and no one think of examining it So many blows by a hatchet would have made mince meat of the scalp.

HK135
Letter, handwritten in lead.

A MAN NAMED RODMAN OF BOSTON HAD A SISTER WHO WAS SICK ABED WITH A COLD. SHE HAD HEART DISEASE AND THE DOCTOR SAID SHE MIGHT DIE ANYTIME OF HEART DISEASE. LIZZIE BORDEN WAS HER FRIEND AND WAS ALONE WITH HER WHEN SHE DIED - AFTER HER DEATH BLACK MARKS WERE FOUND ON HER NECK AND HER JEWELRY WAS GONE. NOT A GREAT AMOUNT OF JEWELRY. <u>AT THE TIME</u> LIZZIE BORDEN WAS NOT SUSPECTED. THIS MAN HAS A PARTNER NAMED HARDY WHO I THINK IS AT BEDFORD SPRINGS.

HK136
Letter, handwritten in ink.

Mr Pillsbury,
    I desire to address a few words to you. No greater responsibility has ever rested upon your shoulders than rests upon them now in your connection with the future disposal of the Borden Case. The papers have recently given

to the public what appears to be a <u>conciliatory</u> message, in which it is said "your attitude toward the case is still one of inquiry only." The same letter stated that Miss Lizzie Borden will be fairly and considerately dealt with." I have been deeply interested in that statement and wonder whether I am in Massachusetts or in Russia.

In the same letter is the statement that the Attorney General speaks in high terms of Judge Blaisdell and Attorney Knowlton. But before your complimentary notice of them reached the public eye, another very important view of <u>their</u> proceedings had been widely circulated in the Boston Journal. The author of that article a prominent Boston gentlemen speaks of the Decision to send Miss Borden to jail, as, "what seems like professional conspiracy". Now this letter has been widely copied and circulated. Why should there be such a gulf between his opinion of the Fall River officials and yours?

A gentleman told me yesterday that the people everywhere in the State will rely upon you, to deal with the Borden Case properly and I asked him how they could rely upon you when you approve of Blaisdells and Knowlton's action and Miss Borden is held to day with out cause, this being the opinion of one of the most learned Judge's in this state. But this gentleman seemed to think the case a very difficult one, and that you make every effort to solve such.

I wonder if the officials of the law who have to deal with the Borden case realize what a powerful public opinion has been aroused. It is not the rabble with their pikes and guns who stand knocking at the doors of justice. It is the <u>moral</u> forces of the state the legal, the religious and the literary, representatives who are ready at a minutes notice to unite for action. While Miss Borden faces the tribunal over which you preside the officials of that tribunal <u>face</u> an aroused public opinion whose verdict may roll in on those Fall River officials in high over-lapping waves!

People seem to have confidence in you but they do not understand how you can uphold Blaisdell and Knowlton?

The papers announce that the Fall River Police are alert. The friends of <u>Miss Borden</u> and of <u>Justice are alert, yes indeed</u>!

Respectfully yours,
Citizen of
Massachusetts

HK137
Letter, handwritten in lead.

Dear Sir
aboat one year ago one member of our Familee after a hard Sicknes lost his mind so far that we hav to keep strickt watch ofver him - in the neight of betwin 3 a 4 thate morgon som was so fatal to the Bordn familie after wi had several Theims looking in his Room and seing no sign of mowing wi remowing the cowering of the bead - wi saw he had cunningle rapt up the Covering so to apair that he was aslep but hav not ben in ther att all. wi starting out to look for him and after 3 a 4 hours of hard driving and look- ing' wi att last se a terible objeckt, bloody, torn and ragged heiding among the brush and fences - wi know him at once - but how to get him - was another thing he was wild and had a pice of wood from a wagon with a Iron rung on the end, also - wi had to be careful I on with a gwick tempo drew a Blancket of wer him and a strugle it was befor we got in the Carige and den the driwe hom and our old freind the Docktor got him to rest it was fear full --- for som theim we had to care for him neight and day - wi for manny weeks had no theim for news papper or anny thing - at last our Docktor told uss about the trial of L. B. and hiss belief that our poor relatiw had som thing to do with it % wi caugt him on the road from Bordens wild bloodiy muthering to himself - fearful things so far wi can count wi get him betwin 10 a 11 - wi be all so owerworked could not notice theim -- our Docktor sad wi cannot make this public for the Raporter Sharks will kill uss all envading the house without regard to the famillee - and will kill not only him bout our dear mother to., our theorie is [?] afther he get out had runn god distance - be attacked of som boddy - struck down he had bigg [?] wound cross the Head and the blood was stif and hard - hiss pocket was torn out som thing missing and then afther he recovered had started towards B- house get in som way heiding der hear Somboddy stirring and fearfull of new attack stricking down the first he see - and afterwards running out ther wi caught him and now owr old freind say that wi has to make somthing for the poor girl - he saees the can never say her gulty but the Can make her Insane -% and now he is weak but gaining strenght but a Shock will drive him madd if he should pass away be sure I will gif you the fackts full on your honor that you spare the familee this is written of owr maid a Emegrant som Cant read the news paper and I som she suppose read this from a book -for to lern English you know -.-once more I assure you that if he pass away - I will gif you all the fackts for you att = ackt som you thinck best

Yours

My Name and hand I will <u>not</u> gif you at present
wi go now to Europe

HK138
Letter, handwritten in ink.

District Attorney Knowlton.
        Fall River, Mass.
Dear Sir:
    At the time of the Almy murder & search I predicted that he would be captured within a mile of the house.
    And now through no supernatural means or inspiration I predict that in the case of Lizzie Borden that she is not guilty in the sense of actual perpetration of the deed.
    But believe that she and possibly the servant Bridget know of the guilty party. And that the imprisonment of the servant might bring out revelations new to the case.
    Write this in belief that the murder was committed by some man - known to both servant and mistress.
    That's partly in consideration that the fact the dispatch and finish with which the deed was executed, points to no unfamilar hand with an axe, <u>beyound attainment</u> of the <u>feminine hand</u>.

HK139
Letter, handwritten in ink.

UNITED STATES SENATE,
FOLDING ROOM
WASHINGTON. D.C.,   **,189**

J.S. HICKCOX,
SUPERINTENDENT.
W. P. BROWNLOW,
ASST. SUPT.

Dist. Atty. Knowlton
        Fall River
                Mass.

Dear Sir:
    I share the universal interest in "Borden" mystery and concur in your view that the crimes were committed by some one who expected to be benefitted by them, and that the person who did the killing was a woman.

I have a theory in regard to these crimes that you may deem worthy of your consideration. It is as follows; 1st. Lizzie Borden had a female accomplice, and this accomplice with her, did the actual killing. 2d. Her accomplice would be benefitted by the death of the Bordens, either by inheritance, or by agreement with Lizzie to share in the benefit she would derive from the crimes. Either may have instigated the crimes. 3d. The accomplice was secreted in the Borden residence and Lizzie kept watch to guard against detection, and to facilitate the escape of her accomplice. 3d. The accomplice was in disguise. 4th. If the accomplice wore womans clothes, she was a near neighbor and after committing the crimes returned to her home and destroyed the evidence of her guilt. 5th. If she was disguised as a man she may have lived near or remote from the Borden residence.

My view is that the accomplice was disguised as a Man. The reasons for my theory are 1st. If Lizzie Borden did the actual killing, the evidence of her guilt would have been plainly apparent or easily discovered. 2d. The means used in committing these murders. The violence, and the instrument with which the killing was done, were intend to establish in the minds of people the belief that the crimes were committed by a Man, and logically, any other agency to prevent detection and facilitate escape, such as disguises etc. adopted in this plot, were all in the direction of the confirmation of this belief.

You of course know that secret murders are usually committed in the most subtile manner and rarely by persons who have the best opportunity to do them, and to whom suspicion would naturally avert, and when the criminal is detected he, or she, is often found to be a person which circumstances would show had the least possible chance to have committed the crime.

Respectfully Yours
J. S. Hickcox

HK140
Letter, handwritten in ink.

Mr. Moody Dear Sir
No doubt you will consider this the work of a "crank" but pardon me nevertheless for making the few suggestions <u>which might not come to your mind</u>.
1st would any person (out-side the family) intending to commit that murder of <u>brought</u> an axe or hatchet <u>with them</u>?

2nd Is there one person out of one hundred thousand fool enough to take a bloody axe or hatchet through the streets with them (after commiting such a foul deed), not knowing but the alarm would be given at once and a search made for the guilty one, and they have the proof of their guilt in their possession. Its absrud to think of

3rd If the murderer had been concealed under the bed could it be possible for him to get out without making some nois, enough to attract the attention of Mrs Borden (so little room beweeen the bed & floor) and would he been likely to of killed her so near the bed, Now if he had been concealed in the closet and came out & killed her would he been likely to of <u>crawled under</u> that bed with the <u>bloody axe in their possession</u>? If so how could he of know when Mr Borden returned (over an hour after he killed Mrs B.) and kill him soon as he laid down to take a rest; would any person be such a fool to tramp through the house in broad day light with a bloody axe in their possession try to find Mr Borden to kill? (with the liability of the Murder of Mrs Borden being found out and the alarm given) to kill Mr Borden soon as he laid down to take a rest.

4th would anyone be fool enough to go through the house hunting for Mr Borden to kill (with a bloody hatchet in their possession) and not knowing who they might come in contact with. Do murders often take such chances. The statement in the hearing before that a Dr - (friend of the family) was in Lizzie Bordens room with her (Lizzie) and I think the Dr's wife and some of our Fall River officers tried the door to enter the room and the Dr said "you cant come in now"? and he didnt get in for some time after. Now what were they doing that they were afraid to let anyone in. If they were not trying to conceal some of L-- guilt

Hoping you will take no offense I am a Lover of justice and a former <u>old resident</u> of old Essex Co. <u>who takes great pride in your work you are doing</u>

HK141

Letter, handwritten in ink.

~~Is it not possible that the older daughter Emma - 6 yrs. older committed the deed. She cordially disliked her step-mother   Where was Emma at time of murder?~~

Opinion Rendered in case of Lizzie Borden in re murder of step-mother and father.

Three persons look suspicious - Bridget Sullivan, unknown man who was seen by boy & a Dr. on the street, and lastly ~~by~~ Miss Borden.

These are the only 3 persons who could have done it, except Morse who was brother of Mr Borden's first wife. You must find out if he can prove alibi - & say & prove where he was at time of murder. Morse left the house after breakfast & was soon followed by Mr Borden.

First duty of detectives is to see Morse & find out if he can produce witnesses to prove where he was at time of murder. If he committed the murder, a motive could be seen at once - He was brother of Borden's first wife. Borden was wealthy & this step wife stepped between him & a fortune. This is not probable, but possible. Borden was about making his will. 2nd There is Bridget Sullivan - a strong woman, who may have been hired by Miss Borden to kill the aged couple. I speak of this because Miss B. pleaded not guilty - It is to be noted that Miss B. had no lover. She was 31 yrs old - not bad looking, educated to a certain degree, travelled in Europe. Who supposes she did not get a "mash" while abroad about whom the inhabitants of Fall River know nothing. This lunatic may have done the work, she being the accomplice. Motive - love for the man - his motive <u>money</u>. This clew is good but rather a hard one to work up, but the hunt for this man should go on. 3 Is the Dr. & boy any special friends of Miss Borden? If so - it may be only a idea to put off the right scent. 4th Miss B. the actual actor in the fearful drama. Motive is plain. Had tried all kinds of things, art, painting, music school - failed in all - record - bad - She was a failure in ~~all~~ one & all. Went to Europe against Fathers will - spent a great deal of money. This is bad. Here begins career of crime. Know of a case, exactly like. When child travels & spends money goes in bad company when away from home - would in desperation, commit murder, for money - case - analogous. Quiet town of Fall River did not suit the Miss Borden - had tasted of apple of knowledge. Wanted more money to go abroad with. Knew she could not get it - for her Father refused to honor a draft on him - for ten days - from her, when she was abroad. Hence motive was easily money to gratify her desire for a life of luxury & travel, probably with questionable company, if she went alone. Her purchase of hydrocyanic acid is proof positive of her intent to commit murder, either by poison or some way. Poison failed to act, all family sick, but her - here lies proof that the poison was given, but was not successful. Drug clerk can identify her, as person who bought acid - Analysis of stomach after death, fails to show poison - why - because this acid is volatile, and 20 minutes after death will evaporate & show no traces. This is a paticularly bad poison to sell. Drug clerk should not have sold it to her, without her signing her name that she bought it & also the use it was to be put to. Two blood spots found on her skirt. She was probably a skillful Page 143 & neat butcher & was careful that no blood got on her. I have an idea this poison was given in a handkerchief to the nose as chloriform & then the hatchet was used - because her mother would have struggled & yelled - calling the attention of the servant girl. The hacking of the victims is perfectly natural work of some novice - an old hand would have given one or two deadly blows & left for fear of detection. The fact that the safe was not broken open or rifled points to either an accomplice living within the house who would reward the outside party committing the deed, or else the party in the house did the deed without help, unless her younger sister helped her, which I am inclined to think she did. This latter must be proven. Murder will out & on trial all things will be proven. Children of wealthy parents are beginning to be very wicked, using money they did not earn, & getting false ideas of life.

That a child will get so bad as to kill its own parents I believe - for I have seen cases, when only fear of presence of others, kept them from doing so. If it is proved that this young woman did this deed, with her sister's help thro' fear that the Father would leave his property to the step- mother, or thro' the motive of a desire for the use of the money at once these two motives, either of which look probable - are sufficiently strong to induce a person out of employment who didn't attend church, & who was jealous of her step mother, to put them both out of the way, so as to get the money & have a free & easy time. The case looks bad for Miss Borden, unless the clew of the pale faced man turns up to be something.

The case of Alice Mitchell was settled by calling her insane, but it is doubtful if she was insane, in the way we look at insanity. She selected her victim, while insane people select anyone who gets in their way. Partially insane she no doubt was, & deserved imprisonment for life. Such cases as Mitchells induce other dissatisfied people to commit murder with a chance of being sent to Insane Asylum for 2 yrs or so. Imprisonment for life at hard labor or hanging is the best penalty.

Such people are not fit for society & hence the best thing to do is to give them a painless death.

      Yours Truly
      Wallace L. Folsom

P.S. I am sorry for this Miss Borden but she is one of many spoilt & vicious characters - whose parents have money & they want it. If she was let off, she would only go on & do worse. She is ruined for life & if society let her live she would only be a nuisance to herself & society. Of course it is for society to decide whether to meet out justice to her or mercy.

Such dangerous persons must needs be guarded - if allowed to live. Insane asylum is the place for her for life. They will look out there she dont murder anyone & she has money enough to pay for her Keep – N. B. Athough the hatchets have no blood on them what about the towels or rags found in the cellar covered & soaked in blood? Nothing has been said in the trial ab't them. Could not the hatchets have been wiped so clean that they showed no traces of blood? In one a/c Miss Borden tried to send the detectives to the farm hands & put the murder on them & offered $5,000 reward. Now - the evidence yesterday was that she told people that she knew they did not do it. To the <u>direct</u> question if she knew who killed her father & mother she gave no answer but said only - she was not my ~~step~~ mother but step-mother. You have the right party & dont let her go - Her religious pretences are only cloaks to hide her real nature. Hold her for grand jury - as you have evidence enough.

If she did not do it, she was an accomplice & accomplices are as responsible as murderers - I should make the trial an extended one taking plenty of time & bringing out all the facts. Dont be in a hurry & act as tho' she was innocent & you will catch them knapping-
                      Yours
                      W. L. Folsom

1893 **Dated Documents**

HK142
Document, typewritten.

MASSACHUSETTS REFORMATORY
Concord, Mass., Jan. 9, 1893

Alfred A. Smith, a boy sixteen years old, son of Robert Smith, of Suffolk St. Fall River, Mass. who was sent from Fall River, Second District Court for Breaking, Entering & Larceny on Dec. 28, 1892, made the following statement to me, in the presence of Deputy Superintendent Charles Hart.

I formerly worked for the Globe Street Railway Co. Fall River, part of the time at the North barn, Bowenville and part of the time driving a lead horse on cars from City Hall, throught South Main St. to Morgan St.; the horse I used I had to get from the horse-car barn on Broadway, and the last trip at night I had to return to the barn.

On the Thursday in August, the day of the Policemen's Excursion, I was cutting hay up stairs in the North barn; when I got through I went down stairs, through the barn, towards the South, out of barn and over the fence on to Turner St. up Turner St. to Main St. got on a horse-car and rode down to City Hall. I left the car and walked down South Main St. as far as Stanton Bros. Boot and Shoe store, that store being just South of Spring St. and on the West side of South Main St. I went into the store and tried to buy a pair of Lawn-tennis shoes but could not find any that suited me. I came out crossed over South Main St. and went up Spring St. to Second St. turned to my right on Second St. and went as far as John Roberson's Candy store which is on the East side of Second St. and opposite St. Mary's Church, where I bought five or six cents worth of molasses candy; came out of store came down Second St. on the East side towards City Hall.

When I got in front of the Borden house, I saw a woman looking out of the window, as if looking up and down the street; there were lace curtains at this window, and she was moving the curtains aside with her hands; the window was not open; I have known this was the Borden house for some time. When she saw me she backed away from the window, I do not know who the woman was, she had bangs on her forehead, I think I would know her face again if I saw it.

I continued down Second St. as far as the Academy of Music, I then turned and went back, and when in front of the Borden house, I saw the same woman a little way from the same window, she was untying a bundle. I should say the bundle was about eighteen inches long, and strong paper around it, looked as if it was cloth of some kind; saw her take out some kind of wooden handle, when she saw me she backed away from the window toward the South of the room, and I went on to Roberson's Candy store again. I bought more candy, came out of store and came down Second St. towards City Hall again, when passing the Borden house I saw lying just inside the front fence, and near to the fence on North side of lot a hatchet and a pair of kid gloves; the gloves were all covered with blood; I went in and picked up the gloves and put them in my left hand coat pocket; I picked up the hatchet the blade was well covered with blood, and there were stains of blood on the handle. I put the hatchet under my coat and buttoned it up, as I turned to come out of the yard, I saw the same woman that I saw at the window, halfway out of the door, this door was on the north side and at the east end of the Borden house, as soon as she saw me looking at her she drew in quickly and shut the door.

I ran out of the yard and down Second St. as far as the entrance in the rear of the Post Office, this entrance is where the mail wagon's drive in; I went into the Post Office yard & went to the stream at the South of the yard and washed the hatchet and gloves.

Question. What did you think about the blood on these articles?

Answer. I thought some carpenter had been using the hatchet, and cut his hand and threw it down in the yard where I found it.

After washing the gloves and hatchet I placed them back where I first had them in my coat; came out of the yard crossed Second st. through Market St. to horse-cars in front of City Hall, got on the car and rode North to Turner St. Got off the car and went down Turner St. went into the barn same way I came out, and hid the hatchet. Came out of the barn went West on Turner St. to Davol St. went into Thomas Haggerty' Boot and Shoe store on Davol St. and bought a pair of lawn-tennis shoes, came out and went North on Davol St. until I came to an open field on East side of street, went across the field to the Old Colony Railroad track crossed the track and went to President Ave. to my sister's Mrs.Geo. Davis, who lives in a large brown block on the Avenue. She gave me a pair of stockings of mine that I had previously left at her house. I put them on and put on the lawn-tennis shoes that I bought, my sister said I had got them too small you should have got them wider.

I had something to eat, then went back to the horse-car barn; went up into the hay loft lay down upon the hay I think it was after twelve o'clock noon. I fell asleep and slept until I was awakened by Gus Bunker; asked me if I had been to dinner, he then told me about the murder of Mr. & Mrs. Borden, I went down and took the lead horse, and took the depot car up French's hill as far as Dr. Lucy Hill's house then brought the horse back as far as the barn; this I did for a boy named Kelly, who drives the lead horse on French's Hill.

1893 Dated Documents

Trial Exhibit #33: "Second Street, looking South," 1893. Residences identified as: left, front to back, Mrs. Adelaide B. Churchill, the Borden House, Dr. Michael Kelly; right, second from front, Southard H. Miller, Dr. Seabury W. Bowen. *Photograph by James A. Walsh, Fall River, Massachusetts.*

Trial Exhibit #35: "Second Street, looking North," 1893. Residences identified as: right, front to back, Dr. Michael Kelly, the Borden House.

I then took a horse car and came down to City Hall, went through Pleasant St. to Second St., up Second St. to the Borden house, found a large crowd of people in front of the house; stayed there quite a while, then I went back in front of City Hall, took car and went down to horsecar barn on Broadway; this would be about half past three P.M.

Took my lead horse and came up through South Main St. to City Hall, and went to work towing cars up South Main St. as far as Morgan St. took my horse back to barn on Broadway & got through about 10:55 p.m. Took the car and came back to Bowenville barn; went into the barn got the hatchet and took it home; kept it about three weeks. The edge of the hatchet was smooth having no nicks in it, but in using it at home to break up a dry goods box I dulled it and nicked it very badly. I sold it to Thomas Connors who keeps a little store near Fulton St. School; he gave me ten cents worth of candy for it.

The gloves I used to drive horse with, one of them got wore out and I threw it away, the other I think is at home in the bureau drawer, I am not sure but I think it is. The gloves were too long in the fingers and too small in the wrists for me. I think it is the left hand glove that is at home.

Question: Why didn't you tell the police about this hatchet and gloves when you heard the Borden's had been murdered?
Answer: Because I was afraid to do so.
Question: What was you afraid of?
Answer: I don't know, but I was afraid.
Question: Did you ever tell anyone in Fall River what you had found?
Answer: No I never told anyone.
Question: Who was the first one you ever spoke to about it?
Answer: To the Officer who has charge of the room I work in at the Reformatory; also to Deputy Superintendent Hart.
Question: Why didn't you tell me when you was in the lock up in Fall River?
Answer: Because I was afraid to.

I was going to tell my father, when he came to see me in the lock-up, but he only stayed a minute or two and I did not have time to tell him.
Question: What was the cause of your telling the Officers at the Reformatory?
Answer: Because I kept thinking about it and couldn't get it out of my mind.
Question: Did anyone tell you or talk with you about making up this story?
Answer: No, nobody whatever.
Question: What time did you leave the barn to go up to Stanton Bros.?
Answer: I should say it was 10 a.m.
Question: Which window of the Borden house did you see the woman first looking out of?

Answer: It was at the South window on the front of the house downstairs.
Question: What window was she at when you saw her the second time?
Answer: The same window.
Question: Did you notice whether the blinds were closed on the other window on the front of the house or not?
Answer: I think the white shutters were closed on the inside.
Question: Did you notice how the windows up stairs were?
Answer: I think they were shut also the white shutters on the inside.
Question: How was the woman you saw at the door dressed?
Answer: I don't know.
Question: When you went into the gate after the hatchet which way did you turn to your right or left?
Answer: I turned to my left and went North towards the other house.
Question: How close to the other house was the hatchet?
Answer: It was within three or four feet of the fence, next to the other house.
Question: Is there a fence there?
Answer: Yes: a board fence with some bushes or vines growing on the North side.
Question: If you should see the Borden house could you tell it? Answer: Yes: (here the picture of three or four houses was shown him and he selected the Borden house, also the window where he saw the woman; he also pointed to the place where the door would be, where he saw the woman, when he was picking up the hatchet. He said there were steps at this door and they run up to dorr from both sides. He also identified the barn, and Dr. Kelly's house and the Buffinton house.
Question: Did you see anyone sitting on the steps of the house North of the Borden house?
Answer: No, I did not.
Question: Did you see a team across the street directly opposite the Borden house?
Answer: No, I did not.
Question: Do you know where the grocery store is South from the Borden house on Second st.?
Answer: I do.
Question: Did you see any men or boys in front of that store?
Answer: I did not. I think there was a grocery team standing in front.
Question: Did anyone see you pick up the hatchet and gloves?
Answer: Nobody that I know of but the woman I saw standing in the door of the Borden house.

Question: Did you speak to anybody after you picked up the hatchet before you got to the horse-cars?
Answer: No, I did not.
Question: Did you make this story up or is it the truth you are telling me?
Answer: No I did not make it up. It is just as I have told you and is the truth.
Question: (By Mr. Hart) Has anyone in the institution said anything to you about this matter before you spoke to them about it?
Answer: No: nobody.
Question: (By Mr. Hart) Do you know that this is a pretty serious affair for you if you have made this story up and it is not the truth?
Answer: Yes sir I do; but it is the truth.
Question: (By Mr. Holliard) Now Alfred all that you have told us is the truth?
Answer: Yes sir.
Question: You are sure of it are you?
Answer: Yes I am it is the truth.
Question: You say you have never told anyone of it until you came to the Institution.
Answer: I did not tell anyone before I came here. I was going to tell my father but did not. I thought of telling the Officer, when he brought me here, when we were in the cars.
Question: Why didn't you?
Answer: Because there were so many talking I did not get a chance to do so.

This ended the conversation.
A mark on the hatchet
        1
       C. Hammond
        Phila.
        Cast Steel.

HK143
Affidavit, typewritten, with notations handwritten in ink, notarized.

State of New York,
City and County of Albany, ss:
  Joseph W. Carpenter Jr, being duly sworn, says that he resides in said City and County; that from the 18th day of July 1892 to the 13th day of August 1892, both inclusive, he occupied a room in the premises Nos. 33 and

35 Maiden Lane, in said City every night during said time, and that he was not absent therefrom on any night during said period.

Sworn to before me this 24th day of January 1893.

Joseph W. Carpenter Jr.

   Wm. F. Beers
      Notary Public
         Albany Co. N. Y.

State of New York,
City and County of Albany, ss:

Victoria A. Foreman, being duly sworn, says that she resides in said City and County, and occupies the premises Nos. 33 and 35 Maiden Lane in said City, and rents furnished rooms in said premises; that she knows Joseph W. Carpenter above named, and rented said Carpenter a furnished room in said premises during the period mentioned in his affidavit; that she had read the foregoing affidavit by him subscribed, and knows the facts stated therein, and that the same are true to her own knowledge.

Sworn to before me this 24th day of January 1893.

Victoria A. Foreman

   Wm. F. Beers
      Notary Public
         Albany Co. N. Y.

HK144
Telegram, typewritten.

TELEGRAM

FR 22 BN:0   P14 paid   2:47pm
   Fall River, Mass   Mar 8th 93
      Attorney General's Office,
         Boston, Mass.

Will attorney general be at home Wednesday or Friday if not when wire answer.

         Andrew J. Jennings

HK145
Telegram, handwritten in ink.

THE WESTERN UNION TELEGRAPH COMPANY.

Boston, March 8, 1893

To: Andrew J. Jennings Esq.
   Fall River, Mass.

Mr. Pillsbury is away from home for several weeks.
   C.N. Harris
   2nd Asst. Atty. Genl.

HK146
Leaflet, printed, with comments handwritten in lead.

SENATE. NO. . . . . . 301.

COMMONWEALTH of MASSACHUSETTS.

Senate, April 12, 1893

The committee on the Judiciary, to whom was referred the Bill relating to the compensation of attorneys appointed by the court in murder cases (Senate, No. 84, introduced on leave), report that the same ought to pass in a new draft herewith submitted.

   For the Committee,
      WILLIAM M. BUTLER

COMPENSATION OF ATTORNEYS. Apr. '93.
Ch. 394

COMMONWEALTH of MASSACHUSETTS.

In the Year One Thousand Eight Hundred and Ninety-three

AN ACT
Relating to the Compensation of Attorneys assigned
by the Court in Murder Cases.

Be it enacted by the Senate and House of Representatives in General Court assembled, and by the authority of the same, as follows:

SECTION 1. *Reasonable* Expenses incurred *and paid* by any attorney assigned by the court for the defense of a person indicted for murder *such person being otherwise unable to procure counsel* shall be paid by the county in which the trial or other proceedings take place, provided such expenses have been ~~authorized~~ *approved* by any justice of the superior court *sitting in the trial or other proceedings in the case.*

SECT. 2. Any justice of the superior court *sitting in the trial or other proceedings in the case* may allow reasonable compensation for the services rendered by any attorney who is assigned to defend any person indicted for the crime of murder, *such person being otherwise unable to procure counsel,* which shall be paid by the county in which the trial or other proceedings take place.

SECT. 3. This act shall apply to cases now pending.

Approved May 26

HK147
Letter, typewritten.

ROBINSON & ROBINSON,

ATTORNEYS AT LAW,

GILL'S BLOCK.

George D. Robinson.

Walter S. Robinson.

Springfield, Mass, April 14, 1893.

Hon. A. E. Pillsbury,
Attorney-General, Boston, Mass.
Dear Sir:—

Your favor which you mailed me from Washington was duly received, and I would have replied, but I saw that it was not important, and besides I did not know where to address you. This I write because I desire to have a word with you as soon as convenient after your arrival in Boston. The case of Commonwealth vs. Borden has been standing now a long time, and naturally the defendant feels that she is entitled to an early trial. Of course, I understand the sufficient reasons for the delay thus far, but I hope that it will be possible for you to arrange for an early date, and as soon as you are in your office again and ready for a conference, I will be glad to know it so that I may inform my associates and con- fer with you as to the proper time. This much may be done in anticipation of the arraignment and the possible direction to be given by the Court.

Yours truly,
Geo. D. Robinson

HK148
Letter, typewritten.

ATTORNEY GENERAL'S DEPARTMENT,
COMMONWEALTH BUILDING,

Boston, April 21, 1893.

Hon. George D. Robinson,

    My Dear Governor:-

        On my return home I find yours of April 14th, and while I am not yet in condition to take up the full line of my work, I will reply to it as soon as I am able to confer fully with the district attorney, which of course, under the circumstances, is indispensable.

    Very truly yours,

        Attorney General.

Springfield, Mass.

HK149
Letter, handwritten in ink.

#160 W. Brookline St.
Boston, April 23/93

Attorney Gen'l Pillsbury,
Dear Sir:
    Permit me, in the interest of justice, to call your attention to one point of the evidence, in the Borden tragedy, which neither the public nor the

press seems to have taken any notice of for its significance- namely: Why was Lizzie Borden not afraid to stand inside of that screen door with every reason to believe the murderer of her father still upon the scene - lurking behind anything that could possibly conceal him - and thinking he might have killed her mother too!

How could she send Bridget upon this and that errand, awaiting her return alone within those terrible walls, -why did she not rush, terror stricken, from that house as fast as she could go - just as any other woman would have done under the circumstances of finding her father murdered as she represents them?

Very Respectfully,
Mary A. Maxwell

HK150
Letter, typewritten.

HOSEA M. KNOWLTON. ARTHUR E. PERRY.
COUNSELLORS AT LAW.
OFFICE:
38 NORTH WATER STREET.

{Dictated}.

NEW BEDFORD, MASS. April 24, 1893.

Hon. A. E. Pillsbury, Attorney General:
    My Dear Sir:-
                I have thought more about the Lizzie Borden case since I talked with you, and think perhaps it may be well to write you, as I shall not be able to meet you probably until Thursday, possibly Wednesday afternoon.

Personally I would like very much to get rid of the trial of the case, and fear that my own feelings in that direction may have influenced my better judgment. I feel this all the more upon your not unexpected announcement that the burden of the trial would come upon me.

I confess, however, I cannot see my way clear to any disposition of the case other than a trial. Should it result in disagreement of the jury there would be no difficulty then in disposing of the case by admitting the defendent to bail: but a verdict either way would render such a course unnecessary. The case has proceeded so far and an indictment has been found by the grand inquest of the county that it does not seem to me that we ought to take the responsibility of discharging her without trial, even though there is every reasonable expectation of a verdict of not guilty. I am unable to concur fully in your views as to the probable result. I think it may well be that the jury might disagree upon the case. But even in my most sanguine moments I have scarcely expected a verdict of guilty.

The situation is this: nothing has developed which satisfies either of us that she is innocent, neither of us can escape the conclusion that she must have had some knowledge of the occurrence. She has been present- ed for trial by a jury which, to say the least, was not influenced by anything said by the government in the favor of the indictment.

Without discussing the matter more fully in this letter I will only say as above indicated that I cannot see how any other course than setting the case down for trial, and trying it will satisfy that portion of the public sentiment whether favorable to her or not, which is worthy of being respected.

June seems to be the most satisfactory month, all things considered. I will write more fully as to the admission of her confession after I have looked the matter up.

Yours Truly,
H M Knowlton

HK151
Letter, typewritten.

ATTORNEY GENERAL'S DEPARTMENT, COMMONWEALTH BUILDING.

Boston,   April 25, 1893.

Dear Mr. Attorney;-

Please see me Wednesday, if possible, as Gov. Robinson and Jennings have both called since I saw you and are very pressing; and I told them that I should see you Wednesday, and that they should hear from me immediately afterward.

I am here for the present only in the forenoon, but if you will let me know at what hour you will come, if in the afternoon, I will meet you.

Very truly yours,

Attorney General.

Hon. H. M. Knowlton,
    New Bedford, Mass.

HK152
Telegram, handwritten in ink.

THE WESTERN UNION TELEGRAPH COMPANY.

RECEIVED at 109 State Street, Boston.
Dated New bedford Ms. 4/26 (93)
To Hon. A E Pillsbury
          Attorney Genl Boston
Shall be engaged in fourth session till four o'clock. send word where meet you after that.
H. M. Knowlton.

HK153
Telegram, handwritten in lead.

THE WESTERN UNION TELEGRAPH COMPANY.

Boston 26 Apl. 26 1893

To: Hon. George D. Robinson
        Chicopee, Mass.

We will confer with you at four tomorrow or if that is too soon eleven Friday.
A E. Pillsbury

HK154
Telegram, handwritten in ink.

THE WESTERN UNION TELEGRAPH COMPANY.

RECEIVED at 109 State Street, Boston.
Dated Springfield Mass   27 Apl (1893)
To Hon A E Pillsbury
        Atty General Boston

Engaged here today & tomorrow
How about next Saturday ten o'clock Telegraph here so I can notify Jennings & Adams

       Geo D Robinson

HK155
Note, handwritten in lead and ink.

Bro. K
Will Sat. 10 do for you?
    A.E.P.

I had an important appointment for Sat. Try Monday. But of course will come Sat. if necessary

(Note: The response following the initials of Albert E. Pillsbury is in the handwriting of Hosea Morrill Knowlton.)

HK156
Letter, typewritten.

  ROBINSON & ROBINSON,   *George D. Robinson.*

   ATTORNEYS AT LAW,   *Walter S. Robinson.*

    GILL'S BLOCK.

          Springfield, Mass., April 27, 1893

Hon. A. E. Pillsbury,
Attorney-General, Boston, Mass.
    Dear Sir:—

    I have received your telegram stating that Saturday will not do, but suggesting Monday afternoon. That runs against my convenience, and I now ask if you can take either Thursday forenoon or Friday forenoon of next week, May 4th or May 5th, at 10 o'clock. Ascertain please, and telegraph me as soon as you can so that I may notify Mr. Jennings and Mr. Adams. If you and Mr. Knowlton can possibly save both days for my and their refusal, that will, perhaps, make it more easy to agree upon a precise day. I greatly prefer the forenoon because I can be ready early in the morning and will not then be obliged to stay over until another day. I would take an earlier day next week, but there are things in the way and I see no better course than to take the days that I have named. I will therefore, expect your telegram as soon as possible.

Yours truly,
George D. Robinson

HK157
Telegram, typewritten.

THE WESTERN UNION TELEGRAPH COMPANY.

Boston, April 28, 1893.

To: Hon. George D. Robinson,
    Springfield, Mass.

Think we had better say tomorrow Saturday ten. Telegraph if agreeable.
    A.E. Pillsbury
    Attorney General

HK158
Telegram, handwritten in ink.

TELEGRAM

Springfield, Mass 28
Hon. A.E. Pillsbury   April 28, 1893
                Atty. Genl
                Boston

You may expect us tomorrow at 10 o'clock
       Geo. D. Robinson

HK159
Letter, typewritten.

ATTORNEY GENERAL'S DEPARTMENT, COMMONWEALTH BUILDING.
Boston, May 2, 1893.

My Dear Governor:-

I hear from Chief justice Mason, who may have sent you the same information at the same time, that they conclude to have the trial begin Monday not later than eleven; and he evidently still considers New Bedford to be the place.

Very truly yours,

Attorney General.

Hon. George D. Robinson,
    Chicopee, Mass.

HK160
Letter, typewritten.

ATTORNEY GENERAL'S DEPARTMENT, COMMONWEALTH BUILDING,
Boston, May 2, 1893.

Dear Mr. Chief Justice:-

As a first impression of the question suggested by your letter, I am inclined to think either that in the case supposed a trial could proceed before two justices, being a ~~court~~ quorum of three; or if not, (and I agree that this would be a somewhat dangerous experiment, especially if the two judges should divide on any important question) that another judge could be substituted in the case of disability of one of the judges arising during the trial; It may be granted, perhaps, that the jurisdiction depends on the continuous presence of three judges but why is it necessarily the same three from beginning to end of the trial? Of course some practical difficulties or inconveniences might arise from the substitution of one judge for another in medias res; but is there any doubt that in any ordinary case, civil or criminal, any judge has power to hold the court and finish a trial begun before another?

If in any other case, so I suppose in this. But I will immediately communicate the suggestion to the Chairman of the Senate Judiciary Committee, and see at least how it strikes him, cautioning him to say nothing about it unless he acts upon it.

It was agreed before we saw you Saturday upon my suggestion that ~~I thought~~ it was necessary that Miss Borden should be arraigned at as early a day as convenient, to be arranged between Messrs Knowlton and Jennings; and I presume it will be done this week before Judge Hammond, as you suggest.

Very truly yours,
Attorney General

Chief Justice Albert Mason.

Since distating this I have seen Mr. Butler, who thinks the necessary legislation can be had, without doubt, if necessary. But for reasons which will readily occur to you, I incline to hope you will come to the conclusion that it is not necessary, and I will assume this unless I hear from you again. If you still think legislation should be had, I will put it on foot at once.

HK161
Letter, handwritten in ink.

THE SUPERIOR COURT
BOSTON
Tues May 2, 1893

Hon. A. E. Pillsbury Atty. Genl.
    Dear Sir

The justices to sit in the Borden case according to present plan held a conference last evening upon the matters raised on Saturday. Justices Blodgett and Dewey are of the same opinion which I reached upon the exceptional character of local conditions affecting Fall River jurors and what should be the action in the premises.

We are all of opinion that it is best to begin on Monday morning not later than 11 o'clock. There is a train now from Park Square Station at 8 am which reaches New Bedford at 9:50. Judge Dewey is accustomed to come to Boston Sunday night for his eastern work and thinks we may properly ask counsel to do the same.

Albert Mason, circa 1890.

Before the formal order assigning time for trial we all think there should be a plea. Judge Hammond opens the civil sitting at New Bedford today and it would seem practicable to arrange an early day for arraignment convenient to the Dist. Atty. and to the Ct.

There is one matter connected with the jurisdiction of our court in capital causes which disturbs me and if it were earlier in the legislative session I should think it serious enough to bring to legislative attention. The provision of the statute for trials in the Supreme Judicial Court was for trial before the full court or two or more justices. The statute for trials in the Superior Court requires trial before three justices. We cannot well read this not less than three. The S.J.C. considered at times in entering a trial likely to be exceptionally long the expediency of taking an extra man to meet the contingency of one giving out. They never did this and never were caught by sickness of either of the two taken. Your own prostration at Northampton is an illustration of the danger. There are three chances of such prostration of a judge to one of the Atty. Genl. and a trial which promises three weeks duration multiplies the chances of each by three. To enter a trial of this character at the end of a hard years work and in hot weather is attended with considerable risk of a large expense coming to nought from disability of a single judge. True we have a similar danger multiplied by four with the jury, but an agreement to go on with less than twelve is a possible expedient even in a capital cause.

I do not think it would be startling or radical legislation to insert in the fifth line of Sect 2 of Chap. 379 of Acts of 1891 "In case of the death or disability of one of said justices during the trial it shall continue before the two remaining" Very likely some happier phrase to the same end would occur to you. I suppose it is too late to think of this now and all that can be done for the present emergency is to select justices not likely to fail in strength.
I send by the messenger your copy of the Goodwin trial.

                Sincerely

                Albert Mason

HK162
Letter, handwritten in ink.

Newburyport May 2nd.93

My Dear Mr. Pillsbury,
I received your letter last night, and after fully consideration, I am ready for such service in the Borden case as you may ask of me. Having said this much, there is no need of saying more of the reasons which weighed with me.

I am before the Grand Jury this week, but the work of trials I can, if need be, leave with my assistant and can be at your command when you wish. I could call on you Saturday afternoon if there was occasion for it, and from that time on could do any work which you desire.

I will of course heed your injunction as to silence, knowing as I do the uncertainty of the course you may adopt, and remembering your caution.

Very truly yours
W. H. Moody

HK163
Letter, typewritten.

**ATTORNEY GENERAL'S DEPARTMENT,
COMMONWEALTH BUILDING,**
Boston, May 2, 1893.

Dear Mr. Attorney:- .
A letter just received from Chief Justice Mason says that they conclude to have the trial begin Monday not later than eleven. He evidently still regards New Bedford as the place. He suggests also that Miss Borden should be arraigned and plead, and that it will probably be convenient for you and Mr. Jennings to have this done at once before Judge Hammond.

Very truly yours,

Attorney General.

Hon. H. M. Knowlton
New Bedford, Mass.

John Wilkes Hammond, circa 1900.

HK164
Letter, handwritten in ink.

THE SUPERIOR COURT.
BOSTON.
May 3, 1893

My Dear Sir

Yours of today is at hand. Personally I am of opinion that the objections to attempting legislation at the present time outweigh the risks of going on with the statutes as they are. When the matter is considered it should be without haste and with no reference to any particular case. If it can be held that it is not necessary to go through the trial with the same three, there would be no practical inconvenience arising from change. With stenographic report of all the evidence as we now have, it would be entirely practicable to proceed with a change of all three if it were necessary. I am quite sure that judges have generally assumed that such change in the progress of a trial could not be made but we have an every day practice that must rest upon an assumption that it can be. One judge goes in to take a verdict where trial has been had before another, and this on the criminal side as well as on the civil. It is worth a more careful study to see if authority for such changes cannot be found before we ask for legislation.

Sincerely
Albert Mason

HK165
Letter, typewritten.

ATTORNEY GENERAL'S DEPARTMENT,
COMMONWEALTH BUILDING,
Boston,   May 3, 1893.

Dear Mr. Chief Justice:-

I think I may have expressed in my note of yesterday more reluctance to have legislation upon the question which you suggested than I ought to have expressed or really felt, and if you think there is really occasion for it, let me hear from you and it shall be done, or at least attempted. Other things being equal, of course I should prefer to have the change, if needed, made at another time; but of course the objections to the present time are not weighty, and you need not regard them.

Very truly yours,

Chief Justice Alber Mason,

HK166
Letter, typewritten.

ATTORNEY GENERAL'S DEPARTMENT,
COMMONWEALTH BUILDING,

Boston,   May 3, 1893.

My Dear Moody:-

    Yours of yesterday is received and appreciated. I do not feel sure that we shall have to draw upon you, but we may. I am, at present, under strict orders not to undertake more than a certain amount of work, nor anything of an unusually trying character; and although I am getting on well and feel as though I could do a full day's work every day, I do not expect to be permitted to take an active part in this trial, which, as you see, is assigned for June 5th. And I may conclude, or may be advised, that my only safe way will be to keep out of it entirely, as it is exceedingly difficult for me to be on the spot without taking a hand. All we ask at pre- sent, therefore, is that if possible you will stand ready and await further developments, as we are obliged to do. We anticipate that the trial will run into, but probably not through, the third week. If Mr. Knowlton wish- es to draw on you for any special service beforehand, as in looking up any question of law or the like, he will correspond with you.

Very truly yours,

Hon. William H. Moody.

HK167
Letter, typewritten.

ATTORNEY GENERAL'S DEPARTMENT,
COMMONWEALTH BUILDING,
Boston,　　May 3, 1893.

Dear Mr. Attorney:-
　　　　I have just received the enclosed prompt and characteristic reply to my note to Moody, which please return. I have written to him that if you wish any special service of him in advance, you will correspond with him.

　　　　　　　　　Very truly yours,

　　　　　　　　　　　　　Attorney General

Hon. H. M. Knowlton,
　　New Bedford, Mass.

HK168
Letter, typewritten.

ATTORNEY GENERAL'S DEPARTMENT,
COMMONWEALTH BUILDING,
Boston,　　May 4, 1893.

Bro. Cooney:-
　　　　Have you any idea how the Herald got the story about the Trefethen case, on the forst page of this morning's issue? It seems to me that it must have been from some officer.

　　　　　　　　　Very truly yours,

Hon. P. H. Cooney,

HK169
Letter, typewritten.

ATTORNEY GENERAL'S DEPARTMENT, COMMONWEALTH BUILDING,
Boston,   May 4, 1893.

My Dear Governor:-

In view of the coincidence between our conversation and the appearance of the Trefethen story in this morning's Herald, I think I ought to assure you, though doubtless it is unnecessary, that the publication was as much a surprise to me as it could possibly be to anybody; and that I have, of course, no idea from whom it proceeded, but intend to find out.

Please treat this as confidential, and oblige,

Yours very truly,

Hon. John D. Long.

HK170
Letter, typewritten.

HOSEA M. KNOWLTON.   ARTHUR E. PERRY.
COUNSELLORS AT LAW.
OFFICE:
38 NORTH WATER STREET.

{Dictated.}

NEW BEDFORD, MASS., May 4, 1893.

Hon. A. E. Pillsbury; Attorney General,

Dear Sir:-

I return Moody's letter. It is very good of him indeed. The arraignment was to have taken place to-day, but the Judge smashed the docket and went home yesterday afternoon for the week. I have arranged to take it up next Monday afternoon.

I shall want to see Moody and talk it over with him, but would prefer to wait until it is a little more certain that you will be unable to attend to the matter. I still hope that you can be in it. Perhaps you will be willing to spend an evening with Moody and myself when we get around to it.

Yours Truly,
H. M. Knowlton
per E.

HK171
Letter, typewritten.

ATTORNEY GENERAL'S DEPARTMENT,
COMMONWEALTH BUILDING,
Boston,   May 4, 1893.

Dear Mr. Attorney:-

Gov. Robinson and Mr. Adams called to-day to express their desire that the indictment for killing of both should be first tried, as to which, in view of what passed between us the other day, I told them they might assume that it would be unless they heard from you to the contrary; and also to ask about the allowance of experts, as to which I told them that the rule ~~was~~ is that they will be allowed a reasonable number, not usually exceeding two on anyone topic, if reasonably necessary, at a reasonable compensation, and if named to and approved by the prosecuting officer in advance; and I told them also that as to this and all other questions of detail relating to the trial, they should communicate with you. I wish to have it understood by the counsel, even if it is not by the public, that since the transfer of murder to the Superior Court, these cases are as much in charge of the District Attorneys as any other criminal case, unless and until the Attorney General appears at the trial. Of course in any case which the Attorney General was to try, I suppose the District Attorney would naturally confer with him as to all questions of importance, and do not suppose any Attorney General would ever be inclined to refuse his advice or assistance in such matters, as I certainly am not; but in view of the situation of this case, and of my own situation, I trust you will be able to, dispose of these matters without difficulty.

Mr. Burt, the stenographer here, has applied to me to take charge of that department of the trial. He has been in other cases, and is one of the most competent and efficient of our court stenographers. Their prices are abominable, but I found, after a desperate attempt, that they could not be cut, even for large quantities. If you wish to arrange about this or to employ anybody I should be glad to have you do so; otherwise, and if I do not hear from you to the contrary, I should be inclined to employ Burt.

Very truly yours,
Attorney General.

Hon. H. M. Knowlton.

HK172
Letter, typewritten.

COMMONWEALTH OF MASSACHUSETTS,
OFFICE OF THE DISTRICT ATTORNEY
FOR THE SOUTHERN DISTRICT.

New Bedford, Mass., May 5, 1893.

Hon. A. E. Pillsbury:
    Dear Sir:-
        Jennings wants to have his experts see the skulls, and I told him I supposed there would be no objection, and have so written to Dolan.

    They also want Bridget Sullivan's testimony at the inquest. We declined to give it to them before the indictment, but I see no objection to giving it to them now. It is almost identical with her story as told before Judge Blaisdell, and will do us no harm. What do you think?
        Yours truly
        H. M. Knowlton

HK173
Letter, typewritten.

ATTORNEY GENERAL'S DEPARTMENT,
COMMONWEALTH BUILDING,
Boston,   May 5, 1893.

Dear Mr. Attorney:-
    Of course I will spend one or any number of evenings or days, within the limits of my strength, with you and Moody at any time; but I had a talk with Dr. Gay day before yesterday, and it is entirely improbable that I shall be allowed to take any active part in the trial, or perhaps even to attend it; the difficulty with which is that attending would involve taking a more active part than I might be able to without risk.
        Very truly yours,

        Attorney General.

Hon. H. M. Knowlton.

HK174
Letter, typewritten.

**COMMONWEALTH OF MASSACHUSETTS,
OFFICE OF THE DISTRICT ATTORNEY
FOR THE SOUTHERN DISTRICT.**

New Bedford, Mass., May 5, 1893.

Hon. A. E. Pillsbury:
    Attorney General.
        Dear Sir:-
            Your favor of the 4th at hand. I should engage Mr. Burt at once.

    I am very glad to make any of the arrangements that you wish me to, and will do so. In this particular case, however, owing to many reasons which are probably as familiar to you as to me, I should very much prefer that the conferences be had between counsel and yourself. Anything, however, that you desire to refer to me I shall be glad to attend to.

        Yours Truly,
        H. M. Knowlton
            per E.

HK175
Letter, handwritten in ink.

        Court House,
           Dedham, May 8, 1893

Hon. A.E. Pillsbury,
    Dear Sir:
        I have communicated with Mr. Rogers about the Borden case and have just received his reply, saying:
"As things look <u>now</u> we do not see how we can help you."
Awaiting further instructions, I remain
        Yours truly,
           Frank H. Burt.

HK176
Note, typewritten.

ATTORNEY GENERAL'S DEPARTMENT,
COMMONWEALTH BUILDING,
Boston,   May 9, 1893.

Mr. Frank H. Burt.
       Dear Sir:-
            Please give me your terms for the Borden case, three copies, and oblige.

        Yours very truly,

            Attorney General.

244 Wash. st,

HK177
Letter, typewritten.

HOSEA M. KNOWLTON.   ARTHUR E. PERRY.
COUNSELLORS AT LAW.
OFFICE:
38 NORTH WATER STREET.

{Dictated.}

        NEW BEDFORD, MASS., May 9th, 1893.

Hon. A. E. Pillsbury,
   Attorney General:
      Dear Sir:-
          I have the enclosed letter from Mr. Libby. I think you told me that you had already arranged for Mr. Burt to attend to the matter, or would do so very soon. You are better acquainted with the details of this business than I am, having had experience with the various reporters.

        Yours Truly,
         H. M. Knowlton
          per E.

HK178
Letter, handwritten in ink.

My Dear Mr. Atty. Genl-

Moody came down yesterday & from 3 to 9 P.M. we had a careful & very satisfactory Preliminary session. He is going into the case <u>con amore</u>. He is proposing to see personally every witness & prepare the case thoroughly. I again tendered him the stroke oar: but he declined it; prefering to take the junior part. He is ready to devote some substantial time, say a fortnight, exclusively to preparation.

He says he has assignments for the first week in June in Salem: and feels that he must soon ask the indulgence of his opponents: and, if he does, he & I agree that it should be after it has been announced in the proper way that he is in the case: to save a garbled and wickedly sensational, report being made, as is sure to be the case, if the news gets out in a left-handed way. This can be done either with or without the announcement that you are unable to go on with the case. I leave it to you to decide upon such course of action as you think best under the circumstances. I regret more than I can express, not only on my own account; but on yours, that the final decision is that you cannot be with us. You were entirely right in your remark that no possible course we could take in the case would relieve us from criticism, more or less offensive. Of course, we must sit and (as Mark Twain puts it) "simply sizzle" under such wicked articles as that in the Record of Friday. For myself, I should never open my mouth: but if you think it will be of service to you, I will willingly be ~~reported~~ interviewed: and say what ought to be said. Let me know if you desire it.

I find myself seriously and unexpectedly handicapped. Our little 3 year old came down with scarlet fever last Monday. She is doing well: but she is at that age when I would not trust her to hired nurses, for all the world has in the way of reward or glory. That means the home broken up, children out, Mrs. K quarantined, & I under the highest obligation to be at home nights, for six weeks- so the Doctor fixes the time. Isn't it wicked, just at this crisis. That was why I had to have Moody come to New Bedford, instead of meeting him, as I originally intended and appointed, in Boston. There are several things I would like to discuss with you personally about the case; and if it is not too much of a tax upon your patience, I will call upon you some day this week at your office.

      Yours very truly,
      Hosea M. Knowlton

Sunday P.M.
May 14, 1893

HK179
Letter, typewritten.

ATTORNEY GENERAL'S DEPARTMENT, COMMONWEALTH BUILDING,
Boston,   May 15, 1893

My Dear Knowlton:-
     Since writing you this morning, yours of Sunday has come in. I am distressed beyond measure at what you say of your child, and can only hope that the disease will turn the right corner more speedily than you anticipate. As to the time and form of any announcement as to the government counsel, if you are to be here within a few days, I suggest that it may be better to confer upon it. I am at your service day or night for this or any other purpose within my strength. I have not yet undertaken to finally determine the question whether I can undertake any part in the trial, but an interview with Dr. Gay yesterday indicates that it will not be safe to assume that I can. If you are not to be here in season to determine by conference the question about any announcement, please let me know and I will write you about it. If you come please notify me as much in advance as possible, as I have to arrange my engagements so as to avoid undertaking too much in the same day. With my sincerest wishes for your welfare at home, I am As ever,
     Yours very truly

HK180
Letter, typewritten.

ATTORNEY GENERAL'S DEPARTMENT, COMMONWEALTH BUILDING,
Boston,   May 15, 1893

Hon. Andrew J. Jennings,
     My Dear Sir:-
          I have sent your letter of May 13th to District Attorney Knowlton, who alone is in possession of the names in question, and

who is in charge of the case under the statute, and of all details relating to preparation for trial; which circumstance, as you will remember, I called to the attention of the counsel for the defence the other day.

Very truly yours,

Attorney General

Fall River, Mass.

HK181
Letter, typewritten.

ATTORNEY GENERAL'S DEPARTMENT,
COMMONWEALTH BUILDING,
Boston,   May 15, 1893

Dear Mr. Attorney:-
The enclosed is just received, and I have written Jennings that it is referred to you. The cases which appear on the subject are Knapp, 9th Pick. 497, Locke 14 Pick. 485, Waldron 17 Pick. 403: but my practice, and that of my predecessors so far as I am informed, has been to furnish the names of witnesses of any material consequence, notwithstanding the law does not require so much. You will exercise your own judgement, of course.

Very truly yours,

Attorney General.

Hon. H.M. Knowlton,

HK182
List, handwritten in ink and lead.

<u>Witnesses
Survey on</u>

1	~~Dolan~~ -	medical examiner	
2	~~Coughlin~~ -	assisted	
3	<u>Draper</u> -	assisted	
	-	assisted	
4	<u>Wood</u> -	chemist	
5	~~A.G. Hart~~		
6	<u>J.T. Burrell</u>	}	
7	<u>Everett Cook</u>	}	
	C.C. Cook	}	
	Caroline Kelley	}	
8	~~Jona. Clegg~~	}	Movements of Borden
9	~~Shortsleeves~~	}	morning of Aug. 4
10	~~Mather~~	}	
11	J.V. Morse	{	
12	Bridget Sullivan	{	household
13	Emma Borden	{	
14	S.W. Bowen	{	
15	Mrs. Churchill	{	Finding murder
16	Chas. Sawyer	{	o.c.
17	John Cunningham	{	
18	Alice M. Russell	{	

1893 Dated Documents

19	Sarah B. Whitehead	}	Relatives of
35	Hannah H. Gifford	}	family & each other
20	Hiram C. Harrington	}	
21	Frank H. Wixon	}	
22	Lucy Collett	}	
	John Devine	}	
23	Pat McGowan	}	
24	Dennis Sullivan	}	As to not
25	Mrs. Bowen	}	seeing
26	Mrs. Kelley's servant (?)	}	prisoner
27	Mrs. Crapo	}	escape
28	Her girl	}	
29	Mrs. John Gormley	{	
30	Louise Hall	{	
31	Alex H. Coggeshall	{	
32	Robert Nicholson	{	
33	James E. Cunneen	{	
34			
43	Aruba P. Kirby	{	
36	Bence	{	
37	Kilroy	{	Buying
38	Hart	{	prussic
39	Wright - N.B.	{	acid
40	Church "	{	

~~Miss White~~ - Testimony of Lizzie Borden

	Harrington	X	
	Medley	X	
	Doherty	X	
41	Fleet		
	Mullaly	X	Officers
	Hilliard	X	
42,	Allen		
	Edson	X	
	Hyde	X	

Miscellaneous		
Edith Francis	no good	
Frank Eddy		
A. C. Johnson		
Ferguson		
Eliz M. Johnson	X	
Geo. Petty	X	

As to escape		
41 F.A. Pickering	X'	
Mark Chase	X	
L.A. Winslow	X	
Thos. J. L. Brown	X	
C. E. Roger	X	
John Eagan	X	
42 Sarah Gray	X	
Mary C. Macomber	Westport	
Mary Wyatt	X	
Harry Pearce	X	
Wm. L. Hacking	X	

(Note: "Miss Carrie Poole, mad" and "Michael [?]" handwritten in lead on reverse side of list.)

HK183
Document, printed, with additional text handwritten in ink.

No..............
COMMONWEALTH
vs.
Lizzie A. Borden

COMMONWEALTH OF MASSACHUSETTS.
BRISTOL, SS.

To the Sheriffs of our several Counties, or their Deputies, the Constables of any Town or City in the County of Bristol, or any district police officer,
GREETING:

You are hereby commanded to summon *Emma Borden, John V. Morse, Charles S. Sawyer, John Cunningham, Alice M. Russell, Sarah B. Whitehead, Hiram C. Harrington, Frank H. Wixon, Lucy Collet, Eli Bence, Fred B. Hart, Rufus B. Hilliard, John Dinnie, Arubia P. Kirby, Elizabeth M. Johnston, ~~Carrie E. B. Rogers~~, Mary Doolan, Cyrus C. Rounsceville, Hannah Reagan, James E. Cunneen* (if they may be found in your precinct), to appear before the **SUPERIOR COURT** next to be holden at *New Bedford* within and for our county of Bristol, on the *fifth* day of *June A.D. 1893* then and there, in our said Court, to give such evidence as they know relating to any matters which may be inquired of on behalf of the Commonwealth, before said Court, or the Grand Jury.

HEREOF FAIL NOT, and make due return of this Writ with your doings thereon, into the said Court.

WITNESS my hand at *New Bedford* in the County of Bristol, the *sixteenth* day of *May* in the year of our Lord eighteen hundred and ninety *three*

H. M. Knowlton
District Attorney

BRISTOL, SS.   *May 29* 1893

                      By virtue of this precept I this day summoned the within named by reading to each in his presence and hearing the within summons for their appearance at Court as within directed.
        FEES.

Service, - - - - - -   Wm H Medley
Travel, miles, - - -   Constable of *Fall River*
Horse and carriage, miles,
                        $

Frederick Bradford Hart, 1889.
Photograph by James P. Stiff, Fall River, Massachusetts.

HK184
Document, printed, with additional text handwritten in ink.

No..............
COMMONWEALTH
vs.
Lizzie A. Borden

COMMONWEALTH OF MASSACHUSETTS.
BRISTOL, SS.

To the Sheriffs of our several Counties, or their Deputies, the Constables of any Town or City in the County of Bristol, or any district police officer,
GREETING:

You are hereby commanded to summon *Thomas Keiran, Adelaide B. Churchill, Abraham G. Hart, John T. Burrill, Everett M. Cook, Joseph Shortsleeve, James Mather, Jonathan Clegg, Patrick F. Lorrigan, Patrick McGowan, Dennis F. Sullivan, Mrs. John Gormley, Louis L. Hall, Alexander H. Coggeshall, Robert Nicholson, Hannah H. Gifford, Jane E. Gray, Frederick A. Pickering, Margaret D. Crapo, Kate Leary, William H. Medley, Philip Harrington, George W. Allen, John Fleet* (if they may be found in your precinct), to appear before the **SUPERIOR COURT** next to be holden at *New Bedford* within and for our county of Bristol, on the *fifth* day of *June* A.D. *1893* then and there, in our said Court, to give such evidence as they know relating to any matters which may be inquired of on behalf of the Commonwealth, before said Court, or the Grand Jury.

HEREOF FAIL NOT, and make due return of this Writ with your doings thereon, into the said Court.

WITNESS my hand at *New Bedford* in the County of Bristol, the *sixteenth* day of *May* in the year of our Lord eighteen hundred and ninety *three*

H. M. Knowlton
District Attorney

BRISTOL, SS.   *May 29* 1893

By virtue of this precept I this day summoned the within named by reading to each in his presence and hearing the within summons for their appearance at Court as within directed.

FEES.

Service, - - - - - - Wm H Medley
Travel, miles, - - -   Constable of *Fall River*
Horse and carriage,   miles,
$

HK185
Document, printed, with additional text handwritten in ink.

No..............
COMMONWEALTH
vs.
Lizzie A. Borden

COMMONWEALTH OF MASSACHUSETTS.
BRISTOL, SS.

To the Sheriffs of our several Counties, or their Deputies, the Constables of any Town or City in the County of Bristol, or any district police officer,
GREETING:

You are hereby commanded to summon *Mark P. Chase, George A. Petty, Thomas Boulds, Charles H. Cook, Harry C. Pearce, Thomas J. L. Brown, William L. Hacking, Oliver P. Darling, Annie F. Peckham, Angenette Wing, George L. Douglass, Michael Mullaley, Mrs. P. V. I. Bowen, William R. Martin, Frank H. Kilroy, Patrick H. Doherty, John Devine, Dennis Desmond, Jr., Frank L. Edson, Patrick Connors, John Riley, Joseph Hyde Delia S. Manley* (if they may be found in your precinct), to appear before the **SUPERIOR COURT** next to be holden at *New Bedford* within and for our county of Bristol, on the *fifth* day of *June A.D. 1893* then and there, in our said Court, to give such evidence as they know relating to any matters which may be inquired of on behalf of the Commonwealth, before said Court, or the Grand Jury.

HEREOF FAIL NOT, and make due return of this Writ with your doings thereon, into the said Court.

WITNESS my hand at *New Bedford* in the County of Bristol, the *sixteenth* day of *May* in the year of our Lord eighteen hundred and ninety *three*

H. M. Knowlton
District Attorney

BRISTOL, SS.   *June 5th* 1893

                    By virtue of this precept I this day summoned the within named by reading to each in his presence and hearing the within summons for their appearance at Court as within directed.

    FEES.

Service, - - - - - -	Isaac B Wordell
Travel, miles, - - -	Constable of
Horse and carriage, miles,	
	$

HK186
Document, printed, with additional text handwritten in ink.

No..............
COMMONWEALTH
vs.
Lizzie A. Borden

COMMONWEALTH OF MASSACHUSETTS.
BRISTOL, SS.

To the Sheriffs of our several Counties, or their Deputies, the Constables of any Town or City in the County of Bristol, or any district police officer, GREETING:

You are hereby commanded to summon *Mary A. Durfee,* ~~*Martha Chagnon, Mary A. Chagnon,*~~ *Alfred C. Johnson, Frank Eddy, Edward Downs, Alfred Clarkson, George W. Hathaway, Mary B. Wyatt, Joseph Derossier, Adelard Perron, Orrin A. Gardiner, William A. Dolan, M.D., Seabury W. Bowen, M.D., Benjamin J. Handy, M.D., John W. Coughlin, M.D.* (if they may be found in your precinct), to appear before the **SUPERIOR COURT** next to be holden at *New Bedford* within and for our county of Bristol, on the *fifth* day of *June A.D. 1893* then and there, in our said Court, to give such evidence as they know relating to any matters which may be inquired of on behalf of the Commonwealth, before said Court, or the Grand Jury.

HEREOF FAIL NOT, and make due return of this Writ with your doings thereon, into the said Court.

WITNESS my hand at *New Bedford* in the County of Bristol, the *sixteenth* day of *May* in the year of our Lord eighteen hundred and ninety *three*

H. M. Knowlton
District Attorney

BRISTOL, SS. *June 5th* 1893

By virtue of this precept I this day summoned the within named by reading to each in his presence and hearing the within summons for their appearance at Court as within directed.

FEES.

Service, - - - - -
Travel, miles, - - -   Isaac B Wordell,
Horse and carriage,   miles,   Constable of
                                $

HK187
Letter, typewritten.

ATTORNEY GENERAL'S DEPARTMENT, COMMONWEALTH BUILDING,
Boston,   May 17th, 1893.

Dear Mr. Attorney:-

Mr. Knowlton wrote me some days ago that he wished for an opportunity for a joint conference between you and ourselves in the Borden case, for which purpose I told him that I would be at your command at any time day or evening on notice. If such joint conference proves to be impracticable, as I trust it may not, please let me see you at some convenient time in advance of the trial, and oblige,

Yours very truly,

Attorney General.

Hon. William H. Moody,
Haverhill, Mass.

HK188
Letter, handwritten in ink.

Wednesday   **LAW OFFICES**
                        20 PEMBERTON SQ.
                        BOSTON
MELVIN O. ADAMS

Dear Albert,

Knowlton says <u>you</u> have Bridget Sullivan's testimony <u>before Inquest</u> and that we may have it.- Therefore I ask for it - Please send by bearer -

I ought to say that Jennings applied to Knowlton and thro him I get the above -

Very Truly
M. O. A.

HK189
Letter, typewritten.

ATTORNEY GENERAL'S DEPARTMENT,
COMMONWEALTH BUILDING,
Boston,   May 17, 1893.

Dear Mr. Attorney:-

Adams calls on me for Bridget Sullivan's testimony at the inquest, saying that you have referred him to me for it. I am very sure that I have never had or even seen it, and a careful search of the office discloses no trace of it; and there is no one in the office who has any recollection of ever having seen it. I think you are misled by the fact that I have a copy of Lizzie Borden's testimony at the inquest, but I am very sure that I never saw Bridget Sullivan's.

I am looking anxiously for some further news of your home affairs. I sincerely hope they will turn in the right direction, and that speedily.

I had not seen the Record article when I received your letter of the 14th, but did afterward. Where or how it originated heaven only knows. It is of the same character as all the rest of course. The newspaper reporters have let me severely alone since the last notice I gave them to that effect. I hope you and Moody and I can ~~meet~~ get together, and as I said before I am at your service for that purpose at any time on a day's notice or so.

Very truly yours,

Hon. H. M. Knowlton,   Attorney General.

HK190
Letter, typewritten.

ATTORNEY GENERAL'S DEPARTMENT,
COMMONWEALTH BUILDING,
Boston,   May 17, 1893.

Col. M. O. Adams,
My Dear Sir:-

I am sorry that you are put to trouble, but Mr. Knowlton must be mistaken, and I think he has been misled by the fact that I had a copy of Miss Borden's evidence. I am very sure that I have never had or even seen Bridget Sullivan's, and I have had careful search made of the office which does not disclose it, and no one in the office has any recollection of ever having seen it. I have written Mr. Knowlton to this effect.

       Very truly yours,

       Attorney General.

20 Pemberton sq.

HK191
Letter, typewritten.

       Boston, Mass. May 18th, 1893.

Dear Mr. Pillsbury,

 Forgive the persistence of a friend of humanity, and your friend. You said you had no information that Miss Borden or her eminent attorneys desired a noleprosique or would willingly accept one, and that a great howl would go up in any case we all admit. Suppose her attorneys would ask for a noleprosique could you not consistently grant it? I have not seen one of them since my interview or communicated with any one in her interests. It seems to me to block all the courts of justice for a month and deprive a hundred accused persons of a speedy trial in order that Lizzie Borden maybe vindicated, or a disagreement ensue is cruel and unnecessary, the rights of others indicted and in prison awaiting trial are as dear to them and they should not be delayed unless there is reasonable certainty of conviction is the good practice you have always maintained. Her wealth is a secure bond of at least $300,000 should any evidence sufficient for conviction ever be found, her trial now and acquittal would be a bar if such evidence were possible or probable. The weary months is an additional reason why you can act leniently in shortening the term of imprisonment, and why not enter a nole now instead of after a disagreement. You are above popular clamor and we need an Attorney General and a Governor broad enough to do so grand a deed as this will be in the eyes of the noblest and the best. while the circumstances mentioned vindicate it to the worst Mac Henries and Hilliards of society. All good people will approve.

      Your friend
      E. Moody Boynton

Webster Street 27 & 28 Revere House

HK192
Letter, typewritten.

ATTORNEY GENERAL'S DEPARTMENT,
COMMONWEALTH BUILDING,
Boston,   May 23, 1893.

Dear Lovell:-

It will be necessary for Mr. Knowlton to have your proposition at once, if you desire to make one as the matter must now be determined one way or another.

Very truly yours,

Attorney General.

Arthur T. Lovell,
Pemberton Sq.
Boston

HK193
Letter, handwritten in ink.

Danvers. Mass.
May 23, 1893.

H. M. Knowlton, Esq.
Dist. Attorney for Bristol Co.

Sir,

In your argument at the hearing in the Lizzie A. Borden case, you said - "As we listened to Dr. Draper's testimony, we were struck by the fact that it was not a man who did this work.xxxxxxx We see in it, however, the weak, irresolute, imperfect femine hand that only knew the impulse to strike, not with the strength of a man xxxxxx these xxxxxxxx they were all weak, irresolute blows."

These words bear strongly and justly against the prisoner. The bones forming the skull are not so hard and dense as commonly supposed; they contain much "cancellated" structure, and there the bone of the skull is weak. I need not remind you that the skull is often fractured by a club, or a fall on the pavement.

From my study and observation when a student of medicine and surgery - graduating at Harvard Med. School in 1874, but not having practised my profession - I am prepared to say that the wounds found on the head of Mr. and of Mrs. Borden - as described by Drs. Dolan and Draper - show a woman's hand - as you so felicitously said in your argument - the hand of a woman weak from the previous day's illness, and weak from hesitation to kill those who once were dear to her.

Instead of giving Mr. Borden ten wounds, and his wife eighteen - as was done - a man of ordinary strength would have killed his victims with from three to five blows at most, would have had a truer aim than in the cases in question, and would have known when his victims were dead.

<u>If before the trial experiments should be made by an expert in anatomy and surgery by inflicting blows with a hatchet on the heads of dissecting-room subjects. I think it could be shown to the jury that the wounds on Mr. and Mrs. Borden were, undoubtedly, made by a woman.</u>

The importance of such testimony is too evident for comment. Very likely these experiments have already been made.

As to the prussic acid testimony - in addition to the extreme improbability that three witnesses should mistake the identity of the prisoner, is the fact that prussic acid is seldom used in murder, and is a poison that only an educated person - like Miss Borden - would be likely to know of. She, doubtless, knew that it was very quick and most powerful in its action.

<u>Perhaps</u> expert testimony would show that the use of this poison is harder of detection, both before and after death, than that of most others.

Jerome C. (or T.) Borden testified that some time after 6 o'clock in the evening before the murder, he saw Lizzie Borden going down the street, and that soon after, Mrs. Borden told him Lizzie had not been out for all day till then, on account of sickness.

But, doubtless, Lizzie could have slipped out, for a short time in the forenoon, without Mrs. B's knowledge; she did not feel well enough to go to a distant drug store, and, naturally, did not want her step-mother to know that she had gone out; so she went to Smith's store, comparatively near her home - as I infer - though she knew the danger of being identified at Smith's.

But she was willing to run that risk, for, seemingly, she was in desperate haste - as the next day's horrors show - for she knew that Emma might return at any moment from her visit, already of two or three weeks' duration.

The prisoner's voice - low, "and a little tremulous" - when asking for the poison, is significant. I have thought much as to the probable motive in the evident falsehood told by Lizzie respecting the note, and conclude that she intended that her falsehood should pave the way for the belief that she could not have gone upstairs and killed her step-mother, for she thought she had gone out to see her "sick friend."

A lady told me that she thought the strongest argument against Lizzie is her demeanor since her arrest; and also her taking her arrest as a matter of course, as it were, is significant.

It is very suspicious if she said, as stated by a newspaper reporter, that she expected to be arrested.

Very truly your's
Samuel P. Fowler.

HK194
Letter, typewritten.

ATTORNEY GENERAL'S DEPARTMENT,
COMMONWEALTH BUILDING,
Boston,   May 25, 1893.

Dear Mr. Attorney:-

I enclose all the communications I have received as to the reporting of the trial, as somebody ought now to be engaged at once, I think. You will remember that I told you that Arthur T. Lovell had proposed for the job, with the privilege of furnishing a copy to the press, but he has furnished me no figures, although once reminded. You will observe that Burt, who bids 35 cents per folio, cooly asks leave to give (meaning of course to sell) the press a copy, without any diminution of his own price. I can say no more than I said the other day, namely:- that Burt, though high, is competent to my knowledge. Whether the others would prove so I cannot say. The difference of 5 cents or so per folio is worth saving, if it can be saved.

The statement which appeared this morning was more or less perverted from the form in which it was given out in every paper in which I have yet seen it, though perhaps no particular harm is done; but it is singular that newspapers cannot tell the truth, even when it is put before them and they know it is the truth.

Very truly yours,
Attorney General.

Hon. H. M. Knowlton
New Bedford.

HK195
Letter, handwritten in ink.

Danvers, Mass.
May 26th, 1893

A. E. Pillsbury, Esq.
Attorn. Gen. of Commonwealth,
    Boston,
        Sir,

In Dist. Attorney Knowlton's argument at the hearing in the Lizzie A. Borden case you will remember that he said - "As we listened to Dr. Draper's testimony, we were struck by the fact that it was not a man who did this work xxxxxx

We see in it however the weak, irresolute, imperfect feminine hand that only knew the impulse to strike, not with the strength of a man; xxxxx those blows were not even evidences of malice, because they were all weak, irresolute blows."

In corroboration of these words is the fact that the bones forming the skull are not as hard and dense as commonly supposed; they contain much "cancellated" structure, and there the bone is weak.

As you know, the skull is often fractured by a club, or a fall on the pavement.

From my study and observation when a student of medicine and surgery - graduating at the Harvard Medical School in 1874, but not having practised my profession - I feel assured that the wounds found on the head of Mr. and Mrs. Borden - as described by Drs. Dolan and Draper- show a woman's hand, - as the Dist. Attorney so pertinently said - the hand of a woman weak from the previous day's illness, and weak, also, from hesitation to kill those who once were dear to her.

Instead of giving Mr. Borden ten wounds, and his wife eighteen, (as was done) a man of ordinary strength would have killed his victims with from three to five blows at most, would have had a truer aim than in the cases in question, and would have known when his victims were dead.

<u>If before the trial experiments should be made by an expert in anatomy and surgery by giving blows with a hatchet on the heads of dissecting-room subjects, I think it would undoubtedly, be made to appear to the jury that the wounds on Mr. and Mrs. Borden were made by a woman. The importance of such testimony is too evident for comment.</u>

As to the prussic acid testimony, in addition to the extreme improbability that three witnesses should mistake the identity of the prisoner, is the fact that prussic acid is seldom used in murder, and is a poison that only an educated person - like Lizzie Borden - would be likely to know of. She, doubtless, knew that it was very quick, and most powerful in its action.

<u>Perhaps</u> expert testimony would show that the use of this poison is harder of detection, both before and after death, than that of most others.

Jerome C. (or T.) Borden testified that, some time after 6 o'clock in the evening before the murder, he saw Lizzie Borden going down the street, and that soon after Mrs. Borden told him Lizzie had not been out for all day, till then, on account of her (Lizzie's) sickness.

But, doubtless, Lizzie could have slipped out for a short time in the forenoon without Mrs. B's knowledge; L. did not feel well enough to go to a distant drug store, and naturally, would not want her step-mother to know that she had gone out; so she went to Smith's store, comparatively near her home (I infer,) though she knew the danger of being identified at Smith's. But she was willing to run that risk, for, seemingly, she was in desperate haste - as the next day's horrors show - for she knew that Emma might return at any moment from her visit, already of two or three weeks duration. The prisoner's voice, "low and a little tremulous," when asking for the poison, is significant.

I have thought much as to the probable motive in the evident falsehood told by Lizzie respecting the note, and I conclude that she intended that the falsehood should make persons believe that she could not have gone up stairs and killed her step-mother, for she supposed that she had gone out to see her "sick friend."

A lady told me that she thought the strongest argument against Miss Borden is her demeanor since her arrest; taking her arrest as a matter of course, as it were.

It is very suspicious if she said - as stated by a newspaper reporter - that she expected to be arrested.

Very truly yours
Samuel P. Fowler

HK196
Document, typewritten.

(Over the Associated Press Lines)
Boston, May 27
H. M. Knowlton, Esq.
Despatches to Mr. Burt or myself on this matter can be filed with Operator Bolles, Standard Office, free of expense to anybody.
H. H. Fletcher,
Associated Press.

(Over the Associated Press Lines)
Boston, May 27.
H. M. Knowlton, District Attorney,
New Bedford, Mass.,

If I can furnish Associated Press copy of Borden trial report I will make my bid thirty cents. Please answer immediately as it is very important for them to know today, so as to have time to make other arrangements should answer be unfavorable.

Frank H. Burt.

To Mr. Knowlton:- Would you kindly send reply by bearer and oblige,

H. C. Bolles
Assd. Press Operator.

HK197
Letter, typewritten.

ATTORNEY GENERAL'S DEPARTMENT,
COMMONWEALTH BUILDING,
Boston, May 27, 1893.

Dear Mr. Attorney:-

Among the multitude of crank communications the enclosed seems to be worth reading. There are one or two hints in it that possibly may be of service to you.

Very truly yours,

Attorney General.

Hon. H. M. Knowlton,
New Bedford, Mass.

HK198
Letter, typewritten.

COMMONWEALTH OF MASSACHUSETTS, OFFICE OF THE DISTRICT ATTORNEY FOR THE SOUTHERN DISTRICT.

New Bedford, Mass., May 27, 1893.

Hon. A E. Pillsbury:
    Attorney General:
        My Dear Sir:-

The defense have asked for two experts, one on each branch, presumably the chemical and the anatomical. They are to designate their names as soon as they have selected them, probably early next week. This makes it of great importance for us to decide whether we want additional experts, and if so whom. Both Dr. Draper and Wood will take it kindly to be fortified, especially in view of the above fact.

Moody and I will probably be very much occupied from now until the beginning of the trial. Will it be too much to ask you to think over the matter, so that when we call upon you sometime next week you can give us your views both upon the employments of experts, and if so whom to employ.

Dr. Draper is coming round on our side in great shape. All doubts he may have has as to the time of death are now fully dispersed.

        Yours Truly,
        H. M. Knowlton
        per E.

HK199
Letter, handwritten in ink.

854 Broadway
South Boston,
May 27, 1893

Hon. E. A Pillsbury:
    Boston-
My dear Mr. Pillsbury,
Yours at hand, you are very kind to say what you have to me.
If there were one time more than another convenient to you (so busy) I would gladly know it.

If at your own house or at your office I would wish to suit your <u>greatest convenience.</u>

Yours most truly,
W. H. Savary

HK200
Letter, typewritten, accompanied by memoranda.

304 Marlboro' Street,
Boston, May 28th, 1893

H. M. Knowlton, Esq.
    Dear Sir:

    I beg leave to submit the accompanying memoranda in fulfillment of your request of Friday relative to the anatomical proofs of the priority of Mrs. Borden's death.

One matter has occurred to me about which I venture to make a suggestion although it may be impertinent. It is this. Would it not be wise, in the presentation of the medical testimony to the jury, to avoid points which are not essential to the case, but which offer an opportunity for medical disagreement and contradiction? There is much in these two homicides about which a medical difference can scarcely be possible. For example, it is indisputable,

1. That both victims came to their death by fracture of the skull and injury to the brain by blows on the head.
2. That these blows were given with a hatchet.
3. That Mrs. Borden was killed before Mr. Borden.
4. That the bodies were not moved after the killing.
5. That there was no resistance to the assault in either case

These are bottom facts which are definite and beyond controversy and they must so impress the jury.

On the other hand, there are certain incidental questions, which are very fascinating in themselves, but which afford ready opportunity for dis- agreement among the medical witnesses and as they do not touch closely the real problem of the cause and manner of the deaths, they might much better, I think, be left out of sight, to the end that the chance of contradictions would be avoided. At the best, these collateral questions are speculative only and cannot be proved demonstratively. As instances of this sort, I name the following (and I am myself responsible for suggesting some of them at our conferences of the 24th and 26th instant):

1. Which was probably the first blow in each of the two cases?
2. What was the relative position of Mrs. Borden and her assailant when the first blow was struck?
3. What was the probable effect of that blow on Mrs. Borden as to her loss of consciousness at once, her ability to scream or to resist?
4. As to the "instantaneousness" of the death in each case.

Unless these and other such matters affect the relation of the accused to the crime charged, are they necessary and expedient to intro- duce? Do they not in some measure give a chance for medical disagreements and for an argument by Gov. Robinson thereon? Do they not interpose a little dust between the eyes of the jury and the main question, namely, what was the cause of the deaths and who was the guilty agent?

Two of the medical experts for the defence, by the way, have made their appearance. They are Dr. Thomas Dwight and Dr. Maurice H. Richardson. Both are Boston men and both are connected with the Harvard Medical School, the former as Professor of Anatomy and the latter as Assistant Professor of Anatomy. Dr. Richardson is also a surgeon of wide reputation and fully acknowledged ability and skill; he is one of the surgical staff of the Massachusetts General Hospital and has had much experience in court as an expert. Dr. Dwight has had less experience in medico-legal matters; he is a highly accomplished anatomist. Both these gentlemen studied the skulls and the bony fragments at my office, while I sat in a room near by within easy call, but not where I could hear conversation when their door was shut. They did not require any information and we had no communication during their study of the corpora delecti.

This appearance of the defendant's medical experts opens anew the question of the desirability of more medical help on the side of the government. Although those two skulls tell their own story most eloquently and thus greatly narrow the need of much doctors' talk it may seem best to you and to Mr. Moody to have some other help in the line of experts. If such be the case, I do not know anyone who would give you better assistance than Dr. D. W. Cheever, of Boston, or anyone who would better offset Drs. Dwight and Richardson. Dr. Cheever is the Professor of Surgery in Harvard Medical School, has been for twenty-five years a visiting surgeon at the Boston City Hospital and was formerly for many years the Demonstrator of Anatomy in the Medical School. To wide knowledge and experience, he adds a peculiarly cool and impressive manner, and is reckoned here a model witness. If he can be secured, I am sure that the prosecution would be very materially strengthened on its medical side.

Pardon a personal matter in conclusion. Will you kindly put me in com-

David Williams Cheever, circa 1900.

Frank Winthrop Draper, circa 1900.

munication with a New Bedford host or hostess who will take care of my animal wants as to eating and sleeping during my visit to your city? If you will be good enough to give me the name and address of the individual I will make my wants known to him. I take the liberty of asking this indulgence this early, as I have an impression that good accommodations will be at a premium presently, and I am always upset and good for nothing if I am deprived of sleep.

I am very truly yours,
F. W. Draper.

MEMORANDA RELATING to the PRIORITY of MRS. BORDEN'S DEATH.

I. As to the condition of the blood in the two cases. At about 11:45 o'clock, fluid blood, from Mr. Borden's wounds, was "dropping" from the sofa to the floor; there was no clot in sight.

A "few minutes later", the blood on the carpet on which Mrs. Borden's head lay was observed by Dr. Dolan to be clotted.

"In man, blood when shed, becomes viscid in about two or three minutes and enters the jelly stage in about five or ten minutes. Coagulation is generally complete in from one to several hours. The time will be found to vary according to the condition of the individual, the temperature of the air and the size and form of the vessel into which the blood is shed." Foster Physiology, p.38.

II. As to the retention of the body heat in the two cases. Mr. Borden's body when first inspected was nearly as warm as in life. Mrs. Borden's body was cold to the sense of touch at nearly the same time. The difference in temperature was a matter of sensation as tested with the hand only; in the absence of accurate observations with the thermometer, the measure of the difference cannot be expressed in definite terms.

The average rate of cooling of the dead human body, lightly covered, and in a temperature of about 70 degrees, has been determined by the use of the thermometer to be one and three-fifths degrees per hour, being subject however to many modifications.

The most that can be said in the two cases under consideration is that the temperature of the two bodies showed that Mrs. Borden had been dead longer than Mr. Borden.

III. As to the state of the contents of the stomach in the two case Mr. Borden's stomach was found to contain a little fruit pulp with some clear fluid (water). there was nothing remaining of the breakfast meal (mutton, &c.)

In the lower bowels were normal fecal masses.

Mrs. Borden's stomach was found to contain the partially digested remains of the food (meat, &c.) taken at breakfast.

In her small intestines was the usual material (chyle) found there in healthy digestion going forward naturally. Some pieces of fruit skin also were found here. The large intestine was empty, not yet having received any refuse from the morning digestion.

In neither Mrs. Borden nor Mr. Borden was any evidence found of any disease about the digestive organs or of any condition, except their death, that had interfered with their healthy activity.

The difference in the stage of digestion reached in the two cases was evidence of the priority of Mrs. Borden's death.

IV. As to the interpretation of the three preceding data. All these data taken together prove that Mrs. Borden died before Mr. Borden died.

It is impossible to state accurately in minutes the period that elapsed between the two deaths.

But it is correct to say that these data, studied either separately or in their associated relation, are consistent with the view that about an hour passed between Mrs. Borden's death and that of Mr. Borden.

Of the three data, the condition of the digestive process in the two individuals is the most significant and reliable.

HK201
Telegram, handwritten in ink.

THE WESTERN UNION TELEGRAPH COMPANY.

Newbedford Ms.   5/29/93
Hon. A. E. Pillsbury
      Atty. Gen'l Boston
  They have Dwight and Richardson our people suggest Cheever Moody Will see you this morning = H. M. Knowlton

HK202
Letter, typewritten.

ATTORNEY GENERAL'S DEPARTMENT,
COMMONWEALTH BUILDING,
Boston, May 31, 1893.

Dear Mr. Attorney:-

Yours received, and I am sorry not to have seen you Monday. I don't know what you allude to in your last clause, but important please let me know of it. I have heard from Mr. Knowlton about experts, etc... and presume I shall see you both during the week; and, as I have said to him you also may command me at any and all times for anything I can do.

Very truly yours,

Attorney General.

Hon. William H. Moody,
Haverhill, Mass.

HK203
Letter, handwritten in ink.

F. W. DRAPER, M. D.
304 MARLBOROUGH STREET,
BOSTON,

May 31, 1893

My Dear Sir: -

Dr. Cheever and I have had a conference to-day with the Borden photographs and skulls before us. We are in entire accord and he will testify

1. That the cause and manner of the deaths were the same in both cases, namely, fracture of the skull and injury to the brain by blows on the head.

2. That the weapon was an edged tool of some weight, like a hatchet.

3. That the length of the edge of the weapon was about 3-1/2 inches.

4. That Mrs. Borden was killed by blows inflicted from behind, the assailant standing astride the body.

5. That Mr. Borden was killed by blows given by the assailant standing at the head of the sofa just within the door.

6. That the assailant was right handed and used his right hand, or, if using both hands, that the left hand was foremost, or in front of the right hand, on the handle.

7. That Mrs. Borden died first, and that the supposition of an hour's interval is not inconsistent with the facts relating to the stage of digestion, the body temperature and the condition of the blood in the two cases.

8. That the deaths were not instantaneous.

9. That a woman would have sufficient physical strength to inflict the blows, assuming that she was of normal adult vigor. I write especially to inform you of two important discoveries which I made upon a careful examination of the two skulls. On Mr. Borden's skull I found that the blow just in front of the ear left its mark on the base of the skull within the cavity, that its depth was 1-7/16 inches and that it cut directly through the internal carotid artery; this wound was necessarily and immediately fatal from hemorrhage. The other discovery is still more important; on one of the cuts in Mrs. Borden's skull, near the right ear, there is a very small but unmistakable deposit of the gilt metal with which hatchets are ornamented when they leave the factory; this deposit (Dr. Cheever confirmed the observation fully) means that the hatchet used in killing Mrs. Borden was a <u>new</u> hatchet, not long out of the store. Perhaps this is not new information either to you or Dr. Dolan; it was new to me and seemed important enough to justify immediate conveyance to you. The shining deposit can be seen with the naked eye; it is plainly visible with the use of a lens, when once its situation is indicated.

I see by the morning papers that killing people with hatchets is a Bristol County habit. I am sorry that this latest homicide comes just now when you and Dr. Dolan are so much occupied with other matters.

Very truly Yours

F. W. Draper

Mr. Knowlton.

HK204
Letter, typewritten, with notations handwritten in lead.

ATTORNEY GENERAL'S DEPARTMENT,
COMMONWEALTH BUILDING,

Boston,   May 31, 1893.

Dear Mr. Attorney:-

Your letters and telegrams received, and of course I will comply with your requests to the fullest extent on seeing or hearing from

Bro. Moody or the stenographer. I was absent Monday and did not see them.

I wish you would consider a little further the question of my presence at. the opening. I have not undertaken to determine it especially as I wish to defer greatly to your desires and Mr. Moody when you come to a ~~farther~~ *final* conclusion; But it still appears to me that while my absence is properly accounted for, and cannot I think affect the case (except as it is lied about, which of course we can not prevent) if I should appear there and immediately disappear, it might affect the case *unfavorable* as some liars and idiots would then say undoubtedly that I was able to try the case, but did not believe in it et cetera. We will determine the matter when we meet. Command me at all time if I can do any thing for you. If you are to see me this week please give me twenty four hours notice if possible, though it is not absolutely necessary.

Very truly yours,

Attorney General.

Hon. H. M. Knowlton.

HK205
Letter, printed, with comments handwritten in lead.

COMMONWEALTH *of* MASSACHUSETTS
BRISTOL SS,   SUPERIOR COURT, JUNE TERM, 1893, LIST OF JURORS

~~Attleborough,~~	~~Isaac Alger.~~
~~New Bedford,~~	~~Charles N. Allen.~~
"	~~Henry B. Almy~~
~~Easton,~~	~~Hebert Ames~~
"	~~Oliver Ames, 2d.~~
Attleborough,	Millard F. Ashley.
Taunton,	Herbert L. Atherton.
Mansfield,	~~George P. Bailey.~~
~~New Bedford,~~	~~Ansel C. Baker~~
"	~~Eugene M. Barrows.~~
"	Bourne S. Bartlett.
Fairhaven,	Frank M. Bates.
~~No. Attleborough,~~	~~William A. Bennett.~~
Taunton,	Zeba F. Bliss.
~~New Bedford,~~	~~Francis A. Booth~~
Attleborough,	Charles E. Briggs.
Swansea,	Jeremiah N. Brown.
~~New Bedford,~~	~~Gilbert K. Brownell.~~
Taunton,	Ansel O. Burt
New Bedford,	William F. Butler
"	~~Robert H. Carter~~
"	~~Joseph Chausse.~~
~~Taunton,~~	~~Nathan Clark.~~
New Bedford,	Jireh W. Clifton.
"	~~George A. Cobb.~~
Acushnet,	James H. Cobb.
Attleborough,	Frank G. Cole. 9
~~Somerset,~~	~~Matthew Costello~~
~~New Bedford,~~	~~Orville W. Cranston.~~
Taunton,	~~Oliver H. Crossman.~~
~~Somerset,~~	~~Benjamin T. Cundall.~~
Attleborough,	~~George W. Curien.~~

~~New Bedford,~~   ~~Silas D. Dammon.~~
~~Taunton,~~   ~~Elihu M. Davis~~
~~Dartmouth,~~   ~~George W. Davis.~~
~~Taunton,~~   ~~Ezra Davol.~~
Berkley,   Albert E. Dean.
~~Taunton,~~   ~~Henry C. Dean.~~
       "   William F. Dean.   -2
New Bedford,   Charles H. Dias.
~~Taunton,~~   ~~John W. Dixon.~~
~~New Bedford,~~   ~~Daniel F. Driscoll.~~
Swansea,   Oscar R. Douglass.
~~New Bedford,~~   ~~Daniel F. Driscoll.~~
~~Easton,~~   ~~Timothy W. Driscoll.~~
Westport,   Thomas B. Earle.
Taunton,   John C. Finn.   10
~~Mansfield,~~   ~~David Fisher.~~
~~New Bedford,~~   ~~Charles F. Folger~~
Attleborough,   Charles F. Forrester.
~~Taunton,~~   ~~Ezekiel P. Francis.~~
~~New Bedford,~~   ~~Frank W. Francis.~~
       "   ~~Oliver E. Gifford,~~
~~Taunton,~~   ~~Gordon H. Godfrey.~~
~~Mansfield,~~   ~~William Graves.~~
~~Seekonk,~~   ~~Olney Greene.~~
~~Freetown,~~   ~~Eben S. Grinnell.~~
~~Attleborough,~~   ~~Henry M. Gross.~~
~~New Bedford,~~   ~~James Grundy,~~
~~N.Attleborough,~~ ~~Jason T. Guild.~~
~~Raynham,~~   ~~Edwin Gushee.~~
Attleborough,   George A. Gustin.
N.Attleborough,   A.O. Hall,
~~Acushent,~~   ~~John F. Hammett.~~
~~New Bedford,~~   ~~Joseph W. Hatch.~~
Swansea,   Charles F. Hathaway.
~~Taunton,~~   ~~George E. Hathaway.~~
       "   Joseph W. Hathaway.
Freetown,   Stephen A. Hathaway.
New Bedford,   Epiphalet W. Hervey.
~~Taunton,~~   ~~Edmund E. Hill.~~
       "   Henry A. Hodges.

"	Louis B. Hodges.	7
~~Attleborough,~~	~~Harold V. Hopkins.~~	
~~Rehoboth,~~	~~Dexter E. Horton, Jr.~~	
"	~~Gilbert M. Horton~~	
~~Dighton,~~	~~Josiah T. Horton.~~	
~~New Bedford,~~	~~George A. Howe.~~	
~~Dartmouth,~~	~~Gideon Howland.~~	
~~Fairhaven,~~	~~Henry M. Hoxie.~~	
~~New Bedford,~~	~~Henry P. Jenney.~~	
"	~~Henry W. Kenyon.~~	
~~Easton,~~	~~George F. King.~~	
~~New Bedford,~~	~~Charles W. Knight.~~	
No. Attleborough,	Charles Lamphier.	
~~Dighton,~~	~~Dwight F. Lane.~~	
~~Fairhaven,~~	~~Frederick E. Lawton.~~	
~~New Bedford,~~	~~Harry J. Leach.~~	
Mansfield,	Gustavus D. Leonard.	
Fairhaven,	James A. Lewis.	
Norton,	Harrison T. Lincoln.	
"	~~Lloyd S. Lincoln.~~	
~~Somerset,~~	~~George Lynch.~~	
Taunton,	Henry B. Macomber.	
"	John F. McCarthy.	
"	Thomas McKeon.	
~~New Bedford,~~	~~George H. Millikin.~~	
"	William J. Mills.	
~~Westport,~~	~~Augustus M. Mosher.~~	
~~Rehoboth,~~	~~Williard B. Munroe.~~	
New Bedford,	Edward M. Murphy.	
"	George E. Nye.	
"	~~F. WIlliam Oesting.~~	
~~No. Attleborough,~~	~~James O'Leary, Jr.~~	
~~Taunton,~~	~~Lyman Palmer.~~	
~~New Bedford,~~	~~Frederick Parker.~~	
~~New Bedford,~~	~~Francis H. Pasel.~~	
"	James H. Pease.	
~~Freetown~~	~~Walter Pease.~~	
~~Taunton,~~	~~Joseph Peltier.~~	
Westport,	George Potter.	-1
Taunton,	Henry N. Pratt.	

No.Attleborough,	Charles I. Richard.	*11*
Dighton,	Augustus S. Russell.	
~~New Bedford,~~	~~Mortimer Searles.~~	
~~Mansfield,~~	~~Charles L. Seaver.~~	
~~Dartmouth,~~	~~Walter C. Slocum.~~	
Easton,	Elijah Smith.	
~~Norton,~~	~~George E. Smith.~~	
~~No.Attleborough,~~	~~O.T. Springer.~~	*Excused*
~~Berkely,~~	~~John F. Staples.~~	
No.Attelborough,	H.K. Sturdy.	
New Bedford,	Augustus Swift.	
"	~~Ezra J. Swift.~~	
"	~~Edward S. Taber.~~	
"	~~John H. Taber.~~	
No.Attleborough,	Philip Thomas.	
~~Attleborough,~~	~~Leon H. Tingley.~~	
~~Easton,~~	~~David B. Tinkham.~~	
New Bedford,	Otis Tinkham.	
Taunton,	John T. Wade.	
~~Dighton,~~	~~Nathan O. Walker.~~	
~~Raynahm,~~	~~Cyrus Washburn.~~	
New Bedford,	Thomas H. Weaver.	
Seekonk,	William Westcot.	*6*
~~Westport,~~	~~Daniel Whalon.~~	
~~Taunton,~~	~~George H. Wheeler.~~	
"	~~Simeon A. Wheeler.~~	
Raynham,	Frederic C. Wilbar.	*4*
Easton,	Lemuel K. Wilber.	*5*
Somerset,	John Wilbur. -3	
~~Fairhaven,~~	~~Albert M. Wilcox.~~	
~~Taunton,~~	~~John T. Williams.~~	
~~New Bedford,~~	~~William H. Willis.~~	
~~Mansfield,~~	~~George Winslow.~~	
~~Taunton,~~	~~George A. Wood.~~	
Dartmouth,	Allen H. Wordell.	

HK20
Notes, typewritten, with comments handwritten in ink and lead.

Geo Pollu Wralf at	Wm F Drue Taunton	John Wilbur Somerset	Fred E Wilbur Raynham	L K Wilbur Easton	Wm Westcott Seekonk
Chas I Richards Taunton	Aug Swift N. Bedford	Frank Y Cole Attleborough	John C Finn Taunton	Louis A Hodges Taunton	Albert Wardell Dartmouth

Jurors' box diagram.

Charles I. Richards, North Attleboro.
American. Real estate. Republican. ~~Universalist~~ Episcopalian. Quite interested in church matters. Has served on jury. Has wife and children. Has not taken sides in the case, but has *not* made declarations about it.

Remarks by Brown. Is a well appearing man. Will try to get excused for the reason that he is one of the town assessors.

He is about 55 years old.
He has been a witness against me in a railroad case
Is thick with Pond, who is for defense
<u>Doubtful</u>
Cobb says Guild says he would be a (?) straight Kind of man, no matter what
Anyone said to him.
Is now an assessor.

William F. Deane, Taunton.
50. Farmer. Republican. Unitarian. Wife and child. Served on jury. Remarks by officers. Lives out of town. Good man.

Augustus Swift
Residence 75 North st
Nationality American
Business proprietor of the
Acushnet iron company
Politics Rep
Religion Protestant but does
not belong to any church
He will not [?] dont know
his opinion

Family consists of wife and
two children
Doesn't believe in circumstantial
Evidence. Good man
With us

Frank G. Cole, Attleboro.

American. Jeweler. Workman. Republican. No interest in religion. Never served on jury. Wife and no children. Age unknown. Not known whether he has taken sides in the case or talked about it.

Remarks by Reed. All these jewelers are acquainted and all intelligent men and read the papers.

Westcott - Says used to be his neighbor
and is a good man Used to live in Taunton
& was a machinist
By Seaver - good straight man.   Grand Army

John C. Finn, Taunton.

Irish. Painter. Democrat. Catholic. Wife and children. Has not expressed an opinion on the case.

Remarks by officers. Good man: a very intelligent Irishman. Been in city council.

EXCUSED

Louis B. Hodges - Taunton

59 - American Moulder - Republican
Baptist - Member of Church
Wife. Children - Never served on Jury
Think has taken sides in case but
made no declarations about it.
Remarks by Seaver & Westcott - All right

Allen H. Wordell, North Dartmouth.

American. Farming tools and produce: does business in New Bedford. Republican. No interest in church matters.

Never served on jury. Wife and children. 45 years of age. Never has talked about case that can be heard of.

Remarks. Attends strictly to business, and a good man in his family.

Good fellow, but will get out of it if he can
Think he is good - Kirby says

George Potter, Westport, below Hix's Bridge.

An American. Farmer: formerly went fishing. Republican. Universalist: slight interest in religion. Never served on jury. Fifty-three years of age. Has a wife and no children. Has not taken sides nor made any declarations that officer can learn.

Remarks by Kirby. Potter is a Mason. Goes to Fall River to marker every week. Is a man of limited education, but has good common sense.
This man is all right - Kirby thinks
Geo. Potter - carpenter

John Wilbur, Somerset.

58. American. Farmer. Republican. Methodist, but not interested in church. Has served on grand jury. Never talked about the case.

Remarks by Seaver. Good square man for jury.

By <u>Gilmore</u>. Doubtful.

Frederick C. Wilbur, Raynham.

38. American. Carpenter. Republican. Congregational church, but no interest. Wife and children. Says she is guilty.

Remarks by Seaver. Good, fair man.

By Gilmore. Uncertain.

Lemuel
~~Leonard~~ K. Wilbur, Easton.   Centre

An American. Farmer. Democrat. [?] No interest in religious matters. Wife and three children. *Family all go to church* Has served on jury a number of times. Has not taken sides on the case, but <u>does not believe in capital punishment</u>.

Remark by Renny. He is considered a good upright man.

By Cobb - Likes him Knows him good
many years. A business man

Farms on large scale.
Think he will do
His Wife thinks Lizzie guilty

William Westcott, Seakonk.

45. American. Farmer. Independent in politics. Goes to Congregational church. Not interested in religion. Married and <u>second wife</u>. Has not talked about the case.

Remarks by Seaver. Good, practical man.

HK207
Letter, handwritten in ink.

GEORGE W. GAY, M.D.,
665 BOYLSTON STREET, NEAR DARTMOUTH,
BOSTON

Jun 1, '93

My Dear General:

I am not the best man on that subject, or I would go in. Dr. C. B. Porter, 5 Arlington St. & Dr. Cheever would be an excellent team, you could not have a better one. Dr. Collins Warren is also a good man. (58 Beacon St.). Porter was formerly in the School as Demonstrator of Anatomy & is a first class man. Dr. H. H. A. Beach is also a bright man, & a good anatomist.

I will see you soon & suggest others if needed.

Sincerely yours,
Geo. W. Gay

HK208
Letter, handwritten in ink.

June 1, 1894

Mr. Knowlton

Sir. I see by the papers that the trial of Miss Borden is to commence the 5th inst.

If the evidence has been published correctly I think that the gov' hav made a mistake on one point that may be an serious injury to their case.

The papers asserted that it was claimed that the murderer <u>must</u> have stood astride of the victim and have used a broad bladed axe with a short handle, and have struck downward square blows as a man would in striking on the top of a log or low block,

If you believe that a woman can strike a dosen such blows and leave such wounds as have been described in Mrs Borden's skull, let your wife try it on a thin-barked green log and then peel off the bark and see the result on the log. No one but an expert axeman could have handled an axe so described with the result described, and he must have been spattered with blood, But if the murderer had stood <u>beside</u> his victims, and have used a thin bladed sharp axe like a lathing hatchet or a bell faced carpenters finishing hatchet, or what is more probable an <u>Ice</u> hatchet with a straight stick for a handle perhaps 18 inches long and ground sharp such as many families have about their refrigerators, and if the blows had been given in a hacking manner at arms length using only the front corner of the hatchet, the wounds in the bone would have been as described even to the change of direction of one or two of them, and might have had a tendency to throw the blood away from the assassin and would not have required a great outlay of strength,

The weapon might have been thrown into the water tank or carried away. ~~by Miss Russell~~.

It seems to me that ~~she~~ if Miss Borden is quilty she is not alone but that the murders must be the result of a conspiracy of which both sisters are parties and with one or more confederates perhaps both male and female.

I thought that I would drop you these lines as they might assist you. For it seemed to me that the police were depending more upon the opinions of professional men rather than upon those who had any practical knowledge of the handling of axes or hatchets and that you would lose your case in consequence.

Please do not allow the reporters to see this as I do not wish any newspaper notoriety.

Yours &c
Chas J Dean
Lunenburg, Mass.

(Note: The content of this letter indicates that the author's date of "1894" is incorrect.)

Albert Enoch Pillsbury, circa 1890.

HK209
Letter, typewritten.

> *ATTORNEY GENERAL'S DEPARTMENT,*
> *COMMONWEALTH BUILDING,*
> Boston,   June 1, 1893.

Mr. Frank H. Burt.
    Dear Sir:-

        I understand that Mr. Knowlton concluds to employ you in the Borden case at 30 cents per folio, with the privilege of furnishing the Associated Press a copy; this not to interfere in any respect with the quality or efficiency of the government work. I expected to see you yesterday or today, but learn now that you are in Dedham.

        Very truly yours,

        Attorney General.

HK210
Letter, typewritten.

> *ATTORNEY GENERAL'S DEPARTMENT,*
> *COMMONWEALTH BUILDING,*
> Boston,   June 1, 1893.

Dear Mr. Attorney:-

        Not seeing or hearing from Burt yesterday or today, as I expected to, and learning now that he is in Dedham, I have written and telegraphed him that you conclude to engage him at 30 cents per folio, with the privilege of furnishing a copy to the Associated Press; this not to interfere in any manner with the quality or efficiency of the government work. I have nothing in writing from him but the type written copy of his telegram of May 27th to you, but that, with what he had previously written me, seems sufficient, and I did not deem it safe to wait longer.

        Very truly yours,

        Attorney General.

HK211
Letter, handwritten in ink.

Mr. Knowlton,
    My Dear Sir,
    I went into this case rather from a sense of duty, & I want to serve the truth & do my duty- I was led to think, however, that two days detention, & possibly a second call of one day, would cover it.
    I hesitated to undertake it Chiefly because I have been out of order in health all the spring, & have had to keep quiet a good deal, on account of a recurrent diarrhoea.
    This is between ourselves= and I mention it, so that you can favor me with getting home, whenever possible.
                              truly yours
                              D.W. Cheever

June 2, 1893

1- Cause of death?
    homicide -
2. manner of death?
    cutting & crushing blows on skull & brain
3. weapon?
4. length of its edge?
A heavy metallic instrument with a cutting edge of 3-1/2 to 4 inches = bevelled = having sharp angles, & with a lever handle - sharp - This hatchet do
5. position of assailant?
on Mrs. Borden, at first in front then behind, then over her from behind - on Mr. Borden, directly over him, & standing behind top of head - 6. position of deceased when attacked?
of Mrs. Borden, upright = of Mr. Borden, lying down, with head turned on right cheek -
7. priority of Mrs. B's death?
one hour at least, in all probability -
    Mrs. B's body, cool -
    Mr. B's body, warm -
    Mrs. B - blood clotted -
    Mr. B - blood dripping -
    Mrs. B - stomach 9/10 full of 1/2 digested food -
    Mr. B - stomach empty save 1/10 partially digested food

Mrs. B - small intestines empty -
Mr. B. - small intestines full of chyle -
8. Amount of blood spattering?
uncertain, might go anywhere -
9. Instantaneousness of death?
Mr. B. the one blow immediately fatal was through the carotid artery = could hardly have been the first blow -
Mrs. B - no one immediately fatal wound = death due to the aggregate of blows -
10. was assailant right handed?
Mr. B - The cut down into carotid canal must have been given by an assailant standing over & behind head, & is right handed; or if with both hands, with left hand forward - weight of evidence is of right handed blows
Mrs. B-
one scalp cut from front, on left parietal bone, may have been with either hand = all the others right handed - all from behind, except two on vertex, which are doubtful -
11 - Could it have been a woman?
yes, if she had such a heavy cutting weapon as the skull wounds indicate -

---

HK212
Letter, handwritten in ink.

June 2, 1893

Miss Borden told me she had written to Marion that she would come. I don't remember much that was said about the trip, <u>except that she felt depressed, that she felt as if something was hanging over her and she couldn't throw it off</u>. She said that while she was at the table the day she was in Marion, and the girls were laughing and talking, that feeling came over her and one of the girls noticed it and said something about her not talking. That is all I can remember of our conversation about Marion.
Later on she said "father and Mrs. Borden were awfully sick last night. I was too, but not as sick as they were, for I did not vomit and they did. I could hear them in my room. I asked them if I could do anything for them but they said no." I asked Lizzie if she thought it was any thing they had eaten, she said "we don't know, we had some baker's bread for sup- per and all ate some of it but Maggie, and all were sick but her. Don't know whether it was the bread or what it was." I said if it was the bread I should think that other people would be sick too. She went on to say that she had thought perhaps

the milk had been poisoned. I asked her about the milk, how it was brought etc. She told me that they put out an empty can overnight. The milkman took it in the morning when he brought the milk. I asked her what time he came. She said "she thought about 4 o'clock." I said it is light at four, and I shouldn't think anyone would dare to come in and do anything to the can, for someone would be liable to see them. She said "I shouldn't think so." She said "her father <u>seemed to have so much trouble with the men that he had dealings with, that she sometimes was</u> afraid <u>that some of them would do something to him</u>." She added I expect nothing but that the house will be burned down over our heads. I don't know just what I said but she answered by saying "Well they have broken into the barn twice anyhow." I said yes, but of course they were after pigeons, it couldn't be they were after anything else. She answered, "<u>they have broken into the house in broad daylight with Emma. Maggie & me in the house</u>." I said I never heard of that before. She said "no father forbid our telling it." I asked her about it and her story was this, as near as I can remember:

"Mrs. Borden's things in her dressing room were ransacked, and her gold watch & chain, money & cartickets were taken." I think she told me there was something else taken but I can't remember just what. 1 think a pin or a charm. They also found a nail in the key hole. She told me her father reported it to the police but they didn't find anybody. She said "father thought they might catch them by the tickets. Lizzie remarked "just as if anybody would be foolish enough to use those tickets." <u>She also told me about seeing a man</u> run <u>around the</u> house one night. <u>I asked</u> her if she didn't <u>think it</u> was Maggie's <u>company, but</u> she hardly <u>thought so.</u>

She told me about a man that came to see her father. She heard him say I don't want to let my property for such business, and the man answered sneeringly, I shouldn't think <u>you</u> would care what it is let for. She said "father was mad and ordered the man out of the house." She told me of Mrs. Borden going over to see Dr. Bowen.

Mrs. Borden said she was afraid they had been poisoned. Mrs. Borden met Mr. Borden in the entry on her way out, and told him where she was going. Lizzie said "her father did not like it and said my money shant pay for it. But she went over.

I asked her what Dr. Bowen said she replied, he laughed when Mrs. Borden told what she feared, and said it was not poison.

Mrs. Borden had told the doctor about Mr. Borden's being sick and he went over to see him. Lizzie said "the way father used Dr. Bowen - why I was so mortified. I don't know what the doctor will think I am sure."

After he had gone Mrs. Borden scolded. She said I am ashamed for you to use Dr. Bowen so. Mr. Borden said "well I don't want him coming over here Dr. Handy style." Mrs. B. said he didn't come over here Dr. Handy style. I told him you were sick and he came over to see you and I think it is a shame you can't treat him decent. He is all the neighbors we have got and I think it is too bad."

Mr. Moody -
The foregoing is a substantially correct narrative as I remember it of the conversation which you wish me to give you.

Miss Russell

June 2, '93

(Note: "Medley matter" handwritten in lead on reverse side of letter.)

HK213
Letter, handwritten in ink.

Newark NJ.
June 10, 1893.

To the Prosecutor in the
Lizzie Borden Trial
Dear Sir

In the New York Tribune of June 9, under the heading of <u>Mrs. Churchill's Story</u> - I have the impression that Lizzie Borden is lying and playing a game.

Mrs. Churchill, Miss Russell, Bridget, and Lizzie are present. Lizzie tells some one <u>to go upstairs & look for Mrs. Borden</u>. Why <u>upstairs</u>? Why does not <u>she herself</u> rush to tell her mother - to tell her instantly, without delay that her father has been murdered! Why does she wait till several witnesses have arrived and then send them upstairs, if not that she knows very well what they will find up there! Why didn't she send some one down the street for her mother or out to the barn or anywheres else but upstairs.

2. Is it natural to suppose that she could have heard her mother come in and then <u>waited</u> (as long as she must have done) before sending the news to her or pretending to do so.

3. It looks very much as though Lizzie Borden were lying because of this. It has been proved that Mrs. Borden had been <u>dead</u> for an hour or two. How therefore could Lizzie state that "<u>she thought she heard her come in</u>?" No sound could possibly have been made to resemble the entrance of anyone.

And if anyone had entered why could it not have been ~~Mrs. Morse~~ her uncle - Why her mother.

Briefly the points are these-

1. The unnaturalness of not notifying her mother as soon as she thought she had arrived.

2. Sending the searching party underline{directly} to the part of the house where they would find Mrs. Borden.

3. She underline{could not have heard her mother enter} - because she had been dead 2 hrs. Therefore it looks like a lie on her part.

Yours truly
Otto H. Schulte
Principal of the Morton St.
Pub. School

Excuse appearance of this note - It has been written very hastily.

HK214
Letter, handwritten in ink.

New York, Sunday June 11th 1893

HOTEL BRUNSWICK CO.

Mr. Knowlton
    Dr Sir,

I am on a sick Bed, but feel as though I must write you & releive my mind or sufficate. unfortionately I am related to the Bordens through marrige. my husband came to me last August two days after the murder of Mr. & Mrs. Borden & said calling me by name. now you know enough to hang that girl but I warn you to Keep silent. & not mention to anyone the interviews you have had with Mrs. Borden the last 3 months. as we will meaning the Bordens never have the disgrace of that girl being convicted if mony can do it.- What he had reference to was that when I had been to see her wich was very often, as she was very fond of me, & confided in me all her troubles. I had often talked with him about it, & he would say it is wicked that those two people cant live in peace. I wish that fiend, meaning Lizzie would go to Europe again as that was all the time. poor Mrs. Borden felt that she was free with out locking, & bolting the door, she was in mortal terror when Lizzie was in the house. she would always ask Briget Sulliven to stay in & not go out & leave her alone. Oh, my heart aches so when I recal the times. that I have herd that Lizzie Borden abuse that dear old lady, because she would not make her father live in better shape as she called it, & the tears would stream down her face & she would sob & cry, & then would say why should I be treated so by that girl. I have always done everything I could for her. it was poor Mrs. Borden that got her Father consent for her to go to Europe & she Lizzie knew it still when she came back. she seemed more ungratful then ever - I have herd her Mrs. B. say to Mr. B., I do believe that girl would kill me if she got a chance & Mr. B. would try to console her by saying, she dont mean half she says - but when he would get Lizzie alone he would say, if you keep on in this way I will send you away from this house penniless - let me just say right here that girl would not have killed her Father, but she knew full well had he found her dead body up in that spare chamber he would accused that girl at once & I think would have slain her on the spot Oh why should I be sick now at this time, wild horses would not keep me from that court room & when she see me on the stand I think I could cause her to faint, for she would well know that their was blood in my eye - I remember one time after I had a confidenteal talk with Mrs. Borden & she seemed so heart broken to think Lizzie treated her so, I went home & wrote her Lizzie a letter, & told her what Mrs. B. had asked me to say, that if she would go away how much Mrs. B. would contribute towards her letter of credit to travel. I told her I hoped she would consider the matter well, & decide to go - as Mrs. B. was in a very nervous condition fearing she ment to harm her she seemed to be in continuel fear of her life, the answer to that letter came June last. I will not describe the contents of that letter, but had it not been destroyed by my husband since the murder & I could have sent it to you it would have convicted her of killing her mother without other evidence. What I wish to write this for, hoping I may give you some points, this is what I have herd my husband say, & he is a Borden knowing well that Lizzie B. premeditated this murder months before she committed the deed. she had tried poison & failed as Dr. Bowen was on hand to releive them, then she was to go away when Emma did, but found Mr. Morse was coming & knew that Mrs. B. always put the spare room in order after anyone had been their, & then it was she decided to murder that poor women, their is great talk about her not having any blood on her cloaths, why should she. let me give you my version of it, how eassey for her to have changed her dress, after she killed Mrs. B. Briget out in the yard then she came down stairs concocted the story about the note, so Mr. B. & Briget would not be anxious about her. then her Father came in & she was anxious to get Briget out of the way, so to make quick work of him. the conversation I overherd between my husband & Emma B. was that the moment Briget was out of the way she put on this water proof cape that buttoned up from top to bottom, a sweeping cap over her head & long cotton gloves drawn over her hands, & with the same weapon she killed her mother she used with her father as soon as the deed was done she could very soon have taken them of & not a trace to be seen. then as soon as she called B she ran up in the attic with every- thing rolled up in the waterproof & lifted up this board in the floor & put the things that she had used intending to take care of them when all excitement was over but Miss Emma was the one that had to destroy all proofs my husband was the one that took the note to Emma asking her to destroy them in my estimation Miss Emma is implicated. I fear you will not be able to read this badly written letter, but I am very weak & have had to lie back in my Bed severel times, but I have become so nervous the past week as the trial is progressing as all the witnesses contradict themselves, & as for Briget Sullivan I feel sure she has been tampered with for she tells intirely different story from what she did at first & she knows it is false for her to say they were a happy household, & she knows very well that Lizzie Borden did the crime for no other person could have done it, I shall look forward anxiously the coming week, & hope & pray that justice will be done, if I could only tell you some of the brutal things she has done in the past two years, I have kept quiet all these months hoping I might consult with you before the time of trial come up but since being confined to my room, in a delicate situation, I felt that I must write you as I am so afraid she is going to get clear, if my husband knew of this letter it would cause a seperation, & although he is the father of my children if she gets clear of imprisenment for life, I will never see him again, but I am able to take care of myself as I have money in my own right. I only hope you with Mr. Moodys help can convict her & if you do, I will send you a check of one thousand dollars. I do not care to see her hang, only put where she can never enjoy that money that she commited that teribel crime for, I have great hopes of your ability, & if you have the chance to cross question her be sharp & do not leave a stone unturned to impress the jury of her guilt for she is as guilty as ever a woman could be of all that is brutal & cruel. A Friend.

HK215
Letter, handwritten in ink.

Greenville
June 11th 1893

District Attorney Knowlton-
      Sir-
I have been reading the Borden murder trial attentively in the Rhode Island newspapers, and it seems to me you are very anxious to convict the daughter

of the <u>first wife</u> of the late Andrew Jackson Borden of an awful, revolting crime. What is your motive in wishing to condemn an American girl to either States/prison or to an ignominious death? Fall River Mass bears a very bad reputation as to morals outside the State of Mass. You probably remember the murder that occurred there more than sixty years since of a factory girl, the Rev. Dr. Avery being the accused murderer, he went to Ohio afterwards. (Burr & Bleumenhassell,- Ohio River).

You remember the morals of Aaron Burr? And perhaps you remember the Robinson & Jewett case, and the acquittal of Robinson by Ogden Hoffman on the ground of his youth (a boy) & the woman Ellen Jewett a New York prostitute. You probably remember the Nathan murder, (the son died recently in Boulogne, France?) The Walter - Malley murder, the acquittal of Malley as they could not convict in Rhode Island on circumstantial evidence. Gordon (the Irish murderer of Sprague) was the last execution in Rhode Island.

In genealogy I have seen some where the name of Rev. Thomas Knowlton in connection with Winsor (My surname)

My father the late Nicholas Steere Winsor was the son of Duty Winsor and his <u>first wife</u> Abigail Steere the daughter of Jonah Steere and Lydia Whipple of Glocester, R.I. Jonah Steere married was son of Job Steere and Lydia Harding. My father was born October 10th 1797 in Smithfield R I. (on the homestead farm.) Duty Winsor & his <u>first wife</u> had three sons. Duty died in 1837 in March his first wife in 1804. Their three Sons were named William (who was born in 1786), Asa, and Nicholas. William died unmarried aged 28, Asa died in 1870 aged 82 & my father in 1885 aged 87. I have a genealogy of Laban Waterman Winsor published in 1847 for Olney Winsor cashier of the Providence Bank whose <u>first wife</u> was Freelove Waterman. A genealogical dictionary by John Osborne Austin antiquarian of R. I. & a volume of Steere genealogy written by Rev. James Pierce Root for the late Henry Jonah Steere of Providence, R. I.

I do not see why you should be anxious to convict the daughter of the <u>first wife</u> of Mr Borden of an awful crime. We have had a revolting murder in R. I. (The Barnaby Graves Murder) Graves being a soldier in the army & a physician will probably escape conviction, but he deserves hanging quite as much as Miss Borden. I do not see what your motive is in fastening this shocking murder on the daughter of the <u>first wife</u> of Andrew Borden. Its treason and Bar fraud of men who have two and three wives. In Mass. there are several men who have two wives & Ariel Thurston of Mass. had three wives. The first a Hart, the second a Hull, the third a Converse. Then the mother of Ariel

Thurston had two husbands (Thurston & Ireland.). Addison Weld of Sturbridge Mass. two wives, <u>first wife</u> Harriet Foster, (own sister to my mother). Their daughter Rosalie second wife of Edwin Clapp. Albert Lane, Rockport, Mass. Second wife Eliza Winsor, daughter of Edward Winsor (the son of Duty Winsor & ~~Abig~~ Alsa Mitchell, (the second wife of Duty.) I am the granddaughter of Duty Winsor & his <u>first wife</u> Abigail Steere. My father married my mother Elizabeth Sayles Foster (second daughter of William Foster & Elizabeth Smith) November 13th 1837, Rev. Reuben Allen the officiating clergy- man. My parents had four children two daughters & two sons. My sister died in 1848, my brothers in infancy.

I am the sole survivor of Nicholas Winsor and wife, my mother died in 1842, my father in 1885. Now I do not see why Bristol County Mass. should wish to fasten this awful double murder on the daughter of Andrew Borden & his <u>first wife</u> (Morse).

I should sooner attribute it to Siscilly and the Italian Mafia & the Pope of Rome (an Italian Catholic). There are three foreign legion saloons that do that.
Sheehan at Addison N. Y. Tchau in Elmira N. Y. [?] German beer saloon Elmira. Man at Rheims France (Champagne & cider.) Mr. [?] liquor saloon Mass. & Elmira. There its bad men (Jacob Sly and Sarah Parks) William Parks drank liquor, the daughter was disreputable as to character. Mr Pierce of Fall River had a daughter (Cora) who went astray in Elmira, and there are a dozen fallen Women who cause contention. Samuel Thompson Irish sculptor of Burnside monument in Blackwell's Island penal institution, & Levi Wetmore in the Inebriate Asylum in Boston, he married Catharine Turner, an Irish girl, & adopted daughter of Wm. Maxwell an Elmira lawyer. Intemperate men (their name is legion) Patrick Bronte of Yorkshire, England spent every evening carousing in the village tavern, brother of the authoress & son of a minister. Edgar Poe Baltimore & his terrible sprees. I think bad men & women do this as a member of a temperance pledge I can tell who they are.

Now I hope you will weigh well your evidence in Court, & not sentence (the Judge will pronounce the final sentence) the daughter of- <u>first wife</u> that of Mr. Borden for something the second wife might have done Jefferson Davis & his second wife, Capt. Mongomery (Confederate) & his second wife (the South) and Lydia Logan second wife of John Smith Hoffman (Ireland) There is something due America, (namely honor.)
Josephine E. Winsor
P. S.   White of Belfast Maine had two wives, so did the Rev. Thomas Beecher. And so did Andrew Waterman & [?] Steere & Mrs. James Winsor, (sister to Howard King.) Gen. [?] & Solomon Gillet & Deacon Grant. (an English-

man). Irish fraud (Logan) German fraud (Bayard Taylor) & Scotch fraud Murdoch & Pratt.

J. E. W.

    American Nationality
    The Nation
    The Flag of Our Union.
    Fair Play.

HK216

Letter, handwritten in ink, accompanied by newspaper clipping.

Boston. June 11/93

District Attorney Knowlton
    Dear Sir:

    I hope you will pardon me for troubling you even so much as to ask you kindly to read this letter. But I am so anxious for <u>your success</u>, that I am constrained to write and ask you to be sure and not lose sight for a moment of the <u>burnt dress</u>, for <u>that</u> one mentioned was evidently the <u>great</u> and damning evidence of the terrible crime. Did you ever in the cross examination ascertain <u>when</u> and <u>where</u> the Paint was used which made the spots as alleged. It was strange wasnt it also that so many stories were told about the visit to the <u>Barn</u>. There have never been any two statements alike. Gov. Robinson seems to have "<u>Cheek</u>" enough to try every time and <u>set you back as of no account</u>. It is not the custom to give <u>each side "fair play</u>." It seems to one who <u>reads</u> that <u>you are not treated fairly</u>. I remember once going to see Heller the <u>Prestidigitator</u> who called attention to an <u>umbrella</u> in a far corner of the Hall. I said to a friend do you see <u>that</u>? The answer was dont you see that the trick <u>was</u>, to divert attention from the more important <u>one on the stage</u>? And so it was. Dont let anything take your attention from the <u>burned dress</u>. A woman who could thrive under <u>imprisonment</u> for so many <u>months</u>, is hardened enough to have committed <u>just such a crime</u>. And it is to be hoped she will be punished even if She is a <u>woman</u>. Gov. Robinson will get his "fat fee" as there is money enough in the <u>Borden Estate</u>. He can afford to work hard. This is only to <u>help you</u> - pardon me. I am for right also.

Always sincerely,
one who reads, but only a woman

I enclose a clipping which I think <u>quite just</u>.

Clipping:

> Remarkable discernment was displayed in the cross-examination of Miss Russell, and Fleet, the officer who searched the Borden house and found the hatchets. Here were two witnesses who were hostile from different motives. The well-established rule of criminal practice is not to provoke such witnesses. The wily lawyer followed the rule in one instance and disregarded it in the other. Miss Russell, the former intimate friend of the prisoner, has evidently formed a private judgment of the case from having her suspicions excited by the destruction of the dress. She had pondered the matter in silence and finally revealed it to the prosecution, doubtless from a high sense of public duty. The cross-examiner's method was to deal gently with her and to feign an indifference to her story which would tend to minimize its importance. This was good art, for if irritated she would have been likely to harm rather than help the case. With Fleet, the officer who had prejudged the case from professional motives, the method was reversed. The lawyer changed his manner and deliberately exasperated the witness, whose hostility to his client he was anxious to reveal to the jury. The Borden trial offers many opportunities for study of old school practice of the best kind. -- N.Y. Tribune

---

HK217
Letter, handwritten in ink.

Gt. Barrington June 12/93

District Attorney Knowlton
                  Sir:

It is surprising that apparently so little attention is paid to the circumstance of the "note" written by "a sick friend". to Mrs. Borden. Even the very able "staff" correspondent of Tribune in todays summary of the case as presented thus far passes it over as if it were trivial. If any such person exists she can certainly be found and will naturally be eager to support Miss Borden by corrobborating her statement. If that statement prove to be a <u>lie</u>, then it would seem that <u>at least</u> "guilty knowledge" is proven on Miss Borden's part. It does indeed seem incredible that she could have done the deed, but if guilty of a crime unparalleled in atrocity since the days of Lucretia Borgia, no "smart lawyer" should be <u>allowed</u> to come between her and justice. The country in spite of appearances, demands of the prosecution a strong presentation of the case, and of the jury a <u>just</u> verdict.

Respectfully
Mrs. Lucy C. Booth

HK218
Letter, handwritten in ink.

June 12th 1893.

Dist. Attorneys Knowlton & Moody
Dear Sirs:-

If the water in the well on the Borden premises, has never been drawn off and dilligent search made at the bottom, I think it would be well to do so at once. It has always run in my mind that it ought to be done, and as I have never heard of its being done, I write this suggestion.

I do not want any notoriety, therefore will sign

Yours for Justice

HK219
Postal card, handwritten in ink.

Balti.   June 12 . 93

Dear Sir,
Believing you have the <u>right</u> person on trial: but that your office is seriously handicapped by a set of police officers who (some of them at least) deserve knocking on the head for their stupidity, or maybe worse: Was Mallaly "seen" by the defense? at this distance, it appears so; or are the police jealous of Fleet? The whole case, the search etc. at the outset was very badly handled. That "doctor" should have been. taken by the neck when he "held the foot" and flung into a cell: he is pretty near an accessory after the fact. I think two keen officers on that job would have given you a better case.

Yours truly
Justice

HK220
Letter, handwritten in ink.

Presque Isle, Maine.
June 13, '93

To Dist. Atty. Knowlton,
    New Bedford, Mass.
      Sir,
        Pardon me for calling your attention to one point in the Borden case-

1 The Defence assume that Miss Borden is <u>entirely innocent</u> of the murder of her Father & Mother.

2 The <u>2</u> murders were committed probably between 9-1/2 & 11 o'clock- Aug 4,92.

3 <u>All</u> admit Miss Borden was <u>in the house every moment</u> that forenoon - except the <u>30</u> minutes She claims she <u>was in the Barn</u>.

4 But the Mother was killed while Miss Borden was <u>in the house</u> & was lying dead <u>one</u> hour or <u>more before she went to the Barn, by</u> Miss <u>Borden's own statement.</u>

Now the question comes, what is it that <u>conclusively</u> follows from all this, - if Miss Borden be innocent?

1 That these <u>2</u> Murders were either committed by <u>one</u> man, who remained in that house for <u>one hour</u> & <u>a half</u> while Miss Borden & Miss Sullivan <u>were both in</u> & <u>about</u> that house - and no one <u>saw</u> him, nor <u>heard</u> him - & no one <u>saw</u> him <u>come</u> or <u>go</u> of all the neighbors & inmates about - Miss Borden being inside up to the time her father was killed.

or

2 That the <u>2</u> murders were committed by <u>2 men</u> who came in & went out during <u>that hour & a half</u> & <u>no one saw them</u>, & no one <u>heard</u> them .

If <u>one</u> man committed the deeds he must <u>come & go</u>, making <u>2 times</u> he was <u>exposed</u> to view <u>outside</u>.

If 2 men did these murders - then there would be <u>4 times</u> they <u>were exposed to view outside</u>.

Can any man be made to believe that a <u>sane</u> man dare expose himself for an hour & a half in that house <u>in open day</u> & expect to escape detection?

Can any man believe that - still worse - that <u>2</u> men, dare try the <u>hazard</u> of 2 murders, in o<u>pen day light</u> there?

The dangers of detection were both from persons <u>inside</u> the house, & <u>outside</u> also.

No sane man committing murder would dare remain in that house 1-1/2 hours to committ a <u>second murder</u>.

No sane _men_ would _dare_ run the risk of 2 murders covering a space of 1- 1/2 hours in open day.
If the murders were committed by 1 man, it leaves him _in that house 1- 1/2 hours_. If by 2 men; they are _exposed_ to _4 travels in open day_ & to public gaze.

It is an absurd that _one_ man did these deeds & dared remain 1-1/2 hours in that house; & it is _equally absurd_ to suppose that 2 men did the deeds & were exposed to _4 trips in & out of_ that house. Murderers, like Burglars, _plan their modes of escape_ & if these murders were committed by either _one_ man, or by _two_ men; there is no _reasonable means_ of _escape shown_ - & no sane man would _dare_ take such chances. There is only _one_ person who had an _ample chance_ to do these deeds, _only one_ who had a_bundant time_ to carry out the plans & if she be not guilty - it is _idle_ to seek for any human being on whom to place the guilt..

Very Resply. Edmund Madigan

HK221
Letter, handwritten in ink.

Freeland June 13th 1893

District Attorney Knowlton,
    Sir
Would it surprise you if you knew the murderer was a man in connection with a woman and have appeared in court several times. You remember Miss Borden had a presentment of coming evil. honestly you may believe her the party who now write had a presentment last August at the time of the murder & could not rest for several days. the man was masked, intent upon murder. so do not be to hasty in condemning the innocent. the guilty party will soon turn up and you will be astonished that you have befriended the murderer it is a long lane that has no turning. but have patience the turn is coming most unexpectedly as you will be made aware. for the enemies make a tumult and they that hate thee have lifted up the head, they have taken crafty counsel against thy hidden ones. come let us cut them off from being a nation. they have consulted together with one consent. they have been confederate against thee. make them like a wheel. Stubble before the wind. so persecute them with thy tempest and make them afraid with thy storm. fill their faces with shame. let them be confounded forever. that men may know who is Jehovah.

I removed his shoulder from the burden. I answered thee in the secret place. let thy hand be upon the man at thy right side. they walked in their own counsels. defend the poor and fatherless do justice to the afflicted and needy, and rid them out of the hand of the wicked.
Greentree

HK222
Note, handwritten in ink.

June 13th 1893.

Mr. Knowlton,
  Dear Sir
    It is incomprehensible to me why the person who sent the note to Mrs. Borden or the messenger who took it to the Borden mansion do not come forward and verify Miss L. Bordens statement.
B. T. R.

HK223
Postal card, handwritten in ink, postmarked "BALTIMORE, MD, JUNE 14, 1893, 7:30 PM."

Sir,
 Is it not true that the <u>formation</u> of a females <u>shoulder blades are different</u> than man's: somewhat longer, hence a womans inability to throw straight or in like manner as a man can? She always throws <u>overhanded</u> and <u>strikes</u> in the <u>same way</u>! A man delivers a blow <u>different</u> always. Medical experts must know this! Would not this fact account for any difference in the delivery of those blows on the skull? What <u>would seem</u> like a <u>left</u> hand blow, being merely the <u>awkward</u> way a woman has of striking and different from a man: I merely suggest this; would it not strengthen your case to show from the very nature & position & direction of those blows that only a ~~male~~ female could do it? in that way?
 You are trying the right one. I think.
Justice

HK224
Letter with enclosure handwritten in ink.

Concord, N.H.
June 14, 1893

Attorney Knowlton,
    Dear Sir -
    I send you the enclosed to use as you see fit - to publish with or without my name as the writer. The "tobacco spot" had no doubt been <u>made</u> after washing off the blood.
    The everybodies here and in N.Y. <u>believe</u> Lizzie Borden guilty.
        I am very truly yours
        Mary E. Walker, M.D.

Enclosure:

Editor of <u>People</u> & <u>Patriot</u>.
    Dear Sir-
    If you have no room for article <u>today</u>, please give to Bearer as it will <u>not keep</u>!
        I am very truly
        Yours etc.
June 14th 1893.   M. E. Walker, M.D.

HK225
Letter, handwritten in ink.

June 14, 1893.

H. M. Knowlton-
    Sir-
    Why do you not ascertain who the milkman was, who supplied the Bordens with milk for years. He said he knew for a fact that Miss Lizzie decapitated a kitten which belonged to her step-mother. If she would do that for spite, she might do worse.

HK226
Letter, typewritten.

WILTON, New Hampshire, June 14, 1893.
District Attorney KNOWLTON,
Dear Sir:

 I take the liberty of writing to you, having met you at the Court House through a letter of introduction from Mr. Henry M. Rogers, yesterday, June 13, something I have heard which may be of importance in the Borden Trial, if it can be traced to its source. I was told today by some- body that, while she was being manicured today at Madame Rosalie Butler's (over McDonald's confectionery shop) in Tremont street near Winter street, Boston, Mass., by a girl whose name she does not know, but who is known in the shop as "Titia," and has bright color and auburn hair, this girl told the following story.

 She said: a friend of hers told her that she (the friend) was told by a friend of Lizzie Borden's that, while visiting Lizzie Borden at her house one day, she was frightened by a cat's jumping upon her lap, she either being afraid of or not liking cats; she cried out, and Lizzie Borden took the cat in her arms and out of the room. She (Lizzie) was gone about fifteen (15) or twenty (20) minutes; when she returned to the room, Lizzie said to her friend: "That cat won't ever bother you again!" The friend asked: "Why not? What have you done, Lizzie?" And Lizzie answered: "I've chopped its head off!"

 Perhaps the hair found on a hatchet, which Professor Wood said looked like a cow's hair, may have come from this cat. Not wishing to meddle in the matter myself, I write the story to you, thinking that, if you thought it of enough importance, you might send a detective to be manicured by "Titia" and draw further particulars out of her. I beg and entreat you not to use my name in the matter in any way whatsoever, as I write unwillingly, but feeling it my duty to do so.

     I remain, dear Sir, very respectfully yours,
      [?] L. Apthorp

HK227
Letter, handwritten in ink.

WORLD'S CONGRESS AUXILIARY, 1893.
THE INTERNATIONAL
CONGRESSES of EDUCATION
of the
WORLD'S COLUMBIAN EXPOSITION
to be held at Chicago, July 25-28, 1893,
under charge of the
National Educational Association
of the
UNITED STATES of AMERICA.
DEPARTMENT of SECONDARY EDUCATION,
NEW BEDFORD, MASS.,

June 14, 1893.

My dear Mr. Knowlton,

I don't know whether the interdict as to conversation between us on Mr. Paine's case extends so far as to such a letter as this, or not. But I am not going to resist my impulses any longer on that account. If I ought not to write this, by some legal fiction consider it unwritten, or in Mr. Blaine's phrase, "burn it".

We all, Mr. & Mrs. Paine, my wife and I, and the others of his family, are exceedingly grateful for your action, - not only your kind view of the situation itself, but your promptness in entering the nol pros on the very first opportunity which the law and custom afforded. I was staggered by the condition which you imposed, I confess, when I learned of it last autumn; and could not see why it was required. But it now seems to me to have been a wise step, not only on your account, but on Mr. Paine's also. It put him in a more favorable attitude before the public, and was the means of demonstrating clearly that no opposition existed to his being set free.

It may not be worth noticing, but you made a slight error respecting his age. He was born Aug. 7, 1827 and so will be 66 the coming summer.

Let me enclose in this a letter received a few days ago from Mr. Paine, in which he sends a message to you. The spirit of the letter is exactly that which

I have always recognized in him since our first acquaintance. Return it at your leisure.

Yours cordially,
Ray Greene Huling

(Note: The content of this letter indicates that it is not relevant to the Borden case. It is included here to maintain the integrity of the collection, which it is a part. It is interesting to note that, in addition to the responsibilities of Miss Borden's case, Attorney Knowlton still maintained an active private practice.)

HK228
Letter, handwritten in ink.

David D. Toal, M.D.
Office:
151 Avenue B, Bet. 9th & 10th Streets,
opp. Tompkins Square

New York, June 14th 1893

Dear Sir-

I respectfully call your attention to my experience with axe wounds within past 26 years. In 10 cases that I can recall to memory 3 were done by an axe in the hands of infuriated women - 7 by men. In no one case was the Brain substance cut into by the women and in all cases where men yielded the axe the bone was cut through and recovery slow. In one other case an ex-policeman who lives at present within 200 yards of my was struck with a cleaver in the hands of an infuriated man his parietal bone was cut through but he is alive and well today That occured about 17 years ago. I have removed a few pieces of bone since. I have a strong impression that some <u>Insane</u> man <u>at large</u> is the <u>murderer</u> of those people and ere long you will hear of another similar case in your common- wealth. I dont know any person interested in the case yet wishing you success in freeing your unfortunate client
I am yours Resp.

David D Toal MD

(? Why not make some experiments on some cadaver's and in my opinion you will find I am right.)

HK229

Letter, handwritten in ink.

                              Washington, D.C. June 15th, 1893.

To
Messrs Knowlton and Moody,
For the State, in the Borden trial:-
Can it be possible that you are not going to put Emma Borden on the Stand? She <u>knows</u> whether her sister committed that murder or not.

                                From a woman who wonders if there
                                is such a thing as Justice.

HK230

Letter, handwritten in ink.

                          LAW OFFICES OF
                            J. H. FOGG,
                       85 EXCHANGE STREET,
                 OVER PORTLAND SAVINGS BANK.

                                      Portland, Me., June 15 1893

District Atty. Knowlton
New Bedford, Mass.
      Dear Sir

You will pardon me for the suggestion. I have followed the progress of the Borden trial with much interest, and noted especially the skillful manner in which the evidence has been drawn out. There is an apparent disagreement among the medical witnesses as to whether the wounds inflicted on Bordens head were made by blows directed from right to left or left to right, or vertical. If the person giving the blows was what is usually termed right handed and held the ax or hatchet by the handle in both hands the natural direction of the blow would be from left to right, the same as a left handed person would strike if wielding the hatchet with his or her left hand. Would not a <u>woman most naturally</u> in giving those blows to Bordens head grasp the handle of the hatchet in both hands?

In that case you might expect some such variety of blows as the experts have described. Viz: Left to right, right to left and vertical

My theory is that she held the handle of the hatchet ~~and~~ in both hands and thus made her mince-meat.

Yours truly
J. H. Fogg

HK231
Letter, handwritten in ink.

June 15,93

Hon. District Attorney Knowlton,

May I as a citizen of Providence R.I. ask why has not the question arisen. Where was Lizzie Borden the two hours previous to her fathers death? Was not Miss Lizzie and Miss Bridget Sullivan in the house all that morning previous to the murder of Mr. Andrew Borden. Her time in the barn is well canvassed but hours previous where was she when Mrs. Borden was murdered? Where was Miss B. Sullivan was she not around inside the house or outside before the mul'der of Mr. B?

HK232
Letter, handwritten in lead.

108 Hamilton St New Haven, Ct
June 15th/93 -
Mr. Knowlten
      Prosecuting Att.

Points ag't L. Borden -
1st Had not been to church for 3 years or more. Testimony ab't teaching in S. School & member of S. Endeavor S dont am't to anything - She had given herself over to the world, flesh, & devil - in that she had given up the church. What an example to the present young ladies of the day - They will become father & mother murderers under the influence of such an example.

2d Point - She related that she told her Father that her Mother had gone out when she unlocked the front door & let him in - testified to that she induced him to lie down - as his wife had gone out. She knew the life of her stepmother "had gone out", but she lied when she said her mother had rec'd a note that morning: - To cover up her deceit & crime she wore a smile to betray her old & tired Father. So Judas betrayed Christ with a kiss - The Dr's testified that from 1 to 1-1/2 hours elapsed between the killing of Mother & Father, if this is so, she was only gone 20 to 30 minutes to barn. ~~Coul~~ Would she not have discovered some trace of her murdered Mother in 1-1/2 hours -she was only absent 20 minutes in the barn. Granted she did go to the barn - could she not have killed her Father & then gone to the barn too, perhaps to disrobe & take off her bloody clothes. A bundle was sent away fr. the home next day after the murder She could have run out to the barn as an alibi - in case the murder was traced to her. Simplist thing in the world. Her motive was apparent enough - She had $2000 in bank subject to, check but bearing int not over 6% int = $120. & 3 small sums of 400, 200 & 141 - subject to check $741 in all - int at 6% = $44.46 total int

$120.
-44.46 int per month only
$164.46

$ 13.70 per month. This is small for a young lady who does not attend church but aspires to European travel & a life of luxury - far above her present ability. It denotes a craving for extravagant living which she could not gratify but which she desired after once getting a taste - The burning of the dress does not am't to so much - as if it had blood on it she would have burned it privately - Probably the dress she did bury or destroy was another. A neighbor testified to seeing some one upstairs with a hood on ab't the time in the morning that the mother was killed - A waterproof with its hood would have protected her dress fr. harm, but one blot of blood was found on her "the damning spot would not out" one blot - how came it there - of human blood - in spite of her great care to efface all trace of the crime, one blot remained to damn her & she could not explain it - Her own story of the affair must be admitted to review, else she can not be allowed to prove an alibi. Her testimony was not against herself - only the facts prove afterward by the Drs that she told a lie in saying her Mother had gone out - where is the woman her Mother visited? If there was any such one would she not come forward to save a persons life - on this lie the whole case stands for conviction. She told her Father a lie that her Mother had gone out in order to induce him to lie down so she could kill him. If a man had done it he would not need to have him lie down - Either she did the deed or had a man do it for her which is just as bad -

W L Folsom
108 Hamilton St

HK233
Letter, handwritten in ink.

Boston June 16, -93

Mr. Knowlton-
    Honored Sir:
        I have watched the Borden trial closely from first until now and have wondered that two incidents have not been brought into it <u>emphatically</u>.

First,- How could Mrs Borden fall in that room, - a woman of her weight, with Lizzie on the same floor or anywhere in the house, and Bridget at work on the windows and neither hear her. Windows are quick to report a fall of anything in a house. To my mind it would be impossible.

Second,- Why did Lizzie burn that dress at that particular time after having kept it since May when the painting was done. In the midst of that terrible horror what made her think of paint spots that if thought of at all previously were considered harmless, - of no consequence

I have looked eagerly for the effect in Court of these two facts. If they have been noticed excuse me and if not pardon this liberty I take in addressing you.

My only wish in that Case as in everything in life is <u>Justice</u> and I believe there can be no <u>real Mercy</u> that is not based on Justice

I wish she could prove herself innocent and why did she not do it long ago.

Very Respectfully
Mrs M. A. Robbins.

P.O. Station A.

HK234
Letter, handwritten in ink.

Honesdale Wayne Co Pa June 16/93

Dear Sir

I may be doing an unheard of thing in writing you; but hope you will pardon me! I have been deeply interested in reading the Lizzie Borden trial: I believe she is guilty: but do not believe she alone is guilty: The whole Court seem to have their attention directed to <u>her</u>, & to think of no one else! Now I shold like to know what kind of man her Uncle Morse is? He having testified that he had not seen Lizzie! What so unlikely when neither Mr. or Mrs. B. were at all related to him! How about his financial matters? & who besides himself knows his where-abouts at the time of the Crimes. He might have remained up stairs all the time, & when Mrs. B. came into the room have killed her, & remained hidden until a good opportunity offered for the butchery of her husband!

Then his testimony about the Lock on the Front Door. How should he notice what the family had not? & he a transient visitor. Perhaps Lizzie had offered to share her all with him if he would do the job.

Then I have thought of her Dr. who was so offiscious giving her morphine & O. Perhaps he had his carriage a short distance outside & pretended to be driving home & was himself the guilty party! Now these are just my thoughts!

I do hope Justice will be done whoever is guilty! Please do not give this to the reporters, but give it your thoughts.

Mrs Henry Wilson

HK235
Letter, handwritten in ink.

June 16th '93
Evening

Hosea M. Knowlton, Dist. Atty.
    New Bedford, Mass.

No doubt you have received many letters from unknown persons, men and women both, <u>since</u>, and <u>about</u> the "Borden Murder", letters that have been of no consequence to you, some of them, probably this one will be the same, be that as it will, I wish to write it. I want to ask you a question. In Bridgets testimony at the <u>first</u> hearing and this present one also, she said, "Mr. Borden had put on his house coat", which could not have been long after he came home, that day. Lizzie also told you her father had taken off his coat, which of course he did. Now what do you think he <u>done</u> with that coat when he <u>took</u> it <u>off</u>. his "frock coat", the one Dr. Dolan testified to as being under his head after he was dead. Don't you think it likely he would have hung it up somewhere in the place or near it, from where he took his "house coat'? I think <u>that coat</u> was what Lizzie Borden covered herself with. I have always thought it could not have been that she contemplated killing <u>her father</u> at the <u>time</u> and <u>place</u> she <u>did</u>. she could not have <u>foreseen</u> what the situation <u>was to be</u> in regard to those three persons just at <u>that time</u>, Bridget, Morse and her father. The situation of Mrs. Borden happened to be just what it was and it gave her the opportunity to kill her, and that she probably did soon after her going upstairs. Lizzie made up that story about that "note", and "going out" sometime beforehand, and when her father came home, she told it to him to prevent his looking about for his wife, which he probably would have done - if she had not told him that - she did not want <u>him</u> to find her then - She must have had some awful feelings <u>before</u> Bridget went up stairs, when she did go up, <u>then</u> it was, I think Lizzie thought she could kill her father - Just the same way she had her mother - there <u>she</u> was, dead upstairs - her father would have to know it before long, and what must come <u>to her after that</u> - she must have realized, the situation must have looked <u>less</u> terrible for her with <u>him dead</u>, then to have him alive. Mr. Borden was killed quickly, no doubt about that and almost as soon as Bridget disappeared upstairs, Lizzie had not the time to prepare for <u>him</u>. that she had did for her step mother, and had to think of what <u>to do</u>. right then and there. <u>I believe</u> she went and got her <u>fathers coat</u>, and put. it on - nothing could have <u>protected</u> her <u>better</u> - a frock coat would come down rather long, and completely shield her person from head down - covered her hands well - it could be lapped over in front well, whether buttoned or not - <u>any woman</u> can tell how it was, that has ever put on a <u>mans</u> coat - No doubt she took off her shoes, to make no noise in step- ping - as he <u>might not</u> have been <u>long</u> asleep, if he was at all, perhaps that paper that was in the stove was about her head - any small thing could have covered her hair, as not much blood would go there, only a few spatters - In the length of time that elapsed after Bridget went up stairs, until she was called again by Lizzie a good many things could have been done if done <u>quickly</u> - as they probably were. Lizzie Borden <u>could</u> have gone and got that cutting instrument, slipped off her shoes put on that coat, cover her hair, <u>then</u> all was ready for the <u>killing</u> - only a moment or two for that, after that first stuning blow, there was probably no blood on the floor at the <u>head</u> of the lounge, <u>behind it</u>. Such was the testimony - she could have <u>stepped there</u>, and not got any on her feet, as quick as that <u>cutting</u> was done she slipped off that coat folded it up, and put it <u>under</u> the <u>quishion</u>, by putting her hands under the quishion - she would not get much blood on them. I have no doubt but what she slipped off her <u>dress waist</u> before putting on the coat - so if there was any blood on her in front - by putting that coat under him it would be on her under waist - she could cover that up - and no one ever saw what she had on <u>under her dress waist</u>. When Miss Russell went to loosen it, thinking she was <u>faint</u> - Lizzie didn't let her - said she was not faint, there was no <u>struggle</u> - consequently <u>nothing</u> to <u>disarrange</u> her hair - or anything else. Lizzie could have gone to the barn and back where the water was - but not for the purpose <u>she said</u> she went - she could have taken even that hatchet done up, to the barn - and called to Bridget just as quick as she came back to the door. After that coat was off her - she was all right, only to wash her hands - now if anyone thinks <u>all</u> of <u>that could not</u> have been done in <u>ten minutes</u> or <u>little more</u> they can go through the <u>imitation</u> - and they will find out it can be easily - if done <u>quickly</u>, even going as far as that barn was and back, Lizzie could have gone to the barn <u>after</u> the murder! We have only <u>her story</u> what she went there for - or how long she was there - That is the way I think it <u>was done</u> - in regard to <u>Mr. Bordens</u> murder, as to <u>Mrs. Bordens</u> murder - no one <u>knows</u> whether Lizzie had on <u>any clothes</u> or not - or perhaps only her under things it was a hot day - she could have taken anything off, <u>and who was to know it</u>? It was of <u>vital importance</u> to her - not to have any <u>blood</u> found about <u>anywhere</u> that would indicate she was "in it" - she looked out <u>for that</u> - first and last. When she changed her dress that afternoon, no one saw her do it, or knew what was under it, Miss Russell saw her coming out of Emmas room with the "pink wrapper" on that was all. If there was <u>deception</u> in that dress, that was given to the <u>officers</u> as being the one she wore that morning there <u>might have been deception</u> in other things.

No mortal eye saw Lizzie Borden commit those murders, she <u>denies it</u>-and thinks she cannot be convicted - perhaps she never will be - Lizzie Borden never went to that barn, or into it for the purpose <u>she said</u>, or for the length of <u>time</u> she said, but it is <u>possible is it not</u> that she <u>may have</u> walked in the yard - after the murder - to prepare herself a little what to say or do - and then went right into the entry and called for Bridget - there was time for <u>that</u>. Taking <u>that coat</u> - for there was nothing to get rid of in clothes. I <u>believe</u> she did put on that coat - If Bridget had only been asked if he hung up that coat - always - it does not seem that he would fold up his coat <u>himself</u> - and put it there to get wrinkled all up, and he to wear it perhaps in the afternoon. <u>Where is</u>

that coat now? if it had been examined at the time it could have been shown where, the blood was, on it - Now if it had been true about that note, Mrs. Borden would have got ready and gone out - if she hadn't been killed just when she was - telling about that "note" was a bad piece of business for the defence, how they are going to get over it I do not see.

I am a woman - I believe Lizzie Borden to be the guilty one - The God of Justice be with you Mr. Knowlton - no matter who I am - only a woman. Lizzie Borden wanted her fathers money - she can have it now.

I send you the inclosed - if you read the Journal, you may have seen it at the time of the date of it, if you did not you read it now, it cannot help you any at the present time maybe, but it is worth reading as coming from Lizzie herself - the conscientious (though gullible) Mrs. Livermore must have reported it correctly, so we will believe it. If Lizzie Borden said all that - in view of all the facts of the case, it shows she is deceitful, cunning and will lie. She rather over did herself - when she included Bridget in her list of "might have beens", Bridget could not have very well "come in on her for water" in either case - for Mrs. Borden was up stairs in the one case - and Bridget in the other. It has looked as though Lizzie was planning to do that deed in her sisters absence and maybe she had been thinking of the very one - she told Mrs. Livermore she could have done in the night - Morse coming as he did would prevent that - as long as he stayed. One feels a kind of horror in reading what she said, she says she could have done all that in the night, removed all traces of the blood from herself - and gone quietly to bed". well she done about the same thing as it was - only it was in her broad day light" - instead of the night - and now she wonders how people can believe it." She was a cunning person - she looked out for the blood - and as none was found on her - to implicate her she thinks she can boldly deny it, and escape - She hated her step mother with a mortal hatred no doubt - and she and her sister Emma lived a life by themselves in that house, that was not known much, to the outside world of Fall River. One can imagine all the causes that were operating, a great many years to bring Lizzie Borden to be what she was. the prospect of the future, if those two people lived to be very old, all that property tied up - that might have brought the girls so much- one can see it all. I heard one man on the street, at the time of the murder, express it in this way- "Well, it was the result of the old man's methods and he got made "mutton" on for it no business to live so mean" - Perhaps that sums it all up - as well as it can be - in more words - There is no "mystery" or "puzzle" about all this to anyone - that probes the thing to the bottom - the "muddle" only comes in trying to make it out that someone else done it - that can never be done - but how anyone else can believe that it was done by another person - is beyond my comprehension.

Mary Ashton (Rice) Livermore, circa 1880.

If Lizzie Borden told Mrs. Livermore <u>about fixing that pillow</u> for her father, I wonder if she said anything about that coat, <u>folding that up</u> - for him, <u>Lizzie told you</u> she did not do anything of that kind and she probably did not, before he went on to the lounge - Mrs. Livermore, <u>believes her</u>, because she simply <u>asserts</u> her <u>innocence</u> - It is such "<u>stuff</u>" as you read here that she has been loading Mrs. Livermore up with, and others too - in her 'Jail" - but <u>all</u> do not swallow it, I am sure. Read the piece and judge it.

Concord, N.H. for Justice -

HK236
Letter, handwritten in ink.

Referring to item marked on Mrs. Livermore's article, the writer heard the story soon after the murder, that Lizzie, while abroad, ran short of funds and telegraphed to her Father who refused to send her more and that her friend's money brought her home - If such is the case Mrs. Livermore's conclusions are at fault -

One who desires justice -

HK237
Letter, handwritten in ink.

Lancaster, Pa.
June 16th/93

District Attorney Knowlton
Honored & Dear Sir,

Do you with all your talent intend to let that <u>Double Murderer</u> Lizzie Borden slip the Law all the world knows Lizzie Borden murdered in cold blood those two good Old People. She got tired of waiting for their money.

Lizzie Borden is a cold heartless wretch She is a <u>double murderer</u>. Cain killed his Brother & God put a mark upon Cains brow. Cain only killed one person. Lizzie Borden killed <u>two</u> persons. The poor old <u>father</u> when he was asleep. <u>She is</u> a tretcherous wretch. She first killed the step mother she hated, and for fear of her Fathers questions, she hacked the poor old man to pieces.

    Oh the tretcherous wretch. Is she to go free Liz Borden gloats over her murders, her <u>heart</u> is <u>Black</u>. Oh the bosh of her Lawyers, Robinson Jenning & Co. The bunch of flowers they make her carry into court - rediculous and her smile Robinson talks about. I say the Borden woman is a Double Murderer. Will you smile at crime & let her slip. God marked Cain he has marked Lizzie Borden - the cruel wicked woman. No one hated them but her.

HK238
Letter, handwritten in ink.

                                          Fall River June 7th, 1893

Hon. Hosea M. Knowlton
    District Attorney
        Newbedford, Mass.
           Dear Sir

                In your cross examination of Miss Emma Borden yesterday it Developed that the fact that She, Mrs Borden, & Miss Lizzie Borden Each had a waterproof & that Miss Emma Borden took Her Waterproof with Her on Her visit to Newbedford & had it there with Her on the day of the ~~mother~~ Murder of her Father and Mother in this City. But you did not ask Her or anny of the other Witnesses for the Prosecution or the Deffence Whether or not in there Search on the Premises the numerous times they searched them, & in the Dress Closet among the Dresses there Whether or not they found Mrs Bordens Waterproof (Lizzies Stepmother) & Miss Lizzies Waterproof also. I showed Judge Reading the, testimony that of the Different Witnesses that they had not been found and that if Lizzie Committed the two murders which I think She did She must Have Placed these two Waterproofs over Her Outside garments Dresses etc. to Keep the Blood off of Her Clothes & She had one on When She Killed her Father and the other on when She Killed her Mother & then Burned them up with the Blood Stains on them after She had Committed the Murders & which accounts for so Little Blood being found on Her Clothes after the Murders. Now wouldent those two Waterproofs that are missing; being a great point for you to Bring forward in your address to the jury next Monday when you are addressing that. That is a Strong Proof of Lizzie Bordens Guilt and If I were you I would allude to it in your address to them. I also sent you this afternoon Fall River Globe last

nights Issue with a Blue mark against Charles Sawyers evidence & which you ought to allude to In your address to the jury during next Monday.
                    Yours Truly
                    Nathaniel R Lewis

K239
Letter, handwritten in ink.

                    Gt. Barrington Sun. June 17/93
Dist. Attorney Knowlton:
            Sir:
            If Miss Borden is guilty it seems to me she would most naturally have fled to the barn after the murder there to finish concealment of evidence, change dress or wrap etc. I should could I have done so horrible a deed - Allowing 20 minutes she had time perhaps to - She might have had an access of murderous frenzy after beginning as animals are crazed when they begin scent the blood of their victims. Pardon my intrusions.
                    Respectfully
                    Lucy C. Booth.

K240
Letter, handwritten in ink.

                    Milton June 17, 1893
Dear Sir,
    I am moved to write to you concerning the trial now going on and hope I do not intrude in doing so.
I have been disgusted and outraged by the course of journalists and reporters. They have made a studied effort to substitute trial by newspapers for trial by jury - and to create venal obstructions to the orderly administration of justice. I have two or three suggestions to make to you.
I Argue your case as if you profoundly believed it. Have no words which imply that you fear a verdict of acquittal or a division in the jury, or that you consider your case weak at any point. I once carried a case in this way, a manslaughter case, when the Atty General Allen, the presiding judge (Marcus Morton) and all bystanders (as I was told) did not believe I could get a verdict

before I made my argument. My plea was said to be forcible, but evident <u>sincerity</u> and profound <u>earnestness</u> did more.

II <u>Hammer again and again</u> what seems to me as an outsider the most telling part of the case, that while other persons coming up that staircase saw Mrs. Borden's body when their eyes were on a level with the second story, Lizzie too must have seen it. She was up there and all about for an hour or more while it was lying there. What others saw she must have seen, and by not reporting it she shared guilty knowledge. I think you need to recur to this point a dozen times. I am told that some one, the city marshal, I think, says that the body could not be seen except at a peculiar angle and for a moment. I do not know how much force is given to this, but I suppose in going up stairs she must have been at the same angle as the others. Of course she did go up, being up there when her father arrived home.

III Lizzie story about being in the barn for 20 minutes might if believed show an <u>alibi</u> in case of one death, but how can it show absence from <u>two</u> homicides which are <u>an hour or more</u> apart!

~~III~~ IV It is a point to be made that it was the morning when persons engaged in housekeeping are all about the house, not the afternoon when women sit down to sewing or like work. It is reasonable to suppose that two women engaged as Mrs. Borden and Lizzie were should have seen each other several times in the course of an hour.

All I have written has doubtless occurred to you, but what I have said under heads I and II seem so important to me that I felt desirous of calling your attention to them.

Your hardest work probably is to overcome the idea that a well brought up young woman, moving in a good circle, member of the church, not suspected before of capacity for such an awful crime, could not possibly have killed father and stepmother. These you will have to deal largely and philosophically. We are all nearer crime than we think [?] or the prayer would never have been made "Keep back thy servant from presumptuous sins."

If we let the passion of hate stay in our minds it corrodes and poisons the whole moral nature, and in the end we may be able to do anything. Five years ago daughter Lizzie Borden had no more idea of doing such a thing than you or I. But she nourished the hate which some day entered her soul. I have felt all along that while <u>money</u> may have been a part of her inspiration, <u>hate</u> was the main impulse.

The papers say that she had no <u>motive</u> to kill her <u>father</u>. But having killed her mother and being suspected by him, he would have disinherited her, & it became necessary for her to commit the second crime.

I sat one day in court within the bar, but you did not know me. You as well as I have changed in seventeen years.

       Yours truly
       Edward L Pierce

HK241
Letter, handwritten in ink.

      Boston, June 18 1893

Honored Sir
  It seems strange to me that it has never occurred to anyone that perhaps Lizzie Borden was naked when she committed the murder. She could easily, and quickly wash herself.
  That is my idea for I think she is the one.

       Yours Respect
       Clara Brown, Boston

HK242
Note, handwritten in ink, accompanied by newspaper clipping.

      Boston, June 18th 1893.
This item was cut from the "Boston Herald" of yesterday.

Clipping:

ATTORNEYS ROBINSON AND KNOWLTON
(From the Providence Telegram.)

Speaking of Gov. Robinson and his conspicuous and creditable part in the Borden trial, the BOSTON HERALD remarks that he has perceptibly increased his reputation as a just man and one who has the strength of character to enforce his sense of what is right in a great and critical trial. We may admit this and also the other remark of the HERALD that:

he has had the force of conviction to speak out and insist that the rights of Lizzie Borden are respected and maintained, and . he has had the people with him by his independence and manly assertion of her priveleges which he has maintained in court. important as this trial is as a testing of the strength of the Massachusetts bar, it is still more important as an illustration of the character which a great lawyer ought to maintain.

But why single out the ex-Governor, who is making such a reputation for himself? Is he the only man who has a force of conviction? Has not Dist.-Atty. Knowlton, the calm, self-contained man who is not making himself famous, but is working as he has been for months to secure what he believes will be a triumph of justice, convictions just as strong as Gov. Robinson's? Is he not manly and independent, and does not he maintain the attitude a lawyer in an important case should maintain? The man who beat Ben Butler for Governor is making a harder fight than he did then, and more eyes are upon him than were then. But even those who believe his client is innocent ought not to exalt the purity of his motives at the expense of the reputation of the counsel for the state. Mr. Robinson himself would not do that, we know. And, while the rights of the prisoner must be protected, so must those of the people. Cold facts are what are wanted, no matter who is crushed.

HK243
Postal card, handwritten in ink.

Boston June 18 1893

Dear Sir if you had half wit you could not Be Guiltey of sutch foolish undertakings God elp the foolish ones if you cale yourself a smart one

---

HK244
Letter, handwritten in ink.

June 18, 1893

<u>Strictly Confidential.</u>
Friend Knowlton;

You do not know who it is that is now writing these lines to you and it may be just as well that you do not, for I am not going to "give myself away" until you have finished your work on the Borden trial, then I may reveal my incognito. Suffice it <u>now</u> to tell you that I knew you years ago, when your father was settled at South Boston, and was well acquainted with all of the coterie of boys and girls with whom you were intimate at that time. I have taken particular interest in the Borden trial, partly from your connection with it, and I have special reasons, obvious perhaps, to you, for not wanting my identity known just now, and you must receive what I write you on trust, as emenating from sincere motives in the interest of Justice. I am minded to give you a pointer on the "exclusive opportunity" theory in the Borden trial, and I thought to pen it to you, this day, so you might make use of it in your argument, if you thought it of any value. It is this:

It has been quite an enigma to me, given the "exclusive opportunity" theory to be true, How it were practicable, in so thorough a manner, for the accused to remove all bloody evidence from her person, <u>twice</u>; first, after the killing of Mrs. Borden and then after the killing of the father. It occurred to me last night, how it could be done, at least in the <u>first</u> killing, leaving only the bloody evidences to be <u>once</u> removed, and that in the last killing, and here is my theory. The accused had her room on the same floor, opening from the same entry way as did the room of Mrs. Borden. How easy it would have been, under the circumstances, for the accused to have gone into her own room <u>before</u> the first attack, divested herself of a part of her clothing, or perhaps all, or nearly all, and in that condition have attacked and killed the woman. Then afterward, donned her outer clothing and appeared and talked with the other inmates of the house. As I remember, the accused objected when offer was made, to having her dress loosened when appearing to faint, sometime, soon after the killing, though of this I am not quite certain. This is significant. I have now given you all I need to give you by way of suggestion, and I do it only on the presumption that you may not, in your multiplicity of work, have thought of it. It may enable you to remove a difficulty that it has enabled me to see through.

I know the wiles and scheming of those under the influence of mania (or the Devil) is very prolific and it would be a matter of curiosity to see the face of the accused, when this theory were touched upon in your argument, if you do so, as I do not believe it has ever been put on paper before this.

I do not understand why mention has not been made of a <u>motive</u> for murder, in the immediate heirship (jointly with her sister) to the father's entire wealth, thus preventing future disinheritance, in case of father's <u>later</u> decease, and his willing the greater part of the property to the stepmother.

Very sincerely yours,
Justice.

HK245
Letter, handwritten in ink.

Dist. Atty Knowlton:-

    I saw today a statement that you proposed to argue that Lizzie Borden was nude on the morning of the Borden murders. Did it never occur to you that if she had been dressed in <u>male attire</u> many strange things could be explained? For example, the "<u>pale young man</u>" whose strange actions attracted attention and the unsoiled condition of L. B.'s clothing. The male attire could have been worn until it was convenient to dispose of it in some way.

    If a new trial is necessary, it may be advisable to investigate this suggestion.

                                      Theorist.

6/19/93.

HK246
Letter, handwritten in ink.

UNION PUBLISHING COMPANY,

STANDARD PUBLICATIONS.

                                      Boston, June 19th - 1893.

Hon. H. M. Knowlton.
       Atty in Lizzie Borden Case
           New Bedford, Mass.

My old friend & pupil:

    I have watched this very remarkable Trial, of which you bear some so important a part, as Trial Justice for the Commonwealth of Mass.

    You have in my opinion a good show to display to the Public that as <u>Dist. Atty</u>, you mean to see <u>Justice done</u> so far as <u>your</u> province lies, in the maintainance of <u>order</u> and <u>Safety</u> in the "Old Commonwealth of Mass." to life and <u>liberty</u>! God bless you <u>friend Knowlton</u>! Whether you win or lose, in this case, none can lay to your charge, any unfaithfulness to see the rights of citizenship sustained, through the Laws which are so ordained.

It would afford me much pleasure as your "old School-Master", to listen to your Plea, to the jury in your argument presented But I shall read it in the Papers. Be Cool! Deliberate, distinct; convey to the gentlemen of the jury, by your looks, words, and acts, that you are not in sympathy with that style of Law, ('The Ex-Gov. Robinson Style.) I may call it, which as Shakespeare says, "would strive to make the false appear the better reason!"

But it will not become me friend Knowlton to speak farther on this subject. When you come next to Boston, if you will inform me when, I shall be happy to meet you for a brief time at Young's or whichever Hotel you are accustomed to stop. Hope your family are all well. Wishing you, my dear sir, success in all your lawful pursuits, and health, and happiness in all respects through life. I am

Sincerely your old friend & Teacher,
Joseph W. Cross Jr. T.M
Broadway House,
Chelsea, Mass.

To Hon. H. M. Knowlton
Atty. at Law
New Bedford, Mass.

HK247
Letter, handwritten in ink.

ATTORNEY GENERAL'S DEPARTMENT,
COMMONWEALTH BUILDING,
Boston,   Tuesday morning 1893

My dear Knowlton:

Robinson gave you a magnificent opportunity and you are making a magnificent use of it. There is but one voice about this. He never came up to the level of the case for a moment. You are surprising even those who know you best. From the first word of opening to the last of argument the conduct of the defense has been inferior to that of the prosecution at every point. I shall never apologize again to you or to Moody for putting this case upon you. It has given you both an opportunity to make a reputation which will outlive you both, and you have both done it.

Yours ever,
A. E. Pillsbury.

HK248
Letter, typewritten.

WM. B. FRENCH,
COUNSELLOR AT LAW,
89 STATE STREET.

Boston 20 June, 1893.

Dear Hosea;

    I have not yet had time to read the whole of your argument printed in the morning papers, but I hasten to congratulate you upon the masterly way in which you presented the Government's case. I have always believed the defendant guilty of the crime of which she is charged, and think you have proved it beyond a reasonable doubt. This argument should make you the next attorney general, and that is not my opinion only, but that of many others.

    I hope to see you when you are next in Boston.

                               Yours very truly,
Hon. H. M. Knowlton,   W. B. French
    New Bedford, Mass.

HK249
Letter, typewritten.

COUNSELLORS AT LAW,
Geo. L. Huntress.   **SEARS BUILDING,**
Homer Albers.   **199 WASHINGTON STREET**
BOSTON.

June 20, 1893

My dear Hosea,

           Good for you old man. I have only had chance to read a couple of columns of your argument in this morning's "Herald" but I read far enough to see that you have reduced Robinson's argument to just its proper dimensions and have risen fully to the great occasion. The con- founded newspapers have been maddening for the past ten days, and everything that Robinson has said, every time he has moved has been called a point in favor of the prisoner, or a coupd'etat or a masterly performance, but you got your inning yesterday and are having it again this morning and to me it is very refreshing.

I have only time for a few words but send them with the heartiest good will.

> Very truly yours,
> Geo L Huntress

Hosea M. Knowlton Esq

HK250
Letter, handwritten in ink.

OFFICE OF CLERK OF UNITED STATES DISTRICT COURT, DISTRICT OF MASSACHUSETTS

94 P. O. Building   Boston, 6/20 1893

My dear Knowlton

A reporter came to my office this morning, before I had read the part of your address to the Jury which has been printed, and answered my enquiry what people said of the Borden case, with the reply that every body was talking about Knowltons address - expressing admiration of his good taste, eloquence and skill. He added that many people who have thought the accused innocent, had changed their minds and now believe her to have been guilty, and reiterated the praise of you on every bodys tongues.

Since then I have read the published part of your address and I write to tell you that I think you deserve all the encomiums that the reported said had been spoken by the public. I think that your address will rank among the best that I have ever read or heard, made to a jury.

From the very first, when I learned that you had decided to prose- cute the woman I <u>knew</u> that there must be a strong case against her, and from that moment till now I have never changed my mind.

I am impelled to write you this and my own humble praise of the noble, honorable and high toned manner in which you have performed a duty which must have been an exceedingly painful one to you.

Respectfully and cordially your friend

> Frank S. Fiske

HK251
Letter, handwritten in ink.

OFFICE OF
JOHN DAVIS,
31 CENTRAL STREET,

Lowell, Mass., June 20, 1893.

Hon. H. M. Knowlton Dear Sir

I have just read your argument and although a stranger to you I can- not help writing a word to you in praise of, and in thankfulness for, such an example of most able and noble fulfillment of duty. As a logical effort it seems to me just comparison in our annals. The most sacred rights of the defendant, throughout, are guarded as carefully, yes, more carefully than by the courts. The profession owes you a quick and hearty acknowledgment for such a service. This slight tribute comes from an humble member of our bar, but it is in my heart and I hasten to say it. In the sense in which this is written the verdict is unimportant. It is not yet rendered.

Very Respectfully John Davis.

HK252
Letter, handwritten in ink.

Boston June 20/93

District Atty. Knowlton
Dear Sir

Your plea in the Borden case is simply <u>magnificent</u> and I do not understand how any jury can decide against you - Your assertions are all true. Gov. Robinson appeals to the sympathies or <u>tries to do so</u> but he fails altogether in his arguments. My opinion of him has changed very materially as I think he has often stooped to cast personal reflections upon yourself - He has however "left no stone unturned". and his deceit has been protected by him to the sacrifice often of <u>facts</u> - He of course has not always kept truth on his side <u>which ought to be against</u> him he however will be paid enough at last from the estate to satisfy all claims - of course <u>todays</u> ending is still to be and it is perhaps not safe to conjecture the end. But it is to be hoped if this jury fail to convict or disagree that the case will be carried to a Higher Court. for I know there are hundreds who believe that <u>the three women did the work</u> or at least that all <u>knew</u> about it. The ridiculous stories which the "<u>Assassin has told</u> stamp her guilt. Again allow me to say your argument has been <u>grand</u> and strong I wish you <u>all</u> success <u>always</u>.

Yours (one who reads)

P.S. I have just read in a local paper not far from Boston the statement of a man who has always known the Bordens and he says he has not the slightest doubt of Lizzie Bordens guilt. and he also says he thinks "Uncle John knows all. So does probably <u>Gov. Robinson</u>.

HK253
Letter, handwritten in ink.

Brookline, June 20, '93.

My dear Knowlton,
    A strong argument and a creditable one.
    I congratulate you.

Yours truly,
James R. Dunbar.

Hon. Hosea M. Knowlton,
New Bedford.

HK254
Letter, handwritten in ink.

NORCROSS, BAKER & PARKER
ATTORNEYS AT LAW
140 MAIN STREET.

Fitchburg, Mass., June 20th 1893

Hon H. M. Knowlton -
My Dear Mr. Knowlton -
    Will you permit me to express to you the great admiration I feel as a citizen and a lawyer for the splendid conduct of the Borden case by you and Moody. The undue expressions of the newspapers, by way of sentimental sympathy for the defendant - and the almost hostile at best hypo- critical attitude of the press towards the prosecution, has tended to make your work more trying - and more difficult. As a lawyer I have been dis- gusted also with the puerile and fulsome flattery of Gov. Robinson - now faded away however in disappointment over his argument - which to my mind is entirely unworthy of him - and not at all

what might have been expected from even a mediocre lawyer - I have been most deeply impressed with your dignified - powerful - yes charitable, and manly argument for the Government. Every citizen ought to feel - and doubtless will - that only a stern sense of duty has governed you. Surely they must know - that the interests of the people, have been protected and guarded by men, more than equal to cope with what was supposed to be an invincible array of counsel for the defense - Whatever be the verdict - you and Moody have done splendid and brave work - with a calm courage and dignity, which has most deeply impressed me and all other lawyers with whom I have talked. This case is one presenting a thousand opportunities to the defense - but full of the most difficult - and exacting problems for the prosecution.

With my most earnest and hearty congratulations and regards - I am most faithfully yrs.

    Herbert Parker

Do not trouble yourself to reply to this letter. You will have other and more important matters to occupy your mind.

HK255

Letter, handwritten in ink.

                                34 Mt. Vernon St.
                                Tuesday Evening
                                Boston June 20, 1893

My dear Knowlton

Let me congratulate you on your magnificent argument in the Borden case - It was a credit to the profession and a masterly marshalling of the facts - It is always a pleasure to see anything well performed - Looking at it as a work of art, in my judgment your argument was excel- lent & your English, your style, your construction of the edifice all gave me pleasure as I read as a lawyer what you had to say.

The verdict to my mind does not detract in me least from the encomiums you deserve. I venture to say your argument carried moral conviction to a great many minds -

Sitting at home here to-night it is a pleasant duty to send greeting to a brother who has performed his part so well.

                                Yours truly
                                James P. Farley Jr

H. M. Knowlton Esq
New Bedford Mass

Herbert Parker, circa 1895.

HK256
Letter, handwritten in ink.

FRANCIS R. JONES,
20 PEMBERTON SQUARE,
BOSTON.
June 20, 1893.

My Dear Mr. Knowlton:

It may be presumptuous in an old pupil to offer his praises to his learned Preceptor, but your great argument has awakened such deep admiration in my heart that I cannot refrain from giving expression to it. I know your intense feeling & your firm adherence to duty, both of which shone out from every sentence of your closing, which was instinct with the best of feeling, & eloquent with it. And I cannot help congratulating you upon the end of your labors, whatever that end may be. I firmly believe, however, that conviction is to follow, & that you are to be relieved at last from all the ignorance, imbecility and wantonness of the newspapers. Surely at such a time, it is not bad taste or bad manners to express one's hearty admiration & faith - even if you have totally forgotten

Yours very truly,
Francis R. Jones.

HK257
Letter, handwritten in ink.

Brockton
June 20, 1893

My dear Knowlton -

We have just now the news by Telegraph of the verdict of "not guilty" - but I want to congratulate you upon your clear cogent & eloquent argument. It is conclusive as it seems to me as to every thing but the legal guilt of the def't & I suppose after the exclusion of testimony by the Courts you hardly expected a verdict of "guilty" - Some time I want to look over the question of "exclusive opportunity" with you - It presents to my mind a question that Mr R seems not to have viewed as I view it -

In haste &
Very Truly
J. M. Day

HK258
Letter, handwritten in ink.

LAW AND NOTARY OFFICE OF
WM. A. YOUNG,
COLLECTING A SPECIALTY.

P. O. Box 694,

Danville, Ill. June 20, 1893

Hon. H. M. Knowlton
New Bedford Mass

Dear Sir-

I have watched with great interest the case of People vs. one Lizzie Borden. As I am to some extent engaged in Criminal Law I would be please to have a copy of your speech for Prosecution and the one made in defense will you kindly inform me if speeches were reported in full: and where: and of whom I could obtain copies. by answering you will confer a favor on your humble servant. with great respect, I remain &c

Yours very Truly
Wm. A. Young
P. O. Box 694
Danville, Illinois

HK259
Letter, handwritten in ink.

THE HEUBLEIN

Hartford, Conn. June 20, 1893.

Hon. H. M. Knowlton
New Bedford, Mass.

Dear Sir.

Tonights paper tells us the verdict in the "Celebrated case" is "Not Guilty."

I enclose you an editorial published in one of the leading evening Journals of this city, "The Hartford Post" which I think reflects the sentiment of thousands of persons who like myself have followed this case & all along have been on your side & who do not, because they can not, change their minds simply because the verdict is as it is.

I have been reading your presentation of the case in today's Boston Herald & await the next edition that I may get the closing portion in full & I want to tell you that I think it a masterly argument, beside which Gov. Robinson's should not be mentioned.

His is ordinary - very much so - yours forceful & extraordinary, tremendously so - & I would have given a good bright dollar to have heard it.

If your Argument is ever put in pamphlet form I would be glad of a copy & proud to pay whatever charge there might be.

Very Resf'y yours
E. B. Worrell
#3 Trull St.
Dorchester, Mass.

HK260
Letter, handwritten in ink.

OFFICE OF
H. L. PARKER,
COUNSELLOR AT LAW,
405 MAIN ST.,

Worcester, Mass. June 21, 1893.

My dear Mr. Knowlton

The verdict was right, but I want to congratulate you upon your <u>masterly argument</u>.

It has given you a reputation of which you may well be proud.

Yrs. very truly
H. L. Parker.

HK261
Letter, handwritten in ink.

LAW OFFICES OF

STEELE & PRESCOTT,

ATTORNEYS.

A. B. STEELE,
W. C. PRESCOTT

Herkimer, N. Y., June 21, 1893

Hon. Hosea M. Knowlton
    Dear Sir:-
  Please accept hearty congratulations on your magnificent address. The New York papers speak very highly of it. I have not been able to get a paper which gave it in full. If any of your papers gave it in full or the-substance of it, please send me one. The charge of the Judge was a stronger plea for the defendant than Robinsons -
A woman <u>could</u> have committed the crime. Did you ever hear about the "Druse" case tried in this county. Mrs. Druse killed her husband cut his head off & burned most of his body. Steele & I prosecuted. She was convicted and was executed.

      Yours in [?]
      W. C. Prescott.

HK262
Letter, handwritten in ink.

      Batavia N.Y.
      June 21 1893

District Attorney Knowlton Esq
  New Bedford Mass.
    Dear Sir,
      I have carefully read from day to day the report published in the Newspapers on the trial of Miss Lizzie Borden. I have also read with interest the report of the address of Ex Gov. Robinson to the Jury in her behalf and your very able and Eloquent and forcible address to the Jury as prosecuting officer. She has been acquitted by

the Jury and their verdict corresponds with my opinion of the case and that of many members of the bar in this vicinity. There was one strong point if the evidence was reliable against her that with the evidence adduced it was difficult to get over. That was that from an examination of the food in the stomach of Mr & Mrs Borden and its digestion that Mrs Borden must have been killed and died one hour or one hour and a half before Mr. Borden. But was that Evidence reliable? I think not and it has misled all parties in the investigation of this murder by its fallacy. I had occasion some years ago to defend a pysician charged with poisoning a child and the chemist claimed and swor he found 39 grains of Muriatic acid in the childs stomach & that it would cause the death of the child. As a fact corroborating the chemist's testimony the stomach of the child had become more or less digested. I inquired of several reputable Physicians, if there was at death a considerable quantity of gastric juice in the stomach before death if it would not digest the food in the stomach and even the stomach itself. The Answers I got was "No it would preserve the stomach." Being somewhat of a chemist myself having taught chemistry I took no "stock" in those answers. I procured books one a standard work upon Physiological Chemistry or Chemistry applied to Physiology (I have forgotten the title of the book & name of Author) and there I found it laid down as a fact that the gastric juice would put forth its properties after death and if there was a considerable quantity in the stomach at death it would digest even the stomach itself. If this be so the amount of food digested in one stomach more than in the other would be no reliable indication of the period of relative death of the two. If there was more gastric juice or fluid in one stomach than in the other the digestion would continue for a period at least after death. As I think the conclusions of the physicians from the digestion of food in the two stomach's unreliable & misleading I venture to call your attention to this. I have practiced law for over forty years - was admitted in 1848 and have had to do with and take part in six or Eight cases of accusation of murder. In the above case by a careful cross examination of the chemist his analysis was shown to be wholly unreliable & Doct Sweeny was acquitted. This was about 40 years ago.

       Yours Respectfully,
       N. A. Woodward

P. S. I trust you will pardon me for writing you this letter. I believe the guilty party to this double murder may yet be found, at least I hope so.

HK263
Letter, handwritten in ink.

COMMONWEALTH OF MASSACHUSETTS, DISTRICT ATTORNEY'S OFFICE, MIDDLE DISTRICT.

Worcester, Mass. June 21, 1893.

My Dear Knowlton,
    I congratulate you on your magnificent argument. It was the work of a Master.

Yours,
F. A. Gaskill

HK264
Letter, handwritten in ink.

HENRY B. PEIRCE
ABINGTON, MASS.

June 21, 1893.

My Dear Bro, Knowlton.
    You don't need congratulations or commendation for you know that you have done your full duty in the Borden case, but I feel like saying that in my judgment no one could have done better. I consider your closing address to the jury a masterpiece.

    I said originally "Hosea Knowlton never would have taken the stand he has taken until he became satisfied in his own mind that Lizzie Borden was the murderer and he will show a reason for the faith that is in him before he is through with the case." This you have done and in a way that will convince thousands, as it has convinced me, that you was right.

Yours sincerely,
Henry B. Peirce

HK265
Letter, handwritten in ink.

BENNETT & HALL
COUNSELLORS AT LAW,
CROCKER BUILDING.

Taunton, Mass., June 21st 1893

My Dear Sir,
    I could not conscientously say that she was proved guilty, but I can conscientiously say that yours was a splendid argument, and ought to make you Attorney General, even tho it failed to convict her.
    When the time comes, if I can be of any service to you in the direction suggested, command me.
                        Very Truly Yours,
                        Edmund Bennett

HK266
Letter, typewritten.

N. SUMNER MYRICK.
COUNSELLOR AT LAW.
FARLOW BUILDING, STATE ST.
BOSTON

June 21, 1893.

Dictated.
Hon. Hosea M. Knowlton,
        New Bedford,
                Mass.

Dear Knowlton:-
                When I saw that the Court had decided to exclude Miss Borden's evidence given at the preliminary trial and thereupon concluded that the defence would not put her upon the stand, I feared that Gov. Robinson was going to reap more than the lion's share of the honor and reputation to be gained by association with the case. But upon reading the arguments as printed in the papers, there can be no doubt of the position you have earned

during the trial. Permit me to congratulate you on your effort, which was masterful and comprehensive in every respect, and, at the same time, dignified and fair. You certainly had more in the disposition of the Court and its atmosphere to contend with than any public prosecutor has had in the trial of a capital case in this State for a number of years.

After the dust and smoke of the battle have cleared away, the calm judgment of the people of the State will award to you very high praise for your conduct of the case. I can well understand that you are experiencing disappointment. I can understand it, because personally I am disgust- ed. Miss Borden seems to have "hoodoed" the Court and jury, not forget- ting the newspaper men. Had Bridget Sullivan been on trial, I venture to say that she would at this moment be confined in a convict's cell. But, however, your reputation is safe, and I am glad of it.

> Yours very truly,
> N. Sumner Myrick.

HK267
Letter, handwritten in ink.

> Tufts College
> June 21, 1893

Hon. Hosea M. Knowlton,
    My Dear Sir:

I yield to an impulse to tell you that, in my judgment, your presentation of the case in the trial just ended, was masterly in its use of facts, and in the cumulative power of its argument. Then, too, so far as I am able to see, there is not a word in it that one would wish you had not uttered.

The best friends of Gov. Robinson may wish that his plea had been free from what, without much strain upon a word, might be called flippancy. Thank God that, in that awful place, you showed so much <u>reserve</u>, and humanity - delicate severity.

You are not a man to care much for the effect of all this upon your- self. I trust, however, that you will not deem me intrusive when I say that safe & good men everywhere, will declare: He lost the case, but he gained the Esteem & Even the affection of the world.

> Faithfully,
> C. H. Leonard.

HK268
Letter, handwritten in ink.

Boston
June 21, 1893

H. M. Knowlton Esq.

Dear Mr. Knowlton.
  When you can get round to it conveniently will you kindly send me up the type-written Evidence that was used in McDermott vs. OCRR. I took it from the Railroad Commissioners office, and feel under obligations to return it Soon. I want to offer you my sincerest admiration for the splendid argument of the Borden case. it was the most impressive heard in our courtrooms for many years, as I hear on every side.

Yours very truly
Chas. F. Choate Jr

HK269
Letter, handwritten in ink.

F. W. DRAPER, M.D.
304 MARLBOROUGH STREET
BOSTON.

June 21, 1893

My Dear Sir:-
  Will you permit me to be among the great company of those who desire to express their admiration for your very able closing argument in the recent trial. Among the many noteworthy incidents of this memorable affair, your address to the jury stands out conspicuously. From all sides, I hear warm praise concerning it, and the praise comes alike from those holding very diverse opinions about the relation of the defendant to the crime. The conditions under which the argument was delivered made its force and keenness the more distinguished, and I am sure that nothing about the Borden case will survive in memory like that closing chapter which you so ably contributed.
Yours very truly
F. W. Draper.
H. M. Knowlton, Esq.

HK270
Letter, handwritten in ink.

BALLOU & JACKSON,
ATTORNEYS AND COUNSELLORS AT LAW,
NO.4 WEYBOSSET STREET.
DAN'L R. BALLOU.   FRANK H. JACKSON.

Providence, R.I. June 21, 1893.

My Dear Knowlton,

I feel it my duty to write you today and I must say that in the case Commonwealth of Massachusetts vs. Lizzie A. Borden you have done your duty like a brave man & an honorable & able Lawyer, and I congratulate you on your honorable <u>cause</u>. You must feel gratified that it is over. As to the result I have not anything to offer except only that if a man had been in the Defendant place pressing the same evidence I am of the opinion that the jury would have returned a different <u>verdict</u>. She has been acquitted by a jury of her <u>peers</u>. You did all mortal <u>could</u> do - did it well & honorably & your brethren of the Bar are all proud of you.

I am truly yours
Frank H. Jackson.

HK271
Letter, handwritten in ink.

PROBATE COURT, COUNTY OF BRISTOL.

Taunton, Mass., June 21, 1893.

My Dear Mr. Knowlton,

You rose to the occasion and your plea was masterly. I congratulate you upon the golden opinions won by you in this case. Gov. Robinsons argument was a disappointment. You fought your case through without much encouragement from anybody. Everything was against you from the beginning, but your argument is fit to be classed among the best things in the history of jury trials.

Very truly yours,
John H. Galligan

Charles Francis Choate, Jr., circa 1895.

HK272
Letter, handwritten in ink.

JESSE C. IVY,
COUNSELLOR AT LAW
113 DEVONSHIRE STREET.

Boston, Mass., June 21st 1893.

My dear Sir,

I have read with care the opening, evidence, arguments, and charge in the Borden case, and, although a conviction was not obtained, still your conduct was not only justifiable, but has also been without spot or blemish and with excelling ability.

The evidence leads to the irresistible conviction that the accused is guilty of the crime charged. She must have been in the Guest Chamber when her stepmother fell from a death wound prone to the floor, and she ceased her ironing to translate her aged father from a gentle sleep into the presence of the Eternal I am. There is genius in crime as in poetry, Law and Science. Just beyond the border line of sanity there seems to be a dearth of perceptions as to moral right, the accused inhabits the land beyond that line - not an exceedingly rare order of being, but exception- ally rare in this respect, that she has calculation, intense and deep cunning, abnormal will power, and abundant courage to execute her will.

This case ought to be preserved in permanent form, especially your argument. This last would be a witness of your fearless and conscientious discharge of duty and an unanswerable demonstration of the indictment. The charge in this case will always be painful for lawyers to read. If it had been delivered within the Bar, it would have been unobjectionable, but it has no proper place in the impartial administration of the law.

I trust you will pardon this letter if any of it seems objectionable, but I felt, as a lawyer, I ought to say to you that I commend your conduct of this case.

Yours truly
Jesse C. Ivy

To H. M. Knowlton, Esq.

HK273
Letter, handwritten in ink.

HARVARD MEDICAL SCHOOL
CHEMICAL LABORATORY
Boston, June 21st, 1893

My dear Knowlton

I wish to congratulate you with all my heart upon your masterly argument in the Borden case, and to assure you that the feeling of every- one with whom I talk, is that you have done your whole duty and have done it to perfection, notwithstanding the unfavorable verdict.

Certainly more than 75 percent of the thinking people believe that Lizzie Borden was guilty, and I find many who think that the verdict would have been different had the interests of the Government been properly upheld by the Court.

I regret very much that I could not be present to hear your argument.

Hoping that you will soon be in Marion where you can obtain a much-needed rest, and that I shall soon see you in Pocasset, I remain

Very sincerely yours,
Edward S. Wood.

HK274
Letter, handwritten in ink.

OFFICE OF
ALPHONSO A. WYMAN,
COUNSELLOR AT LAW,
131 DEVONSHIRE STREET,
ROOM 15.
Boston, June 21st, 1893

Hon. Hosea M. Knowlton,
    New Bedford, Mass.

Dear Sir:

Allow me to add my congratulations to the many you must already received for the manner in which you conducted the great trial which has just been ended.

In my opinion, formed from a careful examination of the arguments, your address in both language and logic, surpassed that of the ex- Governor.

Yours etc.

Alphonso A. Wyman.

HK275
Letter, handwritten in ink.

CHARLES P. GREENOUGH. 3   **9 COURT STREET,**
COUNSELLOR AT LAW.   **ROOMS 22 AND 23**
Boston, June 21st 1893

Dear Knowlton

I cannot refrain from expressing my admiration of your argument in the Borden case. It seemed to me one of the most admirable legal efforts that I can remember. I read every word of it & if it is published under your correcting I should like to read it again.

As Cato said "Tis not in mortals to command success but we'll do better we'll deserve it"?

C. P. Greenough.

HK276
Letter, handwritten in ink.

Plymouth,
Personal   June 21, 1893.

My Dear Knowlton:

I have read your argument in the Bordon case.

I have had a great sympathy with you on account of the abuse of you by the newspapers!

You may or may not become Attorney General, but I would prefer to be the author of that argument, than to be Attorney General.

I see the papers have turned around at the time of the argument, and say Gov. Robinson's argument was a disappoint, [?]

Very truly yours,

E. J. Sherman.

HK277
Letter, handwritten in ink.

> 1645 K St. NW. June 21, '93
> Washington, D. C.

My dear Sir,

In your argument and professional methods, and in the descriptions of your character read in the daily journals, you remind me so forcibly of my father, the late Lincoln B. Knowlton, of Illinois, that I am forced to write and ask you what relationship you bear to Col. Thomas Knowlton, of Revolutionary fame, if any. My father was called the "Harry Clay of the Illinois bar." He died when I was quite a child, too young to remember him. The older lawyers and statesmen of Illinois remember him with pride and affection.

I followed the Borden trial with great interest. Before you began your very fine argument I had said that to my mind the most damaging thing against Lizzie Borden was the failure to find that note, and if a note had been written by some friend, would that friend not be very apt to come forward and state that she was its writer. That was evidently a story hatched for the occasion. It seems to me if Lizzie Borden was not guilty of the murder of her stepmother by her own hands, she was in collusion with somebody whom she hired to do the deed. The step-mother was the objective point - the father's murder an afterthought, made necessary by the first crime.- There was not enough evidence to convict but I cannot smother the suspicion that Lizzie Borden is the head and front of the offending, however the matter was executed and by whom.

With very Kindest esteem, allow me to remain

> Very truly yours,
> (Mrs.) Louise Wolcott Knowlton Browne.

HK278
Letter, handwritten in ink.

> 4 Depter Row
> Boston
> Mass.
> 21 June '93

Dist. Att'y. Knowlton
My Dear Sir:

Not because you are in need of it but because it is in my heart to do it, I write you, wholly a stranger to me, to express, my great

George Dexter Robinson, circa 1890.

admiration of you, in the performance of your (I may say) terrible duties at New Bedford. I specially justify myself in this expression because I have not been able to conceive Miss Borden guilty and therefore am wholly in sympathy with the verdict rendered.

Of course I have only <u>read</u> your argument but from that, I gather so much assurance not only of a fidelity of which all good citizens should be proud - and of ability commensurate with the demands of your office, but also of a spirit and bearing commanding my enthusiastic and grateful admiration, that I am simply impelled (selfishly if you please) to send you these words.

I am a Congregatiional clergyman past 50 years of age at present residing here though not pastor of any church. I was ten years pastor at Haverhill and know Mr. Moody your associate well and am proud of him. As I intimate in my first sentence I am sure you are in no need of sympathy or commendation but may consider yourself worthy of all praise from greater, wiser men than your present correspondent.

Yours very Truly
Henry E. Barnes,

HK279
Letter, handwritten in ink.

CLERK'S OFFICE OF SUPERIOR COURT,
NO. 54 COURT HOUSE, PEMBERTON SQ.

Boston, 21 June 1893,

My dear Mrs. Knowlton,
When Mr. Knowlton will have a leisure minute will you tell him of the deep admiration which his manly effort in behalf of justice & <u>truth</u> has excited in the hearts of his friends. For my part I feel proud to know him & will consider it an honor to shake his hand. As a bit of Court gossip I will cite the remark of L. S. Dabney Esq. who replied to a remark as to Miss Borden's innocence, that if she did not do it, "it did itself,"

Alec sails on the 29th of this month "across the pond," If he knew that I am writing to you, he would send his "best love" to you & yours. I hope to see you sometime this summer and trust that you will not repudiate me as a writing nuisance.

Aline Delano

Three cheers for Mr. Knowlton.

HK280
Letter, typewritten, with newspaper clipping affixed.

RESIDENCE, CANTON, MASS.
WHEN CONGRESS IS IN SESSION, ADDRESS
"THE SHOREHAM," WASHINGTON, D.C.

Canton, June 21st, 1893.

To Hon. Hosea M. Knowlton,
New Bedford, Mass.

Dear Knowlton:-

That argument of yours was a masterly one. And I desire to tender you my congratulations. You couldn't overcome the serious defect in the evidence as set forth by me in the inclosed little interview of the Boston Journal of this evening. And although you lost---I was proud of you--- because you played your part well, and that address of yours will be historical.

Embracing this opportunity to assure you of my continued friend- ship and very kind regard, I beg to remain,

Yours sincerely,
Elijah A. Morse

Clipping:

CONGRESSMAN MORSE TALKS.
He Expresses Great Satisfaction at the Outcome of the Trial.

Congressman Hon. Elijah A. Morse was seen by a representative of the Journal, and was glad to give expression to his satisfaction at the outcome of the great trial. He said that he spent two days at the trial, and had conversation with John V. Morse and both Misses Lizzie and Emma Borden.

He said, "Mr. Morse impressed me as an honest, straightforward, upright man; in private conversation with me he affirmed his solemn belief in Lizzie's innocence; he met the Government contention that no assassin could have got into the house unseen, by saying that he went in and out that house twice on that fatal day, unseen."

In reply to the question if there was any relationship between his family and that of John V. Morse, he said: "Mr. Morse's family and my own are connected in the early history of our country. The prisoner and her sister impressed me," he continued, "as cultured, refined and ladylike persons.

"Gov. Robinson showed his great skill as an advocate: First in cross-examination of the witnesses and his arguments to the Court; second, in getting down from the scholar and the states- man and the jurist that he is, to being hail-fellow-well-met with the honest-farmer jury before him, speaking in their dialect and drawing his illustrations from the New England farm and home.

"District Attorney Knowlton's plea was an eloquent, masterly presentation of the Government's case. I served with him in the Legislature eighteen years ago, and he has grown very much since. The fatally weak point in the Government's case was the absence of blood on the defendant, and the very short time between the murder of Mr. Borden and the alarm, giving her insufficient time to change her clothes and destroy the evidences of guilt if she committed the murder.

"The letter, and the failure to materialize of the writer, messenger or sick person, was the most damaging evidence against the defendant; next in importance was her presence in the house and up stairs, with no knowledge of the dead woman for an hour; but that could not overcome with the jury and the serious defect in the Government's case that I have mentioned.

"The Government's case was hurt by proved falsehoods - 'false at one point, false in all' - first, by the police about the handle of the hatchet; second, the Matron's alleged story of a quarrel.

"On the whole, I am sure the country will approve the verdict, for it is better than ten guilty persons escape than that one innocent person should suffer. Lizzie Borden's previous good character and reputation and connection with the church and missionary enterprises went very far, undoubtedly, in securing her acquittal."

(Note: Newspaper clipping from The Boston Journal, Evening Edition, June 21, 1893.)

HK281
Letter, handwritten in ink.

THE VIRGINIA HOTEL,
RUSH & OHIO STREETS,
CHICAGO.

June 21, 1893.

Dear Knowlton

I have just learned of the Verdict & seen an outline of your argument a perusal of which has only confirmed my belief in the prisoner's guilt; and that if you could have made the argument before public opinion had become so manifestly crystalized in her favor you would have had at least a disagreement if not conviction.

I dont know how you feel about such things but acting on the theory of the Golden Rule I take the liberty of expressing my sympathy with you on having been so handicapped in the trial of the case and my resentment at the thoughtless criticisms which have emanated from some of the sensational papers.

"The Press" as such I think will (if it has not done so already) do you justice & credit you with having earnestly ably & honorably presented this "cause celebre" for the consideration of the jury of public opinion & per- formed your full duty to the Court the prisoner & the people

Yours
Walter Clifford

HK282
Letter, handwritten in ink.

MILTON REED,
ATTORNEY AT LAW,
SECTION A, GRANITE BLOCK

Fall River, Mass., June 21st 1893

My Dear Knowlton:

I wish I could have been by your side when you finished your <u>magnificent</u> (for that's just the word to use) argument, so that I could have congratulated you. It was one of the finest arguments I ever read. I wonder you could have done so well when your case had been "curtailed of its fair proportions" by the rulings of the Court.

Well, the strain is over. The dead past must bury its dead.

Truly yours
Milton Reed.

HK283
Letter, handwritten in ink.

Haverhill June 21

My Dear Knowlton,

I know that you will be pleased to learn that in this county, with those best qualified to judge, your argument is receiving praise without measure.

What is said of it is beyond anything you have heard at home. In spite of all newspaper talk it is not true that she is believed to be innocent.

I met Burley to day (Burley is [?] the leader of our Bar) just after he had finished reading the charge. It has rarely been my fortune to see a man so full of indignation. I verily believe that judge Deweys misconduct will be seen by the Bar.

A local paper is impressed with several things of mine which have challanged the admiration of the country but cant quite see why every- body is rating your speech so much higher than Robinson's. You see we have "our Hosey" down this way too.

I dont know whether you have an invitation to Shermans house Saturday. If you have I hope you will come.

With regards to Mrs. Knowlton and best wishes for the children I am
      Yours very truly
      W. H. Moody

HK284
Letter, handwritten in ink.

      434 West 24th St.
      New York, June 21./93

Hon. H. M. Knowlton
New Bedford Mass.
Dear Sir

The Great North American <u>Blower</u> informs me this morning that Miss Lizzie Borden has been "Set free" by a jury of her peers-and I will remark, after --what is it called? O, "a speedy trial"!

What a damnable outrage! Say, why did you not adopt my opening to the jury with which I sent "Bill Church? and you made a great mistake in not taking for an assistant my friend Barney!

For further particulars see my correspondence with A S. Cushman Esq.

I am in some haste for Court. Expect a trial of my case today before one of those played out nuisances called a jury! <u>Chumps</u>.
     Very Truly
     Yours'
     Wm M Hall

HK285
Letter, typewritten, with notations handwritten in ink.

*Law Offices
of*
JAMES B. OLNEY,
*Catskill,
Greene Co.,
N. Y.,*

Catskill, N. Y., June 22, '93

Dist. Att'y Knowlton,
   Sir,

  The charge has ~~often~~ been made that a N.Y. Court is often organized to convict. The reverse seems to be the rule in- the famous Borden ~~case~~ *trial*, and the learned Judge is in a position to be congratulated on winning his case.

The professional world will, no matter what the newspaper fiends and the counsel opposed to you may say, give you worthy and just applause for the bold and fearless ~~manner you have followed~~ *pursuit of this criminal*. Under the outcry raised and all the fierce efforts to secure acquittal, it could hardly be expected any different result ~~could~~ would be reached but the unerring finger of Justice points to her as the only possible perpetrator of this fiendish murder.

You displayed brilliancy and fertility of resource of a high order, and I cant help telling you of our opinion, as we read and formed our judgment. I say "We", for our Bar are, unanimous on the subject.

      Yours Truly, *In Haste-*
      James B. Olney.

HK286
Letter, handwritten in ink.

**ALBERT B. COLLINS,
COUNSELLOR AT LAW & CONVEYANCER
44 NORTH WATER STREET.**

      New Bedford, Mass., June 22, 1893.

Dear Mr. Knowlton:
  May I take the liberty of expressing in this way what I may

not have the opportunity or facility of expressing personally, -my pro- found admiration for your summing up in the Borden case.

I did not - and my infirmity of hearing would not allow me to - hear you, - but I have anylitically read and reread all the newspaper reports. I have been led to critically compare your argument with that of Sherman in the Goodwin Case: with Clifford at the Webster Trial. Judge Advocate Holt in the trial of Mrs Surralt: Atty. Genl. Brewster in the Star Route cases and Lord Plunket at the trial of Emmet and, of course, the great model, Webster in the White Murder case and in my judgment your argument, for dignity, power, fairness and Justness for the best type of the most difficult form of forensic oratory rose to the height of any of these diverse examples and with perhaps the exception of Webster was far and away above them all.

It was a great argument. It should make you famous-

Yours Truly
A. B. Collins

HK287
Letter, handwritten in ink.

Dedham June 22 1893.

Hon. H. M. Knowlton
My Dear Sir:
I feel impelled to express to you personally, my profound admiration of the manner in which you discharged your official duty in the Borden case. I read carefully all the evidence as published in the <u>Boston Herald</u>, which was the only report, that purported to give the testimony as it fell from the witnesses. In all other newspapers I found nothing but garbled statements and perversions, made apparently to cover up the truth.

The case upon the Evidence for the government, was one of great strength, and to my mind conclusive. But it needed your argument to bring out all its force. It was a great occasion, such as comes to few men in a lifetime, and you nobly proved yourself equal to it. Not only in its thorough grasp of details, but in the higher quality of making clear the exact relation which each fact bore to the main question, it seems to me your argument was one of wonderful cogency and power. It is amazing that it failed to impress either the court or jury. Can it be possible that the case was too great to be comprehended by either?

When the artificial clamors of the hour have passed away and thoughtful minds shall consider what was the real force of the evidence against the prisoner, it will then be clearly seen that on your argument lies the only solution of the apparent mysteries of the Borden murders.

Pardon me if these words seem superfluous and uncalled for, but I have thought while the press is flaunting other opinions it was fitting for you to know, that many men of our profession whose judgments are entitled to respect, as I personally know, join in cordial admiration of the service you have rendered to the Commonwealth and to the administration of justice.

     Sincerely Yours,
     Erastus Worthington

HK288
Letter, handwritten in ink.

    WALTER I. BADGER,
    COUNSELLOR-AT-LAW
    718 EXCHANGE BUILDING,
    53 STATE STREET
    BOSTON,
          June 22d 1893

H. M. Knowlton Esq.
  New Bedford, Mass.
My dear Sir-

 It may be presumptuous on my part but I cannot let the opportunity go by without extending to you my hearty congratulations upon the manner in which you handled the prosecution of Miss Borden and upon your magnificent argument. My only regret. is that business prevented my being present when the argument was delivered.

 I have followed the trial closely and was much impressed with the strong fight that you made. Please pardon the liberty that I have taken but I did want to "shake your hand" as it were - and I have done so.

     I am as ever
     Yours very truly
      Walter I. Badger.

HK289
Letter, handwritten in ink.

Thursday,
June 22.

My Dear Mr. Knowlton,

I am absolutely incapable of expressing my deep admiration and thorough respect for your conduct of the Borden case, but I feel constrained to make the attempt, because every day I appreciate how handicapped you have been and how nobly you led such a forlorn hope as the case has seemed ever since judge Mason showed a disposition to exclude whatever Mr. Robinson demanded of him. From the first I have firmly believed in Lizzie Borden's guilt. I was in Swansea the day the murder occured; & on Sunday, I read an article in a Providence paper commenting on the wonderful knowledge of the house & the habits of its occupants, the murderer had shown. There was no hint of Lizzie Borden's possible connection with the crime; but I said "Horrible as it is to say it, I believe the daughter did the deed." The old lady whom I then visited, said "Can there be such a daughter!" The idea could find no lodgment in her simple, honest mind, & I did not wish to convince her. I have not seen her since, until last May, and I was much impressed to find that this conservative, just woman, had in the retirement of her country home, thought the matter over till she, too, had come to agree with me. She told me of a family in Swansea, whom Lizzie visited in younger days, and who tell, with bated breath, of her one day having taken a nest of robins, and "chopped off their heads," because she "wanted to have a funeral." From an entirely remote, but equally authentic source, I am told of a lady, who called at the Borden house one day, and was much annoyed by a kit- ten, who kept jumping into her lap. It became so troublesome that Lizzie finally took it from the room, and on her return said, 'That kitten won't trouble you any more. I've chopped off her head."

These sound like fairy tales, but I have every reason to believe them true, & taken together, they are, to say the least, significant. It was impossible for me to follow all the testimony. I, however fully appreciated the motive of Mr. Robinson's "objections"; the discouragement, to you, in the judge's "exclusions"; and I have felt that any criticisms as to bias & unfairness, in the first trial, have been fully met & overbalanced by the obvious prejudice & determination to give the prisoner every chance for the acquittal in this last trial. I read one day "Lizzie Borden is being defended not as an innocent woman but as one who cannot be convict- ed." I agree with that as I agree with the verdict of the Recorder's special jury; -"Not proven." However I think you proved Lizzie Borden to have murdered Mrs. Borden, in your one point that having been in the house she

<u>must</u> have heard Mrs. Borden fall. I believe you are entirely right in your theory of how & why Lizzie Borden killed her own father. I believe she knew him to be the only person who would immediately suspect <u>her</u>. Your strongest evidence of her guilt, the story of the note, was so weakly met by Mr. Robinson, that I am surprised the jury were not influenced by that alone, to a "disagreement." The mere fact of her having given the State, the wrong dress, can be construed only as guilt. It is a pity that the state's witnesses were not more consistent: but it is nothing unusual for honest well-meaning witnesses to be led into discrepancies & contradictions. I have failed to see why, in this case, it is specially amusing & peculiar. I firmly believe in Matron Reagan's truth & that your explanations of her apparent denial is the correct one. If I could reconcile my belief in Bridget Sullivan's alleged stupidity, with such a supposition I should be sure her last evidence had been carefully "prepared," by someone else. If the report is true that she will soon go to Europe with the Borden sisters, it would argue that to be the price for learning her lesson so well.

Mr. Knowlton, I might write pages telling you what I think, but I realize that it cannot specially interest you; save the fact that I am one of many who agree with you perfectly; who believe you to be perfectly justified in the course you have taken; & who admire you more for the fight you have made in the face of defeat than had you done the same noble work, assured of success. With sincerest wish that some day Lizzie Borden's guilt will be established, & your position thereby vindicated, I am

Very truly yours,
Mrs. Geo. O. Walker

HK290
Letter, handwritten in ink.

New Bedford 6/22 '93

My dear Mr Knowlton
I leave this p m for the Worlds Fair, but before I go want to send you a line to tell you how fully I sympathise with you in the arduous work you have had to do, in the face of some absurd and hostile criticism. It is of no account. - But you have with a strong and steady hand grasped the opportunity which seldom comes to anyone & perhaps never but once in a lifetime. You have in a masterly manner pleaded the cause of the Commonwealth in behalf of <u>justice</u>. You have placed yourself at the Head of the Massts Bar and won for

yourself the commendation & admiration of all whose good opinion is of value. I congratulate you, and unite most heartily in all the good wishes & kind words which must come to you from all quarters.

Sincerely Yrs
W. J. Rotch

HK291

Letter, handwritten in ink.

Pawtucket, R. I. June 22,1893.

Hosea M. Knowlton, Esq.
New Bedford, Mass.
      Dear Sir:

Allow me to say this: that I believe you per- formed your whole duty in the Borden case. The chain of circumstantial evidence against Miss Borden was and still is very strong, but as I am informed she cannot be tried again. Lawyers, doctors, clergymen, and judges are but men. Miss Borden's immovable cheek aided her at the trial.

      Very truly   J. O. Whitney, M. D.

P.S. You may recall that I was a witness in the Mercy Ellis will case 5 or 6 years ago. Since then I have fallen into very poor health - do not go out, and I have other troubles which I would relate if it would do me any good. I read the papers - mostly the Providence Journal.

HK292

Letter, handwritten in ink.

My dear Mr. Knowlton,

      Allow me to be one of the many to congratulate you on your fine and eloquent speech on the "Borden case", and altho the verdict was, or it seemed to us, right, we were sorry you lost your case.
As my neighbor said, "While I believe Lizzie Borden innocent, Knowltons speech almost made me believe she was guilty."

                     Annie L. T. Williams

June 22nd.   700 Washington St.

                     Brighton Hill

HK293
Letter, handwritten in ink.

June 22, 1893

Mr. H. M. Knowlton,
My Dear Sir,
Doctor Draper tells me you wish for my bill, which I enclose - I am glad, also, of the opportunity to express to you my appreciation of your Courtesy, and Consideration for my comfort.

In spite of unfavorable rulings and charges, I cannot fail to recognize the fortitude with which you conducted a losing cause -

Those qualities must, elsewhere, ensure the success you deserve - And it will be no little satisfaction to you to reflect, that you have done your whole duty as a public prosecutor, in the most remarkable case of modern times.

very truly yours
David W. Cheever.

HK294
Letter, handwritten in ink.

Mr. H. K. Knowlton

Permit me to congratulate you on your able and eloquent argument.

The Judges by excluding evidence and <u>arguing</u> "the charge" won the verdict.

Behind these twelve jurors there are a multitude that have not acquitted and are not able to believe what <u>they wish</u> that she may not be guilty

Yours Resply
W. E. Sparrow
Mattapoisett
Mass. June 22 '93

HK295
Letter, handwritten in ink.

Bridgewater June 22, 1893.

Bro. Knowlton,

Having been at Plymouth attending Court and busy most of the time I have just been able to complete reading newspaper reports of your argument. Allow me most sincerely to congratulate you on your fair, faithful and honorable discharge of your duties in the Borden trial and upon your most masterly argument. It certainly was most admirable in every way and the best that could possibly be made. I am proud of it and the more I think of it the more able its seems to me. You certainly can have no possible reason for entertaining even the shadow of a doubt but that <u>your</u> duty was <u>fully</u> performed.

Yours truly
Hosea Kingman

HK296
Letter, handwritten in ink.

87 Milk St., Boston.
June 22, 1893.

My dear Knowlton:

You made a splendid fight - Your argument, every word of which I read, was consecutive, logical and <u>convincing</u> - No fact was misstated, and no circumstance urged beyond its legitimate bearing - In style and temper it was unexceptionable - nevertheless, the verdict was "not guilty" - and I am not disposed to criticise the finding - From the start it was a losing fight - You had everything to contend against - Antecedent probability, popular clamor, the senseless drivel of the press, a <u>woman</u> to be convicted, the exclusion of important, and (as I believe) <u>competent</u> testimony, and, finally, a charge to the jury which was a stronger argument for the prisoner that her counsel presented; these combined made a conviction impossible - But you did your duty faithfully and manfully - Even those who have abused you the most are now compelled to admit that!

It is safe to say now, that for <u>constitutional reasons</u>, if for no other, the perpetrator of the Borden murder will never be brought to justice in this world. Alas, that it should be so! Trusting that this expression of opinion

from an old friend will not be unwelcome, and hoping that you will not fail to take a well earned rest now that the weary struggle is over. I remain
Sincerely Yours
<u>Asa French</u>

Hon. Hosea M.. Knowlton

HK297
Letter, handwritten in ink.

Amherst, Mass.
June 22nd:
1893-

Dist. Atty. Knowlton
   Dear Sir.
      A word of explanation as to the reason of this missive -
With intense interest I have followed from the beginning your conduct for the Commonwealth of this mystery of the 19th Century -
If I may say so, sir, you have stood in a most difficult position. Confronted upon one side with an irresistible belief in the guilt of Lizzie A. Borden, and on the other with a deplorable lack of <u>legal</u> evidence -
Likewise you have been obliged to face the fickle tide of human prejudice sweeping now & again to your very feet, and finally you have been compelled to plead a losing cause in the teeth of popular misjudgment, unable to appeal to that very flood of human sympathy to which the prisoner at the bar owes her acquittal; yea her life itself!
And so, Mr. Knowlton, you have lost your case: but you have gained hundreds of admirers wherever your masterly logic has been disseminated-
You have not flinched! You have had no $20,000 to allure you to sacrifice the truth for the fee of wealth -
You have been on the unpopular side, but you have won our respect & admiration.
I believe that Lizzie Borden is guilty in the sight of God & her own conscience.
  Why?
1st. Her own at testimony proves her so - tho. excluded by legal technicalities.
2nd. Circumstances prove her so - like a game of chess, in which certain moves must indicate a given line of procedure.

Hosea Kingman, circa 1895.

3rd. The testimony of those who stand nearest to her condemns her, "nolens volens." But pardon me, I am not to give my view -

Again, I have learned that you - or at least the police of Fall River - were in possession of certain evidence, which from its very nature could not be produced in a court room in presence of a woman whom it incriminated -

One thing more -

Will you tell me if there is any possibility of further procedure contra late prisoner -

You will regard this communication as utterly personal - as merely a tribute of one man to another.

Of course I shall not be surprised to receive no answer from you -

      Yours very truly
      William D. Marsh
      Amherst, Mass.

A. T. My grandfather was one of Harvard Law School's first graduates.

HK298
Letter, handwritten in ink.

22d June '93

THE BUFFALO CLUB,
388 DELAWARE AVENUE.

Dear Sir,

I was very much interested in reading your plea in the Borden case. It was refreshing to get something at last beside the "rot" of newspapers and get at the exact case of the people, so finely presented by you. I was summering at Wianno last year & read very carefully Miss Bordens testimony on the preliminary hearing. From her answers alone, I judged her guilty and I have in no wise changed my opinion by any fact adduced on the trial. I have however felt from the start she was insane, with one delusion, - who in such cases is never apparent to the general observer, and may be concealed for years.

This delusion may have been originated and fed in the 3 years she did not speak to Mrs. Borden -

The hacking of the bodies seemed also the work of a lunatic, also the work of a woman, of some neophyte so to speak, who could not judge the effect of his first blows and dreaded a return to life & a witness against him. Then too the position of Mr. Bordens body on the sofa indicates he had been struck by one he did not dread. If a stranger had come in the room he would have risen.

But I write this dear sir, more to congratulate you on your splendid presentation of the peoples case, and to ask you if it be ever printed in pamplet form if you will kindly send me a copy - If Miss Bordens testimony aforesaid is printed I should very much like a copy of that also - May I also ask if it be true that the day of Miss B's first arrival at the police station for her [ex J she laid down & slept half an hour awaiting your arrival, that seemed to hint at insanity, in fact that alone seems to explain her extraordinary nerve, her apparent unappreciation of the crime etc.

      Yours truly
      Henry H. Seymour
     U. S. Commissioner of jurors
   & Northern District of N. Y. Lecturer
     Buffalo Law School
    331 Franklin St. Buffalo, N.Y.

Mr. District Atty. Knowlton.
New Bedford

HK299
Letter, handwritten in ink.

MINISTER'S STUDY,
FIRST UNITARIAN CHURCH,
STONEHAM, MASS.
      22 June, 1893.

Hon. H. M. Knowlton,
 New Bedford, Mass.
Dear Sir:

 I venture, though a stranger to you, to offer my sincere congratulations on the masterly argument you addressed to the Borden jury on Monday and Tuesday of this week. It may be of some slight interest to you to know that I received a careful legal education and practised at the New York bar for two years before deciding to change my profession. It has been my fortune to hear the most powerful advocates of that bar, - among them Charles O'Conor, James T. Brady, John Van Buren, William M. Evarts, John K. Porter, Noah Davis, Sanford E. Church, William A. Beach, and Lyman Tremain. I have, of course, read the most famous speeches of Erskine, West, Pinckney, Webster and Choate. With the single exception of Webster's address to the jury in the White case at Salem I have never read an address to a jury at a trial for murder with greater admiration than I felt for your great effort in the Borden case. I think I was unusually well prepared to ~~enjoy~~ appreciate it. The outrageous conduct of the larger part of the Boston press in advocating the defendant's innocence before the evidence had been given, the undisguised hostility of the Herald, Globe and Journal to the prosecution; the constant adulation and lionizing they bestowed upon Governor Robinson; their unjust, almost savage attacks on the Fall River police; the extraordinary liberties taken by Governor Robinson in his cross examination, his numerous asides and ad captandum interjections; the contrasted dignity and fairness of the counsel for the Government; and finally, the ill-concealed disappointment of the defendant's personal and press friends in Gov. Robinson's address to the jury, all united to give me a keen relish for what you had to say. I thought Mr. Moody's presentation of the case to the jury almost a model of its kind. I knew the evidence had not fully supported his claims at every point. I regretted the absence of the Attorney General, whose brilliant address in the Trefethen case had greatly enhanced his reputation. I knew you had a good name as a lawyer of learning and ability. I did not know that you deserved a great name as an advocate. I began reading your address with great interest, proceeded with increasing admiration and respect and finshed with the thought that it was second only to the greatest efforts of Erkine and Webster. I was immensely pleased to notice that the Boston Journal, Herald and Globe were compelled to praise your address.

There are many paragraphs in your speech that deserve a permanent place in literature. Strong in statement, luminous in illustration, convincing in logic, yet fair, courteous, even chivalric, throughout, your address must take very high rank among the ablest productions of its kind in our age. Your illustrations were particularly happy. I do not recall in all my reading a more powerful ~~and controlled~~ passage than the one in which you describe the difficulties - amounting to impossibilities - that an assassin from outside would have to encounter in doing his dreadful work. - The verdict was what was to be expected, especially after Judge Dewey's one- sided charge to the jury - a charge that seemed to be only a thinly disguised advocate's plea for the defendent.

But nothing can rob you of your great and deserved reputation as an eloquent, learned and high-minded advocate.

I am a stranger to you, but I do not feel that you are a stranger to me. Again I congratulate you most heartily on your magnificent address to the jury in the great Borden trial.

With profound respect,
Yours most cordially,
J. Herman Whitmore.

HK300
Letter, handwritten in ink.

LAW OFFICES OF
BENJ. F. BUTLER
WASHBURN AND WEBSTER
NO. 6 ASHBURTON PLACE
ROOMS 1, 4, 5 & 6

FRANK L. WASHBURN   **PRENTISS WEBSTER**

Boston, June 22nd 1893.

My Dear Sir
    I have not the pleasure of your acquaintance personally yet feel that I do not infringe the courtesies of a brother attorney when I extend to you my warm appreciation of your able argument in the Borden case. I took occasion to read it carefully and throughout believe that I followed your reasoning, which was well put without words lost.

                     Believe me most truly
                     Prentiss Webster

Hon. Hosea Knowlton
    New Bedford, Mass.

HK301
Letter, typewritten.

ARTHUR LORD   **53 STATE ST., ROOM 506**
  COUNSELLOR AT LAW

                     Boston, Mass., June 22d, 1893

Hon. H. M. Knowlton
    New Bedford, Mass.
My Dear Knowlton,
    I have read with great interest and pleasure your brilliant argument in the Borden case. It was a great speech, worthy of a great occasion. It will gratify you to know how generally it is commended by the profession here, and how favorably it is contrasted with Governor Robinson's. It is easy to win laurels when the jury are with you, but it is a great triumph to win them when the jury are on the other side. After so much ill natured and

ignorant criticism as you have been subjected to, it must be very gratifying to have the unanimous approval of the Bar of Massachusetts.

With hearty congratulations I am,

Very truly yours,
Arthur Lord

HK302
Letter, handwritten in ink.

4 Park Street.
Boston June 22, 1893

Hosea M. Knowlton Esq.
My dear Sir-

I desire to express to you my appreciation of your masterly effort before the jury in the Borden murder Trial. So manly, so fair, so courteous, so considerate, so kind, yet with all so just, so clear, so conclusive, so convincing and I may say so <u>convicting</u>.

Very truly yours
Geo. B. Reed.

HK303
Letter, handwritten in ink.

Boston Mass June 22 1893

Hosea Knowlton Dist Attorney Bristol Co
Dear Sir: -

I am entirely unknown to you - being only one of the larger Jury that have been listening to the evidence in the Borden case - as it comes thro the papers - I want to thank you for your speech which to my mind was remarkably convincing & able. It was spoken out of a manly heart, and revealed the delicacy as well as the strength of your nature, moved as you were by a high consideration for woman - and also by your deep conviction of the truth of your cause - I could not help saying as I finished reading it - Thank God for such a man who believes in truth & righteousness.

The verdict is a matter of the greatest wonderment to me - They have allowed the greatest of criminals to go free - although so much was proven that her conviction seemed to me a foregone conclusion, especially after I began to read your summing up. It is my impression that if you had boldly claimed the handleless hatchet to be the instrument you would have carried the day. & they could not have got rid of the conviction that she did it - It fitted exactly & they could not deny it. No outsider would have put it where found.

I like to see justice prevail - but the public sentiment created by the press seemed to fill the very atmosphere - and favored her acquittal notwithstanding 9/10ths of the people believe she did the horrible deeds - I regard it as a perversion of power and influence.

I am inclined to think the day will come when she will be known to have done these deeds - even in this world - but if not, the great day will reveal it.

I trust you will excuse me for taking your time but I felt that you deserved commendation for your faithful fearless exposure of (as I believe) the real criminal in this case - Of course they have great rejoicing at the acquittal - but you have the satisfaction of having nobly done your duty to the State & as one of your fellow citizens I thank you for it. This is not worthy of any reply & was not sent to get your autograph.

Believe me sir. Very Truly Yours
J. F. Eaton
28 State St

HK304
Letter, handwritten in ink.

96 South Eleventh St
Newark NJ
June 22, 1893

Dear Cousin: Will you Kindly allow me to tender you my assurances of deep respect for the able, thorough and conscintious manner in which you discharged the unpleasant duties of your office.

We have followed closely the trial, and feel very indignant at the unkind motives ascribed to you - you, who of all men, are most tolerant and liberal in your thoughts and feeling towards all classes of men, and creeds of mankind.

I do not wish to discuss the issue of the case in any way. I only want to say I do not see how you could have done less in any particular and been faithful in the discharge of your official duties.

With kindest remembrances from all to Sylvia and the Children I am yours with admiration.

Rob't B. Elder

To Hon. H. M. Knowlton.
New Bedford, Mass.

HK305
Letter, handwritten in ink.

SOUTH CONGREGATIONAL CHURCH.

Matunuck, R. I. June 22, 1893.

My Dear Mr. Knowlton:

I had hoped to have a chance to speak to you after the close of Court on Tuesday.

It seemed to me that it was a duty to thank you and Mr. Moody as well, for the dignity and honour - as well as the care and vigour with which you and he discharged your difficult, honorable and painful duty.

I had had every word of the case - and on Tuesday was so fortunate as to hear the close of your masterly and convincing argument. You know, much better than I do, - how admirably it filled the requisitions of your official duty. But I have a right to speak of the new credit which comes to the Commonwealth from the noble, - and as I said dignified - presentation of her case, as it was made by the gentlemen to whom she entrusted it. I should not write this, I believe, but from the recollection of what you said of the pain the duty gave you. Such a man has a right to know what you ought to know, how highly the People, whose interest he has had confided to him, respect him - and how heartily they sympathise with him.

I am not wholly a stranger to you, though you will not remember this. I enjoyed the friendship of your honoured father, - and saw you once or twice when you were a youngster at Tufts College.

With great respect
Yours Truly
Edward E. Hale

HK306
Letter, handwritten in ink.

CHAS. H. HASWELL,
CIVIL AND TOPOGRAPHICAL ENGINEER,
AND CITY SURVEYOR,

New York, June 22"/93
42 Broadway.

Dear Sir

Some people may censure your course.
To such I would ask,
1st   What was the motive of the murder?
2nd   Where was the one who murdered Mrs. B. during the interval of the arrival of Mr. B.?

A percussive blow upon live flesh cauterizes the opening if one is made & blood does not immediately flow.

To assume that those murders involved the spraying of blood upon the perpetrator and the one such a woman as Miss. B. is preposterous.

The instrument or axe if not already found will be upon a proper search for it.

HK307
Letter, handwritten in ink.

Personal   Washington, D.C.
                                          June 23, 1893.
District Attorney Knowlton,
Fall River, Mass.
Dear Sir:

While the press, and it seems to me almost everybody else, is wallowing in the bloody filth to applaud Lizzie Borden I beg the comforting privilege of paying my tribute of respect and gratitude to you as the prosecutor.

I should hesitate to do this if I had any suspicion that your views of the case were less positive than mine, for I have no shadow of doubt that the judge and jury at New Bedford acquitted an assassin.

Your presentation of the damning facts, grand as it was, is not wholly the reason why I say this, for my opinion is founded on the undisputed evidence, every word of which I read in the perverse Boston Journal - per- verse and adverse and grossly unfair.

The conduct of the press is a mystery indeed. It looks like the result of a combination or common obligation in its monstrous unfairness & unanimity. The hostility to the police, which appears to underlie it all, looks like an anti-Irish movement. You know there is a strong secret order of that character in existence.

It seems to me that your statute regulating the matter of charging the jury needs overhauling - or the judges do. Was Judge Dewey's talk as to matters of fact merely "stating the testimony"!! He chose and ignored what facts of the testimony he pleased, and twisted them like a pettifogger - see his romantic suggestions about the note, so silly as to be almost incredible that he could have uttered them. The fact is <u>the law should absolutely prohibit any discussion of the matters of fact</u> - the law, and that only, should be treated in the charge. This is no new born notion of mine. I have held it ever since the first time I saw a judge cheat the counsel of the fruit of their work, and dictate the verdict of the jury.

Well, the assassin has been acquitted. Talk about now "hunting the murderer!! There is but one. No other ever was or ever will be suspected. You are at least sure of that fact, and whatever consolation it may afford - quite considerable to me at any rate. You ought also to have universal commendation.

      Very respectfully yours,
      Horace L. Piper

P. S. I take the additional liberty of addressing to you a little pamphlet - not inviting you to read it, but as a sort of personal identification.

HK308
Note, handwritten in ink.

      Middleboro, Mass.,
      June 23, 1893

Hon. H. M. Knowlton
  Dear Sir
  Please accept my sincere congratulations upon your clear, interesting and eloquent presentation of the "Borden case" for the commonwealth.

Yours Truly,
Benj. C. Knowlton

7 Rock St.

HK309
Letter, handwritten in ink.

H. THOMAS.   **J. C. SEGER.**
OFFICE OF
THOMAS & SEGER.
COLLECTIONS MADE IN ALL
STATES & TERRITORIES.
SUITS ENTERED & PROSECUTED   De Soto, Mo June 23rd 1893
TO FINAL SETTLEMENT IN ALL
THE STATES IN THE UNION.

Atty. Knowlton
       New Bedford Mass.
Dear Sir!-
    While congratulations are pouring in to Lizzie Borden by those who profess to be Christiens allow me to extend my moast hearty congratulations to you for the able manner in which you conducted the famous trial, and done your duty in upholding the piece honour and dignity of the great commonwelth, & may public sentiment look upon your efforts with a law abiding patriotic spirit
                        Yours Truly,
                        J. C. Seger,

HK310
Letter, handwritten in ink.

Friday June 23d, 1893

Mr. Hosea M. Knowlton,
            My dear Sir;
                        I greatly fear that I am doing an absurd and unwomanly thing in continuing to address you, but I have taken such an interest in the recent trial and been so indignant at some of the newspaper comments, that I find it impossible to hold my peace any longer. I can well believe that you are so weary of the case by this time that any reference to it must be unwelcome, but I see on all sides how ex Gov. Robinson has been receiving telegrams and letters of congratulation, and I wondered how many kind words had been said to you; for your speech seemed to me so infinitely superior in every way to that of the counsel for the defense. And I was perfectly furious when I read the editorial I enclose. (I have sealed it up, for I did not want it to catch your eye until you had glanced at my letter). It is from the Philadelphia Inquirer - a sixteenth rate paper altogether, in my estimation, but still one of the prominent dailies. You have probably never seen a copy of it, and you sustain no loss thereby.

I only see the Phila. Times and New York Post regularly but my father (who considers Miss Borden a persecuted innocent) brought me yesterday's Inquirer, thinking to convince me of the error of my ways in holding as firmly to my belief in the daughter's guilt as I did before the trial.

And I am not moved thereto by anything in the evidence so much as by her own conduct. She has never acted as if she were innocent. Putting aside the fact of its being well nigh impossible for her to have seen or heard nothing of such a crime if committed by another person, why did she not make it as clear as the noonday just what she was doing with herself during that hour and a half?

Instead of sitting weeping in her place while the court wrangled over the question whether her contradictory testimony was to be admitted or not, why did she not cut it all short by springing to her feet and declaring that she wanted to testify - that she wanted to make it as clear to everybody just how she spent every moment of that time as it was to her own conscience and the eye of God?

I believe it was because she dared not. If a jury of women had pronounced upon that case there would have been no such hasty verdict of acquittal. I did not expect a conviction on the evidence - I could see it was insufficient - but

I hoped for a disagreement. I have thought so much about the famous trial of Phineas Finn, this last week and yesterday I spent two hours re-reading the chapters devoted to it in Phineas Redux. You are doubtless as familiar with every page of that book as I myself and remember as clearly some of the things poor Phineas said to his friends and his counsel, above all to Mr. Chaffanbrass on the eve of the trial, and his manly bearing in court. My brother, who is himself a Prosecutor, laughs at my fashion of going to my favorite authors for information and consolation and proofs of the justness of my opinions and prejudices, but mine is an unfaltering faith.

I <u>hope</u> you will be able to regard this in the way I have honestly meant it - as a tribute to what I consider a most able and convincing closing argument in a case remarkable alike for the impossibility of any other theory as to the commission of a crime being entertained while furnishing no satisfactory proof as to the guilt of the person accused.

Believe me, My dear sir,
Most respectfully and sincerely yours,
Anna E. Blackwood.

166 Broad St.
Bridgeton, New Jersey.

HK311
Letter, handwritten in ink.

Worcester June 23d/93

Hon H M Knowlton
    Dear Sir
I have followed the trial of Miss Borden very closely, and I cannot refrain from sending my congratulations to you, for the masterly plea you made for the Commonwealth. I hear from men who are judges and some who are strangers, to you speak in the <u>higest</u> complimentary way of what you said at the trial. It does not alter the case who killed the Bordens with me. Father, <u>Mother</u> has gone to a <u>sick friend</u>, and that <u>Mother</u> was dead upstairs. You have had enough of this. My great regard for you caused me to write.

Truly
George D. Gifford.

"District Attorney Knowlton summing up the evidence for prosecution."
Illustration by "Norman," Boston Post, 1893.

HK312
Letter, handwritten in ink.

COMMONWEALTH OF MASSACHUSETTS
OFFICE OF COMPTROLLER OF COUNTY ACCOUNTS,
NO. 7 PARK STREET,
Boston, June 23 1893

Dear Mr. Knowlton

    I want to express to you my appreciation of your conduct and very able argument in the Borden case. But for the previous trials and acquittals of Miss Borden by the Press, you would have split the jury, and that in my judgment would have been a satisfactory result. I remember no case in this country where the conduct of the Press has been so outrageous; as in this one. The public servant who does his full duty has scant appreciation in these latter days-

                Very truly yours,
                Edward P. Loring

HK313
Letter, handwritten in ink.

                Cottage City, Mass.
                June 23d, 1893.

"Well done, good & faithful servant."-
Mr. Knowlton.
    Dear Sir:
    I was present during three days of the recent Borden trial. Heard most of the testimony - was present on the last day. And was never more surprised in my life, that in one hour, a Jury could have collated & digested all the telling facts in the case, and the prisoner's guilt appear without a reasonable doubt. - either as the prime actor or as an accomplice.
    Had the jury remained in, during the night, the verdict would have commanded more respect & consideration in the minds of reasonable men.
    But you, dear sir, have faithfully performed a painful duty, and your fellow citizens thank & honor you for it.
    I am a resident of Atlanta Ga. but feel as much interested in the main-

tanance of wholesome law, as tho' I were a citizen of the old Bay State. - I am a Northern man.

Very sincerely yours,
L. Graves

HK314
Letter, handwritten in ink.

Boston June 23/93

Dear Mr Knowlton: I enclose my bill for the work done for you during the trial. I told Mr. Burt the amount I meant to charge and he agreed it was fair. I hope it will meet your approval, too.

 I suppose you are taking a needed rest. You truly had a severe and very responsible and wearing task to perform: and Judge Blodgett yesterday said to me that your argument was to him a very strong and able one. Nearly all of us - the younger men - wanted to see the girl cleared, as the crime was only attributed to her by inference; and had I been a newspaper worker, I should no doubt have used the power a reporter has to help her cause, though I should not have exaggerated as some of the men have, the conduct of the chief workers in the government's cause. I do not think any of the correspondents had any resentment towards you - I never heard them say one bitter word about you and I notice the Boston Herald has editorially paid you some deserved compliments, and Joe Howard, in the Globe, referred to the trying time you had with the two little ones sick at home. I hope they are getting on well, and that, freed from the exhausting strain, you are recovering your old time ruggedness and good cheer.

Yours truly,
W. B. Wright

HK315
Letter, handwritten in ink.

Adams Nervous Asylum
Jamaica Plain Mass
6 . 24, '93

To Hon. H. M. Knowlton
 New Bedford
Dear Sir,
 I address you as a stranger, though with feelings of becoming deference;

as one who would do the like if a Gov. signed a bill for Womens Suffrage, or was instrumental in any other measure beneficent to mankind; as one who has from the first of this most exciting case, - used their best powers to get at the facts, to arrive at just conclusions, to be calm in both the processess of investigation & elimination of possibilities & probabilities, through intelligent observation, experience, history & individual characteristics, so far as they can bear on individual action, - & the evidence presented, as a woman who, pained at the unwise course of [?] women, urged by loyal sentiments to justice & the noble endeavor to work out its behests, & surprised at both pulpit & press, the result of thoughtlessness & ignorance. The defense desired nothing better nothing more efficient - fighting battles they could never fight or win - public <u>sentimentality</u> in her favor. Everyone in authority has been hounded from the Gov. down because she was not <u>allowed bail</u>, forsooth. This is sufficient to betray the ignorance, - & yet it does honor to the nobility - of men's hearts & to women's, & to that better day when copying that noblest & most disinterested loyalty of men to each other we call esprit de corps, that challenges the admiration & makes better all, - women shall have come to hold it as strong & true as men. So have I been content because too ill to write & get into controversy, - have kept silence. It has been a time when feeling ruled, & moderate judgment held in check; though in honor bound to say few knew what I knew - or had given it the careful thought.

Nothing has escaped my inquirie. Legal points, - Lizzie Borden's character, the family's & its inharmonious state the past five years - from persons wholly disinterested & lived above petty gossip. - & <u>may it please your Honor</u>, I enquired all about you. New Bedford was once my home & I feel a true interest in its people; & in the file of this [?], lawyers, clergy- men & the intelligent citizen ranks alone for none other has been sought.

I have not changed my opinion from the first. Lizzie Borden's "dominant characteristic has always been secretiveness" the Boston Record said. - I learned for 5 years she has not called her step-mother mother had been open in expression at least <u>occasional outbursts</u>. She expressed of her father a wish that could be born only of hate; I know whereof I do affirm - but the woman would not say it or have it known because she is ill, & would not be drawn into the dreadful maelstrom or her husband have her - & I tell you that you may feel justified, & I know you will not betray me.

A clergyman a D. D. who had preached in Fall River many years, - excellent in character & able - said Miss B - had always been thought a "peculiar girl" "that the family troubles were <u>well known</u>", that Mrs Borden was held to be a very amiable woman."

The moral turpitude of the woman who wrote the note in not appearing - made it impossible for one to have been written. It would have been on the plane of the murder. The burning of the dress on Sunday morning & the contradictory stories. The prussic acid. The stain on skirt, on right side & <u>its coagulum</u>. The menstrual blood <u>cannot coagulate</u> under ordinary circumstances & if caused by it the stain would have been on the inside. The reason it cannot coagulate <u>is, it passes through secretions that so modifies</u> its character that it is chemically impossible, - <u>unless</u> the flow is <u>very</u> rapid & overcomes the action of secretions through which it passes. Physicians agree with me that it was a suspicious circumstance. I believe also the blood would have shown whether it was menstrual - if that particular thing had been considered at the right time - but in this I may be mistaken. It may have been part of the plan to commit the deed at a time when she could account for any damaging clues. One thing I wish to say - that Gov. R made use of an old time & erroneous thought, that women's minds are gloomy & unstable at during this function. It must be very abnormal to produce such a state. nature is always on check & never taken by surprise; & God is never mocked. & the more important the work He means nature to perform the <u>more gaurds</u> he puts <u>around</u> it. I do not wish to bore you but have studied this exhaustively.

Judge Pitman has told me many times that women are no better than men. I have come to know it - as my profession has made me drink deeply of life's dregs. Judge Pitman was a life-long friend & a noble man. & held women in a poet's atmosphere. I agree with you that nature not giving women the strength of men - has compensated by power of invention, because it is a <u>universal law</u>. & simple justice & furthermore, he has given her <u>plasticity</u> which [?] is the embodiment of the law of the survival of the fittest. Lecky says "men bear & break but women bear & <u>bend</u>," else many of our best women would die early. This was essential for the conservation of energies to perpetuate the species. Prof. Wood would have said the hatchet was recently sharpened. Lizzie Borden received her friends the night she arrived in a <u>black silk dress</u> & while Emma swore she had none - I think.

Ex Gov. R. made much of the Police promotion. & now the fact comes out that Judge Dewey was made such by him - who made the <u>unique</u> charge - to acquit the prisoner - I had supposed "<u>the charge</u> should be <u>absolutely unbiased</u>. I close with saying - what I learned of you - that you were "a wise & cautious man" "an able & tender man" "a Christian gentleman" I thank you because you were just & did your duty like a man - without fear or favor as one might have addressed a Roman Tribunal - alone, unaided, but by a

guiding sense of duty - & the "noblest Roman of them all. Mr. Pardon Devoll is a cousin & Rev. Benj. Bachelor knows me well -
Please pardon the pencil & anything else you see -
Respectfully
Sarah W. Devoll M. D.

If reaction is equal to action - there will be much serious thinking done - & wider differences of opinion.
P. S. I wish to thank you for your tenderness. Geo. Elliot says "On our death-bed we never regret our tenderness." Your argument bristled with points. The justice of the common law - & that a woman's a woman for a' that & a' that, made for rich & poor alike, <u>but not always</u> by any means applied in that lofty spirit.
Mrs. Robinson has had no word from pulpit or press - nor the woman who failed to return the day of death of an illegitimate child, while the co-worker in iniquity paid $1,500 bail & that's the last of him, & the poor woman is left to shift for herself an outcast & no woman (I believe) has stretched forth a hand for her. I asked the Sec 'y of State W. C. T .U. if any- thing had been done for Mrs R & she said none but one woman had been to see her. They make much of reform work. The inference is apparent. They are a very partisan org. even tho dear Miss Williard [?] called V. P. [?] Morton a <u>saloon keeper</u> & <u>kept it up</u> - because he owned a hotel - let it - & the prop. had a bar. If Miss B. had been a poor girl she would have been convicted. The papers keep up Borden case. If high the billows rise 'tis but to fall as low. Already the weakness of the defense in saying nothing to account for the murder of Mrs. B & bending shafts [?] in portraying circumstances <u>suspicious</u>, are rather often the sledgehammer sort.

    The dress story again from a women's point of view 1st soon after being made, the dress was covered considerably on front & side widths with paint, & accounted for by defense, as that she was around paint pots when the house was painted. It seems to me she should have <u>spilled</u> the <u>paint</u> & <u>wiped it up</u> - or <u>wiped</u> off <u>the pots</u>. 2d - She wore a dress in that condition till it was <u>badly soiled</u> & <u>faded</u> - which would not be tolerated in a servant, because it would not be common decency
3d - After such penuriousness she burned it, when she could have it - or used it for the cellar, or outside steps, for which uses in ordinary house- holds such are put. The testimony of one of her co-travelling companions - now comes out, that Miss B. was below all the party in knowledge of facts, in intelligence & power to observe. She has strength of mind & purpose, but has been trained in other directions. The defense did not put this one on the stand –

[?] had only one blood stain on him. The Prov. Journal thinks a great opportunity has been lost in experts not being able to say how he would have been covered with blood. The W.C.T.U. are not generous in their support of women physicians. Miss Willard has not. – but they do much gratuitous work.

I hope you will not set me down as a bore.
Very truly
S. W. Devoll

HK316
Letter, handwritten in ink.

JOHN K. GOLDSMITH,
ATTORNEY AT LAW,
NEWBURGH, N.Y.

June 24, 1893

Hosea M. Knowlton Esq
Counselor at Law
Dear Sir,

I am a criminal lawyer here. I send you a copy of my opinion in the Borden case, published at the request of the Newburg Daily News on <u>Monday June 20th</u>, 1893, and <u>before</u> I read your speech.

I congratulate you on your summing up in that case. It was as great a speech as ever was made in a criminal case by any lawyer in this or any other country.

I never read a speech or heard a speech, by a District Attorney I admired so much. <u>Believing fully</u> in Lizzie Borden's guilt, <u>as I do</u>, your speech awakened within me the highest admiration and the greatest appreciation. It was superb,- it was grand,- it was masterly,- it was <u>perfect</u>.

I read your speech twice, in the <u>New York Sun</u>, and in the <u>Albany Argus</u>, which papers gave full and complete copies of it.

That magnificent speech places you among the greatest of lawyers and jury advocates.

I was <u>provoked</u>, when I read Judge Dewey's charge to the jury, to see how <u>tremendously</u> he charged <u>in favor</u> of the Defendant, and <u>improperly summed</u> up the case for the Defense.

Do you believe that Lizzie Borden <u>used the handleless hatchet</u> to kill, and then <u>broke off</u> the handle? and did she <u>burn the handle in the stove</u>?

Do you believe, the dress she burned on Sunday morning in the presence of Emma Borden and Miss Russell, was the <u>one she wore while Killing</u>? or do you think she burned <u>one</u> or two dresses right after Killing the parties.

Do you believe she wore <u>that handkerchief around her head</u>, which was found saturated with blood near Mrs. Borden?

I would like to make your acquaintance. If you ever come to Newburgh, call and see me.

With the greatest respect,
and highest esteem, yours etc.
John K. Goldsmith
Brewster Building
Newburgh, N. Y.

HK317
Letter, handwritten in ink.

UNION CLUB, BOSTON
8 PARK STREET

June 24, 1893

Dear Knowlton,

    I am going to presume upon my slight acquaintance to express my thanks to you as a lawyer and as a citizen for your argument. I hope I may never find it my duty to undertake such a burden, but if I ever do, I can only hope my manhood may be shown as clear as was yours.

Yours Sincerely
John Woodbury.

HK318
Letter, handwritten in ink.

201 BEACON STREET.
Boston, June 24 1893.

My dear Mr. Knowlton,

I want to express to you my appreciation of your efforts in behalf of the Commonwealth in the recent trial at New Bedford.

A moral conviction of the guilt of the prisoner, despite the talk of the newspapers, is almost universal among intelligent people, whom I meet.

Your closing argument I consider just, honest and convincing, a splendid effort. I am very respectfully Yours

Francis B. Harrington

HK319
Letter, handwritten in ink.

53 Equitable Building
Boston, June 24, 1893.

My dear Mr. Knowlton,

I wish, if a little late, to express to you my admiration for the very able manner in which you presented the case of Commonwealth v Lizzie Boyden to the jury. It is the general opinion among people whom I meet, members of the bar and others that that was the one thing that came up to the subject and the occasion. If the newspapers had treated your effort as it deserved and had less to say about the commonplace efforts of some others engaged in the trial I should never have troubled you with this note.

Success, I know, is sometimes associated with results, but results do not always measure ability, and I can assure you that you have received much sincere praise from multitudes who have no personal acquaintance with you. I enclose you some editorial comments taken from the Boston Transcript which I thought you might not have seen.

Sincerely yours,
T. E. Grover.

HK320
Letter, handwritten in ink.

Coventry, Vermont, June 24/93

Attorney General Knowlton:
Dear Sir;

I am a woman away up in Vermont, but I am also an invalid and have much time for thought and reading. I have read the Borden trial very closely from the first, the arguments pro & con and have seen very few papers but the Boston Daily Journal, so you see that naturally the bias would come on the side of Miss Borden's innocence as that paper has been very partisan in its utterances.

From the first I have been convinced of her guilt and to my mind your conduct has been impartial, courteous and with a desire to do your duty. I cannot see why so many profess to see that she has been badgered, or forced into misstatements. An innocent person retains the consciousness of innocence. She is a member of my own church (Congl') but I know how often religion cloaks the vilest heart. I know also how relent- less and unreasoning is jealousy. There are in this world and since this trial I have been led to believe they may be rare, because so many refuse or cannot see it in the case of Miss Borden there are certain combinations of traits that produce the subtlest kind of torture for their friends who live with them while outwardly their conduct is irreproachable. Whether Miss Borden was one of those there is no one now to testify.

I am glad for your sake she was acquitted in the state of public feeling and I believe that you are also, but if she is guilty "God can bring every secret thing to light." I have written this as one of God's great family may write to another. I think you have done your duty nobly and that your pleas were eloquent and true to the facts of the case. Many in this little town believe as I do, and the end has not come. Should she ever be proved innocent I shall always maintain that it was one of the seemingly impossible things that sometimes are made possible, but that the facts were strong enough against her to warrant the belief of so many in her guilt.

Yours respectfully
Elvira M. Daggett

HK321
Letter, handwritten in ink.

Providence R.I.
25 June 1893.

Dear Mr. Knowlton

   I enclose a few extracts from many favorable notices of your conduct of the "Borden" trial.
I have no doubt of your utter weariness of the whole business, and so I will not afflict you with a long letter, as indeed I have no right to claim your attention at all, but I could not forbear to give you some slight intimation that at least one person who knew you was completely loyal, and not by any means dominated by the silly "Boston gush" that has broken forth from that prolific fountain, in such copious profusion. I am glad to say that I am somewhat acquainted with a few of the criminal lawyers of this City and I have not heard any of them say but what your course during the whole trying ordeal was just what it should have been, and only what might have been expected from the chief law officer of the commonwealth connected with the case. Hoping the "Borden" mystery will be speedily made plain and your whole course fully vindicated -, if indeed it needed any vindication -I am,

Yours sincerely,
V. B. Kinney

HK322
Letter, handwritten in ink.

PASTOR'S STUDY
FIRST CONGREGATIONAL CHURCH
JACKSON, MICHIGAN
June 28, 1893

Dear Mr. Knowlton

   I have read through your remarkable summing-up in the Borden case. I cannot well forbear to express my astonishment and admiration for that masterly piece of work. An unsuccessful prosecution conducted against so great public prejudice with such ability, might easily react against the prosecutor even if pursued as a duty. To have conducted it so as to present the full strength of the case in such an array of argument as will take its place among the great annals of criminal law, and at the same time to deserve and win the respect and admiration even of a prejudiced public and of the defense itself, was a triumph of oratory and of legal skill that ought to send its author to the highest place his profession can boast.

It is spoken of even in this region among lawyers, in the most extravagant terms of praise.

May I be permitted as a sometime friend to extend my sincere congratulations

Very Truly
William Curtis Stiles

HK323
Letter, handwritten in ink.

Dorchester, June 29, 1893.

Hon. H. M. Knowlton
                Dist. Atty. Bristol Co.
Dear Sir:

Possibly you are too busy to read even letters of approval in relation to the Great Borden trial, if, in fact, you care to hear anything more about it any way. Probably consciousness of duty done - of devotion to the <u>truth</u>. in the matter may make unnecessary if not unwelcome any words of commendation for that devotion, so manifest to my mind. But there has been so much pernicious unthinking nonsensical criticism of the prosecution on the one hand and praise of defense on the other that a word of approval now and then may in some degree counteract this pernicious and careless condemnation and and make it less likely to be a shield of guilt, or a peril to innocence and justice in the future.

The people are not done with talking of this case, nor will the pre- sent generation cease to think about it, and I predict that as the months go by the belief will continue to grow in the popular mind that after all the splendor of the acquittal <u>your theory was the truth</u>, and the spirit of merciless and unthinking criticism of all who had to do with pressing the investigation will give way to a feeling of self condemnation of these critics for having been possibly and in my opinion <u>unquestionably</u> instrumental in defeating justice. In discussing the force of circumstances proved, I have discovered that to certain minds the strongest evidence in the case is no evidence at all. No amount of their kind of thinking will ever give to such minds a perception of the force of the circumstances in this case, while to minds differently constituted and educated, capable of <u>candidly obeying their own logical conclusions</u>, the evidence would have been all but conclusive, if not quite so, of guilt. This peculiar character of the evidence handicapped you with the jury you had. Had it been composed of men educated in the common sense processes of reasoning necessary to "get anywhere" in such an investigation there must have been a different result. As things were it might have been different but for the death penalty. When such a jury is appealed to as by Mr. Robinson in this case, - <u>That the acquittal of deft though guilty would not be much of a mistake</u>, because they would have a life time in which to compensate society for such a mistake it requires pretty positive evidence to hold them to duty. The jury probably <u>held to his view on this</u> point. To my mind the evidence is startling in its force and distinctness.

These murders were done by <u>one</u> of <u>two</u> parties. Either by the party <u>in the house</u>, or by some one, a stranger from outside. Call the outsider best fitted of all men in the world to do what was done and escape, by the name of Smith. Call the party inside Jones. Now it was Jones or Smith. This we <u>know</u>. If Smith did it Jones did n't, If Smith did n't Jones did. Jones was there we know and could have done it easily as compared with Smith. Jones says it was Smith. But Jones did not see Smith there or see a track or trace of him Jones was there but did not hear or see anything of Smith or any vestige of him or of a motive. To believe Smith did it, we must believe almost the <u>impossible</u>, - <u>physically impossible</u>. To believe Jones did it we have nothing impossible and nothing in its character improbable. To believe Smith did it we must believe a stranger with enmity to kill Mrs. B. and hate to hack her would have chosen that most perilous hour of the day for the deed. For he could not know the where- abouts of the members of the household nor their habits nor the habits of neighbors market men &ct. Could not have known but that some one was coming into the hall or chamber or any other hiding place at any moment. We must believe that Smith was reckless of his own safety thus to enter a house at that morning hour, and kill Mrs. B. and then hide and wait for his other intended victim, not knowing but that he must wait until night and that the alarm might be given any moment and the house be taken possession of.

We must believe he hid himself somewhere in some small place without stain- ing anything (impossible) that after waiting an hour or so he came forth to slay Mr. B. not knowing where the other members of the house- hold were, and though a stranger so take in the plan of the house that he could approach Mr. B. and strike as the assassin did.

We must believe that Smith would have wasted time any second of which might cost his life - hacking his dead victim Mrs. B. and then again waste time more precious hacking Mr. B. We see the assassin, be it <u>Jones</u> or <u>Smith</u>, <u>had a sense of security</u>. How could Smith have had a sense of security.

We must believe that a 200 lb person could fall and not be heard by either of the two parties then <u>in</u> the house - one certainly - or just outside. We must believe a person struck facing her assailant would utter no cry to be heard by Jones who was, at the time, going around from room to room perhaps, doors all open except outside doors.

We must believe that Smith in some way covered the marks upon him, washed of his hands &c. or went forth as he was, without being seen by Jones who was out in the yard or by any of the people around who saw so many other things around the Borden house that morning.

We must believe Smith had the same enmity and hate for Mr. B. that he had for Mrs. B. or else that he killed Mr. B. to cover his tracks - to avoid detection of his first crime? Would Smith have waited an hour or so for such a purpose? Which, Jones or Smith would have had such a reason for killing Mr. B.? Now is it easy to believe Smith did all these things without a vestige of evidence of sight or sound that he was there, not the slightest bloodspot on any thing any where, neither in his hiding place in closet or corner, or on the floors or doors or outside, not a <u>thing</u> disturbed to indicate anybody but Jones had been there all this time. For which would it have been easier, Smith the stranger of which there is no trace whatever inside or outside, or for <u>Jones</u> who was <u>there</u> and perfectly familiar with the premises inside and outside, and with the habits of the family and neighborhood and the whereabouts of every thing and every body. Of which is there the most reasonable doubt? Of both? That cannot be. Of Jones? Then it must have been Smith. Of Smith? Then it must have been <u>Jones</u>. Without noticing in detail how much easier at <u>every</u> point it would have been for Jones, especially with what motive was clearly shown, there are some very queer things about these deeds which the guilt of Smith will not explain but the guilt of Jones will explain. Who of all the world but Jones could have so feared to face Mr. Borden that he would risk his neck by waiting an hour to kill him? If Lizzie <u>was</u> "coming <u>slowly</u> from the barn" what about the <u>groan she heard</u> in the house? How a jury could fail to see the force of the circumstances, or could so ignore it, if the did see it, is a mystery to me. Possibly their heads are clearer than mine.

Pardon my writing. I have written ten times as much as I ought even if any can be excusable. I am told by a Boston Editor that expressions of suspicions that "Jones" was guilty are libels. If a deft in libel suit could prove his statement it would be a novel re-opening of the case. If Bridget Sullivan could now be charged there might be a more effectual <u>raking over</u>. I have often wondered whether or not there was an old <u>outhouse vault</u> in the yard or barn, which has <u>never been searched</u>. I have wondered why Lizzie's Uncle <u>Harrington</u> was not called.

But I beg pardon for writing so long, if at all.
Respectfully,
G. B. Buffington

HK324
Letter, handwritten in ink.

Concord, N. H. June 1893

Bro Knowlton

I read your masterly argument as well as those of Gov. Robinson but had before come to the conclusion from the evidence that while it might possibly have been otherwise, there is no reasonable doubt of guilt - that both could have been killed without her knowledge is a little too steep. My purpose in writing is to suggest whether Mr Borden may not have been killed by Morse.

It is very improbable that he came to the house [?] [?] over night within a few feet of his niece, without once speaking with her - If she is guilty as the evidence shows, she did not become a murderer by a single step and their relations may have been such with each other, as to eventually break down her purity and moral sense.

If the reporter is to be trusted she showed more anxiety when he was called, than is to be accounted for by anything to which he testified.

I suppose from Mr. Borden's habits he might be expected to return to the house about the time he did return, and Morse govern himself accordingly.

On what legal principle the court could strike out the purchasing of a deadly poison the day before is beyond my comprehension.

I never knew a case of such or so much manufacturing of public opinion by newspaper correspondents (or could [?] for no doubt) in my life.

From your first movement against her, you and the governments case were assailed through the press.

Perjury in behalf of the defense was to be expected when there was so much money to buy up witnesses I regret that money or position should have turned aside the course of justice but you and your associate Mr. Moody have acquitted yourselves right well.

Very respectfully,
C. R. Morrison

HK325
Letter, handwritten in ink.

Phila. June 1893

Gentlemen of this cort i will just say that i wer talking With a medium last night and she said that no One but that lizzie borden Did that crime and if she were not condemend and punished that the Hole cort would be condemened it shall be burned down at the next term of cort Fire started from outside and all burned up in it for anyone with an Eye can plainly see that no one but her did it as the mother was found to be stiff cold and blood clod- ed as it were. The one i were talking to is no bluff either she can tell the name collar hight size and all she dose not Work for less than 25 Dollars if a murder had of done the deed he never Would of left the watch and chain on him an money in his pocket also not a thing in the house was disturbed and when she gave the alarm she never shed a tear not fainted that showes she is guilty. why did she wait till the crime was Done before she burned the Dress why did she not make some effort to look for Mrs. borden when she found her farther dead Why did she say she was out when she knew she was up stairs dusting the spair room do Justice or suffer afterwards for she is guilty.

HK326
Letter, handwritten in ink.

COOLEY'S HOTEL
Springfield,Mass. Aug 2 1892

Dst Attorney Knowlton
        Fall River Mass.
Dr Sir;

Was reading your closing argument in Republican from which I get an idea which I commend to your consideration and investigation. You said "Then she takes out her things to begin to <u>iron</u>. Bridget went upstairs leaving Lizzie ironing at 3 minutes before 11 nearer to her father etc.etc. In five minutes her father is dead.- "Prussic Acid out of the way how was the deed to be accomplished By <u>Pistol</u>? <u>No</u> and so the <u>steel</u> was used,-We have never yet found the wrap that covered Lizzie <u>Nor found the hatchet</u>" I submit that you have not found the wrap <u>or hatchet</u> because none were used.

<u>Acting upon impulse and sizing the opportunity at hand a flat iron was used</u> with its sharp corner or edges. Sharp enough and heavy enough to cut the hairs and skull bones, but to crush and bruise rather than clean cut the veins and arteries and tissue therefore there was probably no immediate <u>spurting</u> of blood Some witness said there was something seen in the stove, the ashes of something of something burnt. Could it not be a cloth used to wipe the blood from the iron <u>She did not need the time</u> to go down cellar for hatchet or axe
<u>Look at those irons</u>

Yours, <u>Transient</u>

(Note: The content of this letter indicates that the author's date of "August 2, 1892" is incorrect.)

HK327
Letter, handwritten in ink.

**UNITY CHURCH,
NORTH EASTON, MASS.
W. L. CHAFFIN, MINISTER**

Aug. 10, 1893.

Dear Mr. Knowlton,

I have often intended writing you a word to express my feeling of perfect confidence in your honor and fair dealing in the great trial you conducted, and of admiration at what I regard as your <u>masterly</u> presentation of the case at last. It has given me great pleasure to stand by you more than once in discussions on the subject, and to do what I could to assure friends that your treatment of Miss Borden would be honorable and manly even if severe and searching.

As for myself I must say that until the attempt to buy poison, the burglary incident, the note, the extra locked door, the noise necessarily made when Mrs. B. fell, the burning of the dress, the search for sinker etc, are more satisfactorily explained, I cannot acquit her of a hand at least in the affair.

I know of her saying in a house where she visited in New Bedford, when the subject of step mother came up - "I have a step mother and I <u>hate</u> her." Rennie told me that Marshall Hilliard told him that he (Hilliard) found the missing things of Mrs. B. after the "burglary" in Lizzie's room.

Did you ever hear (you have no doubt heard everything & more too) that a relative of Lizzie died in Providence & Lizzie soon appeared & claimed the white skirts of her friend as having been promised her & <u>took</u> them, <u>including the best one which was then on the body</u>, before it was in the coffin! A friend of mine heard it from the dead girl's cousin, the aunt of the deceased who took care of her having told her. I heard that yestedays. The fact that Mr. Borden once was an undertaker & the girls helped him, makes it easier to believe this.

I have often wanted to tell you that I belong to those who stand by you, both as to your motive, your manner and your great ability in the conduct of the case.

       Faithfully Yours
       W. L. Chaffin.

If you have a copy of your plea in convenient form will you kindly send me one.

HK328
Letter, handwritten in ink.

       New Bedford Nov. 30th

Mr. Knowlton:

    Dear Sir. In your speech at the close of Lizzie Bordons trial before being sent up to await the action of the grand jurors, you made some very singular remarks.

    "All the devils on the earth or under the earth could not make me believe that some" men in your standing would have made them, but you, a stump of pigheadedness, "I could believe it of".

      From an advocate of justice

1893 Undated Documents

HK329
Transcript, typewritten

OUIJA

Q. What about the Borden case?
A. Axe - Turkey red - vest - suds - stairs.

Q. Was it her father's vest?
A. His vest

Q. What about Turkey red?
A. Paint

Q. What dress did she wear?
A. No dress

Q. Didn't she wear anything?
A. Yes, trousers.

Q. Who wore them?
A. She

Q. Bridget?
A. No; Lizzie

Q. What did she do with the things?
A. Bury

Q. Where?
A. Yard -

Q. What part of the yard?
A. Cellar - furnace - underneath earth

Q. Are they buried there?
A. Yes.

Q. All?
A. No; some burned

Q. Where did she burn them?
A. Kitchen - wet clothes - trousers bury

Q. Did she kill both her father and mother?
A. Undoubtedly

Q. Did she bury the axe?
A. No - burn handle

Q. What did she do with the rest of it?
A. Box

Q. You mean she put it in a box?
A. Yes

Q. Will they be found?
A. No - too sharp

Q. Who hid them?
A. J. Morse hid things under the earth

Q. Does Dr. Bowen know anything about it?
A. All

Q. Did Lizzie tell him?
A. In her chamber let it out

Q. When did Morse bury things?
A. Thursday - 8 P.M.

Q. Did Morse spend Thursday night there?
A. Went out to hotel at 9 P.M.

Q. What about note to Mrs. Borden?
A. No none

Q. Lizzie made it up?
A. All

Q. Was Mrs. Reagan's story true?
A. Yes

Q. Will she be found guilty?
A. Never

Q. Will Emma's testimony save her?
A. Lies

Q. Were the hat and trousers buried in yard with Mr. and Mrs. Borden's clothes?
A. No

Q. Are the things still buried in the cellar?
A. Still

Q. Could we find them?
A. Yes

Q. Any trace?
A. Puddle

Q. Where?
A. Cellar

Q. Puddle of what?
A. Mud

Q. Where?
A. Cellar

Q. What part?
A. Furnace

Q. What about Morse and vest?
A. Stairs - J.M. knows

Q. What about Prussic acid?
A. First intent

Q. What about furs?
A. No furs

Q. Didn't Morse help?
A. Innocent

Q. Any one help?
A. No accomplice

Q. Why did she do it?
A. 200 M

Q. Do you mean money?
A. Money

Q. Will the verdict be "Not Guilty?"
A. Perhaps

Q. Will the jury disagree?
A. Who knows?

Q. _____?
A. J. Morse - vest

Q. What about Morse's vest?
A. Stairs - note

Q. What about note?
A. Investment

Q. What about investment?
A. Mother

Q. Investment for Mrs. Borden?
A. Talked over

Q. What became of it?
A. Murder

Q. Did Lizzie find the investment in her father's pocket?
A. Heard.

Q. Has Morse got it now?
A. No

Q. Has Lizzie?
A. No

Q. Was it burned?
A. No

Q. Was it buried?
A. No

Q. Where is it?
A. Led to murder

Q. Is it now in vest?
A. No note - darn!

Q. What became of vest?
A. Investment

Q. And Morse knows of it?
A. Yes - talked over night before with Mr. and Mrs. Borden.

Q. Lizzie heard it?
A. Night

Q. Where was she?
A. Dining-room

Q. Hidden in the dining-room?
A. Accident

Q. You mean she heard by accident?
A. Yes

Q. She said nothing to Morse?
A. No

Q. What investment?
A. Mills

Q. What mills?
A. Real Estate

Q. Did Lizzie have a cat?
A. Yes - yellow cat - departed - violent

Q. Who killed it?
A. She - axe

Q. Whose lap did it jump into?
A. Jim Wilder - July 7 - 90.

Q. Where did he live?
A. No. 2 Second street, Fall River

Q. Whom did he tell it to?
A. Susy Wilder - she told it to Tish Thomas - manicure - at Rosalie Butler's - Tremont street.

Q. What hotel?
A. Fall River House

Q. What time did Lizzie murder her mother?
A. 9:30

Q. What did she do afterwards?
A. Worked

Q. What time did she murder her father?
A. 10:45

Q. What did she do afterwards?
A. Put trousers that she wore in tub in cellar sink

Q. Why weren't they found?
A. Stupid

Q. What did she do after putting the trousers in the cellar sink?
A. Then dressed and called

Q. What about barn?
A. No barn

Q. What else did she wear besides trousers?
A. Hat

Q. What color hat?
A. Dark

Q. Any gloves?
A. No gloves

Q. Anything on chest and waist?
A. Nothing but trousers and hat

Q. What about paint?
A. Turkey red - smooch on dress burnt - from mop-board in kitchen – May, 1892.

Q. Will she be convicted?
A. Perhaps by Russell - and Bridget at door

Q. Who took trousers from tub in cellar?
A. Morse took trousers from tub night of murder

Q. When did Lizzie burn the handle of the hatchet?
A. Immediately - then put ashes on hatchet

Q. What about suds?
A. Vermicelli - suds - soup-tureen - Wednesday dinner

Q. Why did she put suds in the soup?
A. Sick

Q. Mother and father sick?
A. Yes

Q. Did Lizzie eat any?
A. Tasted

Q. What about vest?
A. Father's vest - stew-oven - Uncle John vest - going up stairs murder day

Q. Anything else?
A. No - tired - see Herald - Emma.

Q. Did Lizzie wear a water-proof?
A. No - pa's trousers and hat.

HK330
Letter, handwritten in ink.

The murder was the work of a <u>woman</u>. A man kills & stops. This murder- er killed the victims half a dozen times.

Miss Borden on the morning of the crime was altogether too clean with her white hands and orderly dress – she what more natural than that she should have blood on her dress? A lady says "how could she help having blood upon her dress or shoes if she had acted as a woman should?" She was too well groomed.

Her townspeople & acquaintances by their lack of sympathy indicate that they consider her <u>capable</u> of the crime - a very strong indictment -

Bridget the servant knows more than she tells & has probably been bought off - The office of public prosecutor is the most thankless - The whole pressure of the public is brought to bear upon him, as though he were attempting by artful means to entrap the innocent - Counsel & police are chased up like mad dogs when all they are doing is to bring the guilty to punishment as their duty demands.

Lizzie Borden may escape but she will still remain as the most probable murderer - 3 or 400,000 will do much.

N.Y.

HK331
Letter, handwritten in ink.

Commonwealth of Massachusetts,
DISTRICT ATTORNEY'S OFFICE,
Eastern District.

W. H. MOODY	ALDEN P. WHITE
HAVERHILL	SALEM
DISTRICT ATTORNEY	ASSISTANT

My dear Mr. Pillsbury,

I readily detected the difference between the genuine and perverted announcement. I saw some things which, in yesterday's Globe, I was reported as having said some weeks or months ago. so far as they contain anything beyond a mere statement that I had and expected to have no connection with the case, they are without a shadow of foundation.

From some things which have happened and did happen here yesterday I am beginning to share your opinion of newspaper reporters.

Very Respectively Yours,
W. H. Moody

HK332
Letter, handwritten in ink.

That "note."

Of the 80,000 people of Fall River, not one, during all the ten months, has ever come forward, in the interests of justice, friendship, or humanity, to say that they
(1)   <u>wrote</u> that note,
or <u>caused</u> it to be written,
or <u>sent</u> it – or by whom;
(2)   Nobody has ever come forward to say that a note for Mrs. Borden was intrusted to them that day, and was delivered, & to whom;
(3)   Nobody of the <u>hundreds or thousands acquainted with Mrs. B.</u>, or with her marked personality, for 30 years' past, has ever come forward to say that they spoke with her, or met her, or saw her, on the streets, coming or going, on that day.

(Rev.) R. M. Devens.

HK333
Letter, handwritten in ink.

Not a Crank

If a note had been sent to Mrs. Borden why dont the party sending it come forward every body in Christindom knows of the Borden murder. If Mr. Borden had enemies why should Mrs Borden be murdered how could a person or persons be in or about the house in the earlier part of the morning when every body was astir & be waiting in the house till Bridget took her morning nap and Miss Borden was looking for sinkers in the barn an usual time in the day for a domestic to be taking a nap, in the forenoon If well & why was there no preparation for the noonday meal & if some one unknown did it would they carry the weapon away with them they could not have gotten far with it and Miss Emma Borden absent these are knotty questions for the defense to answer If Lizzie is innocent why dont she get up in court & say so she cant appear very guilty <u>If she is realy innocent.</u>

A constent reader of the trial

HK334

Letter, handwritten in ink.

Dist Atty Knowlton
   Dear Sir
   I think if you have a few more able boddied officers sherrifs & lawyers come to your rescue & suggestion you may be able to carry your point of conviction in the Borden case.
   I would not let ones Life suffer just for the notoriety of being the big Lion for this is the way you have seemed to the whole world excepting the Professional you & Judge Blaisdell better let some other one try the case that has not the sharp pregidist shown by you.

HK335

Letter, handwritten in ink.

Much stress is laid by the defense upon the fact that no blood appears upon the defendant. If she were innocent she would be bloody. Coming in from the barn & confronted with her bleeding & stricken father her natural impulse would have been as an affectionate child to rush to his aid raised his head or in some way assist. The fact that she did not go near him (as shown by ~~want~~ absence of blood) & never even stepped close enough to her wounded parent to soil shoes or dress is unnatural. Proves too much.

William Henry Moody, 35th U.S. Secretary of the Navy, 45th Attorney General of the United States, Associate Justice of the U.S. Supreme Court, 1907.
Prints and Photographs Division, Library of Congress.

HK336
Letter, handwritten in ink.

Attorney for Prosecution:
                    Lizzie Borden Case.

Dear Sir:-Does it not occur to you sir - that it being almost an utter impossibility for any other person than Miss Lizzie Borden to have been the murderer of Mr. & Mrs. Borden - that this young woman who has shown such wonderful nerve all thro' her imprisonment & trial might have had foresight and nerve enough to have stripped herself entirely nude to avoid bloodstains upon her clothing, and afterwards burned the dress with paint on it for effect? What think you?
    Is it not something to think about?
                            Curiosity

HK337
Letter, handwritten in ink.

Cooley Hotel
Springfield Mass

Dist Attorney Knowlton
    New Bedford Mass
Dear Sir;
    You may remember that I wrote you from here several months ago suggesting the <u>flat iron</u> theory as a probable weapon in the Borden murders (if done by Lizzie). By an odd coincidence I am here again to hear the report of the verdict- "<u>Not Guilty</u>". for the reason that you could not make any connection of the <u>hatchet or axe theory,</u> either with Miss Lizzie or with the wounds. Miss Lizzie was inseparably connected with the flat irons by her own words or statement at different times, and by Bridget and Miss Alice Russell when asked on the stand "What else did you see in the cupboard besides a part of the old dress." answered "<u>flat irons</u>". Flat irons all but spoke to you in this case, but "having ears you did not hear. and justice is buried with the old people. It only remained for you to connect the flat irons with the wounds to make Lizzie's conviction certain.
    The testimony of those Doctors - the nature of the wounds - the different dimensions of the cuts - the <u>one sided bevels</u> - the breaking in of the skull - the <u>number</u> of blows, a small percentage of which went through - <u>the triangu-</u>

lar cut xc. xc. although this testimony was given by the medical men laboring under the delusion of the <u>hatchet</u> theory and trying to confirm it satisfies me that if the flat iron theory had been given due consideration the veil would have been lifted from the mystery.

Of course it is too late now although there is probably evidence of blood on a flat iron that a chemist could find around the Borden House now, and untill it is established there is danger of some body else being hung for these murders - some crank by confession or other person by force of circumstances to develop.

Yours truly,
Observer

HK338
Letter, handwritten in ink.

Mr. H.M. Knowlton
        New Bedford
Dear Sir.

    this is not what you might term a letter but a Brotherly Warning in your desperate effort to convict poor Lizzie Borden dont forget poor Marston, an unseen Spirritt stoped him in his desperate effort to convict poor crazy Freeman, [?] Taylor was called away rather than poor innocent Thizl Should be hung. Hundreds of Such cases might be recalled every year, you know that Lizzie Borden is not guilty. why dont you arrest Brigett Sulavan and may be rather than be hung herself she would tell of some Irish enemy of poor Mr Bordens that she Secreted in that house that he might get revenge. her chances were good the opertunities offered her were all Suficient. a man of rather low degree was seen leaveing the House. Miss Borden never had anything to do with low coarse looking men. then is it imposable that someone about that house might not secreted that man in the House untill his time came to commit the awfull deed, why is not that man look for that wanted to rent the Store. he must of been a rumseller or of some low degraded Buisness or Mr Borden would not of Sent him away So abrubtly. do you know he was not a particular Friend of Brigett Sullavans I guess not. your chances will not be hurt for the attorney Generalship by doing your duty if it does hang an Irishman. I hope Brother Knowlton that you are not so affraid of offending Irish voters that you will not thourghly investigate this Irish posibility. I repeate it this Irish Posability. Lizzie is not Guilty.

Your Brother

HK339
Letter, handwritten in lead.

Sad as is the fact that horrible murders are on the increase - a still sadder fact stares us in the face as one <u>cause</u>.

Men learned in the law instead of searching for the facts in mysterious murder cases sometimes use art and trickery to so muddle and mistify ajury, that their client is finally set free to repete their diabolical deeds on a helpless people!

While a lawyer should do all that is honest to clear a client of an unjust charge, yet when he undertakes to fasten his client's crime upon even an unknown person, he is worse than the criminal.

The success, or even the labored attempt of Attorneys to clear criminals under the plea of "duty to their clients", right or wrong, is an encourager of crime; and if there is large gains for winning, it matters not how high the position of the attorney for the criminal, it is all used as a means of strong force on an honest jury, who do not see the greed for money, that is as great as that of the criminal, therefore, against their judgement, and out of respect for an attorney of high position & great renown, they yield to lawyer sophistry, that they cannot combat.

The attempt to identify the Portuguese who killed Miss Manchester as the murderer of the Bordens, and perhaps to get him to testify that he <u>was</u> the murderer of both of Lizzie Borden's parents, may be made. It is very clear that the Portuguese loves money well enough to be hired to swear that he killed the Bordens, since he committed murder for money, for while all liars are not murderers, all murders are liars for sale.

Jurors might be talked into believing him, even in the face of such facts as Lizzie Borden telling one person that she was in the bath at the time and another that she was "in the barn" - that she was <u>not</u> in the barn was shown by it being impossible for anyone to have been where there were no traces of feet until the searchers were there, and found that no one could have been there without having left some tracks.

That the Portuguese who killed Miss Manchester was about the size of Officer Hyde, looks as though there was a plan on foot to get that criminal to swear that he was in the closet that was in the hall.

A thousand cents, or no money inducement, but simply a promise that he should be cleared of the Manchester murder when condemnation is shure, if he does not tell this particular salvation lie, that would be expected to clear Lizzie Borden, may be contemplated.

Whether George A. Petty who testified that "the blood was fresh at 11 o'clock on Mr. Borden, and dry on Mrs. Borden," will be approached with money to induce him to disremember these facts, remains to be seen.

Perhaps the Dr. and the lady friend who were so securely locked in a room on important business with Lizzie Borden, and kept the officer waiting, will be able to inform the public whether this lady friend wore away some of Lizzie's clothing or sewed them up in one of the matresses or feather beads?

That people do not burn up old dresses when they are solied, even with paint, as they make just as good scrub cloths, every woman of even a want of economy can see. But that pains should be taken to carry an old dress to a kitchen closet to deposit, and take pains to rip and tare, and burn, shows motives that can not can not blind the most obtuse, since well to do people either give cast off garments from any cause, to servants, poor women to cut over for children, or relegate them to depositories where they can be had as window or floor cloths for cleaning. Bridget Sullivan may be able to tell whether a well to do young woman's blue dress was so completely covered with paint that it was not even fit to be put into an economical New England house rag-bag? Perhaps Lizzie's sister might be induced to give more of an elaborate opinion about the burning of that dress, and why she considered it was "one of the worst things her sister could possibly have done."

The story told by Lizzie that "a note had been brought by a boy that induced her mother to go to visit a sick friend" and a want of surprise when her mother was found so horribly murdered, is in keeping with a stolid appearance of one who had pretended to be ill, when her father and mother were suffering from the effects of poison!

A mangled cat or dog in ones own family could not be seen by women of the family without emotion and the stolid indifference of Lizzie witnessing such horrible scenes, could only be shown by one capable of committing the crimes! This is not the time or place to consider the combination of motives that induced coolly studied crime. But it is in place to assert that one not sure of property would have at leased grabbed Mr. Borden's watch, and thus gained somthing for his trouble if frightened in his work - but here we are confronted with the fact that Mrs. Borden had been killed some time previously, so that the blood on her face was dry, and yet although there had been no haste, there had been no robbery of valuables. Is there a person who ever had a dozen thoughts who would. believe that any knave would kill Mrs. Borden, and then wait for the uncertain return of Mr. Borden however great his enmity for Mr. Borden? As the uncle was not at .home when Mr. Borden was murdered, perhaps he was when Mrs. Borden was - perhaps one ax was used by two different persons, at different times of day? The public would not object to information regarding the time of day that the kind "protector of the orphan girls" left the house on that morning and all his moves until he returned after Mr. Borden's pillows were so unusually and kindly arranged on the lounge by Miss Lizzie, who no doubt told her father that Mrs. Borden "had gone to see the sick friend".

While it is true that the lies of identity by the Warden's, and lie confession of crime by Abbott, hung the latter, no jury knowing that this "cue" was taken by the defense to influence them, would believe that the Manchester murderer was also the Bordens murderer. A knave among the jury may hang them, but eventually truth would reign supreme, and a woman murderer would not be set free to marry and give to the world, children to follow in the footsteps of their illustrious(?) mother.

Is it not about time that the propigation of known criminals cease?

HK340
Letter, handwritten in ink, with newspaper clipping affixed.

The people in Fall River do not burn up old dresses because a little paint may stain them. Certainly not such a family as the Bordens. When a dress is spoiled for wear, in the front, the back being still good is, usually, made up into aprons, dusters & etc., and the useless parts put in the rag- bag to be sold. There is not, probably, a house in F. R. or any other place, that does not keep a ragbag. It is absurd to declare that any woman ever burned up an old dress, that was available for so many purposes in house- keeping. The trouble is to <u>keep in rags</u> for general use. Even tho' I am boarding, I do not burn up anything that will do for "house cloths & etc. I give them to <u>housekeepers</u> who are glad to get them. And what if Lizzie did buy red paint before the murder? The question is did she <u>use</u> it, and what for. Let them produce the articles. Why not burn the skirt in the presence of witnesses? - <u>They</u> could testify that it was spoiled with "<u>paint</u>!" That was the object in doing it.- For the reason given, the Bordens never burned up anything that could be used in necessary housework. To them it would be extravagent waste. I believe that the accused did the murder; but thus far I see nothing but acquital for her. As she is of my own sex, I think I shall be glad of it, - altho' the crime is so henious it ought to be punished.

Yours for justice
D.B.

Clipping:

> These paint spots form one of the strongest points in the case for the defendant. Lizzie Borden's counsel will admit that she burned a skirt some days after the murder but they propose to prove that the skirt really did have paint upon it, and that was not the first time a stained dress was burned in the Borden house. They claim to have ready the testimony of a shopkeeper, that Lizzie Borden bought red paint from him a few days previous to the murders. They will make a strong point out of the fact that Lizzie burned the skirt in the presence of two witnesses. "If she were guilty," they argue, "would she not have destroyed the dress in secret?"

HK341
Letter, handwritten in lead.

When officer Fleet asked Miss Lizzie if she had any suspision of anyone that would kill her father and mother was the answer she gave (that she was not her mother) an answer that expressed sympathy or unfriendly feeling toward her murdered Step mother. Why was she so anoyed when the officers wer trying to find out who had so brutally murdered her father and mother and Did she manifest that willingness to assist them in the performance of their duties that an innocent person would in such an awful Case. I dont think she did. To the contrary she says she wished the men would keep away and not ask so many questions. Would not the officers of the law been welcome visitors at either one of your homes if you had suddenly found your father and mother brutally murdered, as Lizzie had found her parents. And would you not assist them in every way in your power to detect the asassin. And I beleive either one of us would do this without resorting to such unresonable falshoods as the defendant has. Why dont she tell the truth. it would be just as easy for her to do so. I can see no reason for her telling such falshoods except the reason that the truth would surely convict her of this awful crime. Some may say Miss Lizzie was confused or dased by being questioned on this matter. But do you think that she who has not shed a teer even at the first sight of her butchered father or shown any emotion since, would be any more likely to be so confused or dazed than Bridget who has been put to as severe a test in this case as Lizzie. And I think you all beleive what Bridget has told us to be the plain truth. I think she has told us all she knows about this terrible affair. When Mr Borden returned to his home on that fatal day he was let in the front door by Bridget who saw Lizzie standing at the top of the front stairs. This was a few minutes before 11 O Clock. After Mr Borden came in Lizzie came down stairs and tells her father that her mother had received a note from a sick friend and gone out. Then she says her father took of his shoes and put on his slippers and lay down on the sofa. This we know was not so. His shoes wer on when found dead. Then she goes into the dineing room and gets ready to do her ironing. And Bridget says Lizzie was ironing when she went up stairs to her room on the third floor. But immediatly after Bridget had gone Lizzie suddenly conceives the idea that she had better get that lead to make some sinkers. So she drops her ironing (most surely in a very heated condition for the ladies all say ironing is very hot work.) And goes out to the barn goes up staires in one of the hottest places that she could find up under that roof that the sun shone directly uppon (as it was nearly noon) And one of the hottest days we had in the month of August. And she (as I have said before) in a heated condition from the effects of standing over hot flat irons, stays (as she says) at least 15 or 20 minutes eating pears or looking for lead in a box that stood on the work bench. This box she tells us about we find to be a basket a great deal larger than the box she describes and contained no lead. We find a box containing some lead down stairs where she could have got all she wanted for sinkers in 2 or 3 minutes. But did she get any of that lead. She says she stood at the west window some time straightening some of it. What did she do with what she straightened. did she bring it to the house or what did she do with it. I dont think she can tell what she done with it. If she went out there to get lead why did she tell some that she was out there after Iron and others that it was tin or zinc to fix her window. They tell me the windows are all in perfect order through that whole house. When Lizzie called Bridget she says somebody has killed father and wished Bridget would look up stairs and see if they had killed Missis Borden, For she thought she heard her come in. Now if Lizzie had been out in the barn since her father came home when could she heard Missis Borden come in. You know she told her father just before she went out to the barn that Missis Borden had gone out. so she could not have come in before this time. When Lizzie gave the alarm why did she call Bridget and not Missis Borden. If either one of you should find your father brutally murdered in his home do you think you would call the servant before calling your mother. I think not. Why did Lizzie say that she was in the kitchen when her father came home and later say that she was up stairs in her room. Dont you suppose she knew where she was. Bridget says when she let Mr Borden in at the front door she saw Lizzie up the front stairs and heard her speak. Now we all know that Lizzie stood at this time in plain sight of the prostrate form of Missis Borden. The note Lizzie tells about. Who wrote it or who delivered it at the house. no one knows. If there was any such note sent by a friend either the one that wrote it or the one that delivered it would been found before this time and gladly tell the public the circumstances. Which would forever put to rest what is now evident to be another untrue story told by Lizzie. If there had been a note sent to Missis Borden that morning the one that delivered it would been seen by Bridget or the neighbors. And if Missis Borden received any note calling her out she would surely told Bridget before she went out. Bridget says Missis Borden always told her when she was going out. Now we find there is no one but Lizzie that knows anything about this note, and she says her mother said it was from a sick friend. Now does it seem at all reasonable to suppose that Missis Borden would withhold the name of that sick friend or that Miss Lizzie would not ask who the sick friend was that want- ed to see Missis Borden. Under the same circumstances I know that I would inquire to know who it is that is sick. Now in regard to the Prussic acid Miss Lizzie tried to buy. there are three men who see and heard her ask for 10cts worth of Prussic Acid at D.R. Smiths Apothecary Store only a few days before the murder. Two of these men are clerks at that store. The other a medical student who had called there to see Mr Bence (the head cleark.) Each one of these gentlemen tell us on the stand that they know it was Lizzie who they saw ask for the poison. Then we have Mr Wright a New Bedford Apothecary tell us he thinks Lizzie came into his store and asked for Prussic Acid on a date that Lizzie and her sister Emma were in that city. Emma says she left Lizzie in New Bedford while she went over to Fairhaven. So it seems she tried to get the drug there as well as in Fall River. But did not succeed in getting it in either place. After failing to get the desired drug she desided to use the hatchet. I have not the least doubt in my mind (after seeing the wounds on the heads of these poor victims of the asassin) that they were inflicted by a woman. They wer blows that were not such as would be struck by a man. They were not the clear blows of the strong arm used to instruments of that kind. But the imperfect chopping and hacking that is characteristic of the weaker sex. What could been the motive for this awful deed. We fail to find that Mr or Missis Borden had an enemy in the world. But we hear that Lizzie Quarreled with her father and Stepmother about some property some time ago. And that there has been unpleasant feelings existing ever since. What do you suppose Mr Borden cut that slip from the news- paper for and preserved it so carefully in his pocket book. Dont it look as if he intended to coppy from it in the disposal of his property. and that Lizzie might knew he had preserved it and was afraid he might make practical use of it. I think he had preserved that peice of paper for a practical purpose that probably would not be as beneficial to Lizzie as she would like. In regard to conceiling the weppon who could had a better chance to do so than Lizzie. She could conceild it on her person. I dont think they serched her clothes or person. I must say that I fail to see how a person could or would enter that house at that time of the day, and go up stairs and kill Missis Borden. Then wait 1-1/2 Hours at least in the house where Lizzie was all the time And the possibility of other members of the family being there to. then kill Mr Borden and go out unseen or unheard through doores that were locked. And in plain sight of the neighbors and passers by who saw every one that went in or out of that house on that fatal day. And who is there in this world that would take such chances for the sake of revenge. With Lizzie in the house and Bridget out in the yard and neighbors all around that would be sure to see them. And now Mr. foreman and gentlemen after weighing the evidence presented in this case and circumstances connected with it, I feel that we have now a sad duty to perform. And that there is but one thing more for us to do in the conclusion of that duty, and that is to find a Bill against Lizzie A. Borden for the murder of her father, Andrew J. Borden, And step mother Abby Borden.

HK342
Note, handwritten in ink with newspaper illustration affixed.

"The most horrible of all crimes—a parri-"

<u>Dirty Coward</u> who attempts to destroy the reputation of an innocent woman. This mug should addorn the rogues galery instead of holding office in this commonwealth.

HK343
Letter, handwritten in ink.

9P.M.

My dear Mrs. Knowlton,
I have just finished reading Mr. Knowlton's grand argument. Whatever that jury may have said – <u>she's</u> guilty.
                                   Yours very truly
                                   E. P. Briggs.

Letter HK345, written by Lemira C. Pennell.

HK344
Note, handwritten in ink.

My dear Knowlton,
    Notwithstanding your attempt to prove that Lizzie did the killing, I am strongly of the opinion that she did it. If you are at all disturbed over the result, I beg to assure you of my admiration of the way you have borne yourself under conditions severely trying. How plainly, as I read your argument, I can hear the echo of utterances scattered along a course of almost thirty years!
    May the summer's rest refresh you.
                      Truly
                      W. R. Shipman.

HK345
Letter, handwritten in ink.

I do not believe at all that Lizzie was the criminal it may have been some victim who is cursing as I <u>am</u> on [?] which permit a person charged with insanity as I was <u>falsely</u> from being <u>treated</u> much worse than anyone is when arrested for crime: And I have been so badly <u>wronged</u> by people of wealth and influence that many a one finds plenty of [?] on the dainty cushions of his dusty bed or in the stately mansions too late that there are
          Copyrighted, 1886 by L. C. PENNELL
no pockets in their [?]. Women especially have been so <u>mean</u> I am <u>glad</u> the woman was killed first. I often planned to go and see the Bordens as Mr. Wright[?] at the State House [?] My <u>need</u> is so great I <u>may</u> [?] [?] the meaning from it in my Books
                    L.C.Pennell
        present address being at Portland

(Note: The copyright information in the text above appears on the original letter, which was written on the back of a book title page. See illustration.)

HK346
Poem, typewritten.

<u>We are all with you!</u>
Tweedle-dee And Tweedle-dum.
Inspired by Ex-Governor Robinson's Philanthropy. (?)

Says Justice, "Behold, I was made for the Poor,"
Says Law, "for the Rich I am Might;
They can turn me and twist me and have me done o'er,
Till they make me prove Wrong Is all right."

Says Justice, "the Poor Man shall be overta'en,
And his Error resemble a Crime;"
Says Law, "the Rich shall have during my reign,
The good of his Lucre sublime."

Says Justice, "you come of excellent stock,
You are delicate, sensitive, kind;
But if you just happen our statutes to shock
And are Poor, no pardon you'll find."

Says Law, "you may live as the savages do,
You may be your own valet and maid;
If the Coin is all there and the ring of it true,
Protection shall not be delayed."

Says Justice, "we never do things half and half,
We call everything by its name;"
Says Law, "we unbend to the bright, Golden Calf,
For the Law(years) of old did the same."

Says Justice, "Let Matricide, Parricide, be
The foulest of registered Crime;
A life for a life, or for two lives, we'll see
Shall bring the Red-Handed to time."

Says Law, "we admit that Parricide may
A Crime all unparallelled seem;
But cast in the Balance with Gold to outweigh,
The former must sure kick the beam."

APPENDICES

APPENDICES

Appendix A

The following notes on the Inquest Testimony of Miss Lizzie Andrew Borden were handwritten in lead by Hosea Morrill Knowlton, Esq., on four 8" x 10" ruled notebook sheets.

Numerals following some comments refer to page numbers in the original stenographer's minutes of the inquest, August 9 to 11, 1892:

Page 1:

    points cost by ex. of Jng. (ex, AJJ.)

    conveyance and reconveyance   p. 47 et. seq.

    had detectives   47

    nobody bad terms with Mrs. B.   49

    Relations with Mrs. B   50 et. seq.

    not at home when Morse came   53

    locked front door Wen. night   54 & 55

taken care of
    Father's bed room door and
    door to my room locked
    always - broken open Thursday   57

    had 8 or 10 hand. to iron   58

Page 2:

dont [?]
    dont think front door unbolted
        that morning   60
                         67

    heard father speak to
        Maggie as he came in   60

she denies it
    was coming down front stairs   60

Mrs. B. going to put on pillow shams	62
Mrs. B. told me of note	64
Didn't hear her go or come back	65
When I came from only trip down cellar Father was reading paper "there"	66

Page 3:

did not go upstairs after Father went out	66
was not away from house until Father came in	66
putting stick in fire	68 78
sinker story	69 et. seq.
screen hooked when went to barn	69
window in barn not open	74
didn't call Mrs. B because thought she was out	78 83

Page 4:

didn't know Father was dead	78
conversation about Mrs. B. going out & c	80
flea bite only explan.	88
denial prussic acid	90 93
dress given to officers is dress of Aug 4	91

Appendix B

The following remarks on witness testimony pertinent to the Commonwealth of Massachusetts vs. Lizzie Andrew Borden were handwritten in lead by Hosea Morrill Knowlton, Esq. These notes are contained in the partial remains of a 6 1/2" x 8 1/2" ruled notebook of 58 pages with 31 sides inscribed.

Numerals following some statements refer to page numbers in the original stenographer's minutes of the trial, June 5 to June 20, 1893:

Page 1:

Lizzie stood <u>inside</u> of screen door, and never went out or even opened it

she would not let Bridget see the corpse
B.S. 244

Sent for <u>Dr Bowen</u> & <u>Miss Russell</u>
only accidentally that Mrs. Churchill saw it.

As to eating together
BS cross 255-256
B.S. cross 266

Sick & they visited her not
B.S. 255-294

Dr. Bowen saw the form as he stood in guest chamber door
S.W.B. p.

Page 2:

    <u>Dr. Bowen</u> as to color of dress
        S.W.B. p.   Read it

    The desperate nature of a defense
    that tries to [?] the testimony
    of a defendant by showing that
    she was crazy when she testified
    by Bromo-caffeine.
        S.W.B. p. 329

    Read the cross-examination & direct
    of Mrs. Churchills description of the
    dress

    Lizzie has told us another lie
    worse than a lie - a confession!

Page 3:

    "She generally lets me know when she
    goes" says Bridget
    what she told Mrs. Churchill
        Mrs Church. p.

    Officers were searching
    "To see if anyone was there"
        Alice Russell cross ex - p.

    The burning of the dress & the way
    it was[?] is an excellent
    illustration of circumstantial evidence

    Bridget Sullivan said when she
    went out to vomit she found the screen door
    hooked.   B.S. p. 225

    The table near Borden had no blood on
    it   Allen p.

Appendix B

Page 4:

    View showed little blood on mop board
    & bureau in the bed room -

    Lizzie had a front door key &
    went in and out of it herself
                    Morse   129.

    Morse heard no noise that night
                    Morse   129

    Morse says he staid in the sitting room
    but some one else came down
                   p. 133

    Remained in the sitting room till breakfast

    Went back to sitting room till he
    went away
                   p. 134

Page 5:

    When Morse went out Borden unhooked
    the door for him & hooked it up again
                  Morse   136

    When Morse went up stairs he saw
    Mrs. B before he reached the head of
    the stairs

    Morse was there 24 hours & did
    not see Lizzie Borden
                 140

    Morse says barn door was closed
    when he went into the yard

    Hart saw him 9.30
                <u>Hart</u> - p. 165

Burrill 9.45 or before 10   168
Cook 9.45 staid 10 minutes p.
Clegg left his shop 10.29   173
    <u>there</u> 8 or 9 minutes   172
Martin - there at 10.40
      dont think he staid 5 minutes   190

Page 6:

Hadnt had a horse for a year -   193   B.S.
After that didnt use the barn   194   B.S.

Bridget Bolted the back door Thursday   198
& kept it bolted   199

Screen door hooked Wed. at 5   199

When Bridget let Bowen in the spring
door was only on at front door   200

Lizzie came in herself see above
Borden expected to - see Mrs. Kelly's   213

When Bridget went away Wed. night
she left screen back door locked spring lock
Locked when she returned   201
Locked both back doors   "
when she went to bed   202
NO noise Wed. night   204

Page 7:

Bridget came down at 6.15   205
After she took the milk in she hooked
the screen door

Door between kit and sit room
always shut -   207
between din room & sit room
always open   207

Appendix B

Sat down to Breakfast at 7.15
                                 B.S.   221
7 to 7.30   Morse 133 - 134

Bridget put front door with three locks
when she let Borden in   235

5 minutes after Lizzie came
down stairs   236

Then

Page 8:

Order of events
Bridget got up at 6.15 -   205
Mrs. Borden came down at (6.30 to 6.40)   209
went into the sitting room   208
Borden came down 5 minutes after went out   209
emptied his slop & opened the
barn ~~6.30 to 6.40~~,   210 put his
key on shelf, 209   unlocked screen   210
door & went out   210
They eat breakfast & left the room   222
Borden let Morse out   223
Borden cleaned his teeth
& took his key & went up
stairs   223
Then 5 minutes after   (224)
Lizzie appeared -   224
Maggie had been washing windows   224
Bridget went out in back yard
to vomit   <u>224</u>
left Lizzie then   <u>224</u>
UnHooked screen door to get out   228

Page 9:

staid 10 minutes & came back

& all out of sight
Hooked screen door when she
came back   225
<u>Cross. ex</u> "generally locked it   262
I know I must have locked it   263
came back into kitchen &
finished her work - fixed her
dining room table & then saw
Mrs Borden   221   I place
This was about 9 oclock   227
Then after finishing her work
she went into the sitting room &
dining room & dining room [?]   228
As she went out Lizzie appeared
at the door & had talk   229
& told her "she would be around here"
After she came in she hooked
the door -   233
As she was washing the
first sit window she let B in   234

Page 10:

then 5 minutes after Lizzie appeared   235
Borden went up back stairs - &
as he came back B. finished sitting
room & Borden went into it   236
Then Lizzie began to iron
got her ironing board & went
to dining room & began to iron   237
Told Bridget to be sure & lock
the door for Mrs. B. has gone out   237
Told her about the cheap sale at
Sargents that day   238
Lizzie calls
Maggie come down quick
Father is dead. Some body came in & killed him
                                                    240
10 or 15 minutes past 11 -   240

Appendix B

Page 11:

    Bridget says that she had a dress of
    light blue with a sprig on it of darker blue
                                                             241

    Bridget says Miss Lizzie where was you didnt I
    leave the door hooked?
    I was out in the back yard & I heard
    a groan & came in & the screen door
    was wide open   249

    imperfect examination
            Fleet cross p.

    86 spots scarcely show on
    dark paper

    Produced the dress Sat P.M., day
    before burned the other dress

Page 12:

    Horrible sight
            Harrington - cross ex. p.

    Doherty said her hands were
    out   Bowen said he pulled
    the hand out to feel of the pulse

    She was probably dressing
    when ~~the door was open~~ she closed
    the door to Doherty
                      Doherty p.

    Offer to let jury have this
    testimony of Lizzie Borden

    She went upstairs & changed
    her dress alone   NO ~~officer~~ body
    saw her & she even sent Miss
    Russell off on an absurd errand

Page 13:

>Bridget can hear the door slam
>in her room   p. 239
>
>Said she heard her mother come in
>   B.S. p. 247
>Wont you go <u>up stairs</u> to see
>   B.S. p. 247
>
>When Bowen went up after sheets
>they had to get key from shelf
>   B.S.   248
>
>Could even hear the rattling of a key in
>the front door
>   B.S.   234
>
>Never had to let Mr. Borden in before
>   B.S.   281

Page 14:

>As to where Lizzie was Wed. A.M.
>   B.S.   292 - 3 - <u>294</u>
>
>The barn loft was the only sure
>place where Lizzie could not
>possibly see or hear
>
>Many places had no blood on them
>at all -
>   stand - Allen p.
>   carpet Wood p.
>   mop board up stairs view
>
>At the view the windows & doors
>were closed
>
>Pile of ashes close <u>back</u> by the
>box
>   Medley cross ex   p.

Appendix B

Page 15:

    Man <u>Fridays foot</u>steps - Medleys discerning

    ~~She~~
    <u>Dining room table</u> was 5 feet

    Dr. Bowen has social as well as
    professional relations with the family for
    12 years (though he seldom visited the house)
    [?] he is not called as to harmony
                        p. 297
    Dr. Bowen saw Lizzie g---
    Bowen stood in the door and saw
    Mrs. Borden
                        Bowen p. 308

    <u>As to dress</u>:   Bowen
                        p. 310 to 312
    This dress a dark blue p. 314

Page 16:

    Lizzie Borden's statements
    "In the barn looking for some irons or iron"
          to Bowen at once -p. 304
    She was afraid her father had bad trouble
    with the tennants
                   Bowen - p. 304

    Her mother had received a note
    that [?] to visit a sick friend & had
    gone out

    Oh Mrs. Churchill come over - Some
    one has killed father
                  p. 347

    what she told Mrs. Churchill   p. 348
                                     also p. 367

~~See 1~~
what she told Miss Russell
                    p. 381

Page 17:

Jury might never have seen
a drop of blood in the house before
it was shown them

False

What about Cone Leary & Draper

<u>chiefs on & she ate</u>

<u>[?] man going out of doors</u>

Break at that point not accidental

Page 18:

Bowen said inside shutters were
partially closed
                    p. 320
Both loosely drawn together
                    p. 320

Bowen told Lizzie to go to her room
and this was directly after he saw Mrs. B.

Example of contradictory storys

Dr. Bowen

Mrs. B. ~~usu~~ "generally told Bridget
when she was going"   308

They will argue about her correcting
Portuguese to Swede
                    p. 369

Appendix B

Page 19:

    Mrs. Churchill relations social
                                    p. 343

    She saw Mr. Borden about 9 o clock
                                    p. 344

    Saw Bridget going across the street
    fast <u>thought some one sick</u>
                                    p. 396

    Went to window and saw her
    appearance
                        p. 347

    Saw her as she came up stairs
                          p. 357

    <u>Never saw tears</u> -   p. ~~357~~ 351

    Dress described   p. 357

    Thought they were sick   p. 357 cross

Page 20:

    Mrs. Churchill says if there had
    been blood on the dress I should think
    if it was in front I might have seen
    it I couldn't help it, I dont think   p. 366

    Saw the dress shown by Jennings
    before the public hearing
                                p. 371

    Had talk with Jennings Probably
    told him it was just not the dress
                                371

Page 21:

    Miss Russell used to see Lizzie in the
    guest chamber she used it as her
    sitting room   p. 374

    Talk the night before   377 to

    Sent Alice out to get undertaker
                            p. 383

    came back & dress changed
    coming out of Emmas room   383

    Door between her & ~~Liz~~ old
    folks locked & hooked
                            385

    Lizzie screwed it in again   386

    Went down cellar with Alice
                         387
    clothes were there   387
    & Lizzie went into the wash room   388

Page 22:

    Went back & was out of her
    sight 15 or 20 minutes & Lizzie
    must have gone down <u>front way</u>

    Sunday was ironing dress
                  p. 390

    Bowen looked for note and
    Lizzie said "she must have put it
    in the fire"
                  p. 394

    Miss Russell describes dress
                395

Appendix B

　　B. Forebade telling of the burglary
　　　　　　　378

Page 23:

　　HandkerChiefs partially ironed
　　　　　　Alice Russell x p. 399
　　4 or 5 ironed & 2 or 3 sprinkled to
　　be ironed

　　As to seeing blood - looked all
　　right <u>as far as I saw</u>
　　　　　　　　　p. 400

　　A.R. Couldnt see the rest of the
　　dress sufficiently to know whether
　　it was soiled or not - might have
　　been soiled with a number of things
　　　　　　　　p. 416 417

　　Our testimony comes from Lizzies friends

Page 24:

　　Cunningham found cellar
　　door locked　　426

　　Geo. W. Allen - says quarter past
　　eleven was discovered 11.15
　　　　　　　　　432

　　Front door was locked with chain
　　locks & <u>bolted</u>

　　Allen saw as soon as he got on a
　　level with stairs

　　Get Miss Russell - I cant be
　　alone in the house <u>245</u>

[?] 1885 - 379 - was [?] June
19 1885 by G.D.R.

Page 25:

Jennings Opening

Insane person

Always laid at her door -
Hilliard said followed every [?]

Circumstantial evidence
Nobody saw [?] of [?] [?]
killed - never do
   Water into ice

As to womans nature. what a large
proportion of the spectators are women

Out of a billion of cases there
may be one or two in which it has
somewhat uncertainly appeared that
the circumstances did [?] [?] the
case Thousands of cases of direct
   evidence from false

Page 26:

Deacon [?] [?] kissed the
corpse on the day of the funeral
Cornelius Holmes, day of funeral

She wore the blue dress Friday & Saturday
but not   Mrs. Holmes
but not Wednesday
   B.S. ~~Holmes~~ cross

Hilliard - 11 - 1119
   21 - 1122
   10 - 1125

Appendix B

Coughlin - 11 - 1163

Miss Gifford - 14 - 1169

Lucy Collett - 1179 - 1180 - 1181 - 1183
                read this

Page 27:

Bowles - washing carriage from 11 to 11.15 in Churchill yard

Mrs. Kirby - in kitchen & sink room
Jos. Derosier -
Dewey -

Desmond -   20 - 719
                18 - 720 - 721 - 723 - 751

<u>Seaver</u>   Blood spots - 741

Difference of
Wood - 18 - 995
    10 - 1013

Blood spattering   Wood - 1029
Blood spattering   Wood - 1030
                      Draper - 1059
91 does not fit the mark   1067
Cheever - 1089

Page 28:

As to Medley

<u>Steven</u> says he got there at same
time as Mullaly -   1384
Mullaly got there at ~~11.47~~ 11.37 - 610
      Looked all over the yard   1388
      Went into house

came out & found barn door open
Left barn went to the back &
right back again & it was 12 o clock

Clarkson got there at 11.40 & was
[?] talking 7 or 8 minutes
says he went in with Wixon
Wixon says he didn't go in   456

Page 29:

Lowinski - cant give us when
put the team up
Gardner thinks he left at 10 minutes
after   1428
maybe [?] 11.55   1429

Mrs. Raymond   ~~1582~~ -   9 - 1582
Mrs. Bowen -   9 - 1589

Page 30 through 56 blank.

Page 57:

I do not attempt to disguise my
participation in the feeling that we
are trying a heart wrenching case.

Page 58:

Rebuttal

As to Bridget on congeniality   p. 258 - 259
As to   "   locking screen door p. 261 -

Appendix C

INDEX OF CORRESPONDENTS

AUTHOR/POINT OF ORIGIN	*DOCUMENT NUMBER*
ADAMS, MELVIN OHIO Boston, Massachusetts	HK074, HK188
ALLEN, ALBERT E. Boston, Massachusetts	HK028
ANONYMOUS	HK042, HK050, HK052, HK124, HK125, HK127, HK128, HK129, HK131, HK132, HK134, HK135, HK137, HK138, HK140, HK225, HK231, HK334, HK335, HK339, HK341, HK343, HK346
ANONYMOUS Athol Centre, Massachusetts	HK056
ANONYMOUS Boston, Massachusetts	HK006, HK018, HK027, HK041, HK057, HK242, HK243
ANONYMOUS Fall River, Massachusetts	HK113
ANONYMOUS Lancaster, Pennsylvania	HK029, HK237
ANONYMOUS Massachusetts	HK013
ANONYMOUS Peabody, Massachusetts	HK049
ANONYMOUS Philadelphia, Pennsylvania	HK325

ANONYMOUS   HK036
   Springfield, Massachusetts

APTHORP, [?] L.   HK226
   Wilton, New Hampshire

AUSTIN, T.   HK047
   Boston, Massachusetts

B. (*initial only*)   HK003
   Boston, Massachusetts

B., D. (*initials only*)   HK340

BADGER, WALTER IRVING   HK288
   Boston, Massachusetts

BARNES, HENRY ELBERT   HK278
   Boston, Massachusetts

BATCHELDER, MOULTON   HK102

BELL, DORCAS   HK053, HK066
   Brooklyn, New York

BENNETT, EDMUND HATCH   HK265
   Taunton, Massachusetts

BACKWOOD, ANN E. *See LOGUE, MISS ANNIE ELIZABETH BLACKWOOD*

BOLLES, HENRY C.   HK196

BOOTH, LUCY C. (HUNT)   HK217, HK239
  (Mrs. Reuben H. Booth)
   Great Barrington, Massachusetts

BOYNTON, EBEN MOODY   HK191
   Boston, Massachusetts

BRIGGS, E. P.   HK343

Appendix C

BROWN, CLARA HK241
   Boston, Massachusetts

BROWNE, LOUISE WOLCOTT (KNOWLTON)
(Mrs. William H. Browne) HK227
   Washington, District of Columbia

BUFFINGTON, GEORGE B. HK323
   Dorcester, Massachusetts

BURT, FRANK HUNT
   Boston, Massachusetts HK196
   Dedham, Massachusetts HK175

CHAFFIN, WILLIAM L. HK327
   North Easton, Massachusetts

CHEEVER, DAVID WILLIAMS HK211, HK293

CHOATE, CHARLES FRANCIS, JR. HK268
   Boston, Massachusetts

CLANCY, JOHN J. HK035
   Newark, New Jersey

CLIFFORD, WALTER HK281
   Chicago, Illinois

COLLINS, ALBERT B. HK286
   New Bedford, Massachusetts

COWLES, EDWARD HK078
   Hanover, New Hampshire

CROSS, JOSEPH WARREN HK246
   Chelsea, Massachusetts

D., A. B. (*initials only*) HK112
   Brattleboro, Vermont

DAGGETT, MISS ELVIRA M. HK320
   Coventry, Vermont

DAVIS, JOHN HK251
  Lowell, Massachusetts

DAY, JOSEPH MUENSCHER HK257
  Brockton, Massachusetts

DEAN, CHARLES JOHN HK208
  Lunenburg, Massachusetts

DELANO, ALEXANDRIA PAULOVNA (KUSMISCHEV)
(Mrs. James Haskell Delano) HK279
  Boston, Massachusetts

DEVENS, RICHARD MILLER HK060, HK088, HK332
  Norton, Massachusetts

DEVOLL, SARAH WOOD (HOWLAND)
(Mrs. Zebedee A. Devoll) HK315
  Jamaica Plain, Massachusetts

DRAPER, FRANK WINTHROP HK007, HK200, HK203, HK269
  Boston, Massachusetts

DUNBAR, JAMES ROBERT HK253
  Brookline, Massachusetts

EATON, JOHN FRANCIS HK303
  Boston, Massachusetts

ELDER, ROBERT B. HK304
  Newark, New Jersey

FARLEY, JAMES PHILLIPS, JR. HK255
  Boston, Massachusetts

FISKE, FRANCIS SKINNER HK250
  Boston, Massachusetts

FLETCHER, HERBERT HERVEY HK196
  Boston, Massachusetts

FOGG, JOHN HASKELL HK230
  Portland, Maine

Appendix C

FOLSOM, WALLACE L.   HK141, HK232
New Haven, Connecticut

FOSTER, AARON AUGUSTUS   HK072
Powderhorn, Colorado

FOWLER, SAMUEL PAGE, JR.   HK193, HK195
Danvers, Massachusetts

FRANKLIN, GEORGE   HK017
Boston, Massachusetts

FRENCH, ASA   HK296
Boston, Massachusetts

FRENCH, WILLIAM BRADFORD   HK248
Boston, Massachusetts

GALLIGAN, JOHN H.   HK271
Taunton, Massachusetts

GARDNER, PROF.   HK011
Boston, Massachusetts

GASKILL, FRANCIS ALMON   HK263
Worcester, Massachusetts

GAY, GEORGE WASHINGTON   HK207
Boston, Massachusetts

GIFFORD, GEORGE DAVIS   HK311
Worcester, Massachusetts

GOLDSMITH, JOHN K.   HK316
Newburgh, New York

GRAVES, L.   HK313
Cottage City, Massachusetts

GREENOUGH, CHARLES PELHAM   HK275
Boston, Massachusetts

GROVER, THOMAS ELWOOD   HK319
Boston, Massachusetts

H. (*initial only*)   HK055, HK058
Lowell, Massachusetts

HALE, EDWARD EVERETT   HK305
Matunuck, Rhode Island

HALL, WILLIAM MOSELY   HK284
New York, New York

HARRINGTON FRANCIS BISHOP   HK318
Boston, Massachusetts

HARRINGTON, PHILIP   HK065
Fall River, Massachusetts

HARRIS, CHARLES NATHAN   HK024, HK145
Boston, Massachusetts

HASWELL, CHARLES HAYNES   HK306
New York, New York

HICKCOX, J. S.   HK139
Washington, District of Columbia

HULING, RAY GREENE   HK227
New Bedford, Massachusetts

HUNTRESS, GEORGE LEWIS   HK249
Boston, Massachusetts

HURD, FREDERICK ELLSWORTH   HK120
Boston, Massachusetts

INGALLS, MISS BELLE   *See LOVEJOY, MAYBELLE INGALLS.*

IVY, JESSE COLEMAN   HK272
Boston, Massachusetts

JACKSON, FRANK HUSSEY   HK270
Providence, Rhode Island

Appendix C

JELLY, GEORGE FREDERICK   HK030
Boston, Massachusetts

JENNINGS, ANDREW JACKSON   HK016, HK084, HK086, HK094,
Fall River, Massachusetts   HK095, HK115, HK121, HK144

JONES, FRANCIS RICHARD   HK256
Boston, Massachusetts

JONES, W. S.   HK045
Worcester, Massachusetts

KINGMAN, HOSEA   HK295
Bridgewater, Massachusetts

KINNEY, VAN BUREN   HK321
Providence, Rhode Island

KNOWLTON, BENJAMIN C.   HK308
Middleboro, Massachusetts

KNOWLTON, HOSEA MORRILL
Barnstable, Massachusetts   HK083
New Bedford, Massachusetts   HK015, HK021, HK022, HK025,
HK034, HK051, HK067, HK069,
HK082, HK083, HK089, HK096,
HK097, HK100, HK106, HK114,
HK118, HK123, HK150, HK152,
HK155, HK170, HK172, HK174
HK177, HK178, HK198, HK201

KNOWLTON, JOSEPH D.   HK020
Van Buren, Arkansas

L., E. (*initials only*)   HK133

L [?], HENRY   HK026
City Mills, Massachusetts

LEONARD, CHARLES HALL   HK267
Boston, Massachusetts

LEWIS, NATHANIEL R.   HK238
   Fall River, Massachusetts

LOGUE, MISS ANNIE ELIZABETH BLACKWOOD
   Bridgeton, New Jersey   HK310

LORD, ARTHUR   HK301
   Boston, Massachusetts

LORING, EDWARD P.   HK312
   Boston, Massachusetts

LOVEJOY, MAYBELLE INGALLS   HK126
   Haverhill, Massachusetts

MC HENRY, NELLIE S.   HK023
   (Mrs. Edwin D. McHenry)
   Providence, Rhode Island

MACKEY, THOMAS J.   HK031
   New York, New York

MADIGAN, EDMUND COTTRILL   HK220
   Presque Isle, Maine

MARSH, WILLIAM DWIGHT   HK297
   Amherst, Massachusetts

MASON, ALBERT   HK161, HK164
   Boston, Massachusetts

MAXWELL, MARY A.   HK059, HK149
   (Mrs. Charles B. Maxwell)
   Boston, Massachusetts

MOODY, WILLIAM HENRY
   Haverill, Massachusetts   HK283, HK331
   Newburyport, Massachusetts   HK044

MORRIS, HENRY D.   HK044
   Newburgh, New York

Appendix C

MORRISON, CHARLES ROBERT   HK324
Concord, New Hampshire

MORSE, ELIJAH ADAMS   HK280
Canton, Massachusetts

MYRICK, NATHAN SUMNER   HK266
Boston, Massachusetts

NORTHEND, WILLIAM DUMMER   HK068
Salem, Massachusetts

OLNEY, JAMES BROWN   HK285
Catskill, New York

OSBALDESTON, EDWIN PYE TURNER ONSLOW
New York, New York   HK040

OWEN, FRANKLIN PIERCE   HK092
Providence, Rhode Island

PARK, MICHAEL M.   HK070
Toledo, Ohio

PARKER, HENRY LANGDON   HK260
Worcester, Massachusetts

PARKER, HERBERT   HK254
Fitchburg, Massachusetts

PEIRCE, HENRY BAILEY   HK264
Abington, Massachusetts

PENNELL, LEMIRA C.   HK345
(Mrs. Francis Pennell)
Portland, Maine

PIERCE, EDWARD LILLIE   HK240
Milton, Massachusetts

PILLSBURY, ALBERT ENOCH
   Boston, Massachusetts   HK002, HK032, HK038, HK054,
                                           HK073, HK075, HK077, HK093,
                                           HK099, HK100, HK101, HK105,
                                           HK107, HK116, HK119, HK122,
                                           HK148, HK151, HK153, HK155,
                                           HK157, HK159, HK160, HK163,
                                           HK167, HK171, HK173, HK176,
                                           HK180, HK181, HK187, HK189,
                                           HK190, HK192, HK194, HK197,
                                           HK202, HK204, HK209, HK210
                                           HK247
   Toronto, Canada   HK014

PILLSBURY, ALBERT ENOCH   HK087, HK090, HK103, HK108,
   Office of   HK117, HK165, HK166, HK168,
   Boston, Massachusetts   HK169, HK179

PIPER, HORACE L.   HK307
   Washington, District of Columbia

PRESCOTT, WILLIAM COWAN   HK261
   Herkimer, New York

PSEUDONYM
   "An advocate of justice"   HK328
      New Bedford, Massachusetts

   "Attentive Reader"   HK061

   "Citizen of Concord"   HK104

   "Citizen of Massachusetts"   HK136

   Concord N.H. for Justice"   HK235
      Concord, New Hampshire

   "A constent reader of trial"   HK333

   "Curiosity"   HK336

   "Detective Daniel"   HK039
      Boston, Massachusetts

Appendix C

"A Friend" New York	HK214
"Greentree" Freeland	HK221
"In Haste" Providence, Rhode Island	HK001
"Justice"	HK244
"Justice" Baltimore, Maryland	HK219, HK223
"Justice" Providence, Rhode Island	HK043
"New York Ladies" New York, New York	HK037
"N.Y."	HK330
"Observer" Springfield, Massachusetts	HK337
"Old resident of Essex County"	HK140
"One who desires justice"	HK236
"One who reads, but only a woman" Boston, Massachusetts	HK216
"Success"	HK080
"A Suggestion" Yarmouth, Nova Scotia	HK081
"Theorist"	HK245
"Transient" Springfield, Massachusetts	HK326

"Voter"   HK064

"A woman who wonders if there is   HK229
  such a thing as justice.
  Washington, District of Columbia

"Your Brother"   HK338
New Bedford, Massachusetts

"Your Obedient Servant"   HK076

"Yours"   HK013
Massachusetts

"Yours for Justice"   HK218

"Yours (one who reads)"   HK252
Boston, Massachusetts

R., B.T. (*initials only*)   HK222

REED, GEORGE BOWLAND   HK302
   Boston, Massachusetts

REED, MILTON   HK282
   Fall River, Massachusetts

REED, PHILIP GORDON   HK012
   Albany, New York

ROBBINS, MRS. M. A.   HK233
   Boston, Massachusetts

ROBINSON, GEORGE DEXTER   HK147, HK154, HK156, HK158
   Springfield, Massachusetts

ROTCH, WILLIAM JAMES   HK290
   New Bedford, Massachusetts

RUSSELL MISS ALICE MANLEY   HK212
   Fall River, Massachusetts

Appendix C

SAVARY, WILLIAM HENRY   HK199
   South Boston, Massachusetts

SCHULTE, OTTO H.   HK213
   Newark, New Jersey

SEGER, J. C.   HK309
   DeSoto, Missouri

SEYMOUR, HENRY HASTINGS   HK298
   Buffalo, New York

SHERMAN, EDGAR JAY   HK276
   Plymouth, Massachusetts

SHIPMAN, WILLIAM ROLLIN   HK344

SLOCUM, EDWARD L.   HK085
   Providence, Rhode Island

SPARROW, WILLIAM EDWARD   HK294
   Mattapoisett, Massachusetts

STILES, WILLIAM CURTIS   HK322
   Jackson, Michigan

STORREY, HAMILTON   HK048
   New York, New York

STRAND, JOHN BURNS   HK005
   Worcester, Massachusetts

TOAL, DAVID D.   HK228
   New York, New York

V., J. D. (*initials only*)   HK130

VAN ELDREN, J.   HK010
   Newport, Rhode Island

VON KAMEAKE, THEODORE T.   HK046
   Grafton, Massachusetts

WALKER, MRS. GEORGE D.   HK289

WALKER, MISS MARY EDWARD   HK224
  Concord, New Hampshire

WEBSTER, PRENTISS   HK300
  Boston, Massachusetts

WHITE, ALDEN PERLEY   HK063
  Salem, Massachusetts

WHITEFIELD, EDWIN   HK079
  Dedham, Massachusetts

WHITMORE, JAMES HERMAN   HK299
  Stoneham, Massachusetts

WHITNEY, JAMES ORNE   HK291
  Pawtucket, Rhode Island

WILLIAMS, A. G.   HK033
  Providence, Rhode Island

WILLIAMS, ANNIE L. T.   HK292
  Brighton Hill, Massachusetts

WILSON, DELIA A. (GIBSON)   HK004
  (Mrs. Jason G. Wilson)
  Lynn, Massachusetts

WILSON, MRS. HENRY *See WILSON, SARAH A. (BELCHER).*

WILSON, SARAH A. (BELCHER)   HK234
  (Mrs. Henry Wilson)
  Honesdale, Pennsylvania

WINSOR, MISS JOSEPHINE ELIZABETH
  Greenville, Rhode Island   HK215

WOOD EDWARD STICKNEY
  Boston, Massachusetts   HK273
  Pocasset, Massachusetts   HK019

Appendix C

WOODBURY, JOHN   HK317
   Boston, Massachusetts

WOODWARD, NATHAN ARMSBY   HK262
   Batavia, New York

WORRALL, MRS. H. F.   HK259
   Scotland - Mass - United States

WORTHINGTON, ERASTUS   HK287
   Worcester, Massachusetts

WRIGHT, WILLIAM BEN   HK314
   Boston, Massachusetts

WYMAN, ALPHONSO ADELBERT   HK274
   Boston, Massachusetts

YOUNG, WILLIAM A.   HK258
   Danville, Illinois

GLOSSARIES

Glossary A

Profiles of Textual References

The following biographical and historical information relates to individuals and places appearing in the text of the documents. The Editors have made every attempt to uncover the identity of those mentioned. Cases where positive identification was impossible are noted as such. The men considered for service on the jury but not selected have not been profiled as their role in the case was minimal.

ADAMS, MELVIN OHIO 1850 - 1920: born in Ashburnham, Massachusetts, son of Joseph and Dolly (Whiting) Adams. Educated in the Ashburnham public school system and at Brighton Academy in New Ipswich, New Hampshire, he graduated from Dartmouth College in 1871. He was then employed as a teacher in Fitchburg, Massachusetts, while studying law in the office of Amasa Norcross, Esq. of that city. He graduated from Boston University Law School in 1875 and was admitted to the Suffolk bar, marrying Miss Mary Colony in Fitchburg later that same year. Establishing an office in Boston, Massachusetts, he was soon appointed assistant district attorney for Suffolk County, a position he held until his resignation in 1886 when he returned to private practice. In 1890, he served on the staff of Governor John Q. A. Brackett with the rank of colonel. Well-known in business and literary circles, he served as president of the Boston, Revere Beach and Lynn Railroad and of the General Alumni Association of Dartmouth College. He died in Boston, Massachusetts. He was engaged as associate counsel in defense of Miss Lizzie A. Borden.

ALLEN, CHARLES 1827 - 1913: born in Greenfield, Massachusetts, son of Sylvester and Harriet (Ripley) Allen. Having received his Bachelor of Arts from Harvard University in 1847, he subsequently read law in the office of Messrs. George T. Davis and Charles Devens in his native town. He continued the study of law for a time at Harvard Law School and was admitted to the bar in Northampton, Massachusetts, in 1850. He established an office in Greenfield and practiced there until 1861 when he relocated to Boston, Massachusetts, upon being named reporter of decisions for the Massachusetts Supreme Judicial Court. In 1867, he resigned from that position in order to accept the post of attorney general, a title he held for five years. He continued to practice law in Boston and, in 1880, was made chairman of the commission to revise statutes in Massachusetts. In 1882, he was made a judge of the Massachusetts Supreme judicial Court by Gov. John D. Long, retaining that position until 1898. In 1892, he was awarded the degree of Doctor of Laws from Harvard Law School. A noted author, he numbered among his works *Telegraph Cases*, published in 1873, and *Notes on the Bacon-Shakespeare Question*, published in 1900. He died in the city of Boston where he had maintained a residence for over fifty years.

ALLEN, GEORGE WILLIAM 1838 - 1901: born in South Kingston, Rhode Island, son of William and Elizabeth (Crandall) Allen. A Civil War veteran, he enlisted with the rank of private in Company G, 4th Rhode Island Volunteers, serving a term of thirty-seven months. He relocated to Fall River, Massachusetts, in 1874, being employed as a machinist in several textile mills. He was appointed to the Fall River Police Department as a patrolman in 1889. He held the position of committing officer at the Central Police Station at the time of his death at Massachusetts General Hospital in Boston. The first police officer to arrive at the Borden crime scene on August 4, 1892, his official statement relates that he was sent City Marshall Rufus B. Hilliard to "see what the matter is." He testified as to his observations that day.

ALMY, GENEVRA M. (ALLEN) 1826 - 1903: born in Tiverton, Rhode Island, daughter of Abram and Rachel (Gardner) Allen. Married to William M. Almy, a former business partner of Andrew J. Borden in Borden, Almy and Company, she was widowed in 1885. She was closely acquainted with the first Mrs. Andrew J. Borden as well as the Misses Emma L. and Lizzie A. Borden. She died in Fall River, Massachusetts. "Landscape Place," her property on Gardner's Neck Road in Swansea, Massachusetts, was adjacent to that of Andrew J. Borden, as were the burial lots of their families at Oak Grove Cemetery in Fall River, Massachusetts.

BARNEY, GEORGE W. 1817 - 1893: born in Newport, Rhode Island, son of Rufus and Lydia Barney. He first appears in the Fall River, Massachusetts, city directory circa 1869. A grocer by profession, he was employed in that capacity until 1888, when he appears to have retired from active business. He married Miss Esther Rose of Newport and resided with her in Fall River until his death. Their daughter, Annie, was married to Joseph W. Carpenter, Jr.

BATCHELDER, MOULTON 1836 - 1929: born in Plainfield, Vermont, son of Jonathan and Wealthy (Kitchum) Batchelder. Spending his youth in his native town, he moved to Lawrence, Massachusetts, in 1856, securing employment in the Bay State Mills. In 1862, he enlisted in Company C, 40th Massachusetts Volunteers, as a private and was promoted rapidly, holding the rank of second lieutenant at the expiration of his term of service in 1864. Returning to Lawrence, he was appointed to that city's police force and that same year was commissioned a first lieutenant in the Massachusetts Militia for his district. In 1873, he was named assistant city Marshall and promoted to city Marshall five years later. He resigned from the latter position in 1881 to accept an appointment as detective on the Massachusetts State Police force. During his successful career, he arrested six murderers and prepared the cases for trial, with convictions resulting. He served for twenty-three years as the Essex County agent of the Society for the Prevention of Cruelty to Dumb Animals as well as agent of the Society for the Prevention of Cruelty to Children. In 1896, his wife Mary, a native of Plymouth, New Hampshire, died at the age of sixty. Active fraternally, he held memberships in several organizations at the time of his death in Lawrence, Massachusetts. It was in the capacity of state police detective that he became involved in the Borden case.

BEACH, HENRY HARRIS AUBREY 1843 - 1910: born in Middletown, Connecticut, son of Elijah and Lucy S. (Riley) Beach. As a young child, he moved with his family to Cambridge, Massachusetts, receiving his education in the public schools there. In 1863, he enlisted in the United States Army and was assigned to hospital service with the rank of sergeant of ordinance. Granted an honorable discharge in 1866, he returned to Cambridge and entered Harvard Medical School, receiving the degree of Doctor of Medicine two years later. In 1868, he established a practice in Boston, Massachusetts, that same year being appointed surgeon at the Boston Dispensary. His professional career at his alma mater began in 1869 when he was appointed assistant demonstrator of anatomy, a position he held for the next decade. He married Miss Alice C. Mandell of New Bedford, Massachusetts, in 1871. In 1873, he was elected president of the Boylston Medical Society of Harvard University, serving a one-year term. He was named demonstrator of anatomy at Harvard Medical School in 1879, retaining that position until 1882 when he resigned in order to devote his time to teaching clinical surgery at Massachusetts General Hospital. In 1885, having been a widower for nearly five years, he was married to Miss Amy Marcy Cheney, a noted pianist and composer in Boston. In 1898, he returned to Harvard where he was appointed clinical instructor in surgery, it post he retained until 1900 when he began a career as a lecturer. He maintained a connection with Massachusetts General hospital, serving that institution after 1900 as consulting surgeon. A frequent contributor to numerous professional publications, he served as associate editor of the *Boston Medical and Surgical Journal*, working under Dr. J. Collins Warren from 1873 to 1874. He maintained an active membership in several medical societies in both Boston and Washington, District of Columbia. He was recommended to Attorney General Albert E. Pillsbury by Dr. George W. Gay for consideration as a medical expert for the prosecution in the trial of Miss Lizzie A. Borden.

BENCE, ELI 1865 - 1915: born in Braintree, Massachusetts, son of William and Sarah J. (Hudson) Bence. He began his career as a clerk at several drugstores in Fall River, Massachusetts, employed by D. R. Smith from 1890 to 1895. His career took him to New Bedford, Massachusetts, and later to Pittsfield, where he became proprietor of his first store in 1905. He married twice; his first wife was Miss Sarah J. Mayhurst of Fall River and his second Miss Annie C. Maxfield of Fairhaven, Massachusetts. He held office in several professional and fraternal organizations until his death in Pittsfield. He provided testimony at the inquest and preliminary trial and was summoned as a witness for the Commonwealth; his evidence, ruled as inadmissible in the higher court, pertained to the alleged attempt of Miss Lizzie A. Borden to purchase poison a few days before the murders.

BILLINGS, WARREN T.: an employee of the *Boston Herald* in 1892. In charge of that newspaper's coverage of the Borden murder case, he is said to have arrived in Fall River, Massachusetts, shortly after the discovery of the crime. Due to the itinerant nature of his profession, attempts to uncover biographical details have to date been unsuccessful.

BLAISDELL, JOSIAH COLEMAN 1820 - 1900: born in Campton, New Hampshire, the son of Eliphalet Blaisdell. Educated in the Campton public schools and at the Scientific Institute at Hancock, New Hampshire, he relocated to Fall River, Massachusetts, in 1843 and engaged in the shoe trade. Inclined towards law, he studied in the office of James Ford, Esq. and by 1853 was practicing in Fall River. He quickly rose to prominence and became active politically, serving as state representative, state senator and for nine years on the Board of State Charters. He was mayor of Fall River from 1858 to 1859. He married twice; his first wife was Miss Sarah E. Eddy of Fall River and his second Mrs. Annie (Wilcox) Mitchell. His interest in music and excellent natural singing voice led him to establish singing classes at the Baptist Temple, where he was an active member. Appointed to the post of district court justice in 1874, it was in that capacity that he presided at the inquest into the deaths of Mr. and Mrs. Andrew J. Borden as well as at the preliminary hearing. Resigning from that post in April of 1893, he died shortly thereafter in Fall River, Massachusetts. His son, William, married Miss Minnie Borden, a distant relative of Miss Lizzie A. Borden.

BLODGETT, CALEB 1832 - 1901: born in Dorchester, New Hampshire, son of Caleb and Charlotte (Piper) Blodgett. He obtained his early education at Canaan Union Academy in Canaan, New Hampshire. He then prepared for college at Kimball Union Academy at Meriden, New Hampshire. Entering Dartmouth College in 1852, he graduated in 1856 and began his career as a teacher at the high school in Leominster, Massachusetts. He read law in the offices of Messrs. Bacon and Aldrich, Worcester, Massachusetts, and was admitted to the bar in that city in 1860. Following a brief law partnership in Hopkinton, Massachusetts, he began a successful practice in Boston in association with Halsey J. Boardman, Esq. He married Miss Roxie B. Martin of Canaan in 1865. Dissolving his partnership with Attorney Boardman in 1882, he was appointed associate justice of the superior court by Governor John D. Long, a position from which he retired in 1900. It was in this capacity that he served at the Borden trial in 1893. He was president of the Phi Beta Kappa Society of Dartmouth College and in 1889 received the honorary degree of Doctor of Laws from his alma mater.

BODMAN, HENRY A.: foreman of the grand jury which presented the indictments charging Miss Lizzie A. Borden with murder. Attempts to uncover biographical details have to date been unsuccessful.

BORDEN, ABBY DURFEE (GRAY) 1828 - 1892: daughter of Oliver and Sarah (Sawyer) Gray. She became the second wife of Andrew Jackson Borden on June 6, 1865. Stepmother to the Misses Emma L. and Lizzie A. Borden, she was half-sister to Mrs. Sarah B. Whitehead. She was murdered in her home in Fall River, Massachusetts, on August 4, 1892.

BORDEN, ALANSON 1823 - 1900: born in Tiverton, Rhode Island, son of Isaac and Abby (Borden) Borden. During his youth, his family moved to Cayuga County, New York, where he attended the academy at Groton and later Aurora Academy. In 1846, he moved to New Bedford, Massachusetts, and resolved to enter the legal profession. Following two years' study in the office of Messrs. Elliot and Casson, he was admitted to the bar and subsequently opened a practice. In 1856, he was appointed special justice of police court, a position which he held until 1859. He served two years in the Massachusetts state legislature, then as a trial justice for juvenile offenders and, in

1864, was made judge of New Bedford police court. In 1876, he was elected to the mayoralty of that city. He married three times, his first wife being Miss Mary C. Tapham of New Bedford, his second Miss Mary F. Kent of Washington, District of Columbia, and his third Miss Annie R. Commerford, also of New Bedford. Retiring from the bench in 1897, he returned to private practice in New Bedford, where he remained until his death.

BORDEN, ALMY AND COMPANY- established circa 1853 in Fall River, Massachusetts. A furniture and undertaking business operated by Andrew J. Borden and William M. Almy, it was located at Annawan (later Anawan) and South Main Streets. A third partner, Theodore D. W. Wood, entered the firm circa 1864. The partnership of Borden and Almy lasted in excess of twenty-five years.

BORDEN, ANDREW JACKSON 1822 - 1892: born in Fall River, Massachusetts, son of Abraham Bowen and Phebe (Davenport) Borden. A successful businessman, he was senior partner in the firm of Borden, Almy and Company. Heavily invested in income-producing real estate, he had substantial holdings in several local textile mills and banking houses. He served as president of the Fall River Savings Bank and was director of several Fall River corporations. Twice married, he wed his first wife, Miss Sarah Anthony Morse, in 1845 and his second, Miss Abby Durfee Gray, in 1865. True to his Yankee heritage of frugality, he lived simply and had by the time of his death accumulated a sizable estate. He was murdered in his home in Fall River, Massachusetts, on August 4, 1892.

BORDEN, MISS EMMA LENORA 1851 - 1927: born in Fall River, Massachusetts, daughter of Andrew Jackson and Sarah Anthony (Morse) Borden. Her early education was received in her native city as well as at a female seminary elsewhere. Twelve years old at the time of her mother's death, she vowed at her deathbed to take care of her younger sister, Lizzie. She grew to be a woman of a retiring nature. At a house party in Fairhaven, Massachusetts, on August 4, 1892, she returned home immediately upon receiving a telegram informing her of the tragedy within her family. Her support for Miss Lizzie A. Borden throughout her incarceration and trial was unfaltering and her belief in her sister's innocence persisted throughout her life. Following a falling-out between the two siblings in 1904, she left Maplecroft, the home on French Street in Fall River they had shared for ten years. She relocated first to Providence, Rhode Island, and then to Newmarket, New Hampshire. She made her home in the latter locality, living under an assumed name until her death.

BORDEN, JEROME COOK 1845 - 1930: born in Fall River, Massachusetts, son of Cook and Mary A. (Bessey) Borden. A prominent Fall River businessman, he began his career as a bank clerk before entering Cook Borden and Company, a lumber business founded by his father. He married Miss Emma E. Tetlow in 1870. He served as president of the Union Savings Bank and the Troy Co-operative Bank as well as director of several local corporations until his death in his native city. A first cousin of Andrew J. Borden, he served as one of his pallbearers at the funeral on August 6, 1892. A witness at both the preliminary and final trials, he testified in 1893 concerning his visit to the Borden house on August 5, 1892.

BORDEN, MISS LIZZIE ANDREW 1860 - 1927: born in Fall River, Massachusetts, daughter of Andrew Jackson and Sarah Anthony (Morse) Borden. Educated in the Fall River public school system, she attended high school in that city for three years. In the fall of 1890, she enjoyed a grand tour of Europe in the company of a group of her contemporaries. She was present at the Borden family home at 92 Second Street the morning of the murders of her father and stepmother and was arrested as a suspect on August 11, 1892. Tried for those crimes, she was acquitted on June 20, 1893, after little more than an hour's deliberation by the twelve-man jury. Following the trial, she returned to her Second Street home, remaining there until 1894 when the Borden sisters purchased a house at 7 French Street in Fall River. Located in a fashionable district on "the hill," their new home was given the name Maplecroft. Ostracized by her contemporaries, she began to travel extensively. Her interest in the theatre led to a friendship with the actress Nance O'Neil. She often visited the cities of New York and Boston to attend her friend's performances and was also known to entertain the actress and members of her troupe at Maplecroft whenever their tour brought them to Fall River. In 1904, she and her sister, Emma, experienced a falling-out which caused the latter to leave their shared home. The two did not speak for the remainder of their days. Following her sister's departure, she began referring to herself as "Miss Lizbeth A. Borden." As she grew older, she became increasingly reclusive, maintaining very few social contacts. Seemingly content at Maplecroft, she spent the rest of her life in comfortable seclusion, attended by her staff, in the company of her pet Boston bull terriers, Donald Stuart, Royal Wilson and Laddie Miller, surrounded by fine furnishings and an extensive library to occupy her days. The many volumes in her collection, as well as other personal possessions, were distributed according to her wishes among her family, staff and remaining friends following her death in her native city. She was remembered by some who knew her in later life as a lady or great kindness and generosity, with a fondness for children and animals.

BORDEN, SARAH ANTHONY (MORSE) 1823 - 1863: born in Somerset, Massachusetts, daughter of Anthony and Rhody (Morrison) Morse. She was married to Andrew Jackson Borden on Christmas day in 1845 and was the mother of three children: Emma Lenora, Alice Esther and Lizzie Andrew Borden. She died in Fall River, Massachusetts, the cause of death being uterine congestion and a spinal disease.

BORDEN, SIMEON, JR. 1860 - 1924: born in Fall River, Massachusetts, son of Simeon and Irene (Hathaway) Borden. Educated in the Fall River public school system, he received his Bachelor of Arts from Brown University in 1882 and then entered the law firm of his father in the capacity of clerk. Appointed assistant clerk of courts in 1888, he was admitted to the bar in 1894. In 1896 he was elected by a large majority to the office of clerk of courts for Bristol County, Massachusetts, a position formerly held by his father. He married Miss Minnie W. Hood of Fall River. His business interests were extensive and he served as a director of several Fall River corporations and charitable organizations until his death. He was a distant relative of Miss Lizzie A. Borden, sharing the same grandfather, four times great.

BORDEN, THOMAS JAMES 1832 - 1902: born in Fall River, Massachusetts, the son of Col. Richard and Abby Walker (Durfee) Borden. He was educated in the Fall River public school system and then attended Lawrence Scientific School in Cambridge, Massachusetts, studying both engineering and chemistry. He began his career at Fall River Iron Works Company, a corporation owned by his family. In the ensuing years, he demonstrated tremendous business sense with his varied successful ventures, including the American Printing Company and Richard Borden Manufacturing Company. In 1855, he married Miss Mary E. Hill of Fall River. He was a veteran of the Civil War, enlisting with the 5th Company, Unattached Massachusetts Volunteers, holding the rank of first lieutenant and serving a three-month term. An earnest Congregationalist, he was also involved in several civic and philanthropic organizations. In Providence, Rhode Island, at the time of his death, he was tended to by Dr. Maurice H. Richardson. He was second cousin to Andrew J. Borden.

BOULDS, THOMAS 1845 - 1896: born in England. He emigrated to the United States and was residing in Fall River, Massachusetts, by 1889. He remained in that city until the time of his death. A laborer and gardener, he boarded at 90 Second Street, the residence of his employer, Mrs. Adelaide B. Churchill, in 1893. Washing a carriage in the yard of his employer at the time of the Borden murders, he gave testimony pertaining to his actions and observations that morning.

BOWEN, PHEBE VINCENT (MILLER) 1848 - 1907: born in Fall River, Massachusetts, daughter of Southard Harrison and Esther G. (Peckham) Miller. In 1871, she married Dr. Seabury W. Bowen. They resided at 91 Second Street in 1892, in property owned and occupied by her father, Southard H. Miller. She remained active in the Baptist church and in many civic organizations until the time of her death in her native city. Having been a witness at the preliminary trial, she testified in 1893 concerning her observations of the actions of Miss Lizzie A. Borden at 92 Second Street shortly after the murders.

BOWEN, SEABURY WARREN 1840 - 1918: born in Attleboro, Massachusetts, son of Benjamin and Leafa (Clafflin) Bowen. A successful practicing physician in Fall River, Massachusetts, he was educated in Attleboro public schools and received his Bachelor of Arts from Brown University in 1864. He was graduated from Bellevue Hospital Medical College in 1867 and began his practice in Fall River later that same year. In 1871, he married Miss Phebe Vincent Miller. He held the post of city physician, was on the staff of the Fall River Hospital and held memberships in several medical societies. Having retired from practice, he died in Fall River. He was Andrew J. Borden's family physician. He was a witness at the inquest and the preliminary as well as final trial. His extensive testimony pertained to several aspects of the Borden murder investigation.

BRAYTON, JOHN SUMMERFIELD, SR. 1826 - 1904: born in Swansea, Massachusetts, son of Israel and Kezia (Anthony) Brayton. Educated at schools in the Fall River, Massachusetts, area, he subsequently attended University Grammar School in Providence, Rhode Island. Graduating from Brown University in 1851, he pursued law study in the office of Thomas D. Eliot, Esq., New Bedford, Massachusetts, completing his education at Harvard Law School. Admitted to the bar in 1853, he remained in the, legal profession for fifteen years. During this time, he served in various public offices in Fall River, including a term as city solicitor from I S54 to 1857. In 1855, he married Miss Sarah Jane Tinkham of Middleborough, Massachusetts. Active politically, he was a member of the Massachusetts House of' Representatives in 1856 and served seven years as clerk of courts for Bristol County, Massachusetts. One of the incorporators of Union Hospital in Fall River, he also had extensive interest in textile manufacturing and railroad corporations. He served as a trustee of Amherst College for eight years beginning in 1882 and was a Fellow of Brown University from 1898 to 1904. Responsible for organizing both the First National Bank and B. M. C. Durfee Safe Deposit and Trust Company in Fall River, he was president of both until his death. He provided a statement to district police regarding any knowledge of insanity in the Morse family.

BRIGHAM, DAVID SEWALL 1823 - 1893: born in Randolph, Massachusetts, son of Rev. David and Elizabeth Hathaway (Durfee) Brigham. He began his varied career employed as a clerk in the mill of his uncle, Dr. Nathan Durfee, later venturing into the hardware, lumber and coal businesses. In 1878, he was appointed city Marshall in Fall River, Massachusetts, and served a four-year term. Throughout his life he spent a great deal of time in the western United States but returned to Fall River and was employed by the B. M. C. Durfee Safe Deposit and Trust Company at the time of his death. Thrice married, he wed Miss Eliza G. Chace of Fall River in 1845. His second marriage was to Miss Mary Holland Wady in Delaware, Ohio, in 1854, followed by a third to Miss Elizabeth Williams, a native of Delaware, in 1870. He was questioned as -to any knowledge of insanity in the Morse family.

BRIGHTMAN, FRANK W. 1850 -1901: born in Fall River, Massachusetts, son of Horatio N. and Rebecca L. (Drake) Brightman. He married Miss Abby F. Harrison of his native city. He was employed as a bookkeeper in various Fall River textile mills. Later in his career, he served as treasurer of both the Globe Street Railway Company and the Stafford Mills, the latter his employer at the time of his death. It was his signature which was present on the railway tickets reported stolen from the house of Andrew J. Borden in 1891.

BROWN, THOMAS JOSEPH LEE 1864 - 1954: born in Fall River, Massachusetts, son of Joseph Durfee and Mary T. (Lee) Brown. Educated in the Fall River public school system, he began his business career as a bookkeeper. He was an employee of Arctic Ice and Cold Storage Company for several years. In 1905, he became a partner in the firm of Lee and Brown, express agents and teaming. Following a dissolution of partnership in 1918, he continued in the same business under his own name. He married three times; his first wife was Miss Emma E. Barker of Fall River, his second Miss Eva M. Sewal of Westport, Massachusetts, and his third Miss Mattie G. Blaisdell. Following his retirement, he died in his native city. He was in the vicinity of the residence of Andrew J. Borden the morning of the murders.

BUNKER, AUGUSTUS 1874 - 1933: born in Fall River, Massachusetts, son of Henry M. and Harriet (Begins) Bunker. A life-long resident of his native city, he was employed there as a clerk and, later, as a laborer. A Baptist, he was an active member of his church. He is mentioned in a statement given by Alfred A. Smith, an inmate at the Massachusetts Reformatory, on January 9, 1893.

BURRILL, JOHN THOMAS 1857 - 1904: born in Fall River, Massachusetts, son of John B. and Elizabeth (Richmond) Burrill. Educated in the Fall River public school system, he began his banking career as a clerk and later a teller at the National Union Bank. Following it brief period as bookkeeper for L. Nichols and Company, a furniture dealer, he returned to banking in 1882. That same year, he married Miss Fannie K. Worth of Fall River. Six years later, he became assistant cashier of' the Union Savings Bank and shortly thereafter was made cashier, a position he held until his death. He was a witness at the preliminary as well as the final trial. His testimony described a meeting he witnessed between Abraham G. Hart and Andrew J. Borden on the morning of August 4, 1892.

BURT, FRANK HUNT 1861 - 1946: born in Northampton, Massachusetts, son of Henry M. and Frances A. (Hunt) Burt. Having graduated from high school in Springfield, Massachusetts, he relocated four years later to Newton, Massachusetts. He was employed there with his hither, engaged in publishing the *Newton Graphic* until 1886. He was married to Miss Susie Frances Allen in 1885. Following his employment at the Newton newspaper, he embarked on a career as a stenographer, one that would occupy the remaining sixty years of his life. In that capacity he reported speeches by most Presidents from William Henry Harrison to Franklin Delano Roosevelt. He was also assigned to many of Massachusetts' most famous murder trials, among them that of Miss Lizzie A. Borden. In 1897, he became a member of the Massachusetts bar. The following year, upon the death of his father, he assumed publication of *Among the Clouds*, a summer daily published from atop Mt. Washington, New Hampshire, an occupation he maintained until a fire caused that paper's dissolution in 1908. From 1910 to 1913, he reported on conventions of the International Congress of Religious Liberals held abroad in London, Berlin and Paris. As well as being one of the earliest members of the National Shorthand Reporters Association, he also held membership in the New England Society of Shorthand Reporters, for which he served as president for a time. He was a life member of the American Philatelic Society and was owner of the first United States postcard ever mailed. He was active in various mountain clubs. He died in the home of his son in Arlington, Massachusetts.

BUTLER, MADAME ROSILLA, HAIR GOODS: established in 1873 in Boston, Massachusetts. A hairdressing salon and retailer of hair goods, this establishment was located on Winter Street, near Tremont Street, in 1892. The business remained in operation under this name until 1926. It was at this salon that Tish Thomas, a manicurist, was said to have relayed a story which she had heard concerning alleged peculiar behavior on the part of Miss Lizzie A. Borden.

CARPENTER, JOSEPH WILMARTH, JR. 1855 - 1899: born in Fall River, Massachusetts, son of Joseph Wilmarth and Phoebe A. (Kershaw) Carpenter. A partner for a short time with Z. L. Bruce in the produce business, he was subsequently employed as a bookkeeper by the firm of Borden, Almy and Company, until a dispute between him and the firm's proprietors caused his dismissal. He was married to Miss Annie Barney, daughter of George W. Barney of Fall River. In 1882, he relocated to Holyoke, Massachusetts. After this time, he was employed as a traveling salesman in association with an ink manufacturing firm. He died in Worcester, Massachusetts, at the residence of his sister. Although an attempt was made to implicate him in the Borden murders, he was cleared by an alibi provided to Captain Philip Harrington by Mrs. Victoria A. Foreman of Albany, New York.

CARR, WILLIAM 1821 - 1893: born in Warren, Rhode Island, the son of William and Temperance (Smith) Carr. Following his marriage to Miss Elizabeth Valentine Durfee of Fall River, Massachusetts, in 1848, he and his wife resided in her native city. Among his business interests were the Borden Mining Company and Metacomet National Bank, two corporations for which he served as director. He was also an agent for the Fall River and Providence Steamboat Company. He maintained an active interest in the municipal affairs of his adopted city until the time of his death. He provided a statement to district police regarding any knowledge of insanity in the Borden family.

CASE, RESCOMB 1817 - 1901: born in Westport, Massachusetts, son of Pardon and Ellipha (Macomber) Case. A carpenter by trade, he apprenticed to James Ford and Southard H. Miller in Fall River, Massachusetts. He later worked in that trade for a variety of manufacturers there, among them the American Printing Company from which he retired. He was twice married, his first wife being Miss Alma Manchester and his second Mrs. Louisa Adams.

He was an active Congregationalist. His obituary named him a "venerable citizen of Second Street" due to his length of residence there. He provided a statement to district police regarding any knowledge of insanity in the Borden and Morse families.

CHAGNON, MARIANNE (GIGAULT) PHANEUF ? - 1895: born in Canada. She was the widow of Desire Phaneuf, a merchant from St. Damase, Canada. She became the second wife of Dr. Wenceslas Jean Baptiste Chagnon in 1885, married at Biddeford, Maine. A witness at both the preliminary and final trials, she gave testimony pertaining to a noise she heard coming from the direction of the Borden house the evening of August 3, 1892. Her death came tragically, due to injuries sustained when she leapt from a convent window in St. Hyacinthe, Province of Quebec, Canada.

CHAGNON, M. MARTHE 1873 - ?: born in Canada, daughter of Dr. Wenceslas Jean Baptiste and Victorine (Desnoyer) Chagnon. In 1897, she married Edmund Vadnais, a dentist from North Adams, Massachusetts. Widowed ten years later by her husband's unexpected death at age thirty-three, she is next known to have been working as a nurse at Rhode Island Hospital in Providence, Rhode Island. Boarding there during her length of employment, she later relocated to Montreal, Canada, where three of her sisters resided at that time. She is last known to have been living there widowed in 1936. A witness at both the preliminary and final trials, she gave testimony, as did her stepmother, pertaining to a noise heard on the evening before the Borden murders.

CHAGNON, WENCESLAS JEAN BAPTISTE 1837 - 1912: born in St. Jean Baptiste, Rouville, Canada, son of Antoine and Marie-Ann (Bernard) Chagnon. Educated in Catholic seminaries in Canada, he studied at the University of New York, receiving his medical degree in 1860. This was followed by a one-year course of study at McGill University, Montreal, and an additional four months' of study in Paris, France. He practiced medicine in Canada for eighteen years, ten years of which he also served as a justice of the peace. He held the position of surgeon-major in the Canadian Militia from 1868 to 1878 and took part in the Fenian Invasion during the Franco-Prussian War. In 1879, he emigrated to the United States and settled in Fall River, Massachusetts. Anglicizing his name to "John B.," he established his practice and opened a pharmacy. The father of twenty children, he was married three times. In 1861, he married Miss Victorine Desnoyer of his native town with whom he had thirteen children. In 1885, he was married a second time to

Mrs. Marie-Anne (Gigault) Phaneuf of Biddeford, Maine. He was married for the third time in 1898 to Miss Isabelle Ballou of Fall River, with whom he had seven children. He resided at 31 Third Street, directly behind the Andrew J. Borden residence at 92 Second Street. One of the most widely known French Canadian physicians in New England, he was a frequent contributor to the *Montreal Medical Journal*. Active in the community, he was a member of several medical and charitable societies. He died in Fall River, Massachusetts.

CHASE, MARK P. 1843 - 1921: born in Somerset, Massachusetts. A Civil War veteran, he enlisted as a wagoner in Company H, 3rd Massachusetts Volunteers, serving a nine-month term. He came to Fall River, Massachusetts, circa 1870 and was employed as freightmaster of the Old Colony Railroad steamboat wharf. He left the city in 1887 for Westport, Massachusetts, returning to Fall River in five years' time. He worked as a hostler at the New York and Boston Despatch Company, located a short distance from the Andrew J. Borden residence. Following the death of his wife, Sarah, in 1901, he remained in Fall River an additional nine years before relocating to Togus, Maine. He was a resident of Sterling, Connecticut, at the time of his death. The testimony he supplied at the Borden trial detailed his observations in the vicinity of Andrew J. Borden's property on the morning of August 4, 1892.

CHEEVER, DAVID WILLIAMS 1831 - 1915: born in Portsmouth, New Hampshire, son of Dr. Charles Augustus and Adeline (Haven) Cheever. Receiving his early education at home under private instruction, he entered Harvard University, earning his Bachelor of Arts in 1852. The next year-and-a-half he spent traveling extensively in Europe and, upon his return to the United States, he spent one term at the Boylston Medical School. He continued his studies at Harvard Medical School, receiving the degree of Doctor of Medicine in 1858. His internship was spent at the state hospital at Ramsford Island, where he remained for one year after taking his degree. In 1860, he married Miss Annie C. Nichols in Boston. The following year, he was appointed demonstrator of anatomy at his alma mater, a position he held until 1866, when he was named assistant professor of anatomy. Here he laid a firm foundation for his brilliant career as a surgeon and teacher. Serving as senior surgeon at Boston City Hospital in 1864, he had the distinction of being the youngest member of its medical staff. He was appointed adjunct professor and later professor of clinical surgery at Harvard in 1868, spending seven years in the latter position. In 1882, he was named professor of surgery, a position he retained until he was made professor emeritus in 1893. He maintained a private practice and for five years was surgeon at the Boston Dispensary. In 1894, he was awarded the honorary degree of Doctor of Laws by Harvard University. The author of numerous books, including the five-volume *Medical and Surgical Reports of City Hospital*, he also wrote extensively for many of the leading magazines of the day and was a frequent contributor to various medical journals. He served as president of the Massachusetts Benevolent Society, which provided aid to needy physicians. He personally established several scholarships to assist first-year medical students. Following his death in Boston, Massachusetts, a memorial address was written in his honor by Dr. George W. Gay. A specialist in anatomy, he examined the skulls of Mr. and Mrs. Andrew J. Borden and testified as to his findings.

CHURCH, CHARLES H. 1830 - 1914: born in New Bedford, Massachusetts, son of James L. and Sarah Sherman (Smith) Church. It Seems likely that the name "Church" appearing on the list of potential witnesses with the notations "N. B." and "buying prussic acid" beside it refers to this New Bedford druggist. Educated in the public schools of his native city, he completed one year of high school before beginning an apprenticeship as a sailmaker under his father's instruction. Advised by his family to pursue a different trade, he entered the employ of Charles A. Cook and began to learn the drug business. Working at Cook's establishment for over a year, he then relocated to Boston, Massachusetts, where he gained employment at the apothecary of a Dr. Stevens. He moved again after a year to Brooklyn, New York, where he lived for a time, returning to his native New Bedford in 1852. He purchased an existing drug business from Warren B. Potter, expanding it in 1855. He remained a druggist all of his life and was a founding member of the New Bedford Druggist . Association, an organization for which he served as vice- president for several years. He was married to Miss Sarah L. Wood of Dana, Massachusetts. William R. Martin, one of the witnesses summoned to testify at the Borden trial, was employed at this man's establishment circa 1892 to 1894.

CHURCHILL, ADELAIDE (BUFFINTON) 1850 - 1926: born in Fall River, Massachusetts, daughter of Hon. Edward P. and Comfort (Taber) Buffinton. She married Charles H. Churchill, an employee of the water department in Fall River, and was widowed in 1879. She resided with her only son, Charles, at 90 Second Street in the Buffinton family home. An active Congregationalist, she was involved in church activities in Fall River until the time of her death. One of the first summoned to the Borden house following the murders, she provided considerable testimony at the inquest as well as the preliminary and final trials.

CLARKSON, ALFRED 1846 - 1917: born in England, son of Samuel and Sarah (Rodgers) Clarkson. Emigrating to the United States in 1853, he is first listed in the Fall River, Massachusetts, city directory in 1872, employed as a steam engineer. He was renowned in that area as an inventor by the time of his death. Active fraternally, he was a member of the Odd Fellows Lodge. A witness at both the preliminary and final trials, he gave testimony pertaining to his actions in the vicinity of the barn at 92 Second Street the day of the murders.

CLEGG, JONATHAN 1842 - 1923: born in England. Emigrating to the United States in 1872, he is first listed in the Fall River, Massachusetts, city directory in 1876. Throughout his years of residence there, he was employed in a variety of trades. He operated a gentleman's haberdashery, founded circa 1884, on North Main Street in that city. He married Mrs. Christiana (Francis) Oman of Newport, Rhode Island, in 1892. At the time of the murders, he was in the process of relocating his business to the Andrew J. Borden Building at 39 South Main Street. A witness at both the preliminary and final trials, he gave testimony centering around a final encounter with Mr. Borden in his store on the morning of August 4. Following his years as a haberdasher, he was employed as an insurance agent and, for over ten years, as a collector. He died in Fall River, Massachusetts.

COBB, WENDELL HAMLIN 1838 - 1902: born in Sandwich, Massachusetts, son of Rev. Asahel and Helen Maria (Hamlin) Cobb. Having received his early education in public schools, he subsequently attended Paul Wing's Academy in his native town. He prepared for college at Phillip's Academy in Andover, Massachusetts, and then entered Dartmouth College, receiving his Bachelor of Arts in 1861. He began his study of law that same year in the New Bedford, Massachusetts, office of Messrs. Stone and Crapo. Admitted to the Bristol bar in 1865, he established a practice in New Bedford. Among his professional involvements was the prosecution of Alabama and French Spoliation claims at Washington, District of Columbia. In 1872, he married Miss Isabel Frances Cushman of New Bedford. Active politically in that city, he held the office of city solicitor and was a member of the school committee for several years. An alderman from 1885 to 1888, he served again in that capacity in 1891. Associated with the law firm of Marston and Crapo until its dissolution, he then established a partnership with George Marston, Esq.

In 1896, he was chosen to revise the city ordinances of New Bedford. When the National Bankruptcy Law of 1898 was passed, he was appointed one of its referees for the Commonwealth of Massachusetts. A member of the New Bedford Protecting Society, he also served as vice-president of that city's choral association. He died following a brief illness while a patient at St. Luke's Hospital in New Bedford. At the time of his death, he was considered one of the best-known lawyers in that city.

COGGESHALL, ALEXANDER H. 1840 - 1930: born in Westport, Massachusetts, son of Joseph and Phebe (Mosher) Coggeshall. He married Miss Sarah E. Tripp of his native town. He is first recorded as residing in Fall River, Massachusetts, in 1870, employed as a wood dealer. Shortly thereafter, he became partners with Herbert L. Law in the firm Law and Coggeshall, Stables. Founded circa 1872, this business was in operation for two years, after which time he began his own livery business. His stable at 143 Second Street was a short distance from the Borden house. Summoned as a witness, he was not called upon to testify. Having retired from active business, he died in Fall River, Massachusetts.

COLE, FRANCIS GRANGER 1844 - 1915: born in Rehoboth, Massachusetts, son of George and Nancy (Rounds) Cole. A Civil War veteran he worked as a machinist before entering the jewelry trade in Attleboro, Massachusetts. He married Miss Josephine B. Peck of Rehoboth, was prominent in Attleboro public affairs and was an active worker on behalf of the Baptist church. He remained a resident of Attleboro until the time of his death. He was one of the twelve-man jury that acquitted Miss Lizzie A. Borden on June 20, 1893. Questioned in later life by his great-niece, Mrs. Alice E. (Dexter) Dyer, he said only that he "could not believe that a woman could have done it" and refused to discuss his participation in the case.

COLLETT, LUCIE 1874 - 1900: born in St. Henry, Quebec, Canada, daughter of Pierre A. A. and Georgianna (Verrault) Collett. On August 4, 1892, she was summoned to watch Dr. Chagnon's house in his absence by a clerk in his employ, Jean Napoleon Normand, a man she would marry in 1896. A witness at both the preliminary and final trials, she provided testimony concerning her observations while sitting on Dr. Chagnon's porch that morning. She resided in Fall River, Massachusetts, until the time of her death.

CONE, DWIGHT ELEAZER 1854 - 1927. Born in North Brookfield. New York, son of Benjamin and S. Rosette (Beebe) Cone. Educated in the New

Berlin Academy in New York, he began his professional career as a teacher, a step necessary to accumulate the funds for medical study. In 1873, he entered Albany Medical College at Albany, New York, and completed his studies at the University of the City of New York, receiving his degree in 1875. He practiced medicine in New York and Rhode Island before establishing himself in Fall River, Massachusetts, in 1882. He married his first wife, Miss Nancy Adelin Merritt of Coventry, New York, in 1875, and his second, Mrs. M. Abby (Slade) Sias of Somerset, Massachusetts, in 1919. A founder of the Fall River Hospital in 1886, he maintained memberships in several medical societies. Extremely active in Masonic work, he held positions in several Massachusetts and Rhode Island chapters. He died unexpectedly at a clambake in Swansea, Massachusetts. He served as clerk at the August 11, 1892, autopsies of Mr. and Mrs. Andrew J. Borden.

CONNOR, THOMAS J. 1836 - 1905: born in Ireland. He emigrated to the United States in 1870. He was employed as a weaver in a Fall River, Massachusetts, textile mill from 1880 to 1882. He subsequently opened a variety store in that city, a business he operated with his wife, Margaret. Retiring by 1893, he occupied himself until his death as a winemaker. He is mentioned in a statement given by Alfred A. Smith, an inmate at the Massachusetts Reformatory, on January 9, 1893.

CONNORS, PATRICK 1853 - 1926: born in County Cork, Ireland, son of Owen and Catherine (Hurley) Connors. He emigrated to the United States with his family at the age of fourteen, settling in Fall River, Massachusetts, by 1868. First employed as a laborer, he was appointed a patrolman of the police force in that city in 1879, thus beginning a career in law enforcement that was to last over forty years. In 1884, he married Miss Annie O'Dowd. He was appointed to day duty in 1886 and, seven years later, was made captain. During his long career, he was the recipient of several commendations for his excellent work in conducting investigations. He retired from the force in 1923. A deeply religious man he maintained an active interest in St. Joseph's Orphanage in Fall River and was a benefactor to the religious order of the Sisters of Charity. Following a lengthy illness, he died while a patient in Union Hospital in the city where he had made his home. Summoned as a witness, he was not called upon to testify.

COOK CHARLES H. 1836 - 1911: born in Rhode Island, son of Darius and Louisa P. (Francis) Cook. Spending his youth in Fall River, Massachusetts, he enlisted as a private in Company C, 3rd Massachusetts Volunteers, serving a nine-month term beginning in 1862. Following his term of service, he returned to Fall River, where he was employed as a driver. He was one of the individuals who went inside the Borden barn the day of the murders. Employed in various occupations in his later life, he spent several years working as a coachman. He died in Taunton, Massachusetts. Although he gave a statement to the Fall River police, testified at the preliminary trial and was summoned as a witness, he was not called upon to testify.

COOK, EVERETT M. 1855 - 1931: born in Fall River, Massachusetts, son of William and Esther Cook. Educated in the Fall River public school system, he was employed at the First National Bank following graduation and remained there until his retirement. In his capacity as cashier at that institution, he transacted business with Andrew J. Borden on the morning of August 4, 1892, a fact to which he testified at the preliminary and final Borden trials. A prominent figure in banking circles, he was a member of several business clubs. He was married to Miss Mattie L. Brightman. He died in his native city.

COONEY, PATRICK HENRY 1845 - 1915: born in Stockbridge, Massachusetts, son of Lawrence and Catherine Cooney. At an early age, he moved with his family to Natick, Massachusetts, where he was educated ill public schools. Following graduation from high school in 1866, he entered the Allen English and Classical School in West Newton, Massachusetts. He studied law at Boston University and in the Natick offices of Hon. George L. Sawin and John W. Bacon, Esq. In 1868, he was Admitted to the Suffolk bar and began a private practice in Natick, later adding an office in Boston, Massachusetts. Active in civic affairs, he was a member of the Natick school committee from 1880 to 1883. Appointed assistant district attorney for the Northern District of Massachusetts circa 1884, he served in that capacity until 1890 when he was appointed district attorney. He returned to his successful practice in 1894. He married Miss Sarah Allen of West Newton. Several years his junior, she died at the birth of their only child, who perished with her. He held memberships in several prominent professional and fraternal organizations. He died at his residence in Natick.

COUGHLIN, JOHN WILLIAM 1861 - 1920: born in Fall River, Massachusetts, son of William and Abbie (Maley) Coughlin. Educated in the Fall River public school system, he apprenticed as a steam and gas fitter until his employment in the office of Dr. John B. Chagnon inspired in him an interest in medicine. Following study with Dr. Charles C. Terry he attended the College of Physicians and Surgeons in Baltimore, Maryland.

He received the degree of Doctor of Medicine in 1885 and returned to his native city to open practice. He was elected to the mayoralty of that city for four consecutive terms beginning in 1890 and, for the rest of his life, remained active in political circles there. During World War I, he served on the Frothingham Commission. He was involved in several civic and professional organizations. It was he who first informed Miss Lizzie A. Borden that she was suspected of murdering her father and stepmother. His testimony at the trial recounted his visit to the Borden residence on the evening of August 6, 1892.

COWLES, EDWARD 1837 - 1919: born in Ryegate, Vermont, son of George and Mary (Bradley) Cowles. Receiving his early education in public schools, he entered Dartmouth College, graduating with his Bachelor of Arts in 1859. He continued his studies at Dartmouth Medical School and received his Master of Arts in 1861. Two years later, he was awarded the degree of Doctor of Medicine from Dartmouth as well as one from the College of Physicians and Surgeons, Columbia University. Following his medical studies, he became an assistant surgeon at the Retreat for the Insane in Hartford, Connecticut. At the outbreak of the Civil War, he enlisted in the army, serving as an assistant surgeon with the rank of captain. In 1865, he married Miss Harriet M. Wainwright of Hanover, New Hampshire. Discharged from the military in 1872, he moved to Boston, Massachusetts, accepting the position of resident physician and superintendent of the Boston City Hospital. In 1879, he relinquished his position in Boston to succeed Dr. George F. Jelly as superintendent of the McLean Hospital for the Insane in Somerville, Massachusetts. Instrumental in planning the new hospital facility when it relocated to Waverly, Massachusetts, he remained there as its head until his retirement in 1913. Active as an educator, he was professor of mental diseases at Dartmouth from 1885 until 1914 at which time he was named professor emeritus. In 1890, he received the honorary degree of Doctor of Laws from that institution. He was instructor of mental diseases at Harvard Medical School from 1888 to 1914 and was a non-resident lecturer on the same subject at Clark University. The author of numerous monologues on hospital construction, mental health and like subjects, he held membership in several professional societies in the United States and abroad. He was considered one of the leading alienists in the United States and appeared in that capacity in several important murder trials. He was questioned as to whether he believed the perpetrator of the Borden murders had behaved in a maniacal fashion. He died in Plymouth, Massachusetts.

CRAPO, MARGARET L. (WALLACE) 1829 - 1896: born in Saugerties, New York, the daughter of Alexander and Catherine L. (Miller) Wallace. She married John D. Crapo, a wine and liquor merchant, who died in 1877. She resided at 39 Third Street in Fall River, Massachusetts, in 1892, and remained there until the time of her death. Summoned as a witness, she was not called upon to testify.

CUNEEN, JAMES E. 1832 - 1914: born in New York state, son of Michael and Ann S. (Maloney) Cuneen. His family moved to Fall River, Massachusetts, circa 1839 and at the age of seven he began working there. At the time of the Civil War, he was one of the first from that city to volunteer, enlisting as a private with Company C, 3rd Massachusetts Volunteers, having been promoted to sergeant by the time of his discharge nine months later. He was employed for a time insuring real estate and, from 1870 to 1872, served as an alderman. He was twice married, his first wife being Miss Mary A. Organ and his second Miss Mary J. Kelleher. He was heavily invested in Fall River mills and served as director of several corporations until his death. He was referred to as one of that city's most prominent mill men. He was in the vicinity of the Borden house the morning of the murders, was summoned as a witness but was not called upon to testify.

CUNNINGHAM, JOHN J. 1864 - 1912: born in England, son of Patrick and Margaret Cunningham. A partner in Cunningham Brothers, dealers in newspapers and periodicals, he once had the largest route in the city of Fall River, Massachusetts. Appointed to the Fall River Fire Department as a callman in 1891, he remained with the department until his death. Transacting newspaper business on Second Street the morning of the murders, he was told that someone had "stabbed" Andrew J. Borden. He then telephoned City Marshall Rufus B. Hilliard and the office of the Fall River Daily Globe to report the news. A witness at both the preliminary and final trials, he gave testimony pertaining to his observations that morning.

DABNEY, LEWIS STACKPOLE 1840 - 1908: born in Fayal, Azores, son of Frederick and Roxana (Stackpole) Dabney. The son of the vice-consul of Faval, he attended Harvard University in Cambridge, Massachusetts, and was graduated with a Bachelor of Arts in 1861. The following year he enlisted for duty in the Civil War, joining the 2nd Regiment, Massachusetts Volunteers Cavalry, with the rank of second lieutenant. Serving his final year oil the staff of Gen. C. C. Augur, he was mustered out as a captain in 1865. Study in the office of Messrs. Horace Gray and Charles F. Blake enabled him to be admitted to the Suffolk bar in Massachusetts in 1863. Upon completion of his term of duty in the Union Army, he began to practice law in Boston, Massachusetts. In 1866, he was appointed to serve as assistant district attorney with Richard H. Dana, Esq. He was married to Miss Clara Bigelow the following year. He was active in several professional organizations, among them the American and Boston Bar Associations, the latter of which he served for a time as president. His membership in social clubs included the Beverly Yacht Club, of which he was commodore. A resident of Boston, he practiced law there until his death. His comment on the Borden case is mentioned in the letter addressed by Mrs. Alexandria Delano to Mrs. Hosea M. Knowlton.

DAVIS, MRS. GEORGE W., see **DAVIS, SELINA A. (SMITH)**.

DAVIS, SELINA ANN (SMITH) 1868 - 1957: born in Fall River, Massachusetts, daughter of Robert and Ann (Greenwood) Smith. She married George W. Davis, Sr., a stove mounter employed for a time by the Eagle Stove Foundry in Fall River. Residing at 19 President Avenue in 1892, she was visited by her brother, Alfred A. Smith, on the day of the Borden murders. She moved with her family to Somerset, Massachusetts, in 1915 and made her home there until circa 1940 when she moved to Attleboro, Massachusetts, to reside with relatives. In 1953, she relocated with her family to Plainville, Massachusetts. She died at her home in that town.

DEAN, WILLIAM FRANCIS 1839 - 1904: born in Taunton Massachusetts, son of Enos W. and Elizabeth Jane (Williams) Dean. Educated in the Taunton public school system as well as Bristol Academy, also located in that city, he became a farmer and worked land owned for several generations by his family. A Unitarian, he married Miss Mary Jane Bassett of Grafton, Massachusetts, in 1870. He died in his native city. He was one of the twelve-man jury that acquitted Miss Lizzie A. Borden on June 20, 1893.

DELANO, ALEXANDER JAMES 1868 - ?: born in Marion, Massachusetts, son of James Haskell and Alexandria Paulovna (Kusmischev) Delano. It is likely that the mention of "Alec" in the letter addressed by Mrs. Alexandria Delano to Mrs. Hosea M. Knowlton refers to this young man.

DESMOND, DENNIS, JR. 1854 - 1926: born in Fall River, Massachusetts, son of Dennis and Mary (Desmond) Desmond. He entered the Fall River Police Department as a patrolman in 1881 and in 1893 was promoted to the rank of captain. He served as assistant city marshal J and, in 1903, became captain of the Central Division. His wife, Adeline, died in 1923. By the time of his retirement in 1924, he held the record for having commanded every police department division in Fall River. He then relocated to Somerset, Massachusetts, where he resided the remainder of his life. He was the officer who investigated the burglary at the home of Andrew J. Borden in 1891. His testimony at the Borden trial detailed his participation in the search for evidence at 92 Second Street.

DESROSIERS, JOSEPH 1870 - ?: a resident of Fall River, Massachusetts, in 1892. According to his testimony provided at the preliminary trial, he was living at the "King Philip on Main Street." No one by this name is listed in the city directories of the period as residing at that address. Employed as a laborer, he was working in the Crowe yard, property adjacent to that of Andrew J. Borden. His testimony at the preliminary and final trials pertained to his observations there on the morning of August 4, 1892.

DEVINE, JOHN J. 1852 - 1930: born in England, son of Thomas and Catherine Devine. He married Miss Ellen Corbett. His long career with the police department in Fall River, Massachusetts, began in 1877 when he was appointed patrolman. Upon his retirement in 1922, he held the rank of lieutenant. An active member of several professional organizations, he was a resident of Fall River at the time of his death. He assisted in searching the cellar of the Borden residence the day of the murders and examined the hatchets and axes found there.

DEWEY, JUSTIN 1836 - 1900: born in Alford, Massachusetts, son of Justin and Melinda (Kelsey) Dewey. He received his early education in the public schools of his native town and in Great Barrington, Massachusetts. He then attended Williams College, graduating in 1858. He began the study of law in the Great Barrington office of Increase Sumner, Esq., was admitted to the Berkshire bar in 1860 and subsequently established his own practice. He rose quickly to prominence in his chosen profession. He wed Miss Jane Stanley in Great Barrington in 1865. Active politically, he was elected to the Massachusetts House of Representatives in 1862 and again in 1877. He was also elected to the state senate in 1879. In 1886, he was appointed judge of the Massachusetts superior court by Governor George D. Robinson, the man who would later successfully defend Miss Lizzie A. Borden in the courtroom over which he presided. He died in Springfield, Massachusetts.

DINNIE, JOHN 1858 - ? : born in Scotland. Emigrating to the United States in 1882, he settled in Fall River, Massachusetts, two years later. His wife, Catherine, was a native of Massachusetts. In 1892, he was employed as a stonemason in a yard adjacent to the property of Andrew J. Borden and, by 1905, was advertising himself as a contractor. In 1908, he relocated to the Chicago, Illinois, area. A witness at the preliminary trial and summoned for the final trial, he was not called upon to testify.

DOHERTY, PATRICK H. 1859 - 1915: born in Peoria, Illinois, son of John and Mary (Welch) Doherty. He traveled east with his family as a youth and later secured employment at the Fall River Iron Works Company in Fall River, Massachusetts. Following this, he served as a deckhand and member of the lifesaving crew on the Fall River Line steamer *Bristol*. He was appointed to the Fall River Police Department in 1885. Two years later, he married Miss Nora Coughlin of Fall River. He was a member of various professional and fraternal organizations. Promoted to police captain in 1892, he retired from active duty in 1915, dying shortly thereafter. One of the first officers sent to the scene of the crime on August 4, 1892, he provided testimony at both the preliminary and final trials.

DOLAN, WILLIAM ANDREW 1858 - 1922: born in Shirley, Massachusetts, son of Andrew and Jane (McBride) Dolan. Following his family's move to Fall River, Massachusetts, he was educated in that city's public school system. A graduate of St. Joseph's College in Yonkers, New York, in 1879, he became a student in the medical department of the University of Pennsylvania, receiving his degree in 1882. In 1883, he returned to Fall River and entered practice, that same year marrying Miss Nellie B. Hussey of that city. In 1892, he was appointed medical examiner for the Third District in Bristol County, Massachusetts, and as such was the medical officer in charge of the Borden murder case, testifying in that capacity at both the preliminary and final trials of Miss Lizzie A. Borden. He was active in various professional societies and was still practicing at the time of his death in Fall River.

DOOLAN, MARY: from 1893 - 1896, listed as boarding at 96 (later 240) Second Street, the residence of Dr. and Mrs. Michael Kelly. It is likely that she was a domestic employed by the Kellys and is the person referred to as "Mrs. Kelly's girl" and "servant of" in the documents. Summoned as a witness, she was not called upon to testify.

DOUGLAS, GEORGE L. 1864 - 1923: born in Fall River, Massachusetts, son of James and Sarah (Austin) Douglas. A hostler in the city of his birth, he is first listed in the city directory there in 1892, employed at Douglas Brothers, a livery, boarding and exchange stable on Morgan Street. He remained in Fall River until 1897, when he relocated to New Bedford, Massachusetts, gaining employment there as a motorman. He returned to Fall River for a short time but, by 1907, was again employed as a motorman in New Bedford, where he resided with his wife, Anna. He died in Taunton, Massachusetts. Summoned as a witness, he was not called upon to testify.

DOWNS, EDWARD P. 1877 - 1950: born in Fall River, Massachusetts, son of John A. and Catherine (Hannon) Downs. Employed early in his life as a wood dealer, he began a career as a clerk in 1904. Marrying Miss Johanna Gleeson, he lived in the city of his birth for his entire life. For many of those years, he was employed by Louis P. Drape, Inc., fish dealers. A youth at the time of the Borden murders, he was summoned as a witness but was not called upon to testify.

DRAPER, FRANK WINTHROP 1843 - 1909: born in Wayland, Massachusetts, son of James Sumner and Emmeline Amanda (Reeves) Draper. Educated in the public schools of his native town, he then attended Brown University in Providence, Rhode Island, receiving his Bachelor of Arts in 1862. Upon graduation, he enlisted with the 35th Massachusetts Volunteers as a private, serving in the medical division of his regiment. He saw active service during the Civil War, being detailed with the Army Medical Board. In 1864, he was appointed captain, becoming actively engaged in several southern campaigns. Following expiration of his term of duty, he entered Harvard Medical School, graduating in 1869, at which time he interned at Boston City Hospital in Boston, Massachusetts. He married Miss Fanny V. Jones in Boston in 1870. Establishing a general family practice in that city, he was a visiting physician at both Children's Hospital and City Hospital. Appointed medical examiner for Suffolk County in 1877, he served in this capacity until 1905. A frequent lecturer at Harvard University, he was appointed assistant professor of legal medicine in 1884 and in 1889, professor of medical jurisprudence, holding the latter position until 1903. An authority in his field, he maintained active memberships in several professional organizations and served as president of the Massachusetts Medical Society from 1900 to 1902. He was also a fellow of the American Academy of Arts and Sciences. An editor of several medical journals, he frequently contributed articles for publication. Among his works were *Ergot of Rye: Its Physiological and Therapeutic Relations*, published in 1869 and *A Textbook of Legal Medicine*, published in

1904. He died in Brookline, Massachusetts. Assisting at the autopsies of Mr. and Mrs. Andrew Borden on August 11, 1892, he gave testimony at the preliminary and final trials which detailed his findings.

DRISCOLL, PETER M. 1853 - 1899: born in Boston, Massachusetts, son of Patrick and Ellen Driscoll. Employed as a hairdresser in Fall River, Massachusetts, he became a partner in the firm of Driscoll and Sheffield, Fashionable Hairdressers, in 1880. This partnership dissolved in 1882, at which time he continued in the same profession under his own name for the next sixteen years. He married Miss Harriet A. Read of Westport, Massachusetts, and, following her death in 1882, Miss Hattie D. Vadenais of Fall River, who died in 1898. He followed her to the grave only one year later in Taunton, Massachusetts, the cause of death acute melancholia. His claim that he had shaved Joseph W. Carpenter, Jr. in Fall River on August 1, 1892, cast suspicion on that man, as he was known to be an enemy of Andrew J. Borden.

DURFEE, MARY A. (BENTLEY) 1856 - 1924: born in Newport, Rhode Island, daughter of George and Elizabeth Bentley. In 1876, she married Joseph Franklin Durfee, a clerk for a Fall River, Massachusetts, provisions dealer. She died at her home in that city. A resident of 124 Second Street in 1892, she gave testimony pertaining to a scene she witnessed in which Andrew J. Borden was threatened by a man on the steps of his home.

DURLING, OLIVER H. PERRY c.1873 - ? : born in New Jersey, son of James W. and Charlotte A. (Douglas) Durling. Educated in the Fall River, Massachusetts, public school system, he graduated from Bradford Matthew Chaloner Durfee High School in 1892, holding the rank of major in that institution's cadet force. Employed as a clerk in Fall River, he relocated to Providence, Rhode Island, in 1900 and is known to have lived in Pittsburg, Pennsylvania, employed as a manager, in 1915. He married Mrs. Martha C. Bothwick. Summoned as a witness, he was not called upon to testify.

DWIGHT, THOMAS 1843 - 1911: born in Boston, Massachusetts, son of Thomas and Mary Collins (Warren) Dwight. He spent his early years with his family in Paris, France. Preparing for college at Dr. Epes S. Dixwell's school in Boylston Place, Boston, Massachusetts, he entered Harvard University in the class of 1866. He interrupted his studies there to enroll in Harvard Medical School, from which he received the degree of Doctor of

Medicine in 1867. He studied abroad for two years in Berlin and Vienna, afterwards returning to the United States where he established practices in both Boston and Nahant, Massachusetts. In 1872, he was awarded his Bachelor of Arts from Harvard University and was subsequently appointed instructor in comparative anatomy there. From 1872 to 1876, he also dedicated time to Bowdoin College where he served as first a lecturer in and later professor of anatomy. At Harvard Medical School in 1874, he was made instructor in histology and, six years later, appointed instructor in topographical anatomy. From 1877 to 1880, he served as an out-patient surgeon at Boston City Hospital. He also held the position of visiting surgeon at Carney Hospital in South Boston for a seven-year period ending in 1883. That year, he was successor to Dr. Oliver Wendell Holmes in the Parkman Professorship of Anatomy and Physiology at Harvard Medical School and was presented with the honorary degree Doctor of Laws from Georgetown University in 1889. He also served for a time as an instructor in anatomy at the Medical School of Maine. He married Miss Sarah Catherine Iasigi. He was the author of several books on anatomy, among them *Frozen Sections of a Child*, published in 1881, and *Variations of the Bones of the Hands and Feet*, published in 1907. He contributed frequently to medical and popular monthly publications. He died in Nahant, Massachusetts. A distinguished anatomist, he served as a medical expert for the defense and in that capacity examined the skulls of Mr. and Mrs. Andrew J. Borden.

EAGAN, JOHN J.: son of Owen and Catherine Eagan. First listed in the Fall River, Massachusetts, city directory in 1888, he was employed as a clerk by P. F. Millea, Provisions Dealer, 54 Spring Street, in 1892. Working as a clerk for various firms in that city, he is last listed in 1939 as an employee of A. Yoken and Sons, Grocers. Present on Second Street the morning of the murders, he provided a statement to the Fall River police. He did not testify.

EDDY, FRANCIS WILMARTH 1831 - 1898: born in Fall River, Massachusetts, son of Francis and Betsy (Wilmarth) Eddy. He married Miss Sarah J. Gardner. He was employed as a foreman and hack-driver by Charles T. Kirby and Company, Stables. He remained in that profession until the time of his death. Summoned as a witness, he was not called upon to testify.

EDSON, FRANCIS L. 1855 - 1906: born in Fall River, Massachusetts, son of Daniel and Susan Edson. Employed as a roll coverer, he was appointed to (fit- Fall River Police Department ill 1883 and held the rank of sergeant at the little of the Borden murders. He was advanced to lieutenant in February of 1893 and, in December of that same year, promoted to captain. He married Miss Bertha C. Perkins. He was actively involved in many organizations, both professional and fraternal. He died in Fall River, Massachusetts. His extensive testimony at the trial relayed details pertinent to the search of the Borden property.

EDWARDS, WILLIS: a clairvoyant physician. He is recorded as residing in Lynn, Massachusetts, for two years only, 1892 and 1893. His unusual profession probably caused him to be itinerant. Delia Wilson, writing to Attorney Hosea M. Knowlton, suggested that he be contacted for information on the Borden case as he could provide "every detail even to the names.

FESSENDEN, SUSAN BREESE (SNOWDEN) 1840 - 1932: born in Cincinnati, Ohio, daughter of Sidney and Elizabeth (Mitchell) Snowden. Spending much of her early life in the city of her birth, she later relocated with her family to Covington, Kentucky. She married John Henry Fessenden circa 1861, moving with him first to New England and then to Knoxville, Tennessee. Settling in the midwestern United States, she spent the next eleven years residing with her family in Sioux City, Iowa. Her extensive knowledge of various areas of her native country prompted her to begin lecturing, a vocation at which she achieved considerable success. In 1882, she relocated to Boston, Massachusetts, a city where she was to make her home for nearly forty years. During a year abroad, tragedy struck her family with the unexpected death of her twenty-two-year-old daughter while in Germany. Returning to Boston, she was actively involved in various women's groups. It was through this that she worked in close association with Frances Willard, then president of the Woman's Christian Temperance Union, serving as superintendent for that organization's department of franchise. A supporter of scientific temperance, she lectured widely on that and other topics. Serving as president of the Massachusetts chapter of the W.C.T.U. from 1891 to 1898, she was an associate of several prominent women of the day including Julia Ward Howe, Mary A. Livermore and Lucy Stone. She was a member of the New England Women's Club and the Century Club of Boston. An active Congregationalist, she maintained a strong interest in that church's mission program. In 1921, she left Boston for Northfield, Minnesota, and there spent the remainder of her life. In 1892, she appealed to Attorney Hosea M. Knowlton in regard to the admission of Miss Lizzie A. Borden to bail.

FINN, JOHN C.: son of Thomas Finn. He married Miss Catherine T. Grady of Somerset, Massachusetts. A painter, he was later employed as a clerk at the United States Post Office in Taunton, Massachusetts. He was one of the twelve-man jury that acquitted Miss Lizzie A. Borden on June 20, 1893. Having served for a time as a common councilman, he was said to be a dependable and reputable citizen.

FISK, GEORGE B.: an individual mentioned in a letter to Attorney Hosea M. Knowlton from Providence, Rhode Island. Attempts to uncover his identity have to date been unsuccessful.

FLEET, JOHN 1848 - 1916: born in Ashton-under-Lyne, Lancashire, England, son of Richard and Charlotte (Brown) Fleet. He emigrated to the United States as a youth and was employed at the American Linen Company in Fall River, Massachusetts. He then enlisted as a landsman in the United States Navy in 1864, serving a seventeen-month term. Following the Civil War, he returned to Fall River where he worked at various trades and married Miss Lydia Wallace of that city. In 1877, he was appointed to the police department and rose through the ranks from patrolman to city marshall, retiring in 1915. He died one year later in Fall River. It was as assistant city marshall in 1892 that he was called upon to arrest Miss Lizzie A. Borden for the murders of her father and stepmother. His extensive testimony at the preliminary and final trials concerned the police search for evidence at the Borden residence, providing detailed information about the hatchets found there.

FOREMAN, VICTORIA A. (BANKS): 1856 - 1896: born in Canada, daughter of Lewis and Catherine Banks. A resident of Albany, New York, in 1892, she took boarders in her residence at Nos. 33 and 35 Maiden Lane. Her husband, William S. Foreman, was a headwaiter at Delavan House ' a leading Albany hostelry, which was destroyed by fire in 1895. Following her death in that city, her husband relocated to Niagara Falls, New York. A room in her house was let to Joseph W. Carpenter, Jr. and she was questioned extensively about him by Fall River, Massachusetts, police officer Philip Harrington. Her statement, accompanied by a sworn affidavit, claimed that Mr. Carpenter had paid his rent each week in advance for the period of July 8th to August 13th, 1892, a fact that strengthened his alibi as to his whereabouts on August 4, 1892.

FRANCIS, MISS EDITH A. 1870 - 1944: born in Fall River, Massachusetts, daughter of William and Priscilla (Cluny) Francis. She was employed as a clerk, in 1891, for the Fall River firm of Charles C. Cook and Son and, following that, worked for several years as a bookkeeper with John P. Slade and Son. She was an active member of the Third Baptist Church, serving as deaconess and superintendent of the primary department of the Sunday school there. A life-long resident of Fall River, she maintained active memberships in both the World Wide Guild Home Worker's Society and the Women's Christian Temperance Union and was a member of the Fall River Historical Society. Summoned as a witness, she was not called upon to testify.

GALE, WILLIAM BOYNTON 1829 - 1899: born in Southampton, New Hampshire, son of John Gale. His early education was received under private instruction, furthered by two years' study at Harvard University. Having read law in the Concord, New Hampshire, offices of Gen. Franklin Pierce, Esq. and Hon. Asa Fowler, Esq., he was admitted to the New Hampshire bar in 1853. Shortly thereafter, he relocated to Marlboro, Massachusetts. A member of the Middlesex bar since 1860, he maintained an office in his adopted town until his move to Boston', Massachusetts, in 1878. He practiced law in that city until the time of his death, in rooms at the Hotel Vendome where he made his home. He was a member of the Knights of Pythias. A statement he made concerning the arrest of Miss Lizzie A. Borden appeared in the September 9, 1892, issue of the Concord Enterprise.

GARDNER, ORRIN AUGUSTUS 1867 - 1944: born in Swansea, Massachusetts, son of Henry Augustus and Caroline Cole (Mason) Gardner. A graduate of Warren, Rhode Island, high school, he attended Bryant and Stratton Business College and then Rhode Island Normal School. A teacher in Tiverton, Rhode Island, as well as Swansea and Fall River, Massachusetts, he later served as principal in two Fall River schools. He was employed for a time as an agent of the trustees of the State Industrial School for Boys and, following retirement from that position, taught at St. Andrew's School in Sewanee, Tennessee. He died in Dighton, Massachusetts. A cousin of the Misses Emma L. and Lizzie A. Borden, he was summoned as a witness but was not called upon to testify.

GAY, GEORGE WASHINGTON 1842 - 1931: born in Swanzey, New Hampshire, the son of Willard and Fanny (Wright) Gay. Spending his early life on his father's farm, he was later educated at Powers Institute in Bernardston, Massachusetts. After apprenticing for a year in Keene, New Hampshire, with Dr. George B. Twitchell, he entered Harvard Medical School where he most likely studied under Dr. David W. Cheever, demonstrator of anatomy at that time. In 1867, he secured a post as surgical house officer at Boston City Hospital in Boston, Massachusetts. The following year, he completed his medical studies and received the degree of Doctor of Medicine from Harvard. Also in 1868, having established a medical practice in Boston, he married Miss Mary E. Hutchinson of Milford, New Hampshire. Following his first wife's death, he was married again, in 1875, to Miss Grace Greenleaf Hawthorne of Boston. Senior surgeon at the Boston City Hospital, he lectured on his profession at the Harvard Medical School. He was a clinical instructor in surgery there from 1880 to 1900. He was the recipient of an honorary Master of Arts from Dartmouth College in 1895. A trustee for the Wrentham State School for the Feeble-Minded in Wrentham, Massachusetts, he also served for two years as president of the Massachusetts Medical Society, and was a member of both the British Medical Association and the American Surgical Association. He was a published author and included among his works *The Medical Treatment of Malignant Diseases* and *The Use of Opium in Senile Gangrene*. In 1892, he was acting as personal physician to Attorney General Albert E. Pillsbury.

GIBBS, SAMUEL WHELPLEY 1854 - 1926: born in Fall River, Massachusetts, son of George W. and Susan B. (Whelpley) Gibbs. Educated in the Fall River school system, he went on to graduate from Dartmouth College in 1889. His medical education was obtained at the University of Vermont. He entered practice soon after and became one of the best-known physicians in Fall River, active in the profession until the time of his death. He held offices in several fraternal organizations. He married Miss Susan Wallace Crapo, also of his native city. His home at 39 Third Street was among those visited by Officer Dennis Desmond of the Fall River Police Department as part of his investigation of the Borden burglary in 1891.

GIFFORD, HANNAH H. (BORDEN) 1836 - 1912: born in Fall River, Massachusetts, daughter of Joseph and Hannah (Westgate) Borden. She was a relative of Andrew J. Borden, having a great-grandfather in common with him. She married Perry Gifford, a dealer in dry and fancy goods, and was widowed in 1898. A cloakmaker in Fall River, she counted among her clients Abby, Emma and Lizzie Borden. She was a witness at the inquest into the deaths of Mr. and Mrs. Andrew J. Borden as well as the final trial, where tier testimony pertained to the relationship between Mrs. Borden and her stepdaughter, Lizzie. She moved to Hanson. Massachusetts ill 1904, where she was residing at the time of her death.

GLOBE STREET RAILWAY COMPANY: established in 1880 in Fall River, Massachusetts. The first streetcar line operating there, the cars were drawn by horses until the introduction of electric trolley car service in 1892. It remained in business until 1901 when, through a consolidation of smaller streetcar lines, it began operation as Old Colony Street Railway Company. Several horsecar tickets issued by this company, signed by Frank W. Brightman, were among the items reported stolen from Andrew J. Borden when his house was burglarized in 1891. Alfred A. Smith, a boy interviewed at the Massachusetts Reformatory regarding his observations in Fall River on August 4, 1892, was once employed by this company.

GORMLEY, ELIZABETH A. (BYRNE) 1870 - 1902: born in Providence, Rhode Island, daughter of John and Eliza (Conlon) Byrne. She was married to John H. Gormley, a man who held a variety of occupations during his lifetime. In 1892, they resided at 122 Third Street in Fall River, Massachusetts, he being employed as a saloonkeeper. She died at her home in that city. As she explained to the police in Fall River, she was 'at the home of Mrs. Adelaide B. Churchill when that woman "ran through the house," telling her of what had occurred at the residence of Andrew J. Borden. Summoned as a witness, she was not called upon to testify.

GRAY, ELIZABETH ANN (HOWARD) 1833 - 1907: born in Amesbury, Massachusetts, daughter of James and Ann (Schofield) Howard. She married Nathaniel P. Gray, a master mariner in Fall River, Massachusetts, who for a short time was a partner with Leander D. Wilbur in the firm of Wilbur and Gray, Clothiers. Residing in Fall River, she and her husband shared a house with her sister and brother-in-law, Captain and Mrs. James C. Stafford. In 1870, they relocated to New Bedford, Massachusetts. Widowed in 1879, she was residing in that city with her daughter, Mrs. Annie H. Howland, in 1893. She remained there until the time of her death. Captain Stafford suggested her as a possible source of information on the Morse and Borden families. This is most likely due to the fact that, in 1857, her widowed mother resided at 9 Ferry Street, a neighbor to the Andrew J. Borden family at 12 Ferry Street, Fall River, Massachusetts.

GRAY, JANE B. (NEGUS) 1829 - 1917: born in Massachusetts, daughter of Benjamin and Betsy Negus. She married Ellery Gray, a mariner in Fall River, Massachusetts, and was widowed in 1865. In 1892, she resided at 188 1/2 Second Street. She lived in Fall River for the rest of her life. She provided a statement to the police regarding incidents in the life of Miss Lizzie A. Borden prior to the murders. Summoned as a witness, she was not called upon to testify.

GRAY, MISS SARAH J. 1855 - 1934: born in Manchester, England, daughter of John and Sarah A. (Crowther) Gray. She was a resident of Fall River, Massachusetts, most of her life. Her brother, John Windsor Gray, was proprietor of a paint store located at 103 Second Street. She was at his shop on the morning of August 4, 1892, and provided police with a statement. At the time of her death, she was believed to be one of the oldest residents of the Steep Brook section of Fall River.

GREENE, CHESTER WASHINGTON 1811 - 1896: born in Coventry, Rhode Island, son of William Fones and Abby (Sheldon) Greene. A resident of Tremont, Illinois, in 1838, he married Miss Abby Stone Steadman of Belpre, Ohio. In 1844, they relocated to Fall River, Massachusetts. A prosperous businessman in that city, he later became involved with his son in the insurance and real estate business. He also served for a time as postmaster in the city of Fall River. Remaining active in business affairs, he died in the city where he had made his home. He was questioned by district police concerning his knowledge of Borden family relations.

HACKING, WILLIAM L. 1863 - 1939: born in Fall River, Massachusetts, son of Robert H. and Marion (Harvey) Hacking. Employed as a lineman and, later, a motor inspector, he became a wireman with the Fall River, Massachusetts, firm of Potter and Earle, electrical contractors. Hired in 1905, he remained with the company for over thirty years. He married Miss Mabel Cole Cluny of Fall River. In 1909, he relocated to Somerset, Massachusetts, and resided there until his death. Summoned as a witness, he was not called upon to testify.

HAGGERTY, TIMOTHY, BOOTS AND SHOES: established circa 1870 in Fall River, Massachusetts. Operated by one of the ' best-known residents of the northern section of that city, this boot and shoe-making business, in 1892, was located on Davol Street, near Bowenville train station. The firm's proprietor retired from active business life in 1911 and devoted himself to the manufacture of violins. He is mentioned in a statement given by Alfred A. Smith, an inmate at the Massachusetts Reformatory, on January 9, 1893.

HALL, LOUIS L.: operated L.L. Hall and Company - Livery, Boarding, Sale and Exchange Stable, 129 Second Street, Fall River, Massachusetts, beginning in 1892. According to his statement made to the Fall River police, he was "in view of the Borden house, for some time before eleven o'clock" the day of the murders. He did not testify at the trial. In 1895, he left the city of Fall River for Taunton, Massachusetts.

HAMMOND, JOHN WILKES 1837 - 1922: born in Mattapoisett, Massachusetts, son of John Wilkes and Maria Louisa (Southworth) Hammond. Educated in the Mattapoisett public school system, he prepared for college at the Academy in Mattapoisett and then entered Tufts University, graduating in 1861. He was subsequently employed as a teacher for a brief time before enlisting the following year with Company 1, 3rd Massachusetts Volunteers, during the Civil War. Upon completion of his nine-month term of duty he returned to teaching while pursuing the study of law at the Boston office of Messrs. Sweester and Gardner as well as at Harvard Law School. He was subsequently admitted to the Middlesex bar and began a practice in Cambridge, Massachusetts. In 1866, he married Miss Clara Ellen Tweed in Taunton, Massachusetts. He served as city solicitor for Cambridge from 1873 to 1886, when he resigned to accept his appointment to the bench of the superior court of Massachusetts. In that capacity, he presided over the arraignment of Miss Lizzie A. Borden. He resigned that position in 1898 to become a justice of the Supreme Court of Massachusetts. In 1891, he received the honorary degree of Doctor of Laws from Tufts University.

HANDY, BENJAMIN JONES 1849 - 1929: born in Marion, Massachusetts, son of Frederick Plummer and Sylvia Grace (Berry) Handy. Educated in public schools in his native town as well as Middleborough, Massachusetts, he received the degree of Doctor of Medicine from Harvard Medical School in 1871. He maintained a successful practice in Fall River, Massachusetts, from 1874 to 1913, when he returned to Marion. He married Miss Susan E. Holmes. Active in several professional organizations, he held memberships in both the Fall River and Massachusetts Medical Societies. Having retired from practice, he died in his native city. A 'witness at both the preliminary and final trials, he gave testimony pertaining to a man he observed in the vicinity of the Borden residence.

HARRINGTON, HIRAM C. 1829 - 1907: born in East Greenwich, Rhode Island. He settled in Fall River, Massachusetts, and, in 1854, married Miss Lurana Borden of that city, the sister of Andrew J. Borden. Employed as a blacksmith, he operated a shop at Fourth and Borden Streets. He served on the Fall River city council for two terms, once in

1860 and again in 1864. He served as high priest for the Royal Arch Chapter of the Masons. He died at his residence in Fall River, Massachusetts. Questioned at the inquest and summoned as a witness for the final trial, he was not called upon to testify.

HARRINGTON, PHILIP 1859 - 1893: born in Fall River, Massachusetts, son of James P. and Mary (McCue) Harrington. Educated in that city's public school system, he was employed as messenger boy for the Western Union Telegraph Company. His attendance at St. Lawrence University in Canton, New York, was cut short by reverses in his father's business which necessitated his obtaining employment. His work history was varied until his appointment as a patrolman in the Fall River Police Department in 1883. He remained a member of the night force until, at the request of City Marshall Rufus B. Hilliard, he was assigned day duty. He was appointed captain in December of 1892 and served as a clerk of the Fall River Police Beneficial Association that same year. He provided testimony at the preliminary trial of Miss Lizzie A. Borden. He died unexpectedly in Newport, Rhode Island.

HART, ABRAHAM GIFFORD 1831 - 1907: born in Fall River, Massachusetts, son of Jonathan and Susan (Gifford) Hart. Educated in the Fall River public school system, he was first employed as a machinist in the shop of Marvel and Davol, a position he retained for twenty years. He maintained an active interest in city and state politics and was treasurer of the Union Savings Bank, for which Andrew J. Borden also served as an officer. In 1853, he married Miss Lydia Pierce of Rehoboth, Massachusetts. Active in church affairs as well as several fraternal organizations, he was the first president of the Fall River Veteran Fireman's Association. He died in his native city. A witness at the preliminary and final trials, he gave testimony relative to his meeting with Andrew J. Borden on the morning of August 4, 1892.

HART, CHARLES SUMNER 1856 - 1929: born in Fall River, Massachusetts, son of Abraham Gifford and Lydia (Pierce) Hart. Educated in the Fall River public school system, he was first employed as a clerk in the hat shop of William H. Ashley and, later, that of Jeremiah H. Earl. In 1879, he married Miss Clara Frances Dodge, a Fall River schoolteacher. In 1880, he moved to Palmer, Massachusetts. By 1886, he was residing in Concord, Massachusetts, employed as a clerk at the Massachusetts, Reformatory, a state prison. Appointed deputy superintendent in 1892, it was hi this capacity that he presided over the interview of Alfred A. Smith, an inmate there, concerning that boy's actions the morning of the Borden murders. By 1905, he had been appointed superintendent, holding that position until 1909, when he retired and returned to his native city. He was residing in Fall River at the time of his death. In 1914, his daughter, Miss Clara Louise Hart, became the wife of Dana Smith Hilliard, the son of City Marshall Rufus B. Hilliard.

HART, FREDERICK BRADFORD 1870 - 1941: born in Fall River, Massachusetts, son of William and Betsy (Briggs) Hart. He married Miss Lenora Morse Littlefield of his native city. Employed as a clerk at D. R. Smith's drugstore in 1892, he later worked as a collector and, for over 30 years, as a salesman for the Enterprise Brewing Company in his native city. He was employed by that company at the time of his death. A ninth generation descendant of Governor William Bradford of Massachusetts, he belonged to several fraternal organizations. He appeared as a witness at both the inquest and the preliminary trial and was summoned as a witness for the final trial. He was not called upon to testify.

HATHAWAY, GEORGE W. 1843 - 1925: born in Freetown, Massachusetts, son of Edmund D. and Anna (Terry) Hathaway. Employed as a commercial salesman, he married Miss Emily A. Porter of Taunton, Massachusetts, and settled in Fall River, Massachusetts, in 1882. He remained there until 1917 when he relocated to Assonet, a neighboring town. He died in the home of his son in Fall River. Summoned as a witness, he was not called upon to testify.

HILL, MISS LUCY C. 1839 - 1924: born in Warwick, Rhode Island, daughter of Christopher Hill, Jr. and Hannah C. (Durfee) Hill. Having settled at a young age with her family in Fall River, Massachusetts, she was employed early in her life as a teacher there. In 1888, she went to Boston, Massachusetts, to study medicine for two years. Returning to Fall River, she began a successful practice as a physician with offices at 130 North Main Street. Unmarried, she remained in that city until her death. She is mentioned in a statement given by Alfred A. Smith, an inmate at the Massachusetts Reformatory, on January 9, 1893.

HILLIARD, RUFUS BARTLETT 1849 - 1912: born in Pembroke, Maine, son of David and Elizabeth (Wilson) Hilliard. He attended schools in Newburyport, Massachusetts, until the age of fifteen when he enlisted in the United States Army. He was stationed at various forts along the Atlantic coast during his three years of service. In 1872, he came to Fall River, Massachusetts, and was employed at the American Printing Company. In 1879, he was appointed to the Fall River Police Department, where he received periodic promotions until, in 1886, he was named city marshall. In 1888, he married Miss Nellie Smith Clark of Fall River. Best known for his involvement in the investigation of the Borden murders, he provided extensive testimony at both the preliminary and final trials which detailed his handling of the case. He was also instrumental the following year in resolving the Bertha Manchester murder case. Under his command, the Fall River Police Department grew to be the third largest in the Commonwealth of Massachusetts. He resided in Fall River until his death.

HODGES, LEWIS BRADFORD 1834 - 1905: born in Taunton, Massachusetts, son of Lewis and Sally B. (Round) Hodges. He received his education in the Taunton public schools. In 1861, he married Miss Hannah Elizabeth Godfrey of Norton, Massachusetts. The following year, he enlisted in the army and was appointed first sergeant in Company G, 4th Massachusetts Volunteers. An iron moulder by trade, he figured prominently in the civic affairs of his native city and served for several years as a member of the common council. He died in his native Taunton. He was one of the twelve-man jury that acquitted Miss Lizzie A. Borden on June 20, 1893.

HOLLAND, MRS., see **HOWLAND, ANNIE H. (GRAY)**.

HOLMES, CHARLES JARVIS 1834 - 1906: born in Rochester, Massachusetts, son of Charles Jarvis and Louisa (Haskell) Holmes. He came to Fall River, Massachusetts, in his youth, was educated in the city's public school system and, upon graduation, entered the banking profession. At the age of twenty-one, he was appointed treasurer of the Fall River Five Cents Savings Bank, a position he held until his death. His many and varied interests caused him to figure prominently in the management of several textile manufacturing corporations. He was active for a time in the Massachusetts state legislature, and his civic duties included a sixteen-year term on the school committee in Fall River. He was also a trustee of that city's public library. He married Miss Mary Anna Remington of Fall River in 1858. Highly esteemed in the community, he was an active Congregationalist. He testified at the Borden trial. It was to his home that Miss Lizzie A. Borden repaired, receiving visitors there following her acquittal.

HOLMES, JOHN HENRY: a resident of Boston, Massachusetts, in 1892. He received an honorary Master of Arts degree from Dartmouth College in 1886. The managing editor of the *Boston Herald* during that newspapers coverage of the Borden case, he retained that position for over fifteen years.

In 1907, it is recorded that he left Boston, establishing a residence in Weston, Massachusetts. '

HOWARD, JOSEPH: a syndicated columnist. In 1892, he reported on the Borden trial for the *Boston Globe* as well as various other national newspapers.

HOWLAND, ANNIE HOWARD (GRAY) 1861 - 1938: born in Fall River, Massachusetts, daughter of Captain Nathaniel P. and Elizabeth Ann (Howard) Gray. She was the niece of Capt. and Mrs. James C. Stafford, her mother being the sister of Mrs. Stafford. At the age of nine, she moved with her family to New Bedford, Massachusetts. She married John J. Howland, a municipal official in that city. A member of the Old Dartmouth Historical Society, she was also active in the Woman's Club and the Country Week Society of New Bedford. She resided there until four years before her death when she relocated to the home of her daughter in South Dartmouth, Massachusetts. She was questioned as to any knowledge of insanity in the Morse or Borden families.

HURD, FREDERICK ELLSWORTH 1861 - 1903: born in Wolfboro, New Hampshire, son of George A. and Laura A. (Chapman) Hurd. He received his early education in the Wolfboro public school system. Preparation for college was done at the Boston Latin School in Boston, Massachusetts. He began legal studies at Boston University while reading law in the offices of John H. Hardy, Esq. and Samuel J. Elder, Esq., both of Boston. Admitted to the Suffolk bar in 1884, he was that same year appointed assistant district attorney for Suffolk County. His death came unexpectedly at the young age of forty-one in Denver, Colorado. He was involved in the preparation of indictments for the Commonwealth of Massachusetts against Henry G. Trickey.

HYDE, JOSEPH 1845 - 1933: born in England, son of Cornelius and Arin (Cook) Hyde. Employed as a laborer, he was appointed to the position of day patrolman in the police department in Fall River, Massachusetts, in 1879. He remained with the department until his retirement in 1915. He married Miss Mary E. Burke of Fall River, who later became the first woman there to practice law. He was a resident of that city at the time of his death. His testimony at the trial detailed his observations during the time he spent at 92 Second Street the evening of August 4, 1892, where he was assigned watch until 11:00 o'clock.

Glossary A

JELLY, GEORGE FREDERICK 1842 - 1911: born in Salem, Massachusetts, son of William and Sarah (Tay) Jelly. Educated in the Salem public school system, he continued his education at Brown University in Providence, Rhode Island. Receiving his Bachelor of Arts and Master of Arts from that institution in 1864, he proceeded to Harvard Medical School. Obtaining his medical degree three years later, he began a general practice in Springfield, Massachusetts. He was subsequently employed at the McLean Asylum for the Insane where he served as second assistant physician from 1869 to 1871 when he was promoted to superintendent. He remained there in that capacity until 1879, when he left to establish a private practice in Boston, Massachusetts. In 1880, he was appointed examiner of the insane in that city. Prior to the Borden trial, he corresponded with Attorney General Pillsbury regarding the issue of insanity in that case. He served as chairman of the State Board of Insanity for a ten-year period beginning in 1898. In 1907, he was presented with the honorary degree of Doctor of Science from Brown University. He was a respected insanity expert, providing evaluations in many notable cases including that of Mrs. Mary Baker Eddy, head of the Christian Science Church. Having married his first wife, Miss Ellen A. Parker of Bath, Maine, in 1873, he later married Miss Ann Mary Parker, also of Bath, in 1894. A member of many professional organizations, he retired to Wakefield, Massachusetts, shortly before his death. Among those present at his funeral were Dr. George W. Gay and Dr. Edward Cowles.

JENNINGS, ANDREW JACKSON 1849 - 1923: born in Fall River, Massachusetts, son of Andrew M. and Olive B. (Chace) Jennings. Educated in the Fall River public school system, he prepared for college at Mowry and Goff's Classical School in Providence, Rhode Island. He proceeded to Brown University, from which he graduated in 1872, earning a Bachelor of Arts. He subsequently served for two years as principal of the high school in Warren, Rhode Island. In 1874, he began the study of law in the office of James M. Morton, Esq. of Fall River. He attended Boston University Law School, obtained his degree in 1876 and was admitted to the bar in Bristol County, Massachusetts, that same year. His first partnership was formed immediately with Attorney Morton and lasted for fourteen years. He married Miss Marion G. Saunders of Warren, Rhode Island, on Christmas Day in 1879. In 1890, he opened an office with John S. Brayton, Jr. and, upon that firm's dissolution in 1892, continued to practice alone. He was a member of the school committee of Fall River from 1915 to 1878 and served in both the Massachusetts House of' Representatives and state senate. He was elected district attorney for the Southeastern District of Massachusetts, holding that office from 1894 to 1898. A life-long resident of his native city, he was active in civic and church affairs and was a member of various professional organizations. He served for a time as president of the Fall River Bar Association. He was a trustee of Brown University and was identified with several Fall River corporations, being a director of the Globe Yarn Mills, the Sanford Spinning Company and the Merchants Manufacturing Company. He was also a director of the Union Savings Bank. He acted as Miss Lizzie A. Borden's attorney from the time of her arrest. As a member of the legal team which represented her at the trial, he delivered the opening statement for the defense.

JOHNSON, ALFRED C.: an employee of Andrew J. Borden at his farm in Swansea, Massachusetts. He gave a statement to Fall River police concerning his knowledge of axes or hatchets at the Bordens' Second Street property. Summoned as a witness, he was not called upon to testify.

JOHNSTON, MISS ELIZABETH MURRAY 1858 - 1907: born in Fall River, Massachusetts, daughter of Thomas and Annie (Murray) Johnston. Educated in the Fall River public school system, she furthered her studies at Bridgewater Normal School. She taught school in Myricks, Massachusetts, before returning to her native city where she continued in that vocation for twenty-five years. Beginning as a subordinate teacher, she advanced to serve as principal in two institutions. An active Congregationalist, she was also a member of several professional organizations. Her death came unexpectedly at her residence in Fall River. In Marion, Massachusetts, the day of the murders, she was sent a letter there by Miss Lizzie A. Borden.

KELLY, MARY CAROLINE (CANTWELL) 1861 - 1951: born in Peoria, Illinois, daughter of Edward H. and Caroline (Taylor) Cantwell. A resident of Providence, Rhode Island, she relocated to Fall River, Massachusetts, following her marriage to Dr. Michael Kelly in 1891. She was one of the organizers of the Queen's Daughters, a New England Roman Catholic organization which provided nursing assistance to the poor. She accompanied the first American pilgrimage to the Holy Land, visiting previously inaccessible Christian shrines in Palestine. Late in her life, she relocated to the home of her daughter in Passaic, New Jersey, where she spent the remainder of her days. A neighbor of the Bordens at 96 Second Street, she was a witness at both the preliminary and final trials. She gave testimony pertaining to her observations on the morning of August 4, 1892.

KELLY, MICHAEL 1856 - 1916: born in Ireland. He came to Fall River, Massachusetts, in 1870. Graduating from Holy Cross College in Worcester, Massachusetts, in 1879, with a Bachelor of Arts, he then attended Bellevue Hospital Medical College in New York. He received the degree of Doctor of Medicine from that institution in 1885. Considered a leading specialist in children's diseases in Fall River, he was appointed city physician by Mayor John W. Coughlin in 1890. He married Miss Mary Caroline Cantwell of Providence, Rhode Island, in 1891. He resided at 96 Second Street, next door to the home of Andrew J. Borden, at the time of the murders. He completed his education by returning to Holy Cross College, where he obtained his Master of Arts in 1896. Very interested in Irish home rule, he frequently entertained members of the Irish Parliament in his home. He was a resident of Fall River at the time of his death.

KIERAN, THOMAS: son of Owen and Ann Kieran. A civil engineer, he resided in Fall River, Massachusetts, from 1884 to 1899, at which time he relocated to New York City. He was called upon by the Commonwealth of Massachusetts to make surveys and plans showing relative distances between the house of Andrew J. Borden and various points in the downtown area of Fall River. His blueprints of the Borden house were also entered as exhibits at the trial. In his testimony, he elaborated on details of these plans. He was known to have been residing in New York City in 1917.

KILROY, FRANK H. 1872 - 1912: born in Fall River, Massachusetts, son of John and Julia (Morrow) Kilroy. A student in 1892, he relocated to Boston, Massachusetts, five years later. Upon his return to his native city in 1899, he was employed as a clerk. He was a resident there at the time of his death. As one of those present at D. R. Smith's drug store the day of Miss Lizzie A. Borden's alleged attempt to purchase prussic acid, he was a witness at both the inquest and the preliminary trial., He was summoned as a witness for the final trial of Miss Borden, but not called upon to testify.

KIRBY, ARUBA P. (TRIPP) 1828 : 1912: born in Westport, Massachusetts, wife of Uriah Kirby. In 1859, she came to Fall River, Massachusetts, where her husband gained a reputation as a fine liveryman. She resided in that city for the rest of her life. A neighbor of the Chagnon family on Third Street, she testified as to her actions and observations the morning of the Borden murders.

KNOWLTON, HOSEA MORRILL 1847 - 1902: born in Durham, Maine, son of Rev. Isaac Case and Mary Smith (Wellington) Knowlton. The itinerant nature of his father's profession caused him to be educated in several school systems. Preparation for college was done at high schools in Oldtown and Bangor, Maine, as well as Keene, New Hampshire, then at Powers Institute in Bernardston, Massachusetts. His father's appointment as pastor of the Universalist Church in New Bedford, Massachusetts, in 1866 caused his family to relocate there. Following his graduation from Tufts University in 1867, he read law in the office of Edwin L. Barney, Esq. in New Bedford and also attended Harvard Law School. He was admitted to the bar in 1870 and subsequently opened an office in New Bedford, entering a partnership with Attorney Barney which lasted seven years. He began public service in 1872 when he was appointed registrar of bankruptcy for the First District in Massachusetts, an office he held until its abolishment in 1878. In 1873, he married Miss Sylvia Bassett Almy of New Bedford. He was a member of the New Bedford school committee from 1874 to 1877. He served as city solicitor in 1877, as a representative to the state legislature from 1876 to 1877 and as state senator from 1878 to 1879. Following this, he was named district attorney of the Southern District of Massachusetts, a position he held until January 1, 1894. At this time, he resigned to become attorney general for the Commonwealth of Massachusetts, an office to which he was reelected five times. He served on various boards as a director, among them the Edison Electric Light Company of New Bedford and Citizens' National Bank, also of that city. He was a trustee of Tufts University and, from 1872, a member of the Universalist Society. In June of 1893, in his capacity as district attorney for the Commonwealth of Massachusetts, he headed the prosecution against Miss Lizzie A. Borden, on trial for the murders of Mr. and Mrs. Andrew J. Borden. Though the verdict was not in favor of the Commonwealth, he received praise from a multitude of sources for his masterful handling of the prosecution. He died at his summer home in Marion, Massachusetts.

KNOWLTON, LINCOLN BROWN 1805 - 1853: born in Shrewsbury, Massachusetts, son of Ezekiel and Eleanor (Brown) Knowlton. A graduate of Union College, he studied law in the office of Governor John Davis of Massachusetts, following which he maintained a successful practice in Peoria, Illinois. An elegant public speaker, he was known as the "Henry Clay of the Illinois bar" and maintained intimate friendships with Abraham Lincoln and Stephen A. Douglas. Active politically, he was a delegate to the Baltimore convention in the interest of Henry Clay and was nominated for Congress but expired before the election. In 1834, he married Miss Charlotte Spooner and, following her death, married Miss Lucretia Wolcott. He was a resident of Peoria at the time of his death. He is mentioned in a letter written by his daughter, Mrs. Louise W. K. Browne, to Attorney Hosea M. Knowlton.

KNOWLTON, SYLVIA BASSETT (ALMY) 1852 - 1937: born in New Bedford, Massachusetts, daughter of Benjamin and Sophia (Allen) Almy. A graduate of Bridgewater Normal School, she was employed as a teacher for a time in Westport, Massachusetts, prior to her marriage in 1873 to Hosea M. Knowlton. She had many public interests and was an organizer and second president of the New Bedford Woman's Club. In this capacity, she had the honor of introducing Winston Churchill when he lectured there on his experiences in the Boer War. She passed her later life at her summer home in Marion, Massachusetts, as well as in the Boston area. She was in Newton, Massachusetts, at the time of her death.

KNOWLTON, THOMAS 1740 - 1776: born in Boxford, Massachusetts, son of William and Martha (Pinder) Knowlton. Having spent his youth on his father's farm, at the age of sixteen he accompanied his brother, Daniel, on campaigns in Canada during the French and Indian War. In 1756, he married Miss Anna Keyes of Ashford, Connecticut, and for the next sixteen years lived his life as a farmer in that town. He was active in that area's militia, moving from the rank of ensign to second lieutenant in a short time. In 1773, he was named a selectman for the town of Ashford. Appointed captain of his local militia in 1774, he fought in the Revolutionary War battles of Breed's Hill and Bunker Hill. Promoted to lieutenant colonel, he saved his regiment from capture at the battle of Long Island. He was later promoted to colonel. His son, Frederic, was serving under his command at the battle of Harlem Heights. It is said that, after being mortally wounded at this battle, he lived just long enough to give his son a final benediction. He is mentioned in a letter written by the daughter of Lincoln B. Knowlton to Attorney Hosea M. Knowlton.

LEARY, JOHN HURLEY 1863 - 1901: born in Fall River, Massachusetts, son of Jeremiah R. and Julia A. (Hurley) Leary. Educated in the Fall River public school system, he graduated from Holy Cross College in Worcester, Massachusetts, and later received his Bachelor of Arts from Boston College. After attending Harvard Medical School, he obtained the degree of Doctor of Medicine at Bellevue Hospital Medical College in New York. He first established practice in Newport, Rhode Island, and then in his native city in 1888.

It was there that he was appointed city physician it position he held for several years. He was a patient at Butler Hospital in Providence, Rhode Island, at the time of his death. He served as a witness at the autopsies of Mr. and Mrs. Andrew J. Borden on August 11, 1892.

LEARY, KATE: an individual summoned as a witness. She was not called upon to testify. Attempts to uncover her identity have to date been unsuccessful.

LIVERMORE, MARY ASHTON (RICE) 1820 - 1905: born in Boston, Massachusetts, daughter of Timothy and Zebiah Vose Glover (Ashton) Rice. Following early education in Boston as well as western New York state, she attended Miss Martha Whiting's Female Seminary in Charlestown, Massachusetts. Graduating in 1836, she remained at the school until 1838 employed as a teacher. During the subsequent three years, she was employed as a tutor for a family in Virginia, at which time she developed strong anti-slavery opinions. She then relocated to Duxbury, Massachusetts, where she obtained a position as a teacher. She married Daniel Parker Livermore, a minister there, in 1845. She traveled to various Universalist church pastorates with her husband, including Fall River, Massachusetts, circa 1845. They settled in Chicago, Illinois, where she served on the Chicago Sanitary Commission. A popular lecturer during the Civil War, she was also a noted writer and speaker for woman's suffrage. She returned to the Boston area in 1869, employed as editor of the *Women's Journal*. In 1888, she authored *My Story of the War- A Woman's Narrative*, an extremely successful publication which sold in excess of sixty thousand copies. Her next book, *The Story of My Life* published in 1897, was equally popular. Active in various women's organizations, she was one of the founders of the Massachusetts Woman Suffrage Association. Retiring from lecturing in 1895, she died ten years later in Melrose, Massachusetts. She took an active interest in the Borden case, having been an intimate friend of the first Mrs. Andrew J. Borden.

LONG, JOHN DAVIS 1838 - 1915: born in Buckfield, Maine, son of Zadoc and Julia Temple (Davis) Long. He received his early education in the Buckfield public school system and prepared for college at Hebron Academy at Hebron, Maine. Following his graduation from Harvard University in 1857, he held the post of principal at Westford Academy in Westford, Massachusetts, until 1859 when he entered Harvard Law School. He left Harvard and read law as a student in the Boston, Massachusetts, office of Sidney Bartlett, Esq. and was admitted to the Suffolk bar in 1861. At that time he opened a law office in his native town and then moved to Boston the following year. There he became a partner with Stillman B. Allen, Esq. and Thomas Savage, Esq. in the firm of Allen, Long and Savage. Their successful partnership lasted until 1880 when he left the practice of law for political life. That same year, the honorary degree of Doctor of Laws was bestowed upon him by Harvard University. As a public figure, he served the Commonwealth of Massachusetts in a variety of offices including lieutenant governor and governor from 1879 to 1881. In 1870, he married Miss Mary Woodward Glover of Hingham, Massachusetts. His second wife, to whom he was married in 1886, was Miss Agnes Pierce of North Attleboro, Massachusetts. He served for a time in Congress and was Secretary of the United States Navy from 1896 to 1902. Retiring from political life, he returned to Boston and the practice of law. He received the honorary degree of Doctor of Laws from Tufts University in 1902, that same year being elected president of the Board of Overseers of Harvard University. He served as director of several professional and civic organizations and was the author of numerous books and essays. In 1879, he published a translation of Virgil's *Aeneid*, acclaimed for its faithfulness to the original. Among his other works were *The Republican Party - Its History, Principles and Policies*, published in 1898, *After Dinner and Other Speeches* and *The New American Navy*. He died at his residence in Hingham, Massachusetts.

LORRIGAN, PATRICK F.: an individual summoned as a witness. He was not called upon to testify. Attempts to uncover his identity have to date been unsuccessful.

LOVELL, ARTHUR T. 1859 - 1925: born in Watford, England. He emigrated to the United States as a young man. Residing for a time in Washington, District of Columbia, he then relocated to Boston, Massachusetts. First listed in that city's directory in 1890, he was employed as a reporter for the Boston Journal until circa 1893 when he became a stenographer. He occupied offices in Barristers Hall, Pemberton Square for many years and was associated with several of Massachusetts' important court cases. He was a member of the Veteran Journalists' Association and of the Ancient and Honorable Artillery Company. He died at his home in Dorchester, Massachusetts, where he had resided with his wife, Bessie. One of the court stenographers to approach the Attorney General's office requesting consideration for employment on the Borden case, he was not selected.

LUBINSKY, HYMAN 1874 - 1923: born in Russia, son of Jacob and Bessie (Sinderoff) Lubinsky. In 1892, he was employed as an ice cream peddler by

Charles A. and Agnes S. Wilkinson, Confectioners, 42 North Main Street, Fall River, Massachusetts. He was employed as a packer in that city at the time of his death. He was in the vicinity of the Borden house on the morning of the murders and testified at the trial as to his observations that day.

MC GOWAN, PATRICK 1859 - 1938: born in Ireland, son of Patrick and Mary McGowan. He emigrated to the United States and was first employed in Fall River, Massachusetts, in 1889 as a mason's laborer. He married Miss Mary A. Doyle of that city. He gave testimony pertaining to his actions in the Crowe yard, property near the Borden residence, on the morning of the murders. Later in his life, he worked as a farmer and, in 1928, founded P. McGowan and Sons, Sand and Gravel. He died in Fall River.

MC HENRY, EDWIN D.: a private detective. He resided in Providence, Rhode Island, in 1889, employed as general manager of the Rhode Island Detective Bureau Company, a firm established in 1886. Renamed McHenry and Company Detective Bureau in 1891, the firm dissolved the following year. In 1892, accompanied by his wife, Nellie, he relocated to New York City. The Fall River Evening News of February 7, 1894, noted that "Mrs. E. D. McHenry, wife of the detective who was employed by the government in the Borden case, has obtained a divorce nisi on the ground of adultery." In Buffalo, New York by 1895, he became a partner with Frank H. McDonald in the International Detective Agency, a firm which operated for only a year. In 1897, he was proprietor of McHenry's Detective Bureau, operating two years later as McHenry's Secret Service. He was last known to have resided in Buffalo in 1899. In 1892, he was associated with the *Boston Globe* reporter, Henry G. Trickey, in a scandal which became known as the Trickey-McHenry affair.

MC HENRY, NELLIE S.: wife of detective Edwin D. McHenry. She resided with her husband in Providence, Rhode Island, in 1892. On August 19th of that year she conducted an extensive inter-view with Miss Bridget Sullivan, having gained the confidence of the Bordens' former maid by posing as a relative of the family. The following year she moved with her husband to New York City and, in 1894, resided in a boarding house in Jersey City, New Jersey. The *Fall River Evening News* of February 7th of that year noted that "Mrs. E. D. McHenry, wife of the detective who was employed by the government in the Borden case, has obtained a divorce nisi on the ground of adultery."

MACOMBER, MARY C.: was in the vicinity of the Borden house on August 4, 1892. Standing near Louis L. Hall's place of business, she witnessed Mrs. Churchill as she ran down the street following the discovery of murder at 92 Second Street.

MANLEY, DELIA SUMMERS (MANCHESTER) 1850 - 1919: born in Tiverton, Rhode Island, daughter of William and Rhoda Drake Manchester. Married to Seabury T. Manley in 1869, she and her husband received Primary class instruction from Mrs. Mary Baker Eddy of The First Church of Christ, Scientist, in 1882. The following year, she and her husband, through permission of Mrs. Eddy, began to teach Christian Science in Fall River, Massachusetts. She was a graduate of the Massachusetts Metaphysical College of Boston, Massachusetts. Through her continued study with Mrs. Eddy, she became a Christian Science practitioner and, as such, obtained a charter with her husband to establish the Fall River Christian Science Institute. Widowed in 1904, she continued to practice in Fall River. In 1919, she relocated to the Norwood section of Warwick, Rhode Island, where she expired at the home of her daughter. The aunt by marriage of Miss Alice M. Russell, she was the sister-in-law of Miss Russell's mother. A resident at 206 Second Street in Fall River in 1892, she was a witness at both the preliminary and final trials. Her testimony pertained to her seeing a man near the Borden property the morning of the murders.

MARSTON, GEORGE 1821 - 1883: born in Barnstable, Massachusetts, son of Charles and Nancy C. (Goodspeed) Marston. He received his education in the public schools of his native town. At the age of twenty, he pursued a business career, beginning as a clerk with Howland and Hinckley, a ship-chandlery. After six months, he became inclined toward law and began his studies in the office of his uncle, Nymphas Marston, Esq. While attending Harvard Law School, he taught periodically to cover his expenses. In 1845, he was admitted to the Suffolk bar. Active politically, he held the position of register of probate in Barnstable from 1853 to 1854, at which time he was promoted to judge of probate, a position he was to hold for four years. In 1860, he began a nineteen-year term as district attorney for the Southern District. He relocated to New Bedford, Massachusetts, in 1869, establishing partnerships first with William W. Crapo and, later, with Wendell H. Cobb. He possessed a variety of business interests, serving as president of the Nantucket and Cape Cod Steamboat Company and director of several corporations including the Old Colony Railroad Company and the Citizens' National Bank of' New Bedford. He was married to Miss

Elizabeth Weston of Falmouth, Massachusetts. In 1879, he resigned his post as district attorney to accept the position of attorney general, an office to which he was three times reelected. Declining nomination for a fourth term in 1882, he focused his attention on his private practice. He died at his residence in New Bedford.

MARTIN, WILLIAM R.: first listed in the Fall River, Massachusetts, city directory in 1891. He was employed as a-clerk for William A. Bennett, Apothecary, on North Main Street in that city. In 1892, he relocated to New Bedford, Massachusetts. While residing there, he was employed as a clerk at the firm of Charles H. Church until 1894. Summoned as a witness, he was not called upon to testify.

MASON, ALBERT 1836 - 1905: born in Middleborough, Massachusetts, son of Albert T. and Arlina (Orcutt) Mason. He received his early education in Middleborough public schools as well as Pierce Academy, located in that same town. For a brief period, he was employed by a manufacturing firm in Plymouth, Massachusetts, and there, in 1857, married Miss Lydia F. Whiting. He began his law studies in the Plymouth offices of Edward L. Sherman, Esq., and was admitted to the bar in 1860. He subsequently established offices in that city. In 1862, he enlisted in the 38th Massachusetts Volunteers with the rank of second lieutenant, eventually being commissioned captain and assistant quartermaster. Upon expiration of service in 1865, he resumed his practice and became active politically. He was elected to the House of Representatives in 1873 and again in 1874. Retaining his practice in Plymouth, he formed a partnership with Charles H. Drew, Esq. and, in 1874, opened an office in Boston, Massachusetts. Additional partnerships were later formed with Arthur Lord, Esq. and Benjamin R. Curtis, Esq. He was appointed associate justice in 1882 and, in 1890, chief justice of the superior court. He was one of the judges who presided over the trial of Miss Lizzie A. Borden. He died in Brookline, Massachusetts.

MATHER, JAMES 1860 - 1921: born in Scotland. He emigrated to the United States, being employed in Fall River, Massachusetts, as a carpenter and, later, in the textile mills. He was a resident of that city at the time of his death. Working in Jonathan Clegg's store in the Andrew J. Borden building the morning of August 4, 1892, he witnessed a meeting there between Mr. Clegg and Mr. Borden. His testimony at the preliminary and final trials of Miss Lizzie A. Borden concerned his observations that day.

MEDLEY, WILLIAM H. 1853 - 1917: born in England, son of Joseph and Hannah (Chambers) Medley. Employed in textile mills in Lancashire, England, as a child, he emigrated to Massachusetts and, in 1876, settled in Fall River, finding employment as a mule spinner in textile mills there. He was active in the mule spinners' union and contributed regularly to *The Labor Standard*, a once prosperous Fall River publication. A member of the Fall River Police Department as of 1880, he was a patrolman at the time of the Borden murders. In 1910, he was appointed assistant city marshall and, upon City Marshall Fleet's retirement in 1915, was promoted to that title. Residing in Fall River with his wife, Mary, he was an active member in several fraternal organizations there. A victim of an automobile accident, he died unexpectedly in the city where he had made his home. Among the first police officers to arrive at the scene of the crime, his testimony detailed his observations there that day.

MILLER, SOUTHARD HARRISON 1811 - 1895: born in Middleborough, Massachusetts, son of Alden and Millicent (Lovell) Miller. He came to Fall River, Massachusetts, at the age of sixteen to learn the carpenter's trade and soon, under partnership with James Ford, became engaged as a contractor. Following dissolution of this partnership, he maintained an extremely successful business on his own for several years. In 1836, he married Miss Esther G. Peckham of Newport, Rhode Island. He served for nearly forty years as director of Massasoit National Bank. He resigned that position in 1893 due to his advancing age. Following his retirement, he spent his remaining years in Fall River. He provided a statement to district police regarding any knowledge of insanity in the Morse family.

MOODY, WILLIAM HENRY 1853 - 1917: born in Newbury, Massachusetts, son of Henry Lord and Melissa Augusta (Emerson) Moody. Educated in the public schools of Salem and Danvers. Massachusetts, he prepared for college at Phillips Academy in Andover, Massachusetts, graduating in 1872. He continued his studies at Harvard University where he graduated third in his class in 1876. He studied law at Harvard and in the office of Richard H. Dana, Esq. and was admitted to the Salem bar in 1878. He then began a practice with Edwin N. Hill, Esq. in Haverhill, Massachusetts. Active in civic affairs there, he served on the school board and held the post of city solicitor in 1888 and 1889. He was subsequently elected district attorney for Essex County, a position he held for six years. It was in this capacity that he was appointed by Massachusetts Attorney General Albert E. Pillsbury to serve on the prosecution in the Borden trial. He delivered the opening argument for the Commonwealth of Massachusetts vs. Lizzie A. Borden. In 1895, he was elected representative to Congress for the Sixth District, an office to which he was reelected in 1896, 1898 and 1900. In 1902, he was named Secretary of the United States Navy by President Theodore Roosevelt, succeeding Hon. John D. Long. He received the honorary degree of Doctor of Laws from Amherst College as well as one from Tufts University in 1904. That same year, he was appointed to the position of attorney general of the United States and remained in President Roosevelt's cabinet until he was chosen to fill a vacancy on the Supreme Court in 1906. He retired from the bench due to ill health in 1909 and was residing in Haverhill, Massachusetts, at the time of his death. The following year destroyer #277 in the United States Navy was named for him in recognition of his accomplishments when serving as secretary of that division of the armed forces.

MORSE, ANTHONY 1800 - 1878: born in Somerset, Massachusetts, son of Captain Joseph and Sarah Lawton (Vinnicum) Morse. He was the father of Sarah A. (Morse) Borden and John V. Morse. He was first married to Miss Rhody Morrison in 1822 and, following her death, Miss Hannah C. Almy. At the time of his death, he was a resident of Girard, Illinois.

MORSE, ELIJAH ADAMS 1841 - 1898: born in South Bend, Indiana, son of Abner and Hannah (Peck) Morse. He received his early education in the public schools of Sherborn and Holliston, Massachusetts, where his family had relocated early in his youth. He continued his studies at the prestigious Boylston School in Boston, Massachusetts, and Onondaga Academy in New York. The foundation of his substantial fortune was laid when, as a boy with a small shop in Sharon, Massachusetts, he prepared stove polish. In 1861, he enlisted in Company A, Massachusetts Infantry, and saw active service during the Civil War. Settling in Canton, Massachusetts, at the expiration of his term of duty, he married Miss Felicia Vining of Holbrook, Massachusetts, in 1868. Perfecting his polish formula, he entered into a partnership with his brother and began the large scale manufacture of the widely popular Rising Sun Stove Polish. He was sole proprietor as of 1888 and by 1896 his plant produced some ten tons per day. Taking an active interest in politics, he served in the Massachusetts House of Representatives in 1876 and in the state senate in 1886 and 1887. He was elected to Congress in 1888, 1890 and 1892. A philanthropist and leader in the cause of temperance, he lectured widely and was a noted public speaker. He died in Canton, Massachusetts.

MORSE, JOHN VINNICUM 1833 - 1912: born in Somerset, Massachusetts, son of Anthony and Rhody (Morrison) Morse. As a young man, he was employed for two years by Charles and Isaac Davis in their meat business in Westport, Massachusetts. At the age of twenty-two, he moved to Illinois, remaining there fourteen years before settling in Iowa, where he was engaged in the horse trade. It was his custom to travel east each summer and visit Fall River and New Bedford, Massachusetts. He was a familiar figure in those two cities, kept a boat in New Bedford and enjoyed fishing. He promised himself early in his career that, when he retired, he would spend the rest of his days in comfort. Having been a successful businessman, he was able to do so. He died in Hastings, Iowa. An uncle to the Misses Emma L. and Lizzie A. Borden, he was visiting at 92 Second Street at the time of the murders. A witness at the inquest, preliminary trial and final trial of his niece, he provided testimony of his intimate knowledge of events within the Borden household.

MORTON, MARCUS, JR. 1819 - 1891: born in Taunton, Massachusetts, son of Marcus and Charlotte (Hodges) Morton. A graduate of Brown University, he received his Bachelor of Arts in 1838. He then entered Harvard Law School and was awarded his Bachelor of Laws two years later. After taking his degree, he furthered his legal studies in the Boston, Massachusetts, office of Messrs. Peleg Sprague and William Gray, being admitted to the Suffolk bar in 1841. He established a practice in Boston and married Miss Abby Bowler Hoppin in Providence, Rhode Island, in 1843. He took up residency in Andover, Massachusetts, in 1850 and there became active politically, serving as a representative for that town to the Constitutional Convention in 1853 and the state legislature in 1858. A member of the House of Representatives, he served as chairman of the Committee on Elections. In 1858, he was appointed judge of the superior court of Suffolk County and remained on the bench until the abolition of that court the next year. In the organization of the Massachusetts Supreme Court in 1859, he was elected one of the judges, serving in that capacity for the next decade. In 1869, he was appointed a judge of the Massachusetts Supreme judicial Court and, in 1882, its chief justice. He resigned from the latter position in 1890, having served on the bench of three courts for thirty-two years. He was awarded the degree of Doctor of Laws from Harvard Law School in 1880. He died at his residence in Andover. He was eulogized by Attorney General Albert E. Pillsbury as "brilliant, patient and always accessible."

MULLALY, MICHAEL 1848 - 1908: born in East Taunton, Massachusetts, son of Michael Mullaly. Employed as a longshoreman, he was appointed a night patrolman of the police department in Fall River, Massachusetts, in 1877. He was of particular value because of his knowledge of the water and frequently was assigned waterfront duty. He was married to Miss Margaret Ring. A member of the Police Beneficial Association in Fall River, he died unexpectedly in that city. One of the police officers at the scene of the crime following the Borden murders, he testified at both the preliminary and final trials of Miss Lizzie A. Borden.

NICHOLSON, ROBERT 1843 - 1908: born in Dundee, Scotland, son of Mitchell and Matilda (Keith) Nicholson. After learning the mason's trade from his father, he emigrated to the United States in 1874, settling in Fall River, Massachusetts. There, having gained employment in the construction business, he married Miss Alice Crammond. In 1892, his offices were located at 147 Second Street. In 1895, he was joined in his contracting firm by his son, Mitchell. Active in civic affairs, he was a member of various fraternal organizations in Fall River at the time of his death. Summoned as a witness, he was not called upon to testify.

OAK GROVE CEMETERY: established in 1855 in Fall River Massachusetts. Its initial site encompassed forty-seven acres, later enlarged through various purchases of additional land. Once described as "one of the most beautiful places for burial of the dead" in New England, it was here that many of the city's prominent citizens chose to erect monuments to carry their epitaphs. The mortal remains of Andrew J. Borden and those of his family rest here in lots numbered 172, 173 and 174 on Linden Path.

PEARCE, HARRY C.: son of Nathaniel A. and Mary (Davis) Pearce. He was employed as a teamster in Fall River, Massachusetts, listed in that city's directory for the first time in 1894, boarding with his family at 25 Third Street. Later in his life he was employed at the Fall River Iron Works Company. He relocated to the Chicago, Illinois, area and, by 1923, was a resident of Montreal, Canada. Summoned as a witness, he was not called upon to testify.

PECKHAM, ANNIE F.: an individual summoned as a witness. She was not called upon to testify. Attempts to uncover her identity have to date been unsuccessful.

PERRON, ADELARD 1859 - 1933: born in Canada, son of Francis X. and Luce (LeBoeuf) Perron. He was married to Miss Celia Cloutier. Appointed to the police department in Fall River, Massachusetts, in 1885, he was promoted to the rank of lieutenant in 1893. He retired from the force in 1916 and was in Foxborough, Massachusetts, at the time of his death. Summoned as a witness, he was not called upon to testify at the Borden trial.

PETTEY, GEORGE AMBROSE 1839 - 1906: born in Tiverton, Rhode Island, son of Jireh Bennett and Sarah (Church) Pettey. Early in his life, he voyaged on a whaler, returning to his native town to make a living as a farmer. He married Miss Lydia G. Manchester in 1860. From 1869 to 1879, he was employed as a clerk for his father's firm, Wade and Pettey, Grocers, located on Second Street in Fall River, Massachusetts. In his later years, he was employed as a bookkeeper at the Tiverton Dye Works in Tiverton, Rhode Island. Following his retirement, he died in Fall River. A resident of 66 (later 92) Second Street prior to Andrew J. Borden's purchase of that property, he was in the vicinity of that address on August 4, 1892. He was admitted into the Borden house following the murders and testified as to his observations there.

PICKERING, FREDERICK A. 1849 - 1904: born in Fall River, Massachusetts, son of Thomas J. and Jemima (Cornell) Pickering. He married Miss Ella Ray. A pioneer in electrical engineering, he was employed by the Fall River Electric Light Company for several years. He then accepted a position with a New York firm, assisting in establishing electrical plants nationally. He died in his native city. He was in the vicinity of the Borden house on the morning of the murders.

PILLSBURY, ALBERT ENOCH 1849 - 1930: born in Milford, New Hampshire, son of Josiah Webster and Elizabeth (Dinsmoor) Pillsbury. Educated in Milford public schools, he then prepared for college at Appleton Academy in New Ipswich, New Hampshire, and Lawrence Academy in Groton, Massachusetts, graduating from the latter in 1867. He entered Harvard University in the Class of 1871. He did not complete his course there but did, in 1890, receive the honorary degree of Master of Arts from that institution. He moved to Sterling, Illinois, where he taught school and studied law with his uncle, Hon. James Dinsmoor. He was admitted to the Illinois bar in 1869 and the Massachusetts bar in 1870, settling in Boston and opening a practice. For several years early ill his career, he served as vice-president and president of the Mercantile Library Association of Boston. He was also a member of the corporation of the Franklin Savings Bank and a director of the United States Trust and Safe Deposit Company. He served the Commonwealth of Massachusetts in various capacities as an elected official, in the Massachusetts House of Representatives in 1876, 1877 and 1879, and in the state senate as representative of the Sixth Suffolk District in 1884, 1885 and 1886. He married Mrs. Louise F. (Johnson) Wheeler of Newbury, Vermont, in 1889. He was attorney general from 1891 to 1893 and as such was involved in the case of the Commonwealth of Massachusetts vs. Lizzie A. Borden. His official work received wide attention, notably his argument to the jury in the Trefethen murder trial. He served as professor of constitutional law at Boston University from 1896 to 1908. He was the author of *Daniel Webster, the Orator*, published in 1903. In 1913, he was the recipient of the honorary degree of Doctor of Laws from Howard University in Washington, District of Columbia. He died in West Newton, Massachusetts.

PILLSBURY, LOUISE F. (JOHNSON) WHEELER 1850 - ? : born in Hamilton, New York, daughter of Edward C. and Delia M. (Smith) Johnson. The widow of a Mr. Wheeler, she married Albert Enoch Pillsbury, her third husband, in Newbury, Vermont, in 1889.

PORTER, CHARLES BURNHAM 1840 - 1909: born in Rutland, Vermont, son of James Burnham and Harriet (Griffs) Porter. Having received his Bachelor of Arts from Harvard University in 1862, he continued his studies there, obtaining his Master of Arts the following year. He was awarded the degree of Doctor of Medicine from Harvard Medical School in 1865. That same year, he was married to Miss Harriet A. Allen in Cambridge, Massachusetts. His appointment in 1867 to the post of assistant demonstrator of anatomy at Harvard Medical School began an association with his alma mater that was to last for over thirty-five years. Named demonstrator of anatomy in 1868, he retained that position until 1875 when he was made instructor in surgery. He became an assistant professor of surgery in 1882 and was promoted five years later to professor of clinical surgery. A resident of Boston, Massachusetts, he was there associated with Massachusetts General Hospital for most of his professional life, first as a surgeon to outpatients and, after 1875, as a visiting surgeon. He was a member of various professional organizations, among them the Massachusetts Medical Society, the Society for Medical Improvement and the American Surgical Association, for which he served as vice-president in 1892. He was recommended to Attorney General Albert E. Pillsbury by Dr. George W. Gay for consideration as a medical expert for the prosecution in the trial of Miss Lizzie A. Borden.

PORTER, EDWIN H. 1864 - 1904: born in Glasgow, Kentucky, son of Columbus and Margaret (Davis) Porter. Educated in the public schools of his native Glasgow, he was first employed as a teacher and, later, learned the trade of typesetting. He traveled extensively and for a time was employed by the *Providence Telegram* in Providence, Rhode Island. From there he went to Fall River, Massachusetts, to become city editor of the *Tribune* until its dissolution. He was then engaged by the *Daily Globe*, where he was on staff for a time with Thatcher T. Thurston. His specialty was police work and he became the correspondent to the *Boston Herald* for his district. He married Miss Winnie Leonard of Fall River in 1891. At the conclusion of the Borden murder trial, his book, *The Fall River Tragedy: A History of the Borden Murders* was published. He was in the city of Fall River at the time of his death.

POTTER, GEORGE 1839 - 1909: a farmer, he resided with his wife, Emma, in Westport, Massachusetts. He owned a sizable farm on the river road, approximately twelve miles from New Bedford, Massachusetts. Newspaper accounts at the time of the trial claimed him to be "level headed" and "true as steel." He died in the town where he had made his home. He was the first juror drawn and, as such, one of the twelve men who acquitted Miss Lizzie A. Borden on June 20, 1893.

REAGAN, HANNAH B. (HOWE) 1848 - 1924: born in Ireland, daughter of Henry and Catherine (McCarthy) Howe. She married Quinlan M. Reagan, a stonecutter working in Fall River, Massachusetts. The first matron of that city's Central Police Station, she served in that capacity from 1888 to the time of her resignation in 1909. She was active in several church societies and was a Fall River resident at the time of her death. Her testimony at the trial pertained to incidents which occurred during the nine-day incarceration of Miss Lizzie A. Borden at the Fall River jail.

RICHARDS, CHARLES 1. 1829 - 1910: son of Henry and Fanny (Holmes) Richards. A resident of North Attleboro, Massachusetts, he was employed in real estate. He was one of the twelve-man jury that acquitted Miss Lizzie A. Borden on June 20, 1893. Selected as foreman of that jury, he was said to be a man of good judgment. He died in Attleboro, Massachusetts.

RICHARDSON, MAURICE HOWE 1851 - 1912: born in Athol, Massachusetts, soil of' Nathan Henry and Martha Ann (Barber) Richardson. At the age of eleven he relocated with his family to Fitchburg, Massachusetts, where he obtained his early education. He graduated from high school in Fitchburg in 1869 and entered Harvard University, receiving his Bachelor of Arts in 1873. Teaching at the high school in Salem, Massachusetts, he studied at that time with Dr. Edward B. Peirson. He subsequently attended Harvard Medical School where he was awarded the degree of Doctor of Medicine in 1877, establishing a practice in Boston, Massachusetts, later that same year. In 1879, he married the daughter of his former teacher, Miss Margaret White Peirson. Serving as surgical house officer at Massachusetts General Hospital in Boston, he resigned that position to become private assistant to the demonstrator of anatomy at Harvard Medical School. Later appointed demonstrator of anatomy there in 1882, he retained that post until five years later when he was named assistant professor of anatomy. He served as a visiting surgeon at the Massachusetts General Hospital in 1886 and as consulting surgeon at various other hospitals. In 1895, he was made assistant professor of clinical surgery, gaining his full professorship after eight years. In 1907, he was named to the Moseley Professorship of Surgery, a position he held until his death. Serving for a time as chairman of the surgical section of the American Medical Association, he was also a charter member of the International Surgical Society. A frequent contributor of articles to various professional journals, including *Park's Surgery by American Authors* and *Dennis' System of Surgery*, he was president of the American Surgical Association in 1902. He served as a medical expert for the defense in the Borden trial and in that capacity examined the skulls of Mr. and Mrs. Andrew J. Borden.

RILEY, JOHN 1849 - 1906: born in Ireland, son of John and Ellen (McCormick) Riley. He married Miss Elizabeth Gorman. Employed as an operative in textile mills, he was appointed as a patrolman on the Fall River, Massachusetts, police force in 1880. A member of several professional associations, he served on the force until his death. He was one of the police officers at the scene of the crime on August 4, 1892.

ROBINSON, GEORGE DEXTER 1834 - 1896: born in Lexington, Massachusetts, son of Charles and Mary (Davis) Robinson. Receiving his early education in the public schools of his native city, he attended Lexington Academy and then prepared for college at the Hopkins Classical School in Cambridge, Massachusetts. Graduating from Harvard University in 1856, he accepted the post of principal at the high school in Chicopee, Massachusetts. He began the study of law in 1865 in the Charlestown, Massachusetts, office of his brother, Hon. Charles Robinson. He was married twice, first to Miss

Hannah E. Stevens in 1859 and then to Miss Susan E. Simonds in 1867, both marriages taking place in Lexington. Active politically, he served the Commonwealth of Massachusetts as a member of the House of Representatives, a senator, a congressman and from 1883 to 1886 as governor. In 1884, he received the honorary degree of Doctor of Laws from Amherst College and another from Harvard University two years later. Following his public service he devoted himself to law with considerable practices in Chicopee and Boston, Massachusetts. His professional involvements caused him to decline numerous presidential appointments. He was principal attorney for the defense in the Commonwealth of Massachusetts vs. Lizzie A. Borden. He died in Chicopee, Massachusetts.

ROBINSON, JOHN, CONFECTIONERY: established in 1876 in Fall River, Massachusetts. The business remained in operation until its proprietor's death in 1904. From 1892 to 1893, his shop was located at 112 Second Street. His store was mentioned in a statement given by Alfred A. Smith, an inmate at the Massachusetts Reformatory, on January 9, 1893.

ROGERS, CARRIE E. BROWN 1870 - 1954: born in Fall River, Massachusetts, daughter of George H. and Sophia S. L. (Brown) Rogers. She married Walter Everett Peckham, a dealer in dairy products, in 1898. A member of the Mayflower Descendants, she was ninth in descent from John Alden. She also belonged to the Daughters of the Colonial Wars and the Daughters of the American Revolution. She was a life-long resident of her native city. Employed as a bookkeeper at the time of the Borden murders, she was summoned as a witness, but not called upon to testify.

ROGERS, HENRY MONROE 1839 - 1937: born in Boston, Massachusetts, son of John Hicks and Lucy Catherine (Smith) Rogers. He received his early education in his native city at Adams Grammar School and English High School. Following preparatory work at Boston Latin School, he entered Harvard University, receiving his Bachelor of Arts in 1862. Introduced to President Abraham Lincoln by his friend and classmate, Robert Todd Lincoln, he was a frequent visitor to the presidential mansion in Washington, District of Columbia. In 1862, President Lincoln personally appointed him acting paymaster of the United States Navy, serving on various ships until his discharge in 1865. He subsequently returned to Boston and read law in offices in that city. He continued his studies at Harvard Law School and received his Master of Arts in 1866, followed by his Bachelor of Laws in 1867. He was admitted to the Suffolk bar the following year.

Entering the Boston firm of Messrs. Brooks and Hall, he began a successful career in the legal profession, forming various partnerships over the years. He married Miss Clara Kathleen Barnett of Cheltenham, England, in 1878. A noted singer, Miss Barnett was known in musical circles as Clara Dora and performed across Europe and America. He served as chairman of the executive committee of the United States Employers' Liability Assurance Corporation, Limited, as well as holding executive positions with several other corporations. At the age of ninety, he completed his memoirs, Memories of Ninety Years, a volume of 400 pages. At the time of his death in Boston, he had the distinction of being the oldest living graduate of both Boston Latin School and Harvard University.

ROUNSEVILLE, CYRUS COLE 1852 - 1919: born in Acushnet, Massachusetts, son of Cyrus Cole and Irene P. (Ashley) Rounseville. He moved to East Freetown, Massachusetts, with his widowed mother at an early age. Educated in public schools there, he then attended Bryant and Stratton Business College in Boston, Massachusetts. Following graduation, he relocated to Fall River, Massachusetts, and, in 1869, worked as a clerk for the Narragansett Steamship Company. He subsequently gained employment as an administrator in various textile corporations. His interests also leaned toward banking, where he was vice-president of both Union Savings Bank and Troy Co-operative Bank. He married Miss Mary O. Pitman of Fall River in 1893. Active in both church and civic affairs, he was a resident of that city at the time of his death. Summoned as a witness, he was not called upon to testify.

RUSSELL, MISS ALICE MANLEY 1852 - 1941: born in New Bedford, Massachusetts, daughter of Frederick W. and Judith (Manley) Russell. She was a niece by marriage of Mrs. Delia S. Manley. Employed as a clerk for several years in Fall River, Massachusetts, she later taught sewing in the public schools of that city. In 1908, she was promoted to supervisor of sewing, retiring from that position in 1913. She resided in Fall River for the rest of her life. She was a witness at both the inquest and the preliminary trial but it was not until the grand jury hearing that she revealed her "burning of the dress" testimony. She was also a witness at the trial of Miss Lizzie A. Borden in June of 1893.

SARGENT, FRANK E., COMPANY: established in 1882 in Fall River, Massachusetts. This dry goods business was dissolved in 1894 when its proprietor pursued a career as a cotton broker. The morning of August 4, 1892, Miss

Lizzie A. Borden was said to have discussed a sale of dry goods at this establishment with Bridget Sullivan.

SAWYER, CHARLES S. 1843 - 1907: born in Portland, Maine. Educated in New York, he was determined to become a portrait painter. At the time of the Civil War, he enlisted in Company A, 165th Regiment, New York Volunteer Infantry. Captured by the Confederates, he served time as a prisoner of war. Following the expiration of his term, he moved to Fall River, Massachusetts, where he pursued his career as a scenic artist. He married Miss Mary A. Negus of Fall River in 1872. In 1897, he founded the firm Charles S. Sawyer and Company, House and Sign Painters, on South Main Street in Fall River, a business he operated until ill health forced him to retire shortly before his death. A resident of 78 Second Street in 1892, he was left in charge of the Borden house by Officer Allen the day of the murders. His testimony at the inquest, preliminary and final trials pertained to his observations there at that time.

SHORTSLEEVES, JOSEPH 1846 - 1915: born in Canada. A carpenter by trade, he emigrated to the United States in 1854 and first appears in the Fall River, Massachusetts, city directory in 1892. Listed alternately under the names "Shortsleeves" and "Short," as well as the French "Courtemanche," he resided in that city for the rest of his life. A veteran of the Civil War, he fought with the 4th Regiment, Heavy Artillery of New York and was later a member of the G.A.R. He married Miss Mary Ann Sloan. Engaged in carpentry work with James Mather in Jonathan Clegg's store, he gave testimony at the preliminary and final trials pertaining to his observations when Andrew J. Borden visited there on the morning of August 4, 1892.

SMITH, ALFRED A. 1877 - ?: son of Robert and Ann (Greenwood) Smith. He resided with his father, a foreman and later a baker, on Suffolk Street in Fall River, Massachusetts. In 1892, at the age of fifteen, he was employed by the Globe Street Railway Company as a driver and laborer. He was the younger brother of Mrs. George W. Davis. Sentenced to the Massachusetts Reformatory in December of 1892 on a charge of breaking and entering and larceny, he provided police with a detailed account of his actions and observations in the vicinity of the Borden house on August 4, 1892. To date, no records have been uncovered that provide any further biographical details.

SMITH, D. R., APOTHECARY: established circa 1878 in Fall River. Massachusetts, located at 135 South Main street in 1892, the firm remained in operation until the death of its proprietor in 1923. Eli Bence, a clerk at this apothecary shop from 1890 to 1895, claimed that Miss Lizzie A. Borden had attempted to purchase a quantity of prussic acid there a few days before the murders of her father and stepmother.

STAFFORD, JAMES COGGESHALL 1817 - 1895: born in Tiverton, Rhode Island, son of Peleg and Prudence (Coggeshall) Stafford. He married Miss Esther A. Howard of New Bedford, Massachusetts. First listed as a sea captain in the Fall River, Massachusetts, city directory in 1859, he was then sharing a house with the family of his brother-in-law, Captain Nathaniel P. Gray, their two wives being sisters. He last appears as living in Fall River in 1864 but is known to have been in New Bedford circa 1892, again residing in a house near that of Captain and Mrs. Gray. He was questioned as to any knowledge of insanity in the Borden family. This is most likely due to the fact that his mother-in-law, Mrs. Ann Howard, was a neighbor to the Andrew J. Borden family when residing on Ferry Street in 1857.

STANTON BROTHERS BOOTS AND SHOES: established in 1874 in Fall River, Massachusetts. The business was operated by Michael E. and John Stanton as a partnership. Following the death of Michael in 1898, the remaining brother was sole proprietor until the firm's dissolution in 1904. This business was mentioned in a statement given by Alfred A. Smith, an inmate at the Massachusetts Reformatory, on January 9, 1893.

SULLIVAN, BRIDGET ? - 1948: born in Billerough, County Cork, Ireland, daughter of Eugene and Margaret (Leary) Sullivan. Emigrating to America circa 1886, she was first employed as a scullery maid at the Perry House, a Newport, Rhode Island, hostelry. She remained there about one year, then relocated to South Bethlehem, Pennsylvania, to join relatives who had settled there. Employed by the Smiley family as a domestic servant, she remained in Pennsylvania until circa 1888, when she moved to Fall River, Massachusetts, there obtaining a position as a cook in the household of William Reed. She was subsequently employed as a domestic by Clinton V. S. Remington until November of 1889 when she was hired as servant to the family of Andrew J. Borden. In that household, she was frequently referred to as "Maggie," it apparently having been the custom of the Misses Borden to refer to their domestic help by that name. Her responsibilities there included cooking, cleaning and ironing. Attending to those duties the morning of August 4, 1892, she was one of the last to see her employers alive. She took leave of the Borden household shortly after the murders, residing with friends in Fall River. At the time of the Borden trial, she relocated to New Bedford, Massachusetts, where she was employed by jailkeeper Joshua A. Hunt. She provided key testimony at the inquest, preliminary hearing and final trial. Most likely seeking to disassociate herself from the tragedy once her responsibilities were through, she appears to have looked west. It has been suggested by a relative that having acquaintances in Anaconda, Montana, caused her to relocate there. Legend suggests that she returned to Ireland prior to settling in Montana, the trip to her native land financed by a sum of money provided to her by Miss Lizzie A. Borden. No evidence as yet has surfaced to authenticate or disprove this theory but it is known that she was residing in Anaconda, Montana, by 1897, employed as a domestic. A marriage certificate was issued to John M. Sullivan, a smeltman, and Miss Bridget Sullivan in 1905. Her year of birth was here listed as 1871, paring five years from the age she testified to at the trial, testimony she qualified with the statement that she was only aware of how old she was because she had been so informed. Following her marriage, she continued to be employed as a domestic, living the remainder of her life in virtual obscurity. Circa 1942, in declining health, she moved to Butte, Montana, to reside with a niece. She expired in a Butte hospital and was interred with her husband in Mount Olivet Cemetery in Anaconda.

SULLIVAN, DENNIS F.: an individual summoned as a witness. He was not called upon to testify. Attempts to uncover his identity have to date been unsuccessful.

SWIFT, AUGUSTUS 1831 - 1906: born in Falmouth, Massachusetts, son of Nathan D. and Pamelia C. (Cowen) Swift. He moved to New Bedford, Massachusetts, in his youth to learn the iron moulder's trade. After leaving New England for a period, he returned and gained employment at the Fairhaven Iron Foundry in Fairhaven, Massachusetts. He married Miss Nancy S. Jenney of Providence, Rhode Island, in 1854. He later established the Acushnet Iron Foundry in New Bedford. He was a resident of that city at the time of his death. He was one of the twelve-man jury that acquitted Miss Lizzie A. Borden on June 20, 1893.

THOMAS, TISH: a manicurist in Boston, Massachusetts. In 1892, site was said to be employed at Madame Rosilla Butler, Hair Goods on Tremont Street in that city. Attempts to uncover any biographical details have to date been unsuccessful.

THURSTON, THATCHER THAYER 1860 - 1911: born in Fall River, Massachusetts, son of Rev. Dr. Eli and Julia Ann (Sessions) Thurston. Educated in the Fall River public school system, he prepared for college at Phillips Academy at Andover, Massachusetts, graduating in 1877. He then entered Amherst College, receiving his Bachelor of Arts with honors four years later. Following graduation, he spent four years in New York City employed in the woolen house of George E. Steadman. Returning to Fall River in 1885, he began his career in the newspaper business as a reporter in the Fall River office of the *Providence Journal*. In 1887, he joined the staff of the *Fall River Daily Globe*. He married Miss Ada Elizabeth Dunn of his native city in 1894. His enterprising newspaper work gained him considerable recognition in the field. He resigned his post with the *Globe* in 1896 and accepted the position of editor of the *Fall River Daily Herald*, and for a time was simultaneously employed as a correspondent for the *Providence Journal*. In 1905, he relocated to Providence, Rhode Island, where he became editor of the *Providence Tribune*, a position he held until his death.

TRICKEY, HENRY G. 1868 - 1892: born in Dover, New Hampshire, son of John W. and Betsey E. Trickey. Having relocated with his family to Belmont, Massachusetts, in his youth, he was educated in the public school system there. An honors graduate from Belmont High School, he moved to Boston, Massachusetts, soon after leaving school, there engaging in the study of law in the offices of a prominent attorney. Deciding against the legal profession after less than a year, he obtained a position as a reporter for the *Tribune* in Cambridge, Massachusetts, thus beginning his newspaper career at the young age of seventeen. Shortly thereafter, he became employed at the *Boston Globe*, covering the neighboring communities of Lexington, Belmont and Arlington until his appointment to the Boston staff. He was a successful and enterprising journalist, his career accomplishments ranging from an expose of opium resorts in Boston in 1885 to an interview with Jefferson Davis, former leader of the Confederacy, in 1886. He married Miss Gertrude Melzar of Wakefield, Massachusetts, in 1890. He was an active member of both the Boston Press Club and the Press Cycle Club. In October of 1892, he was the author of an article which contained information allegedly provided by Detective Edwin D. McHenry, exposing new evidence in the Commonwealth of Massachusetts' case against Miss Lizzie A. Borden. Soon discovered to be a fabricated story, it was retracted by the Boston Globe the next day. Shortly following this episode, he left his home in Dorchester, Massachusetts, going first to the home of relatives in Evanston, Illinois, and later to Hamilton, Ontario, Canada, where he registered in a hotel under the name of Henry Melzar.

Conflicting reports exist as to why he left the United States; it has been said by some that he went to Canada out of fear of indictment for the *Boston Globe* article while others feel he was actually in Ontario on business for that newspaper. It was on December 3 of 1892 that, in attempting to board a moving westbound train in a Canadian depot, he fell to his death.

TUCKER, GEORGE FOX 1852 - 1929: born in New Bedford, Massachusetts, son of Charles Russell and Dorcas (Fry) Tucker. Having received his Bachelor of Arts from Brown University in 1873, he continued his education at Boston University Law School. He received his Bachelor of Laws in 1875, after which he established a practice in Boston, Massachusetts, with offices at Barrister's Hall. Active politically, he served as a member of the Massachusetts House of Representatives for a two-year term beginning in 1890. The following year, he was awarded the degree of Doctor of Philosophy from Brown University. He was appointed reporter of decisions for the Massachusetts Supreme Court in July of 1892, a position he was to retain for the next eight years. A resident of Lakeville, Massachusetts, he commuted daily to his law office in Boston. Later in his life, he relocated to Middleborough, Massachusetts, there becoming active in that town's politics. A noted author, he numbered among his works such diverse titles as *The Monroe Doctrine, a Concise History Relating to its Origin and Growth*, published in 1885 and *Mildred Marvel*, a novel published in 1899. In 1907, he was married to Miss Effie Dana Williams. He acted for a time as counsel for the General Claim Agency operated by Albert E. Allen. He died at his home in Middleborough.

WARREN, JOHN COLLINS 1842 - 1927: born in Boston, Massachusetts, son of Jonathan Mason and Annie (Crowninshield) Warren. Receiving his early education in his native city, he prepared for college at Boston Latin School and Epes S. Dixwell's Academy. He entered Harvard University in 1859 and received his Bachelor of Arts four years later, at which time he entered Harvard Medical School. In 1866, he was awarded the degree of Doctor of Medicine. Following graduation, he entered private practice until 1871 when he was appointed instructor in surgery at Harvard Medical School. Thus began an association with his alma mater which wits to last the remainder of his life. He was married in 1873 to Miss Amy Shaw of Boston. That same year, he was appointed editor of the *Boston Medical and Surgical Journal*, retaining that post for the next eight years. He was associated there with Dr. Henry H. A. Beach, who served for two years as his associate editor. In 1882, he was promoted to assistant professor of surgery and, five years later, to associate. Receiving his professorship in 1893, he was named Mosley Professor of Surgery six years later and was awarded the title of Mosley Professor Emeritus in 1907. He served as an overseer at Harvard beginning in 1908, acting in that capacity until late in his life. Throughout his career, he was several times awarded the honorary degree of Doctor of Laws by various universities including Harvard in 1906 and McGill University in Montreal, Canada, in 1914. He was a fellow of the American Association of Surgeons and an honorary fellow of both the Royal College of Physicians in London, England, and the Royal College of Physicians in Edinburgh, Scotland. An active member of several professional societies in his home state as well as nationally, he served as president of the American Surgical Association in 1896. The author of several medical texts, he numbered among his works *Healing of Arteries in Man and Animals After Ligature*, published in 1886, and *Surgical Pathology and Therapeutics*, published in 1895. He was editor and part author of the two-volume *International Text-book of Surgery by American and British Authors*, published in 1900. His death came in the city of his birth. He was recommended to Attorney General Albert E. Pillsbury by Dr. George W. Gay for consideration as a medical expert for the prosecution in the trial of Miss Lizzie A. Borden.

WESTCOTT, WILLIAM 1845 - 1921: born in Seekonk, Massachusetts, son of Valorus and Charlotte (Perry) Westcott. A life-long resident of his native town, he was a farmer by profession, living in his ancestral home on Pine Street. A member of the Congregational church, he married Miss Helen M. Perry in 1869 and, following her death in 1876, Miss Catherine Amelia Turner. He died in the northern section of his native town. He was one of the twelve-man jury that acquitted Miss Lizzie A. Borden on June 20, 1893.

WHITE, ANNIE M.: an official stenographer for Bristol County, Massachusetts, at the time of the Borden trial. A resident of New Bedford, Massachusetts, she is recorded there from 1887 to circa 1894. Summoned as a witness, she was called to testify regarding the notes which she recorded at the inquest, August 9 through August 11, 1892.

WHITEHEAD, SARAH BERTHA (GRAY) 1864 - 1932: born in Fall River, Massachusetts, daughter of Oliver and Jane E. D. (Baker) Eldridge Gray. She was the half-sister of the second Mrs. Andrew J. Borden. She married George W. Whitehead, a man employed as, first, a teamster and, later, a produce salesman in Fall River. In 1912, she relocated to New York City and was at Winnipeg, Manitoba, Canada, at the time of her death. She was a witness at the inquest and was summoned for the final trial but was not called upon to testify.

WILBAR, FREDERICK C., see **WILBUR, FREDERICK COPELAND**.

WILBER, LEMUEL K., see **WILBUR, LEMUEL KEITH**.

WILBUR, FREDERICK COPELAND 1857 - 1928: son of William and Jeminah (Tracy) Wilbur. He married Miss Elvira Caswell. A cabinetmaker by trade and resident of Raynham, Massachusetts, in 1892, he was a respected citizen of that town and lived there for the remainder of his life. He was one of the twelve-man jury that acquitted Miss Lizzie A. Borden on June 20, 1893.

WILBUR, JOHN 1833 - 1915: born in Somerset, Massachusetts, son of Daniel Whitman and Welthy (Hall) Wilbur. A farmer in his native town, he was also employed as a housewright and road surveyor. In 1853, he married Miss Esther D. Mosher of Warren, Rhode Island. Well-known in later life as a breeder of fancy poultry, he spent his last years in Worcester, Massachusetts. He was one of the twelve-man jury that acquitted Miss Lizzie A. Borden on June 20, 1893.

WILBUR, LEMUEL KEITH 1837 - 1912: born in Norton, Massachusetts, son of Oren and Polly (Eldredge) Wilbur. In 1860, he married Miss Elizabeth Hudson Fuller of Easton, Massachusetts. He was a prominent resident of that town and farmed on a grand scale. The owner of several hundred acres of both farm and woodland, he was also engaged for a time as a lumber and charcoal merchant. Reputed to be a businessman of strictest integrity, he died at his residence in Easton, Massachusetts. He was one of the twelve-man jury that acquitted Miss Lizzie A. Borden on June 20, 1893.

WING, ANJEANNETTE (WILBUR) 1849 - 1924: born in Tiverton, Rhode Island, daughter of David and Hannah (Rounds) Wilbur. She married Joseph Wing, a clerk for Cobb, Bates and Yerxa Company, grocers in Fall River, Massachusetts. In 1892, she resided with her husband at 86 Middle Street in that city. Widowed in 1909, she left Fall River and was residing in Cranston, Rhode Island, at the time of her death. Summoned as a witness, she was not called upon to testify.

WINSLOW, LEANDER A. 1859 - 1929: born in Fall River, Massachusetts, son of James H. and Elizabeth Winslow. He married Miss Mary J. Durfee of his native city in 1881. A partner with Edmund J. Sokoll in the firm Sokoll, Winslow and Company, Confectioners, he was later employed as a clerk at the Fall River Electric Light Company. A life-long resident of Fall River, he held membership in various fraternal organizations. Summoned as a witness, he was not called upon to testify.

WIXON, FRANCIS H. 1841 - 1908: born in Dennisport, Massachusetts, son of Captain James and Bertha Wixon. He came to Fall River, Massachusetts, with his family and, at the age of sixteen, entered the apothecary business. After the outbreak of the Civil War, he enlisted in Company C, the 5th Rhode Island Regiment, holding the rank of private under the command of General Burnside. His service was primarily at Roanoke Island. In 1872, his father died after thirty years' service as deputy sheriff of Bristol County, Massachusetts. He was appointed to succeed his father and served in that position until his death in his adopted town. He married Miss Anna D. Estes of Fall River in 1875. He was a member of the G.A.R. as well as various fraternal organizations. At the Central Police Station in Fall River on the day of the murders, he was one of the first on the scene. He testified at both the preliminary and final trials, providing evidence which detailed his observations in and around the Borden residence on August 4, 1892.

WOOD, EDWARD STICKNEY 1846 - 1905: born in Cambridge, Massachusetts. He attended Harvard University, receiving his Bachelor of Arts in 1867. Entering Harvard Medical School in 1868, he received the degree of Doctor of Medicine in 1871 and a Master of Arts the following year. In 1872, he went to Europe to study physiology and medical chemistry in Berlin, Germany and Vienna, Austria. Appointed assistant professor of chemistry at Harvard in 1871, he remained in this capacity until his appointment to a full professorship five years later, a position he held until his death. In 1883, he married Miss Elizabeth Richardson of Cambridge. He was under the care of Dr. Maurice H. Richardson at the time of his death in Brookline, Massachusetts. An expert in the analysis of blood and blood stains, he was called upon to testify at numerous murder trials throughout his career. Having examined several pieces of evidence removed from the Borden household, he gave testimony at the trial detailing his findings.

WORDELL, ALLEN H. 1848 - 1920: born in Fall River, Massachusetts, son of Holder and Rachel Wordell. A resident of North Dartmouth, Massachusetts, he was married three times. In 1893, he was a retailer of agricultural implements and seed in New Bedford, Massachusetts, a member of the firm Wilson and Wordell. He was in New Bedford, Massachusetts, at the time of his death. He was one of the twelve-man jury that acquitted Miss Lizzie A. Borden on June 20, 1893.

WORDELL, ISAAC B. 1856 - 1894: born in Providence, Rhode Island, son of William and Rebecca (Luther) Wordell. He was appointed to the position of patrolman in the Fall River Police Department in 1883. During the reorganization of the force in 1893, he was promoted to inspector with the rank of lieutenant and as such his signature appears on witness summonses issued for the Borden trial. He served as a partner in the police department with William H. Medley and was a member of the force at the time of his death.

WRIGHT, EDWARD E. 1862 - 1931: son of Asahel and Ellen Wright. He was married to Miss Edith M. Shepherd of New Bedford, Massachusetts. It seems likely that the name 'Wright" appearing on the list of potential witnesses with the notations "N.B." and "buying prussic acid" beside it refers to this New Bedford druggist. First listed in that city's directory in 1883, he was employed by 1. H. Shurtleff, Apothecary. He worked in that capacity until 1889, when he began his own business. Known as Wright Drug Company from 1891 to 1893, his establishment is last listed as operating in 1907. It was at this establishment that Miss Lizzie A. Borden was alleged to have attempted to buy a quantity of prussic acid while on a visit to New Bedford with her sister.

WRIGHT, MARY JANE (IRVING) 1832 - 1905: born in Fall River, Massachusetts, daughter of James Irving. She married Andrew Robeson Wright of that city in 1853. She served as matron of Taunton jail in Taunton, Massachusetts, during her husband's term as sheriff of that city from 1886 to 1896. She was in Fall River, Massachusetts, at the time of her death. She was a former neighbor of the Borden family and her daughter, Isabel Mathewson Wright, and Lizzie A. Borden played together as children. In one of life's ironic twists, the matron's term coincided with the period when her daughter's former playmate was being held in that very prison pending trial for the murder of her father and stepmother.

WRIGHT, MR., see **WRIGHT, EDWARD E.**

WYATT, MARY B. 1852 - ? : born in Massachusetts. She was a widow residing above Dr. and Mrs. Seabury W. Bowen at 91 Second Street, Fall River, Massachusetts, in 1892. First listed in that city's directory in 1890, she was last recorded there in 1921. Questioned by the police and summoned as a witness, she was not called upon to testify.

Glossary B

Profiles of Correspondents

The following biographical information relates to individuals whose correspondence was included in Attorney Hosea M. Knowlton's files. The Editors have made every attempt to uncover the identity of those mentioned. Cases where positive identification was impossible are noted as such. Correspondents listed below who are also mentioned in the text of the documents are profiled in Glossary A and are here cross-referenced.

ADAMS, MELVIN OHIO 1850 - 1920: see **GLOSSARY A**.

ALLEN, ALBERT E.: a claim agent and former resident of Boston. Massachusetts. First appearing in that city in 1883, he maintained offices on Washington Street. He relocated to Washington, District of Columbia, six years later.

APTHORP, [?] L.: author of a letter from Wilton, New Hampshire, to Attorney Hosea M. Knowlton. The first name of the author has not been deciphered. It is likely that this person was a relation of William F. Apthorp (1848 - 1913), a prominent music scholar and educator from Boston, Massachusetts. This assumption is made on the basis of the fact that he and his family were known to have summered in Wilton, New Hampshire. As reported in the "Wilton" section of *The Farmers Cabinet*, a Milford, New Hampshire, newspaper, on May 18, 1893, "William F. Apthorp of Boston will occupy the house of Henry Emerson at the Centre during the summer. The help for the house arrived on Saturday." Efforts to obtain a positive identification for this individual within the Apthorp family have to date been unsuccessful.

AUSTIN, T.: a resident of Boston, Massachusetts. Nothing in the content of this letter indicates the positive identity of the author.

BADGER, WALTER IRVING 1859 - 1926: born in Boston, Massachusetts, son of Erastus Beethoven and Fanny (Babcock) Badger. Receiving his early education in his native city's public school system, he prepared for college at English High School and at Adams Academy. In 1878, he entered Yale University, receiving his Bachelor of Arts four years later. While at Yale, he became a noted collegiate athlete and, at that time, formed the nucleus of his life-long interest in his alma mater. He began the study of law in the Boston office of Solomon B. Lincoln, Esq. and entered Boston University Law School, receiving his Bachelor of Laws cum laude in 1885. Following graduation, he was admitted to the bar and established a practice in Boston, specializing in corporate law. In 1887, he married Miss Elizabeth Hand Wilcox of New Haven, Connecticut. Active socially, he was also a member of several professional organizations. He died at his home in Cambridge, Massachusetts.

BARNES, HENRY ELBERT 1832 - 1910: born in Plantsville, Connecticut, son of Henry and Ada (Clarke) Barnes. He graduated from Yale University in 1860 and subsequently entered the Chicago Theological Seminary. After completion of his education, he was ordained a Congregational minister. At the outbreak of the Civil War, he enlisted in the 72nd Illinois Regiment, being appointed as its chaplain. He also served under General Ulysses S. Grant at Vicksburg, Pennsylvania. He was appointed pastor of the Centre Congregational Church in Haverhill, Massachusetts, in 1876. During his pastorate there, nearly two hundred new members were accepted into the congregation and the church edifice was enlarged and rebuilt. In 1886, he relocated to Sherbrook, Massachusetts, remaining there a short while until settling in North Andover, Massachusetts. He remained there for eleven years, leaving in 1904 to accept a pastorate in Brookline, Massachusetts. In 1907, he was elected department chaplain of the Massachusetts G.A.R. and was reelected again to that position the following year. The author of numerous religious and patriotic articles, he lectured frequently on those topics. He was an active member of the Loyal Legion and chaplain of the Chandler Post, G.A.R., in Brookline. Following a brief illness, he died at his residence in his adopted city.

BATCHELDER, MOULTON 1836 - 1929: see **GLOSSARY A**.

BELL, DORCAS: author of a letter from Brooklyn, New York, to Attorney Hosea M. Knowlton. Nothing in the content of this letter indicates the positive identity of the author.

BENNETT, EDMUND HATCH 1824 - 1898: born in Manchester, Vermont, son of Milo Lyman and Adaline (Hatch) Bennett. He received his early education at Burr and Burton Seminary in Burlington, Vermont, as well as at Manchester and Burlington academies. He then attended that state's university, graduating in 1843. He pursued his study of law in his father's office and was admitted to the Vermont bar in 1847. Later that year, he relocated to Boston, Massachusetts, and was there admitted to the Suffolk bar in 1848. He practiced law for a time in Boston but eventually established a residence in Taunton, Massachusetts. where he was associated in a practice with Nathaniel Morton, Esq. which was to last for nearly three years. The following years were spent in various partnerships, including those with Hon. Henry Williams, Henry J. Fuller. Esq. and Frederick S. Hall, Esq., also of Taunton. In 1853, he was married to Miss Sally Crocker. Appointed judge of probate and insolvency for Bristol County, Massachusetts, in 1858, he retained that post until his resignation twenty-five years later. Elected to the mayoralty of his adopted city 1864, he served in that capacity for three successive terms. His interest in the welfare of the community was evidenced by his active involvement with various institutions there. He served as a director of the Young Men's Library Association of Taunton and promoted the establishment of that city's public library in 1866. A member of the board of directors of the Old Colony Historical Society, he was a great contributor to its welfare. He was a lecturer at Harvard Law School from 1870 to 1872. at which time he also became a professor at the Law School of Boston University. That same year, he was presented with the degree of Doctor of Laws from his alma mater. He was involved principally in the literary aspect of law and as such prepared several volumes including the *Massachusetts Digest*. He was named by Governor William E. Russell to the position of chairman of a board of commissioners, appointed to promote uniformity in United States legislation. He also was appointed by Governor Roger Wolcott to head a commission organized to revise the general statutes of the Commonwealth of Massachusetts. In 1876, he was named dean of the faculty of Boston University Law School, maintaining that position until his death. A frequent contributor to numerous professional publications, he served as an editor of the *American Law Journal* from 1870 to 1888. Devoting a considerable amount of time to the Episcopal church, he acted as a delegate to the Diocesan Convention. Between 1874 and 1895, he was elected seven times to be deputy from his diocese to the General Convention of the church. His other involvements included a position on the board of trustees to the Protestant Episcopal Church of the Diocese of Massachusetts and president of the trustees of the Episcopal Theological School at Cambridge. Massachusetts. He died in rooms at the Hotel Vendome where he made his Boston residence.

BLACKWOOD, ANNA E., see **LOGUE, MISS ANNIE ELIZABETH BLACKWOOD.**

BOLLES, HENRY C. 1855 - 1905: born in New Bedford, Massachusetts, son of John M. and Sarah (Burgess) Bolles. Educated in the public schools in his native city, he gained employment in his youth as a message carrier for the Western Union Telegraph Company. His mastery of the Morse alphabet qualified him to send and receive messages and so he obtained his first position as telegrapher, working at the New Bedford freight station for the Boston, Clinton and Fitchburg Railroad. At the age of sixteen, he returned to Western Union, employed first as day operator, and eventually assumed the position of night operator. In 1875, he was married to Miss Annie Briggs. When the Baltimore and Ohio Telegraph Company opened an office in New Bedford, he was hired as manager, retaining that position in 1889 after that company's merger with the Postal Telegraph Company. Having served as the Associated Press operator in the offices of *The Evening Standard*, a New Bedford newspaper, in 1887, he was to continue in employment there as well as at Postal Telegraph until 1896. At that time, he surrendered the position at the latter due to poor health. He remained employed at the *Standard* until circa 1903 when he was taken ill, at which time he traveled to the island of Jamaica in the hopes of effecting a cure. Upon his return, he resumed his post at the newspaper but poor health forced his retirement and he was soon confined to bed. He died at his Borden Street residence in his native city.

BOOTH, LUCY C. (HUNT) 1836 - 1914: born in Great Barrington, Massachusetts, daughter of Charles and Lucy (Beebe) Hunt. Educated at the Maplewood Institute in Pittsfield, Massachusetts, she was also a graduate of the Emma Willard School in Troy, New York. In 1855, she traveled to Peru, Illinois, where she married Reuben H. Booth, a businessman in that city. In 1859, after selling out their business in Peru, she and her husband relocated to her native town. Widowed in 1871, she remained active in the social affairs of Great Barrington and was a member of the Thursday Morning Club. Her son, Charles Hunt Booth, was employed as a cashier at the National Mahaiwe Bank in Great Barrington, an institution at which Hon. Albert Mason served for a time as director. Well-read and literary, she authored several historical papers and was a noted conversationalist. She died at her residence in her native town.

BOYNTON, EBEN MOODY 1840 - 1927: born in Harrisville, Ohio, son of Methusaleh and Abigail (Moody) Boynton. Moving to Massachusetts with his parents when a young boy, he grew to become a noted inventor in Newburyport, Massachusetts. He amassed his fortune from the invention of the "lightning-saw," its M-shaped teeth designed to cut through hard woods. In 1873, he married Miss Anna Bartlett Gale of Newburyport, residing in that town as well as maintaining a summer residence in nearby West Newbury. Gaining prominence in the shipping industry, he served for a time as a state representative and was a noted lecturer, economist and publicist. The inventor of the single rail or bicycle railroad, he spent years persistently attempting to gain the support of the Commonwealth of Massachusetts for its promotion. He claimed that with trains traveling at speeds of up to 200 miles per hour, a fast and safe one-day trip from the Atlantic to Pacific Coast would be possible. He never saw his dreams come to fruition, even though they were considered practical and effective by several railroad men. He expended his considerable fortune, acquired through the success of an earlier invention, in futile efforts to promote another. Following the death of his first wife in 1916, he married Charlotte Densmore Dickson of Boston, Massachusetts. He died while a patient in Massachusetts General Hospital in Boston, Massachusetts.

BRIGGS, E. P.: author of a letter to Mrs. Hosea M. Knowlton. Nothing in the content of this letter indicates the positive identity of the author.

BROWN, CLARA: a resident of Boston, Massachusetts. Nothing in the content of this letter indicates the positive identity of the author.

BROWNE, LOUISE WOLCOTT (KNOWLTON): daughter of Lincoln Brown and Lucretia (Wolcott) Knowlton. In 1888, she married General William H. Browne, a lawyer and distinguished veteran of both the Civil and Mexican wars. A resident of Washington, District of Columbia, she was active in church circles and charitable organizations and maintained an interest in genealogy. Her husband's career as an author and practicing attorney in the United States Supreme Court assured them a prominent position in Washington society. She held membership in several patriotic organizations.

BUFFINGTON, GEORGE B. 1835 - 1906: born in Somerset, Massachusetts, son of Henry Tisdale and Content S. (Sweet) Buffington. First listed in the city directory of Fall River, Massachusetts, in 1876, he resided at the time with his widowed mother and was employed as a clerk. Two years later he held a position as deputy sheriff of that city, working in that capacity until 1880 when he relocated to the neighboring city of Taunton. He was first employed there as a teacher and subsequently was principal of the Cohannet grammar school. He moved to Dorchester, Massachusetts, circa 1884, and resided there with his sister, Miss Mary P. Buffington. A teacher in the Boston, Massachusetts, school system, he was involved in the evening school service there. He died at his home in Dorchester.

BURT, FRANK HUNT 1861 - 1946: see **GLOSSARY A.**

CHAFFIN, WILLIAM L. 1837 - 1923: born in Oxford, Maine, son of William F. and Louise (Shattuck) Chaffin. In his early childhood, he moved to Concord, New Hampshire, with his family following the death of his father. Since his mother was an invalid, he was adopted by an aunt, Mrs. Nancy Chaffin-Fessenden. Entering the Unitarian Theological School in Meadville, Pennsylvania, in 1857, he was graduated four years later. He married Miss Rebecca L. Bagley of Meadville in 1862. Being ordained that same year, he was assigned the ministry of the Second Unitarian Society. The following year, he enlisted in the 58th Regiment of the Pennsylvania Volunteers and as such served in the Civil War campaign that resulted in the capture of Confederate leader John Morgan. Following his term of service, he was made minister of the Unitarian Church in Fitchburg, Massachusetts, beginning there in 1865. He was named pastor of the Church of the Unity in North Easton, Massachusetts, in 1868 and was ministering to that congregation at the time of his death fifty-five years later. Active in town affairs, he served for twenty-eight years as a member of the North Easton school committee and was also secretary of the trustees of the Ames Free Library. He served the G.A.R. as chaplain for a period of time. A member of the fellowship committee of the Unitarian denomination, he held a position for several years on the board of trustees of the Meadville Theological School as well. In 1886, he published a history of his adopted town. Later in his life, he authored other volumes, including histories of both Robert Randall and the Chaffin family. At the time of his death at his home in North Easton, he was the oldest active minister in the United States.

CHEEVER, DAVID WILLIAMS 1831 - 1915: see **GLOSSARY A.**

CHOATE, CHARLES FRANCIS, JR. 1864 - 1927: born in Cambridge, Massachusetts, son of Charles Francis and Elizabeth W. (Carlisle) Choate. Receiving his early education in private schools in his native city, he prepared for college at St. Mark's School in Southborough, Massachusetts. Following graduation from Harvard University in 1888, he entered Harvard Law School. He also read law in the Boston, Massachusetts, office of Josiah H. Benton, Esq. In 1890, he was admitted to the Suffolk bar and, entering the office of Attorney Benton, began the practice of law. He married Miss Louise Burnett in Boston in 1892 and maintained residences in both Boston and Southborough. In 1898, he entered into a successful partnership with John M. Hall, Esq. with offices in Boston. Ralph A. Stewart, Esq. was admitted to the firm in 1904 and the firm's name was subsequently changed to Choate, Hall and Stewart. He numbered among his partners in this firm Joseph W. Knowlton, Esq., son of Hosea M. Knowlton, Esq. He served for a time as corporation counsel of the New York, New Haven and Hartford Railroad. Active in the municipal affairs of Southborough, he was a delegate to the Constitutional Convention in 1917. A director and president of St. Mark's School and the Fay School, he also served on the boards of various hospitals and corporations. His estate in Southborough was noted for its stables and kennels and was the scene of several important legal and political gatherings. He died at Massachusetts General Hospital in Boston shortly after a heart attack brought about his collapse during a trial in the federal court.

CLANCY, JOHN J.: a resident of Newark, New Jersey. He was the proprietor of a shoe store on Market Street in that city in 1892, the address of which appears on his letter to Attorney Hosea M. Knowlton. He last appears in the Newark directory in 1896, apparently the year of his death, as his widow, Mary, is listed the following year.

CLIFFORD, WALTER 1849 - 1912: born in New Bedford, Massachusetts, son of John Henry and Sarah Parker (Allen) Clifford. He received his early education under private instruction and at Friend's Academy in his native city. Having prepared for college at Phillips Academy in Exeter, New Hampshire, he then entered Harvard University and received his Bachelor of Arts in 1871. He began the study of law at Harvard Law School and during his third year there registered as a student in the Worcester, Massachusetts, office of Messrs. Staples and Goulding. He was admitted to the Bristol County bar in 1874, a year before receiving his Bachelor of Laws from Harvard Law School. Immediately after graduation, he entered the New Bedford law firm of Messrs. Marston and Crapo in the capacity of law clerk. Through subsequent changes in the partnership, the firm eventually became Crapo, Clifford and Clifford when his brother, Charles W. Clifford, Esq., joined. In 1878, he married Miss Harriet Perry Randall, a native of New Bedford. In 1877 and 1878, he served as a member of the common council in that city. Attaining prominence through his various successes as an attorney, he became active in municipal affairs, holding the mayoralty of New Bedford in both 1889 and 1891. His administration was noted for establishing the Board of Public Works and for its considerable improvement and development of public buildings. In both 1892 and 1896, he was a delegate to the Republican National Convention, there forming an acquaintance with President William McKinley. He possessed many business interests, serving for several years as vice-president of the New Bedford Five Cents Savings Bank. An active officer and director in several New Bedford corporations, he held membership in social clubs both there and in Boston, Massachusetts. A polished speaker, he was considered one of the best dressed men in his native city, always faultlessly attired. He died at his summer residence in North Dartmouth, Massachusetts.

COLLINS, ALBERT B. 1854 - 1922: born in Fairhaven, Massachusetts, son of Joseph and Sybil (Kennison) Collins. He received his education in the public schools of his native town. A student of law in the New Bedford, Massachusetts, office of Thomas M. Stetson, Esq., he was admitted to the bar in 1877. He immediately established a practice in New Bedford and later was associated in a firm with Lemuel Holmes, Esq. Following dissolution of that partnership, he associated himself with various other attorneys throughout his career. In practice, he specialized in laws governing the conveyancing and holding of property. Upon the recommendation of Hon. Walter Clifford, mayor of New Bedford, he was appointed by the United States government as a special expert. In this capacity, he collated and tabulated mortgage conveyance statistics for the Federal census of 1890 from the Registries of Deeds of New Bedford and Taunton, Massachusetts. He was subsequently employed by Bristol County, Massachusetts, as superintendent of various departments in the Registry of Deeds in New Bedford and Taunton. In 1903, he was appointed Register of Deeds for Bristol County, retaining that position until the time of his death. Active in the municipal affairs of Fairhaven, he served as that town's auditor and was a member of both its school committee and Board of Health. He also held the position of overseer of the poor for a time. He died following a brief illness at his residence in his native town.

COWLES, EDWARD 1837 - 1919: see **GLOSSARY A.**

CROSS, JOSEPH WARREN 1808 - 1906: born in East Bridgewater, Massachusetts, son of Naphaniel and Margaret G. (Bird) Cross. He received his early education in the public schools of his native town. In 1821, he began private instruction under Rev. Pitt Clark, the secular clergyman, at Norton, Massachusetts, remaining with him three years. At the age of sixteen, he entered Harvard University, receiving his Bachelor of Arts in 1828. The next year, he accepted the position of principal at Orleans Academy in Orleans, Massachusetts, remaining there until 1830 when he was appointed head of Chatham Academy, also located on Cape Cod, Massachusetts. In 1832, he gave up the teaching profession and entered Andover Theological Seminary in Andover, Massachusetts. Ordained a Congregational minister in 1834 at the Congregational Church in Boxboro, Massachusetts, he served as pastor to that congregation for the next six years. In 1840, he was appointed minister of the West Boylston Congregational Church, also in his native state, remaining there until his retirement twenty years later. He was married to Miss Sarah Fletcher of that community. A resident of West Boylston for sixty years, he spent the end of his life in the cities of Worcester and Lawrence, Massachusetts. It was noted, at the time of his ninety-sixth birthday celebration, that he read two newspapers each day without the aid of eyeglasses. He had lived long enough to see his great-great-grandchildren, which he remarked was the only incident which made him feel aged. At the time of his death at the residence of his daughter in Lawrence, he was the oldest living alumnus of both Harvard University and the Andover Theological Seminary. He held the distinction of being the oldest Congregationalist minister in the United States.

DAGGETT, MISS ELVIRA M. 1843 - 1924: born in Coventry, Vermont, daughter of Alpheus and Clarissa (Green) Daggett. She probably received her education in her native town, where she was to reside the greater portion of her life. It is likely that she occupied herself at home, tending to the needs of her family. She is remembered by one who knew her as an educated woman very much interested in the affairs of Coventry. She died in Littleton, New Hampshire.

DAVIS, JOHN c.1832 - 1902: born in Lowell, Massachusetts. Educated under the guardianship of a Mr. Watson and, later, Elijah M. Read, he attended the public schools of his native city. Following graduation from Dartmouth College, he returned to Lowell, studying law there in the office of Messrs. Daniel S. and George F. Richardson. Employed as a tutor preparing young men for college, he abandoned his teaching career upon admission to the bar and established a practice. He came to be regarded as one of the best real estate lawyers in the city, his Lowell office specializing in probate and estate settlement. He served for a time as president of the Old Lowell National Bank and, later, as a director of the First National Bank, also in Lowell. During his career, he also was associate justice of police court for a time. Late in his life, he married a Miss Stearns, a schoolteacher. He died suddenly while speaking with clients in his Lowell law office.

DAY, JOSEPH MUENSCHER 1824 - 1897: born in Newton Lower Falls, Massachusetts, son of Joseph Fisher and Mary Ann (Savage) Day. As a child, he moved with his family first to Union and later Portland, Maine. He received his education in schools in Portland where he also studied law. Admitted to the Suffolk bar in 1846, he established a practice in Boston, Massachusetts, forming a partnership with Daniel W. Gooch, Esq. In 1851, he moved to Barnstable, Massachusetts, establishing an office there with Zeno Scudder, Esq. He married Miss Elizabeth Ann Chadwick of Portland in 1852. The next year, he was appointed deputy collector of taxes for Barnstable County, thus beginning his involvement in civic affairs there. Elected register of probate in 1858, he was appointed judge of probate of Barnstable County the next year, serving in that capacity for twenty-three years. He served as a delegate to the Republican National Convention in 1860 and the next year was appointed collector of the Port of Barnstable, resigning from that position after only a few months. In 1862, he was instrumental in forming a company of volunteers and was elected captain. Upon that company's attachment to the 40th Regiment, Massachusetts Volunteers, he was commissioned major. While on duty in South Carolina, he contracted an illness that incapacitated him for further service. Returning home, he continued in his successful private law practice and resumed his judicial duties. He maintained an active interest in politics on a state and national level for the rest of his life. A member of several professional and social organizations, he was one of the earliest members of the Union Club in Boston, Massachusetts. He died at his residence in Barnstable, considered at the time one of that town's leading citizens.

DEAN, CHARLES JOHN: son of Charles and Jane Maria (Wright) Dean. A resident of Lunenberg, Massachusetts, he was most likely self-employed as a farmer. From 1878 to 1890, he paid taxes on a sixteen-acre lot with house and barn. His payment of the poll tax in Lunenberg continued beyond this time to 1895. He was known to have been boarding in Fitchburg, Massachusetts, in 1893.

DELANO, ALINE, see **DELANO, ALEXANDRIA PAULOVNA (KUSMISCHEV)**.

DELANO, ALEXANDRIA PAULOVNA (KUSMISCHEV) 1845 - 1928: born in Archangel, Russia, daughter of Paul Feodorovich and Eudoxia

Porstrovna (Shafrov) Kusmischev. Educated in Russia, she was a graduate of the Patriotic Institute for Daughters of the Nobility in St. Petersburg, receiving a gold medal in 1860. In 1867 in St. Petersburg, she married James Haskell Delano, an American attached to the United States Navy. Emigrating to the United States, she eventually settled with her husband in Massachusetts and, in 1899, was known to be living at the Hotel Dudley in Boston. Widowed the following year, she later relocated to Cambridge, Massachusetts, where she was residing in 1909. A noted lecturer, she wrote extensively for American and Russian magazines and newspapers. Fluent in both the French and Russian languages, she worked as a translator for several leading publishing houses. It is likely that the mention of "Alec" in her letter to Mrs. Hosea M. Knowlton refers to her son, Alexander J. Delano. Following her death, her remains were interred in Marion, Massachusetts.

DEVENS, RICHARD MILLER 1824 - 1900: born in Charlestown, Massachusetts, son of Samuel and Rachel (Noble) Devens. It is likely that his early education was received in the public schools of his native town. Inclined toward the ministry, he studied theology, maintaining connections with the Methodist Protestant and Methodist Episcopal denominations throughout his life. Although he temporarily filled various pulpits, he always declined assignment to a permanent pastorate. He married Miss Catherine V. Oakes of Cambridge, Massachusetts, in 1846 and, following her death, wed Miss Hannah Ellis of Danvers, Massachusetts. At the time of his first marriage, he was employed as an accountant but soon devoted all of his energies towards literary pursuits. Associated with various prominent New York City daily newspapers throughout his career, he often covered important events of the day. A noted author, his works included *Our First Century: One Hundred Great and Memorable Events of Perpetual Interest in the History of the United States, 1776 - 1876*, published in 1876. A resident of Cataumet, Massachusetts, for a time, he moved circa 1885 to Norton, Massachusetts. Plagued by ill health the last decade of his life, he continued to write and developed a keen interest in the affairs of his adopted town, where he was noted for his benevolence. He retired from newspaper work in 1899 and, following his death in his Norton residence, was interred in Cataumet.

DEVOLL, SARAH WOOD (HOWLAND) 1835 - 1922: born in South Dartmouth, Massachusetts, daughter of Bradford and Susan (Law) Howland. She was the widow of Zebedee A. Devoll, a prominent New Bedford whaling captain who lost his life in 1861 in the Civil War. She graduated from New

England Medical College in Boston, Massachusetts. Early in her life, she was an active member of the woman's suffrage movement and as such was a close associate of Mrs. Lucy Stone. She was practicing medicine in Jamaica Plain, Massachusetts, in 1893, and subsequently relocated to Portland, Maine, there opening an office. She later returned to Massachusetts and was residing in Dorchester at the time of her death.

DRAPER, FRANK WINTHROP 1843 - 1909: see **GLOSSARY A.**

DUNBAR, JAMES ROBERT 1847 - 1915: born in Pittsfield, Massachusetts, son of Henry W. and Elizabeth (Richards) Dunbar. Educated in the public schools of his native city, he later attended Williams College, receiving his Bachelor of Arts in 1871. He studied law briefly at Harvard Law School and in the Westfield, Massachusetts, office of Hon. Milton B. Whitney. Admitted to the Hampden County bar in 1874, he formed a partnership with Attorney Whitney, engaging in the general practice of law. He was subsequently admitted to practice in the United States courts. He married Miss Harriet Pierce Walton of Westfield, Massachusetts, in 1875. In 1885 and 1886, he served in the state senate and was active on the committee on the judiciary and served as chairman of the committee on election laws. During his term, he was also chairman of a joint special committee organized to investigate state house expenditures. He was a delegate to the Republican State Convention in 1887. The next year, he was appointed by Governor Oliver Ames to a seat on the bench of the superior court of Massachusetts. He was known to be an influential Republican party leader in the western part of his native state. He moved to Newton, Massachusetts, at that time and, in 1898, he returned to private practice, establishing a partnership in Boston with Messrs. Felix and Charles S. Rackemann. He served as a director of the Boston Safe Deposit and Trust Company, was a trustee of Williams College and held membership in various professional and social organizations. He died at his home in Brookline, Massachusetts.

EATON, JOHN FRANCIS 1842 - 1905: born in New York state. He moved to the Boston, Massachusetts, area as a young man and began to study architecture under Gridley J. F. Bryant, one of the more prominent Boston architects. In the early 1880s he resided in Cambridge, Massachusetts, maintaining an office on State Street in Boston until circa 1901 when he relocated his family and business to Newton Highlands, Massachusetts. He served as a deacon in the Congregational church and was an active participant in church affairs. He retired from his office duties due to ill health and died while hospitalized in Newton, Massachusetts.

ELDER, ROBERT B. 1843 - 1905: born in Flat City, Missouri. A naval veteran of the Civil War, he relocated in his early twenties to the Newark, New Jersey, area, there becoming associated with the Domestic Sewing Machine Company. With that firm for over thirty years, he severed his connection when difficulties forced his employer into receivership. He was subsequently involved in the real estate and insurance businesses, being employed as a special agent for the Prudential Insurance Company. Settling in Verona, New Jersey, in his later years, he was a member of the Second Presbyterian Church and served as a trustee for that institution. Active in the affairs of his church as well as various charitable organizations, he was also a member of the Royal Legion. His death came tragically due to injuries sustained when he was thrown from a trolley car into a trench which had been dug for installation of high pressure water service in the city of Newark.

FARLEY, JAMES PHILLIPS, JR. 1848 - 1896: born in Chelsea, Massachusetts, son of James Phillips and Chloe (Swift) Farley. After obtaining his Bachelor of Arts from Harvard University in 1868, he began his study of law at the Boston, Massachusetts, office of T. C. Wakefield, Esq. Having attended Harvard Law School for a time, he then read law in the office of R. Morse, Esq. in Boston and was admitted to the bar in 1870. The following year he was presented with the degree of Master of Arts from his alma mater. He was married to Miss Mary Eliot Wells. He practiced law in the city of Boston, for a time in partnership with Alfred Hemenway, Esq. He died while a patient at the Massachusetts General Hospital.

FISKE, FRANCIS SKINNER 1825 - 1907: born in Keene, New Hampshire, son of Phineas and Isabella (Redington) Fiske. Educated in the public schools of his native town, he later attended Dartmouth College, receiving his Bachelor of Arts in 1843. Entering Harvard Law School, he was awarded his Bachelor of Laws in 1846 and was subsequently admitted to the New Hampshire bar. Following this, he traveled extensively for several years and, upon his return, married Miss Annie Wilson. Settling in his native town, he opened an office and began to practice law. In 1861, he was commissioned lieutenant-colonel of the 2nd New Hampshire Regiment and the next year, while in command of a Pennsylvania regiment, contracted army fever, forcing his resignation. Returning to Keene, he resumed the practice of law and, in 1865, moved to Boston, Massachusetts. He was admitted to the Suffolk bar that same year. Establishing a private practice, he was appointed to the post of clerk and auditor of the United States Bankruptcy Court in 1871, holding that position for thirty-four years. An active Mason, he was also a member of the G.A.R. Retiring in 1903 due to ill health, he spent his final years at home in Milton, Massachusetts.

FLETCHER, HERBERT HERVEY 1855 - 1941: born in Granby, Massachusetts, son of Erastus and Elmira (Hervey) Fletcher. His early life was spent on the farm and, due to his situation, it was with great difficulty that he received a liberal education. Attending the public schools of his native town, he spent two terms at Wesleyan Academy in Wilbraham, Massachusetts. At the age of seventeen, he became an assistant teacher at Betts Military Academy in Stamford, Connecticut. Here he was granted the privilege of admission to classes preparing for college. In 1875, he entered Williams College where he excelled as a student. The recipient of numerous coveted honors, he was a staff member and later president of the *Athenaeum*, the Williams newspaper. In 1879, he received his Master of Arts with honors, marrying Miss Alice S. Kellogg of Granby that same year. Unable to secure a suitable position as a teacher, he engaged in newspaper work, employed as New England editor of the *Springfield Daily Union*. In 1882, he moved to Boston, Massachusetts, becoming the New England agent for the National Associated Press and, the next year, accepting the same position for the United Press. A tireless worker, he was instrumental in developing the news service of the United Press throughout the New England states. He quickly rose to prominence and, in 1889, was appointed service superintendent for the New England Associated Press, a position he held for the next eight years. In 1897, he accepted the position of assistant managing editor of the *Boston Evening Transcript*, being appointed associate editor the next year. During this period, he was awarded an honorary degree of Doctor of Laws from Norwich University. Appointed managing editor, he gained national fame as the founder of the popular "Churchman Afield" columns, read by all denominations. In 1920, he was presented an honorary Master of Arts from his alma mater. He retired in 1933, ending a career spanning over half a century. The author of several religious texts, he also lectured widely on various subjects. He held active memberships in several press and art associations. He died at his residence in Brookline, Massachusetts

FOGG, JOHN HASKELL 1837 - 1906: born in North Gorham, Maine, son of Daniel and Johanna (Files) Fogg. He received his early education in the public schools of his native town as well as at North Bridgton Academy in Bridgton, Maine. Following graduation, he became engaged as a school teacher while beginning to pursue the study of law. In 1861, at the outbreak of the Civil War, he enlisted as a private in Company A, 7th Maine Volunteers. Quickly promoted through the ranks, he served as sergeant major, second lieutenant and first lieutenant. Resigning due to ill health at the close of the Peninsula campaign, he re-enlisted upon his recovery. Appointed to the rank of captain, he was ordered to duty at Washington, District of Columbia, where he organized and drilled troops for the service. In 1864, a relapse of his illness caused his final resignation from military service. Returning home to Gorham, he engaged in commercial business and resumed the study of law, being admitted to the Cumberland bar in 1871. Active in the civic affairs of his native town, he served as a member of the school board. Moving to Portland, Maine, circa 1872, he established a legal practice, specializing in estate and trust work. Eight years later, he was married to Miss Mary A. Brigham. A member of the Portland city council for three years beginning in 1882, he served as its president in 1885. He was defeated by a narrow margin in his campaign for the Portland mayoralty in 1884. Serving as a member of the state legislature for five years beginning in 1887, he also directed his energies toward his considerable private practice. Highly esteemed in the legal profession, he was appointed, along with Hon. James P. Baxter and Seth L. Larrabee, to administer the estate of Joseph Walker, a prominent Maine philanthropist. Active fraternally, he held membership in several secret orders and societies. He was a member of the Natural Historical Society, the Maine Genealogical Society, the Sons of the Revolution and several professional organizations. He remained active professionally, despite declining health, until shortly before his death at his Portland residence.

FOLSOM, WALLACE L. c.1854 - 1905: born in Fair Haven, Connecticut. Employed as a gardener in New Haven, Connecticut, in 1893, he resided in that city with his wife, Elizabeth. Beginning circa 1894, he gained employment as a clerk and held that occupation for the remainder of his life. He died at his residence in the town of Orange, a borough of West Haven, Connecticut.

FOSTER, AARON AUGUSTUS 1833 - 1921: born in Wakefield, Massachusetts, son of Aaron and Abigail Foster. Self-educated, his brief formal education was confined to a few winter months in the public schools of his native town. Encouraged by his parents, he developed an interest in literature and the written word that was to remain with him the rest of his life. When the call came for volunteers at the outbreak of the Civil War, he enlisted, serving three years with a regiment in his home state. His career in newspaper work began in 1868 when he established the *Wakefield Banner*, a successful hometown newspaper. Later connected with the *Roxbury Gazette* in Roxbury, Massachusetts, he spent several years writing its editorial column. He was also employed at this time as editor of periodicals in both Boston and New York City. By 1883, he had attained a position on the staff of the *North American Review* in the city of New York. Concern for his health caused him to move to the state of Colorado where he became employed as a dealer of mining properties. Throughout his life, he continued as a frequent contributor to monthly publications, chiefly the *North American Review* and the *International Review*. By the early 1890s, he had settled in Powderhorn, Colorado, and, in 1907, moved to Montrose, Colorado, where he was to spend the remaining years of his life. An invalid in his last years, he maintained a remarkable mental capacity and was a noted conversationalist.

FOWLER, SAMUEL PAGE, JR. 1838 - 1915: born in Danvers, Massachusetts, son of Samuel Page and Harriet (Putnam) Fowler. A graduate of Amherst College in Amherst, Massachusetts, he received his Bachelor of Arts in 1861. The next year, he enlisted in Company K, 8th Massachusetts Volunteers, where he served a one-year term. In 1863, he was discharged with the rank of sergeant. Returning home, he continued his studies at the Andover Theological Seminary and was graduated in 1865. He then began a brief but successful career as a preacher and was popular among the many parishes to which he ministered. His interest in medicine caused him to enter Harvard Medical School, receiving the degree of Doctor of Medicine in 1874. It was said that his medical studies were prompted by his desire to cure the illness of his sister, Miss Harriet P. Fowler, an invalid. A noted writer and critic, he maintained a lifelong interest in the municipal affairs of his native town. In his last days a valetudinarian, he died while a patient at Thomas Hospital in Peabody, Massachusetts.

FRANKLIN, GEORGE: author of a letter to Attorney Hosea M. Knowlton. Nothing in the content of this letter indicates the positive identity of the author.

FRENCH, ASA 1829 - 1903: born in Braintree, Massachusetts, son of Jonathan and Sarah Brackett (Hayward) French. Receiving his early education in the public schools of his native town, he prepared for college at

Leicester Academy in Leicester, Massachusetts. Entering Yale University, he received his Bachelor of Arts in 1851. He studied law at Albany Law School in Albany, New York, and Harvard Law School, receiving his Bachelor of Laws from the latter in 1853. He was admitted to the New York bar that same year. Furthering his legal studies in the Boston, Massachusetts, offices of David A. Simmons, Esq. and Harvey Jewell, Esq., he was admitted to the Suffolk bar in 1854. Residing in Braintree, Massachusetts, he established a practice in Boston. He married Miss Ellen Clizbe of Amsterdam, New York, in June of 1855, her death coming suddenly only three months later. In 1858, he married his second wife, Miss Sophie B. Palmer of Boston. In 1866, he served in the Massachusetts House of Representatives. In 1870, he accepted an appointment by Governor William Claflin to the post of district attorney for the Southeastern District, filling a vacancy caused by the resignation of Edward L. Pierce. He was elected to this office successively until his resignation in 1882. During his term as district attorney, he was offered a seat on the bench of superior court by Governor John D. Long, a position he declined. He was on the Board of Commissioners of Inland Fisheries and, in 1882, was appointed as judge on the Court of Commissioners for the Alabama Claims. The next year, he was selected by President Chester A. Arthur as one of the visitors to West Point Military Academy. In 1886, he served one term as a representative in the state legislature. He spent his later life actively engaged in the successful practice of law. He maintained active membership in several professional organizations. He was a prominent figure in the town of Braintree until his death at his residence there.

FRENCH, WILLIAM BRADFORD 1848 - 1912: born in Lewiston, Maine, son of Rev. William R. and Marcia (Bradford) French. The son of a Universalist clergyman, he spent his early years in Turner, Maine. Relocating to the state of Massachusetts as a young man, he was employed at Cohasset High School for two years as principal. While so engaged, he pursued the study of law and, in 1872, entered the office of Daniel C. Linscott, Esq. of Boston. Admitted to the Suffolk bar the following year, he dealt primarily in cases of insolvency, bankruptcy law and trade matters. His career caused him to argue before the supreme courts of both Massachusetts and his native state, federal courts and, in the case of Trader National Bank vs. Chipman, the United States Supreme Court. In 1875, he married Miss Elizabeth D. Southard of Portland, Maine. He became a charter member of the Boston Bar Association the following year. A lecturer for several years on insolvency law at Boston University Law School, he held membership in several professional organizations. Prominent in the Unitarian Society in Winchester, Massachusetts, where he made his home, he was a member of the committee organized to over- see the building of a new church for that congregation. He died at his residence in his adopted town.

GARDNER, PROF.: author of a letter to Attorney Hosea M. Knowlton from Boston, Massachusetts. Nothing in the content of this letter indicates the positive identity of the author. Rev. Elijah Cutler, mentioned as a contact in the text of the letter, was employed as an agent for the Massachusetts Bible Society. Rev. Cutler was a resident of Dorchester, Massachusetts, in 1892.

GASKILL, FRANCIS ALMON 1846 - 1909: born in Mendon, Massachusetts, son of Albert and Anna Smith (Comstock) Gaskill. He received his early education in the public schools of his native town and at Woonsocket High School in Woonsocket, Rhode Island. A graduate of Brown University, he received his Bachelor of Arts in 1866. Spending the next year in Newport, Rhode Island, he was employed as tutor for the children of Clement B. Barclay. He entered Harvard Law School and studied there a year and one-half, leaving to read law in the Worcester, Massachusetts, office of Hon. George F. Verry, Esq. He married Miss Katherine Mortimer Whittaker of Providence, Rhode Island, in 1869, and was admitted to the bar that same year. He entered into a successful partnership with Attorney Verry in Worcester that was to last until that man's death in 1883. He then formed an equally successful partnership with Horace B. Verry, Esq., stepson of his former associate. Dealing primarily in corporate law, he numbered among his clients the Worcester Consolidated Street Railway Company, the Worcester Electric Light Company and the Mutual Life Assurance Company. He began his public career in 1875 when he served as a member of the common council in Worcester, a position he was to assume again eleven years later. In 1886, he was elected district attorney for the Middle District of Massachusetts and held that office by successive reelection for the next nine years. He was appointed associate justice of the superior court of the Commonwealth of Massachusetts in 1889. Following the death of his wife that same year, he was married a second time to Miss Josephine L. Abbott of Providence. He resigned as district attorney in 1895 when he was appointed justice of the superior court of the Commonwealth of Massachusetts, a position he held until the time of his death. In 1899, he was awarded the degree of Doctor of Laws from his alma mater. Serving as a director and president of the Worcester Free Public Library, he was a generous benefactor of that institution. It was through his efforts that the papers and briefs of Richard H. Dana, Esq., a noted Massachusetts attorney and author, were obtained for the library's collection. He was the author of *Civic and Political History of Worcester*. Interested in education, he served as trustee to both Worcester Academy and Brown University. Active in business circles, he was a director of several Worcester corporations. He was a member of the First Baptist Church and was active in various social clubs. His death came unexpectedly while he was a guest at the Passaconaway Inn at York Cliffs, Maine, where he spent his summers. Noted as a man of sterling qualities, at the time of his death he received tribute from the numerous organizations with which he was involved.

GAY, GEORGE WASHINGTON 1842 - 1931: see **GLOSSARY A.**

GIFFORD, GEORGE DAVIS 1833 - 1910: born in Westport Point, Massachusetts, son of Humphrey and Phoebe (Davis) Gifford. After receiving his early education in the public schools of his native town, he entered the retail business, opening a dry goods store in nearby New Bedford, Massachusetts. Employed in that capacity for over twenty years, he sold the store in 1882 and relocated to Worcester, Massachusetts. He retired briefly but, growing restless, returned to work three years later. Entering the employ of Barnard, Sumner and Putnam Company, he held the position of floor superintendent there for over twenty-five years. He was married to Miss Jane Adelaide Liscomb. He was active in the affairs of the Church of the Unity. Retiring in 1909, he died the following year at his home in his adopted city.

GOLDSMITH, JOHN K. 1841 - 1895: born in Little Britain, New York, son of Increase Stoddard Goldsmith. A lawyer by profession, he studied in the New York office of A. S. Cassidy, Esq. He was a resident of Brooklyn, New York, circa 1872 when he married Miss Margaret Bosch, a native of that city. He moved from there to Newburgh, New York, in 1882, where he established a practice. A noted author of prose and poetry, he was frequently published in the city he was to call home. He died in New Windsor, New York.

GRAVES, L: a resident of Atlanta, Georgia, visiting Cottage City, Massachusetts, in 1893. Nothing in the content of this letter indicates the positive identity of the author.

GREENOUGH, CHARLES PELHAM 1844 - 1924: born in Cambridge, Massachusetts, son of William Whitewell and Catherine Scollay (Curtis) Greenough. Having prepared for college at Boston Latin School, he received his Bachelor of Arts from Harvard University in 1864. He served in the United States Navy, assigned to the *U.S.S. Vanderbilt*, engaged in blockading along the North Carolina coast. In 1865, he visited Asia and spent the following two years traveling extensively in the Orient as well as Europe. Upon his return to Massachusetts, he entered Harvard Law School, receiving his Bachelor of Laws in 1869. Admitted to the Suffolk bar that same year, he formed a partnership with Robert M. Morse, Esq. and Richard Stone, Esq. under the name Morse, Stone and Greenough. Their partnership was to last for ten years. During this time, he served as counsel for the Boston Gas Light Company, for which his father was treasurer. In 1871, he married Miss Mary Dwight Vose of Boston. He made a specialty of corporate law and served as counsel for various other gas companies throughout his career. Leaving his law firm, he again devoted time to foreign travel, eventually returning to the United States and establishing a private practice. A frequent contributor to magazines and law journals, he was the author of the *Digest of Gas Cases* in 1883. A member of several historical societies, he served for three years as president of the Antiquarian Society of Worcester, Massachusetts. He was instrumental in establishing and maintaining the Boston Legal Aid Society and served as first treasurer and, later, president of that city's bar association. Beginning in 1895, he became engrossed in the collection and preservation of rare autographs and documents. During his lifetime, his collection grew extensively and was equaled by few in New England. He spent his early married life in Boston, then moved to Brookline, Massachusetts, where he spent the rest of his life.

GROVER, THOMAS ELLWOOD 1846 - 1910: born in West Mansfield, Massachusetts, son of Thomas and Roana Williams (Perry) Grover. Educated in the public schools of his native town as well as under private instruction, he attended the English and Classical Academy in Foxborough, Massachusetts. He began his career employed as a school teacher and later as a clerk. For a brief period, he was a co-editor of *Eagle and Flag*, a Foxborough newspaper. He read law in the Canton, Massachusetts, office of Ellis Ames, Esq. and was admitted to the Bristol bar in 1869. He began a private practice in Canton, operating an additional office in Boston, Massachusetts. In 1870, he was appointed trial justice for Norfolk County, a position he held for the next twenty years. Admitted to the United States

Circuit Court in 1871, he married Miss Frances L. Williams of Foxborough that same year. Engaged in the general practice of law, he served as counsel for several towns in Norfolk County. Active in town affairs in Canton, he served as superintendent of schools as well as in a variety of other offices, including a position on the school committee. In 1889, he was appointed district attorney for Norfolk and Plymouth Counties, filling the vacancy created by the resignation of Hosea Kingman. He began a two-year term as a representative for the Fourth Norfolk District in the state legislature in 1894. During that time, he was appointed chairman of the railroad commission. By 1909, he had been appointed district attorney for the Southeastern District of Massachusetts. A frequent lecturer, he made a specialty of Memorial Day orations and was a contributor to several newspapers and magazines. Active in business circles, he served as a trustee for the Canton Institute for Savings. An honorary member of the G.A.R., he was also active in Masonic circles. He died in Canton, Massachusetts.

HALE, EDWARD EVERETT 1822 - 1909: born in Boston, Massachusetts, son of Nathan and Sarah Preston (Everett) Hale. Educated at Boston Latin School, he entered Harvard University, receiving his Bachelor of Arts in 1839 and his Master of Arts three years later. Pursuing his theological studies, he was licensed to preach and began a career that was destined to bring him national fame. In 1846, he was appointed minister to the Church of the Unity in Worcester, Massachusetts, serving that congregation for the next ten years. He was married to Miss Emily Baldwin Perkins of Hartford, Connecticut, in 1852. Four years later, he was appointed chaplain to the United States Senate, there forming political friendships that were to endure for the rest of his life. That same year, he was appointed minister to the South Congregational Church in Boston, Massachusetts. He served as overseer at Harvard from 1866 to 1887 and was presented with the honorary degree of Doctor of Scientific Theology in 1879. Appointed preacher to his alma mater in 1886, he served in that capacity for two years. A prominent lecturer in national demand, he spoke on religious and political issues. He served as chairman for the Massachusetts Commission for International Justice. In 1901, he was presented with an honorary degree of Doctor of Laws from Dartmouth College and another from Williams College three years later. The author of numerous published stories, speeches, poems and histories, he also served as editor of various literary journals. A philanthropist, he was a promoter of "Chautaugua Circles" and "Lend-a-hand" clubs, acting as editor of that organization's journal. Spending his final years in the city of his birth, he was eulogized by leading political figures and clergy of the day. He counted among his closest friends President and Mrs. William H. Taft, Mrs. Julia Ward Howe and Samuel Clemens.

HALL, WILLIAM MOSLEY c.1806 - 1894: born in Hebron, Connecticut, son of Dickerman and Hannah (Bishop) Hall. Self-educated, he began to support himself early in life, his first job earning him three dollars a month. As a young man he went to sea, serving on the crew of various vessels over the next several years. In 1840, he married Miss Evaline W. Hayden of Hartford, Connecticut. Following his marriage, he moved west, settling in St. Louis, Missouri, where he was employed as an agent for the Lake Steamboat Association which operated between Buffalo, New York and Chicago, Illinois. In 1846, he represented the city of Chicago at the Chicago River and Harbor Convention. The need for improvement of the harbors of several cities in the northeast prompted this convention. The bills passed, which resulted in the appropriation of several thousand dollars by the United States Congress for that cause, were vetoed by President James K. Polk. Upon completing his work at the convention, he presented the city of Chicago with a bill for his expenses in the sum of $576, a sum which remained unpaid at the time of his death over forty-five years later. In 1853, he established a ticket office in New York City for the Michigan Southern and Northern Indiana Railroad. Interested in the expansion possibilities which the railroads offered, he was among the first to contend that a railroad to the Pacific Coast was necessary. He was involved with several major lawsuits involving disputes over steamship and railroad properties. In the final years of his life, he brought suit against Marshall O. Roberts involving $30,000 which represented a share of the money obtained from the sale of the steamship Illinois. He was awarded a full settlement by the jury but a new trial was called and this case remained unresolved at the time of his death. It is likely that this is the case to which he refers in his letter to Attorney Hosea M. Knowlton. Throughout his career, he had accumulated a sizable estate, all of which he lost as a result of poor investments and speculations. An invalid the last decade of his life, he died penniless at his residence in the city of New York.

HARRINGTON, FRANCIS BISHOP 1854 - 1914: born in Salem, Massachusetts, son of Samuel Bishop and Caroline Elizabeth (Hawes) Harrington. A graduate of Tufts University, he received his Bachelor of Arts in 1877 and entered Harvard Medical School where he was awarded the degree of Doctor of Medicine four years later. He established a practice in Boston, Massachusetts, in 1882 and, later that same year, married Miss Abbie Josephine Ruggles of Cambridge, Massachusetts. He served as visiting surgeon and later as consulting surgeon at Massachusetts General Hospital in Boston. He was a member of the administrative board of Harvard Medical School and was medical advisor to the trustees of Peter Bent Brigham Memorial Hospital in Boston. In 1903, he began to lecture on surgery at Harvard Medical School and continued there in that capacity until shortly before his death. He held membership in several professional organizations. By the time of his death in Boston, he was considered one of the most valued members of the medical profession in that city.

HARRINGTON, PHILIP 1859 - 1893: see **GLOSSARY A.**

HARRIS, CHARLES NATHAN 1860 - 1933: born in Port Byron, Illinois, son of Rev. John L. and Sarah (Ebright) Harris. The itinerant nature of his father's employ in various pastorates caused him to receive his early education in several midwestern and eastern United States locations. Preparing for college at Boston Latin School in Boston, Massachusetts, he entered Harvard Law School in 1882 and was admitted to the Suffolk bar that same year. Graduating with a Bachelor of Laws two years later, he practiced for a time in the city of Boston. In 1890, he married Miss Sarah Wyman Bird of Cambridge, Massachusetts. The following year, he was appointed second assistant attorney general of the Commonwealth of Massachusetts, a position he held until 1894. Having prepared a supplement to the Massachusetts public statutes in 1895 by appointment of Governor Frederick T. Greenhalge, he was later named by Governor Winthrop M. Crane to serve on the commission formed to consolidate public statutes. Appointed second assistant register of probate for Middlesex County in 1905, he held that post for eleven years, at which time he was promoted to assistant register. In 1924, he was selected to complete the unfinished term of the register of probate upon the resignation of Frederick M. Esty. That same year, he was elected to serve a full term in that office. Appointed by Governor Alvin T. Fuller to the office of judge of probate for Middlesex County, he served in that capacity until the time of his death. Active in both fraternal and professional organizations, he died in Winchester, Massachusetts, where he had made his home.

HASWELL, CHARLES HAYNES 1809 - 1907: born in New York, New York, son of Charles and Dorothea (Haynes) Haswell. Following a classical education, he was graduated from Joseph Nelson's Collegiate Institute. Subsequently employed by James P. Allaire, a noted steam-engine builder, he was eventually to hold the positions of chief draftsman and designer for that business. In 1829, he was married to Miss Ann Elizabeth Burns. As part of the move to introduce steam power to the United States Navy, he was commissioned to submit designs for engines for the frigate Fulton, after which he was assigned to supervise their construction. Following a brief suspension in 1843 caused by a dispute over a project with newly-named chief engineer Gilbert T. Thompson, he was reinstated but taken from sea duty. The next year, however, he was named to succeed G. T. Thompson as chief engineer of the Navy. He returned to civilian life eight years later and at that time was employed as a consulting engineer in his native city. He worked on various diverse projects as an engineer, from commercial vessels to building and harbor design. He was employed for a time as a surveyor of steamers for Lloyd's of London and the New York underwriters. Actively involved in civic affairs, he was a member of the Common council in New York City for three years beginning in 1855, serving one year as that council's president. A veteran of the Civil War, he was also a trustee of the New York and Brooklyn Bridge. He was frequently published, his most noted work being *Mechanic's and Engineer's Pocket Book*, first printed in 1842. He was the author of numerous other professional publications as well as *Reminiscences of an Octogenarian of the City of New York, 1816 to 1860*, which was published in 1896. His death came as the result of a fall shortly before his ninety-eighth birthday.

HICKCOX, J. S.: author of a letter from Washington, District of Columbia, to Attorney Hosea Morrill Knowlton. In 1893, he made his residence in that city, employed as superintendent of the Folding Room of the United States Senate. Attempts to obtain further biographical details have been to date unsuccessful.

HULING, RAY GREENE 1847 - 1915: born in Providence, Rhode Island, son of John Greene and Huldah S. (Wilcox) Huling. Educated in the public schools of his native city, he spent two years as a student at Providence High School. He prepared for college at Mowry and Goffs Classical School, also in that city, and subsequently entered Brown University. Receiving his Bachelor of Arts in 1869, he furthered his studies at that institution and was awarded a Master of Arts three years later. A resident of Fall River, Massachusetts, from 1869 to 1875, he was employed there as a classical assistant at the high school. At that time, he accepted the position of principal at Fitchburg High School in Fitchburg, Massachusetts, remaining there for the next eleven years. In 1879, he married Miss Ellen C. Paine of Fall River. In 1886, he became principal of the New Bedford High School in New

Bedford, Massachusetts, relocating to that city. He accepted the position of headmaster at English High School in Cambridge, Massachusetts, and moved to that city in 1893, maintaining a summer residence in Marshfield, Massachusetts. That same year, his interest in education led him to undertake post-graduate work at Harvard University. In 1894, he was awarded the degree of Doctor of Science from Brown University and, in 1897, he obtained his Master of Arts at Harvard. A founder of the New England Association of Colleges and Preparatory Schools, he lectured widely on the organization and management of schools. In 1900, he became an examiner at Boston University. He served as editor of numerous professional publications and was a frequent contributor of articles. His service in professional organizations included the presidency of the Massachusetts Teachers Association, membership in the American Institute of Instruction and the High School Master's Club. A trustee of Brown University, he served on the board of several professional societies. He was also active in several religious organizations, serving as both secretary and president of the Boston Baptist Social Union and as secretary of the Boston Baptist Mission Society. His interest in genealogy caused him to maintain memberships in the Massachusetts, Rhode Island and Pennsylvania historical societies. In 1908, ill health forced him to resign his position in Cambridge. At the time of his death in Marshfield, he was considered one of the best-known educators in the United States.

HUNTRESS, GEORGE LEWIS 1848 - 1924: born in Lowell, Massachusetts, son of James Lewis and Harriet Stinson (Paige) Huntress. A descendant on both sides of colonial ancestors, he prepared for college at Phillips Academy at Andover, Massachusetts. He entered Yale University, receiving his Bachelor of Arts in 1870. He studied at Harvard Law School for one year and read law in the Winchester, Massachusetts, office of Messrs. Stephen B. Ives, Jr. and Solomon Lincoln, Jr. He was admitted to the Suffolk bar in 1872 and married Miss Julia A. Poole of Metuchen, New Jersey, three years later. That same year, he became a partner in the firm at which he had studied, remaining there until 1882 when the death of Attorney Ives caused its dissolution. He later became associated with Homer Albers in Boston, Massachusetts, continuing in that respect until 1909. Active in athletics while at Yale, he was president for a time of that university's alumni association. He possessed varied business interests and acted as president of several corporations, among them the North River Lumber Company of Nova Scotia, The Jerguson Manufacturing Company of Boston, and the Bolivia Rubber Company of Boston and Bolivia, South America. He was also a director and member of the executive committee of the Queensborough-Boston Corporation. Having spent his life in Winchester as well as Boston, Massachusetts, he died at the residence of his son in the latter city.

HURD, FREDERICK ELLSWORTH 1861 - 1903: see **GLOSSARY A.**

INGALLS, MISS BELLE, see **LOVEJOY, MAYBELLE INGALLS.**

IVY, JESSE COLEMAN 1847 - 1924: born in Warsaw, Alabama, son of James B. and Sarah E. Ivy. Enlisting in the Confederate Army at the out- break of the Civil War, he served for the duration of that conflict. Educated in the North, he attended Harvard University, graduating in 1874 with a Bachelor of Arts. Continuing his studies at Harvard Law School, he obtained his Bachelor of Laws two years later. He married Miss Sarah F. Hyde. Admitted to the Middlesex bar the following year, he was, by 1895, also a member of the Suffolk bar. He established a practice in Boston, Massachusetts, one which he eventually shared with his son, Malcolm Ivy, Esq. He retired in 1915, returning to his native state. He died at his residence in Geiger, Alabama.

JACKSON, FRANK HUSSEY 1848 - 1903: born in Nobleboro, Maine, son of Joseph Jackson, Jr. and Arletta G. (Flagg) Jackson. His family relocated to Jefferson, Maine, during his early childhood and it was there that he was educated. Following high school, he continued his education at Lincoln Academy, Newcastle, Maine, in 1863 and supported himself by teaching school. His study of law began three years later in the office of Henry Farrington of Waldoboro, Maine, and later with Hon. Lorenzo Clay of Gardiner, Maine. He was admitted to the Kennebec bar in 1867. Following his defeat for election to the office of Lincoln County clerk of courts, he began a practice in 1869 in Hallowell, Maine. Serving that town in the office of solicitor from 1870 to 1878, he relocated the following year to Providence, Rhode Island, and was subsequently admitted to that state's bar. He was married to Miss Ella A. Owen of Waltham, Massachusetts, in 1875. In 1880, he was admitted to practice in the United States Courts. The partnership he formed at that time with Colonel Daniel R. Ballou, Esq. was to last until 1895. Throughout the length of his residency in Rhode Island, he maintained an active interest in the politics of that state but was elected only once, to the office of senator in the fall of 1902. He was a member of various fraternal organizations until the time of his death at his residence in Providence.

JELLY, GEORGE FREDERICK 1842 - 1911: see **GLOSSARY A.**

JENNINGS, ANDREW JACKSON 1849 - 1923: see **GLOSSARY A.**

JONES, FRANCIS RICHARD c.1866 - 1935: born in Boston, Massachusetts, son of Francis and Julia A. (Fletcher) Jones. He prepared for college at Boston Latin School, furthering his education at Harvard University, from which he was graduated cum laude in 1887. Three years later, he obtained his Master of Arts from that institution as well as a Bachelor of Laws from Harvard Law School. He then gained employment as secretary for Hon. Hollis Gray of the United States Supreme Court in Washington, District of Columbia. Eventually returning to his native city, he there became associated with the firm Goodwin, Parker, Raymond and Comstock. He was married to Miss Helen Steele. Having retired from practice in 1905, he remained in Boston and died at his home in that city.

JONES, W. S.: author of a letter written on stationery from the Lincoln House, a hostelry in Worcester, Massachusetts. It is likely that this person was a transient as there is no one listed by that name in that city's directories for that period. Nothing in the content of the letter indicates the positive identity of the author.

KINGMAN, HOSEA 1843 - 1900: born in Bridgewater, Massachusetts, son of Philip D. and Betsey Bump (Washburn) Kingman. Educated at Bridgewater Academy, he prepared for college at Appleton Academy in New Ipswich, New Hampshire. In 1860, he entered Dartmouth College. His education was interrupted when he responded to the call for volunteers during the Civil War. In 1862, he enlisted with Company K, 3rd Regiment, Massachusetts Volunteers, serving one year. He resumed his education, making up his third year's work in his senior year, and received his Bachelor of Arts in 1864. He married Miss Carrie Cole of Carver, Massachusetts in 1866. The next two years were spent studying law in the Bridgewater office of William Latham, Esq. Admitted to the bar in 1866, he engaged in the practice of law, forming a partnership with Attorney Latham. Upon the retirement of Attorney Latham in 1871, he continued in private practice and later expanded with an additional office in Boston, Massachusetts. In 1878, he was appointed special justice of the First District Court of Plymouth County. He was elected commissioner of insolvency in 1884, a position he held for the next three years. During this period, he also served as city solicitor for Brockton, Massachusetts. In 1887, he was chosen as district attorney for the Southeastern District of Massachusetts. He resigned his position as district attorney in 1889 to accept the appointment to chairman of the Metropolitan Sewage Commission. A trustee of the Plymouth

County Historical Society and Bridgewater Academy, he was also active in business circles. A prominent member of the order of Free Masons, he held membership in several professional societies. He died at his residence in the city of his birth.

KINNEY, VAN BUREN 1832 - 1910: born in Griswold, Connecticut, son of Spencer and Lucinda Kinney. During the Civil War, he enlisted with the 2nd Connecticut Regiment. Taking part in a three-month campaign. he reenlisted upon completion of his term, this time with the 10th Connecticut Regiment. Hospitalized for about a year due to a leg wound, he later returned to active duty with the rank of colonel. During his length of service, he participated in twenty-one battles. He relocated to Providence, Rhode Island, circa 1885, residing there with his wife, Amy, employed as a travel agent. Active in several veteran's organizations, he was a member of the Slocum Post of the G.A.R. and the Pawtuxet Veteran's Association. He frequently wrote news for the fraternal columns of the *Providence Journal* relating to these groups. He was also an honorary member of the Ladies' Auxiliary of the G.A.R. Always an active individual, he began to decline in health circa 1907 following the shock of his son's unexpected death in a railroad accident. He died at his home in Providence.

KNOWLTON, BENJAMIN C. 1860 - 1932: born in Liberty, Maine, son of Hiram and Lorraine (Hunt) Knowlton. A resident of Bridgewater. Massachusetts, for several years, he was employed there as a police officer and, later, as an officer at the state farm. Following his retirement, he moved with his wife, Lucy, to Middleborough, Massachusetts. He died while a patient at a hospital in Taunton, Massachusetts.

KNOWLTON, HOSEA MORRILL 1847 - 1902: see **GLOSSARY A.**

KNOWLTON, JOSEPH D.: son of James M. and Clarissa (Borden) Knowlton. Having resided with his parents in Cazenovia, New York, he moved to the state of Arkansas in 1868. By 1892, he had settled in the Van Buren, Arkansas, area, being employed as a conductor by the Saint Louis Iron Mountain Railroad. In 1898, he and his wife saw their daughter, Katie Blanche, buried in the Fairview Cemetery in Van Buren. According to a published family genealogy, he had established himself successfully as a farmer by 1897.

L[?], HENRY: author of a letter to Attorney Hosea M. Knowlton from City Mills, Massachusetts. The surname of the author of this letter has not been deciphered. Efforts made to identify this person in the town of origin of the letter have been unsuccessful.

LEONARD, CHARLES HALL 1822 - 1918: born in Northwood, New Hampshire, son of Lemuel and Cynthia (Claggett) Leonard. Moving with his family to Haverhill, Massachusetts, as a child, he was educated in public schools there. Later a student at Haverhill Academy, he spent part of his time employed as a teacher. It was at this time that he made the acquaintance of John Greenleaf Whittier, as he taught in the schoolhouse immortalized in that poet's work, "Snow-Bound." Following his time at Haverhill, he went on to Bradford Seminary in Bradford, Massachusetts, and later Atkinson Academy in New Hampshire, again dividing his time between his studies and teaching. Employed at Bradford for four years, he received private instruction at that time under a Mr. Taggart of Haverhill Academy as well as the highly respected history and philosophy instructor, E. B. Morse of Newburyport, Massachusetts. Determined to enter the ministry, he changed his denomination from Congregational to Universalist prior to beginning formal study. He spent two years under the instruction of Dr. Thomas Jefferson Sawyer in Clinton, New Jersey, and in 1848 accepted assignment to the Church of the Redeemer in Chelsea, Massachusetts. During his pastorate there which lasted over twenty years, the congregation grew from twenty-nine to in excess of four hundred families. He married Miss Phoebe Ann Bassett of Atkinson, New Hampshire, in 1848. Active in the public life of Chelsea, he served on the school board for twenty-two years and was chairman of the committee organized to oversee construction of a new high school. In 1869, he was awarded a Master of Arts from Tufts University and the degree of Doctor of Scientific Theology from St. Lawrence University two years later. It was in 1869 that he was called to Tufts University by his teacher, Dr. T. Sawyer, to assist in managing the divinity school there. He remained employed in that capacity until 1884 when, upon the retirement of Dr. Sawyer, he was given full charge, being named dean of the Crane Theological School. His efforts there were instrumental in the successful development of the school. He held that position for the rest of his life. The author of several religious texts, he was active in a number of professional societies. He died at his home in Somerville, Massachusetts.

LEWIS, NATHANIEL R. 1844 - 1893: born in Fall River, Massachusetts, son of Nathaniel and Flora (Aldworth) Lewis. His early education was most likely completed in the public schools of his native city. He married Miss Elvira Josephine Fish of Tiverton, Rhode Island. First listed in the Fall River city directory in 1874, he spent his entire career employed in the cotton waste business established by his family. His death came unexpectedly, after a brief illness, in the city of his birth.

LOGUE, MISS ANNIE ELIZABETH BLACKWOOD 1851 - 1905: born in Roadstown, New Jersey, daughter of James L. and Elizabeth (Glendon) Logue. Moving with her family to Bridgeton, New Jersey, as a child, she probably received her education in the public schools there. As was common among women of her position, she likely spent her days at home, tending to the needs of her family. Her brother, mentioned in the letter she authored to Hosea M. Knowlton, was William A. Logue, Esq., a prominent Bridgeton attorney and county prosecutor. A naive attempt at an alias may be what prompted her use of the pseudonym "Anna E. Blackwood," a deception faulted by the correct listing of her address on the communication to Knowlton. She died in the town where she had spent most of her life.

LORD, ARTHUR 1850 - 1925: born in Port Washington, Wisconsin, son of Rev. William H. and Persis (Kendall) Lord. As a young child, he moved to Plymouth, Massachusetts, with his family and was educated in the public schools there. He prepared for college at Plymouth High School. In 1868, he entered Harvard University, receiving his Bachelor of Arts cum laude four years later. He studied law in the Boston, Massachusetts, office of Messrs. Lathrop, Abbot and Jones and was admitted to the Plymouth bar in 1874. That same year, he was appointed trial justice for Plymouth County. He was associated there in business with Albert Mason, Esq. and Benjamin R. Curtis, Esq., also establishing a private practice in Boston, specializing in corporate law. In 1878, he married Miss Sarah Shippin. Active in the community, he was a member of the Board of Managers of the Public Library, chairman for a time on the Board of Health and a trustee, beginning in 1878, of the Pilgrim Society. Serving as representative from Plymouth to the general court in 1885 and 1886, he was a member of the committee on probate and chancery and also held the seat of chairman on the committee on the revision of the judiciary system of Massachusetts. He was also a member of the Civil Service Commission from 1888 to 1899, being appointed by four Massachusetts governors. He maintained his ties with Plymouth, acting as chairman of the board of selectmen there. Active in business circles, he served as clerk and director of C. W. Leatherbee Lumber Company and was a director of several other Boston corporations. Elected president of the Pilgrim Society, he held that office for thirty years. He was a member of both the Massachusetts and American Historical Societies, the American Antiquarian Society and various other historical organizations. He received the honorary degrees of Doctor of

Letters from Brown University and Doctor of Laws from Dartmouth College. He died at his daughter's residence at the Hotel Ludlow in Boston.

LORING, EDWARD P. 1837 - 1894: born in Norridgewock, Massachusetts, son of Ira and Betsey Loring. Educated in public schools, he then graduated from Bowdoin College. He subsequently studied law in the Norridgewock office of Stephen D. Lindsey, Esq. and at Albany Law School in Albany, New York. He was admitted to the bar in Somerset County, Maine, in 1861. Enlisting in the army during the Civil War, he entered the 13th Maine Regiment as first lieutenant and was later mustered out as major and brevet lieutenant colonel. Following admission to the Suffolk bar in Massachusetts in 1868, he established a private practice, also serving as clerk and special justice of the police court in Fitchburg, Massachusetts. He was also president of the common council in Fitchburg for a time. In 1868, he was married in Waterville, Maine, to Miss Hannah M. Stark. Active politically, he was a member of the Massachusetts House of Representatives, serving on both the judiciary and state redistricting committees, and was a member of the state senate from 1883 to 1884. By 1895, he was practicing in Boston, Massachusetts, and there accepted the appointment of the governor to the office of controller of county accounts. He was residing at the Hotel Oxford in West Newton, Massachusetts, at the time of his death.

LOVEJOY, MAYBELLE INGALLS 1859 - 1939: born in Haverhill, Massachusetts, daughter of Sherwin and Ophelia M. (Andrews) Lovejoy. Educated at Robinson Seminary in Exeter, New Hampshire, she also studied at Boston School of Oratory in Boston, Massachusetts. Well-known in the Haverhill area as an elocutionist and entertainer, she was listed in that city's directory in 1892 as an actress, her stage name "Miss Belle Ingalls." It is likely that her professional career ended upon her marriage, in 1893, to James Kellogg Mills III, a photographer in Amherst, Massachusetts. Following her marriage, she resided in Amherst and remained there until the death of her husband in 1925. She returned to her native city at that time and resided in the home of her sister for the rest of her life.

MC HENRY, NELLIE S.: see **GLOSSARY A.**

MACKEY, THOMAS J. c.1828 - ? : born in South Carolina. A veteran of the Mexican War, he enlisted in the Palmetto Regiment from his native state. Wounded during the storming of Mexico City, he was the recipient of two service medals. In light of his future career, it seems likely that he studied law at this time. Enlisting following the outbreak of the Civil War, he served in the Confederate Army with the rank of captain in an engineering regiment. Following the defeat of the Confederacy, he returned to South Carolina and was elected judge of that state's sixth circuit court. He retained this position until his retirement in 1883. According to his letter to Attorney Hosea M. Knowlton, he visited Europe and was in the city of Paris, France, in 1890. The next year, he married his wife, Sarah, and was practicing law in New York City by 1893. In 1898, he was sued for divorce on a charge of bigamy by his wife who claimed that he had married twenty-two-year-old Miss Catherine S. Porterfield of Charlestown, West Virginia, the previous year. He was residing at the Hoffman House in New York City when the former Miss Porterfield learned of the suit brought against her husband by her predecessor. He is last listed in the New York City directory in 1899.

MADIGAN, EDMUND COTTRILL 1835 - 1904: born in Damariscotta Mills, Maine, son of John Cottrill and Elizabeth (Cottrill) Madigan. A graduate of Cambridge Law School, he married Miss Mary Stark Burns in 1868. He lost his wife tragically only nine days after she gave birth to their only son, Joseph, in 1869. A practicing lawyer, he was active in the affairs of Aroostook County, Maine. He suffered tragedy again in 1888 when his son was drowned in Damariscotta Lake. A resident of Presque Isle, Maine, by 1890, he had business interests there that included real estate as well as the Presque Isle Clothing store. Possessing an interest in genealogy, he was the author of *History of the Madigan Family, Damariscotta Mills, Maine*. He died in the place of his birth.

MARSH, WILLIAM DWIGHT 1865 - 1918: born in Bernardston, Massachusetts, son of Rev. Dwight and Elizabeth Le Barron (Clarke) Marsh. A preacher, he graduated from Amherst College in 1888, residing at that time at his parents' residence in Amherst, Massachusetts. Associated with the Northern New York State Holiness Association in the early 1890s, he served congregations in the Brushton, New York, area. By 1895, he was residing in Scroon Lake, New York, where he was actively engaged as a preacher. He married Miss Lillian Adelaide Sawyer, a native of New York, in 1897. He returned to Amherst with his family circa 1912 and resided there in the home of his mother. During his final years, he devoted considerable time to evangelism. At the time of his death, his remains were interred in the family lot in Amherst.

MASON, ALBERT 1836 - 1905: see **GLOSSARY A**.

MAXWELL, MARY A. 1846 - 1926: a resident of Boston, Massachusetts. First listed in that city's directory in 1889, she was for five years the proprietor of Mrs. M.A. Maxwell and Company, an embroidery frame business. She was married to Charles B. Maxwell, a Boston police officer. Relocating to Roxbury, Massachusetts, circa 1898, she was widowed the following year. She last appears listed as such in 1901.

MOODY, WILLIAM HENRY 1853 - 1917: see **GLOSSARY A.**

MORRIS, HENRY D.: a resident of Newburgh, New York. First listed there in 1884, he was employed as a job printer. In 1888, he was involved in the publication of *The Morning Star*, a short-lived Newburgh newspaper. According to records in Newburgh, he moved in 1893 to Troy, New York. No records have to date surfaced to validate his residency in that city.

MORRISON, CHARLES ROBERT 1819 - 1893: born in Bath, Maine, son of William and Stira (Young) Morrison. He prepared for college at Newbury Seminary in Vermont. In 1839, he began to read law in the office of Messrs. Goodall and Woods in his native city. Admitted to the bar two years later, he entered a partnership with Attorney Goodall. He married Miss Susan Fitch of Littleton, New Hampshire, in 1842. Moving to Haverhill, Massachusetts, three years later, he practiced in that city until 1851, at which time he was appointed judge of the Circuit Court of Common Pleas. Serving in that capacity for four years, he then returned to private practice, this time in Nashua, New Hampshire. Shortly after the outbreak of the Civil War, he was commissioned adjutant to the 11th Regiment, New Hampshire Volunteers. Serving for two years, he resigned in 1864, settling in the city of Manchester, New Hampshire. During his years there, he was involved in the preparation of numerous volumes, among them the *Digest of New Hampshire Reports*, *Digest of School Laws* and the *Probate Directory*. In 1876, he relocated to Concord, New Hampshire, residing there until his death.

MORSE, ELIJAH ADAMS 1841 - 1898: see **GLOSSARY A.**

MYRICK, NATHAN SUMNER 1854 - 1930: born in New Bedford, Massachusetts, son of Alexander G. and Huldah (Paddleford) Myrick. A graduate of Phillips Academy at Andover, Massachusetts, he later attended Boston University. He was first employed as a journalist, serving on the staff of the Associated Press. Leaving newspaper work to pursue his interest in law, he attended Boston University Law School and was admitted to the Suffolk bar in 1890. Establishing a practice in Boston, Massachusetts, he maintained an office there for over twenty-five years, residing in Wellesley Hills, Massachusetts. During his career as a Boston lawyer, he developed an interest in the development of the merchant marine, eventually devoting his time exclusively to that subject. In 1915, he was appointed an assistant in the transportation department of the Chamber of Commerce of the United States. He served as counsel for its committee on the Department of Commerce which analyzed the laws governing steamboat inspection and administration. When the United States declared war against Germany in 1914, he was appointed a member of the war shipping committee, later serving as its vice-chairman. He was instrumental in the warship building program. In 1919, he relocated to Washington, District of Columbia, and resided in that city the remainder of his life.

NORTHEND, WILLIAM DUMMER 1823 - 1902: born in Byfield, Massachusetts, son of John and Anna (Titcomb) Northend. Preparing for college at Dummer Academy, he was graduated from Bowdoin College in 1843. Studying law in the office of Hon. Asabel Huntington, Esq. in Salem, Massachusetts, he was admitted to the Essex bar in 1845. That same year, he was married to Miss Susan Steadman Harrod. He practiced law in Peabody, Massachusetts, for three years, at which time he relocated his office to Salem. In a law partnership for many years with Hon. George F. Choate, Esq., he was frequently called upon by the Massachusetts Supreme Court to act as counsel for the defendant in capital cases. He served in the state senate in both 1861 and 1862 and was also chairman of the committee on the Rhode Island boundary. Among his attempts at public office were the Democratic candidacy for Congress in 1868 and the Salem mayoralty in 1887. An overseer of Bowdoin College, he also acted as vice-president of the trustees of Dummer Academy. He possessed a great interest in both history and politics, especially that of the Massachusetts Bay Colony, and lectured frequently on related topics. President for several years of the Essex Bar Association, he died at his home in Salem.

OLNEY, JAMES BROWN 1833 - 1900: born in Hartford, Connecticut, son of Jesse and Elizabeth (Barnes) Olney. During his first year, his family moved to Southington, Connecticut, where he was subsequently educated in public schools. He prepared for college at Lewis Academy in Southington and, in 1850, entered Yale University, attending through his sophomore year. In 1853, he began the study of law in the Windham, New York, office of his cousin, Danforth K. Olney, Esq., remaining there for one year. Entering the office of another cousin, John Olney, Esq., also of Windham, he remained there until admission to the bar in 1855. The next year, he opened an office in Prattsville, New York, and began to practice law. Appointed judge advocate on the staff of Brigadier-General Bassett in 1857, he served in that capacity one year. In 1859, he was elected to the office of district attorney for Greene County, New York, being reelected to that position in 1862. Relocating to Catskill, New York, that same year, he entered into a partnership with his cousin, Danforth, under the name of Olney and Olney. In 1865, a third partner, Hon. Rufus H. King, Esq. was admitted to the firm. Withdrawing from this partnership the following year, he established a successful private practice in his adopted town. He married Miss Julia P. Watson of Catskill in 1870. Active politically, he served as a delegate to several conventions on local, state and national levels. A member of the Catskill board of education for six years, he held the office as president for two of those years. In 1883, he was elected superintendent of the town of Catskill. An active Mason, he was also a founding member of the Rip Van Winkle Club. At the time of his death at his residence in Catskill, he was considered the leading lawyer of Greene County.

OSBALDESTON, EDWIN PYE TURNER ONSLOW c.1829 - 1929: born in Cheltenham, Lancaster, England, self-proclaimed son of the Earl of Onslow, grandson of Admiral Charles Pye Turner of the British Navy. It is likely the case that a good portion of his life story was self-created. His life was referred to as a "veritable Osbaldeston saga" in his New York Times obituary. Accounts of his youth state he received his early education under private tutelage at 12 Hanover Chambers, Buckingham Street, London, England. There he established a friendship with his classmate, Albert Edward, Prince of Wales and future sovereign, King Edward VII. He later attended the Royal Military Academy at Cheltenham, England. Following service in the Crimean War, he went to Australia, obtaining a medical education at Carleton University in Melbourne. It was there that he lost his wife, who went on a hunting trip and never returned. Having embarked on an expedition to try and locate the lost explorer, Dr. Liechard, in the Australian bush, he later traveled to the United States, settling in New York. He established the New York School of Training for Massage and was reputedly one of the foremost massage operators in the country. According to advertisements, he became established in business in 1864 but other accounts reveal that he did not appear in the United States until 1886. He also advertised as a physician and was a practicing chiropodist, numbering among his patients the Duke of Luxembourg and President Ulysses S. Grant. He is last listed as residing and working in New York City in 1896. In Malone, New York, circa 1902, he was implicated in a theft from a store when he came forward to defend one of his female employees. Following her to Germany in response to a challenge to a duel by her fiance, he claimed to have killed both that man and his second. He was exonerated of the crimes but was instructed by Kaiser Wilhelm II to remain in Germany for sixteen months. It is probable that the next years were difficult ones, as by 1910, he was living in a shack by the railroad in Asbury Park, New Jersey, which he had constructed out of soap boxes and crates. A popular figure by the tracks, he entertained passers-by, performing acrobatic stunts on a signal tower over fifty feet in height. He appeared frequently in town wearing a light summer suit regardless of the weather, sometimes walking along the boardwalk until the early hours of the morning. In 1926, he gained national attention when he was arrested as a suspected escaped prisoner. He was accused by nonagenarian Deputy Sheriff S. Foster Black of Binghamton, New York, of being "Edwin Turner," a horse thief who escaped custody by leaping from the washroom window of a moving train in 1881. He was never returned to New York for trial, as Governor A. Harry Moore of New Jersey refused extradition. He always blamed events such as these, which apparently occurred quite frequently, on a half-brother or nephew who bore a strong resemblance to him. In his lifetime, he was said to have been a veteran of both the Boer War and the Boxer Rebellion. In his final months, he became depressed when making inquiries into the expense of arranging his own cremation. The end of his colorful life, caused by self-inflicted gunshot wounds, occurred in his shack in Asbury Park. A package sent to a local funeral director just before his well-planned suicide contained a pair of blue silk pajamas and a note with instructions that these were the clothes in which he wished to be attired when cremated. His final wish was that there be "no funereal gloom, corpse-gazing, tears, black raiment or graveyard grimness."

OWEN, FRANKLIN PIERCE 1853 - 1905: born in Scituate, Rhode Island, son of Elisha B. and Mary E. (Mathewson) Owen. Receiving his early education in the public schools of the village of North Scituate, he later prepared for college at Lapham Institute, located in his native town. Graduating from Amherst College in 1874, he began the study of law with George E. Webster, clerk of the Common Pleas Court of Providence County, serving in that office for several years as assistant clerk. Admitted to the Rhode Island bar in 1883, he began practice four years later as junior member of the firm Page and Owen in Providence, Rhode Island. His partnership with Charles H. Page, Esq. was to last ten years before its amicable dissolution. Active in both town and state politics, he was elected to the state senate in 1888 and 1889.

A member of the lower house of the General Assembly in 1892 and 1893, he also acted as speaker of the house the latter year. In his native town, he held the post of chairman of the board of assessors for several years. In 1901, he succeeded Attorney Page as Scituate town counsel, a position he retained until his death. An early promoter of the Providence and Danielson Railway, he served that corporation as president for two years and, later, as counsel. He was married to Miss Mary S. Fisher in 1877 and to Ida V. Holmes in 1898. He was active in several fraternal and professional organizations. His political activity continued throughout his life. His declining health was said to have been attributed to the strain of campaigning as the Democratic candidate for the United States Congress in both 1902 and 1904. A life-long resident of his native town, he also maintained a winter home in the city of Providence and it was there that he expired.

PARK, MICHAEL M. 1864 - 1945: born in Fairgrounds, Ontario, Canada, son of Philip and Margaret (Watson) Park. The son of a Canadian farmer of limited means, he began to work at a young age. Having received education in public schools, he entered the Collegiate Institute at Vienna, Ontario, at the age of nineteen, graduating with honors two-and-one-half years later. He subsequently entered the Normal School at St. Thomas, Ontario, graduating from that institution in 1885. Teaching school for three years, he continued his studies at the University of Michigan, receiving the degree of Doctor of Dental Surgery in 1891. That same year, he relocated to Toledo, Ohio, and there established the first dentist's office in East Toledo. He was married to Miss Ella M. Gale. His dental practice was maintained for fifty-two years, several of those years in partnership with his son, Harley G. Park. A charter member of the Euclid Avenue Methodist Church, he also held memberships in several fraternal and professional organizations. A member of the Northwest Dental Society of Ohio, he also served as president of the Toledo Dental Society in 1909. Retiring from his practice in 1943, he died after a short confinement in his Toledo home.

PARKER, HENRY LANGDON 1832 - 1910: born in Acton, Massachusetts, son of Asa and Margaret Ann (McCorlistone) Parker. Receiving his early education in the public schools of his native town, he prepared for college at Lawrence Academy in Groton, Massachusetts. A graduate of Dartmouth College in 1856, he read law in offices in Milford and Worcester, Massachusetts. In 1860, he was admitted to the bar and opened an office in Hopkinton, Massachusetts. In 1862, he was appointed trial justice for Middlesex County, serving in that capacity for the next three years. Moving his practice to Worcester in 1865, he became active in civic affairs there and was a member of the school board. He subsequently served as a representative in the Massachusetts legislature from 1886 to 1887 and as state senator from Worcester for a two-year term beginning in 1889. Appointed one of the trustees of the Public Reservations of Massachusetts, he served on various leading committees. In 1893, he was appointed chairman of the committee formed to revise the charter of the city of Worcester. He was an active member of the Episcopal church in Worcester and also served as a trustee of the public library there. An avid horticulturalist, he was appointed president of the Worcester County Horticultural Society in 1889. His first wife was Miss Isabel H. Mason of Northampton, Massachusetts, and his second Miss Helen B. Gooding of Bristol, Rhode Island. He spent his final years occupied by his many interests. At the time of his death in Worcester, he was the oldest member of the Worcester Bar Association.

PARKER, HERBERT 1856 - 1939: born in Charlestown, Massachusetts, son of George A. and Harriet Newell (Felton) Parker. His early education was received at private schools in Philadelphia, Pennsylvania, and by private tutorial instruction. He prepared for college at the Collegiate School in that city. Entering Harvard University in 1874, he was unable to complete his studies and left for reasons of ill health prior to his senior year, traveling at that time to Europe. Returning the next year, he read law in the Worcester, Massachusetts, office of Messrs. George F. Hoar and Thomas L. Nelson, and was admitted to the Worcester County bar in 1883. The next year was spent in Washington, District of Columbia, as a private secretary to Senator Hoar, in whose office he had previously studied, and as clerk on the committee on privileges and elections. Returning to his native state, he opened an office in Worcester, practicing there briefly until 1885 when he began practice in Clinton, Massachusetts. There, he formed a partnership with Hon. John W. Corcoran, Esq. that lasted six years. He married Miss Mary Carney Vose of Lowell, Massachusetts, in 1886, that same year being appointed assistant district attorney for the Middle District. In 1892, he was admitted as a junior partner in the Fitchburg, Massachusetts, law firm of Norcross and Baker, subsequently renamed Norcross, Baker and Parker. Active politically, he served on the Republican State Committee. In 1894, he established a private practice in Worcester and later acted as special justice of the Second District Court of East Worcester. Appointed assistant district attorney of the Middle District, he was subsequently elected to a three-year term as district attorney beginning in 1896. That same year, he was awarded a Bachelor of Arts from Harvard University. During the 1890s, he was a member of the board of examiners for admission to the bar, treasurer of the Law Library Association of Worcester County and secretary of the Association of District Attorneys of the Commonwealth. In 1899, he returned to private practice and in 1901 announced his candidacy for the Republican nomination for attorney general of the Commonwealth of Massachusetts. Overwhelmingly nominated, he held that office, gaining national attention due to his participation in several celebrated criminal cases. In 1905, he returned to private practice, opening a law office in Boston, Massachusetts, which he maintained until his death. Active in the civic affairs of Lancaster, Massachusetts, where he made his home, he was a member of the school committee and a trustee of the public library. He was presented with an honorary degree of Doctor of Laws from Tufts University in 1905. He held membership in several athletic, social and political organizations nationally. At the time of his death at his residence in South Lancaster, he was called the "Bay State's most influential citizen."

PEIRCE, HENRY BAILEY 1841 - 1898: born in Duxbury, Massachusetts, son of Martin Bailey and Mary E. (Wellman) Peirce. His early education was received in the Abington, Massachusetts, public school system and at the Mercantile Academy in the capital city of Boston. In 1861, he enlisted as a private in the 23rd Massachusetts Volunteers and served four years, being mustered out with the rank of captain in 1865. Shortly thereafter, he became engaged in the insurance business in Boston, representing the Manhattan Life Insurance Company of New York and the Travelers Insurance Company of Hartford, Connecticut. He also undertook brokerage work for several fire insurance companies. An active veteran, he was appointed secretary and treasurer of the commission for the care of disabled soldiers. That same year, he was named assistant adjutant general in the Massachusetts G.A.R., being reappointed each year until 1876. Active in business affairs, he was president of the Abington Mutual Fire Insurance Company and a trustee of the Abington Savings Bank. He also served as a director of the Massachusetts Benefit Association in the city of Boston. He was elected secretary of the Commonwealth of Massachusetts in 1875, serving in that capacity until his retirement in 1890. His first wife, Miss C. Elvira Carew, died in 1862, only one year after their wedding. In 1865, he was married a second time to Miss Augusta Arnold, who died in 1882, and a third time to Miss Fanny B. Pease, the next year. Taken ill while making a speech at the silver anniversary exercises of the Ladies Grand Army Circle, he was transfered to his Abington residence where he died shortly thereafter.

PENNELL, LEMIRA C. 1821 - 1893: widow of Francis Pennell. She was the author of numerous pamphlets, published between 1874 and 1891, which decried the treatment of the insane in hospitals, the unjust incarceration of the sane and the corruption she perceived in the church and state. Committed to the Maine state insane asylum in Augusta, Maine, in 1880, she was released after a time but was to spend various periods of her life in institutions. A published author and satirical cartoonist, her works include *The Memorial Scrapbook* published in 1883, *This Remarkable Essay: Sickness vs. Smell* in 1889 and *This Red Book* in 1886. It was from a copy of the last work that she extracted the title page and upon it wrote a letter to Attorney Hosea M. Knowlton. Having resided in Portland, Maine, at the time she communicated with Attorney Knowlton, she died in Augusta, Maine.

PIERCE, EDWARD LILLIE 1827 - 1897: born in Stoughton, Massachusetts, son of Jessie and Eliza S. (Lillie) Pierce. He attended Brown University, where he was a classmate of Erastus Worthington, also a letter writer in this volume. He received his Bachelor of Arts from that institution in 1850. Entering Harvard Law School, he was awarded his Bachelor of Laws two years later. In 1853, he was admitted to the Norfolk County bar and traveled to Cincinnati, Ohio, where he spent the next year in the office of Solomon P. Chase, Esq. He continued in private practice until the outbreak of the Civil War when he enlisted with Company I, 3rd Massachusetts Volunteers, serving a three-month term. Following his discharge, he was employed by the United States government to conduct an inquiry into the condition of the former slaves on the plantations at Sea Islands, South Carolina, submitting an extensive report upon completion of the assignment as well as authoring the book *Negroes at Port Royal*. Returning to his native state, he was appointed collector for internal revenue for the Third District in 1863. His first wife was Miss Elizabeth H. Kingsbury of Providence, Rhode Island, whom he married in 1865. His second wife was Miss Laura Woodhead of Huddersfield, England. In 1866, he held the office of district attorney for Norfolk and Plymouth Counties, retaining that position by successive election until 1869. That year, he was appointed secretary of the Board of State Charities, serving until his resignation in 1874. He was a state representative from Milton, Massachusetts, in 1875 and 1876 and was offered, but declined, appointment to the office of assistant treasurer of the United States in 1878. In his later years, he devoted his energies to his considerable private practice. The author of several volumes on railroad law, his other works include *Two Systems of Government Proposed for the Rebel States*, published in 1867, and *Memoir and Letters of Charles Sumner* in 1881. The next year, he was presented with the degree of Doctor of Laws from Brown University. An extensive traveler, he left the United States three months before his death, spending time with his wife first in Hamburg, Germany, and then Paris, France. His death came in the latter city and was attributed to arsenic poisoning, complicated with other diseases.

PILLSBURY, ALBERT ENOCH 1849 - 1930: see **GLOSSARY A.**

PIPER, HORACE L.: author of a letter from Washington, District of Columbia, to Attorney Hosea Morrill Knowlton. In 1893, he made his residence in that city, employed as an assistant superintendent of lifesaving service. Attempts to obtain further biographical details have been to date unsuccessful.

PRESCOTT, WILLIAM COWAN 1848 - 1931: born in New Hartford, New York, son of Daniel M. and Mary (Wood) Prescott. He received his early education in the district schools of Herkimer County, New York, preparing for college at Utica Academy and graduating in 1867. He then entered Tufts University, receiving his Bachelor of Arts with high honors in 1871, at which time he pursued his legal studies in the Herkimer office of Messrs. Earl, Smith and Brown. Admitted to the New York state bar in 1875, he formed a partnership with Hon. Robert Earl, Esq. and then Samuel Earl, Esq., the latter association lasting for seven years. The following year, he married Miss Frances Maybie Cotton of New York, New York. In 1882, he formed a successful partnership with Abram B. Steele, Esq. in the firm of Steele and Prescott. In 1887, he was named chairman of the board of the police commission of Herkimer, serving until his resignation in 1892. He was elected a member of the legislative assembly of New York that same year and served two consecutive two-year terms. Active in civic affairs, he was a trustee of the Chamber of Commerce and of the public library. Held in high esteem by his community, he was elected president of the village of Herkimer in 1896 and also served one year as village attorney. Following the death of Attorney Steele in 1913 after a thirty-one-year partnership, he became professionally associated with Essie R. Henderson, Esq. Prominent in the affairs of his church, he was also an active Mason, serving in various official positions within that order. He was active in many professional organizations and was a founder of the Herkimer Historical Society. In his later years, his legal involvement was primarily in estate work and the surrogate court. He died at his residence in his adopted town. In 1884, in association with Attorney Steele, he participated in the sensational trial of Mrs. Roxelana Druse, tried and convicted of the brutal murder of her husband, William. This case bore similarities to that of the Bordens, as an axe was used to remove the head of Mr. Druse after he had been shot by his wife. Convicted, Mrs. Druse was hanged on February 28, 1887.

REED, GEORGE BOWLAND 1829 - 1907: born in Montpelier, Vermont, son of Thomas and Mary (Bowland) Reed. Relocating to Massachusetts, he began a bookselling business in Boston, making his home with his wife, Clara, in nearby Cambridge. Beginning circa 1869, he operated the business as such for four years, at which time he began to deal exclusively in law books. After fifteen years, he became involved in the publication business. He died in Arlington, Massachusetts.

REED, MILTON 1848 - 1932: born in Haverhill, Massachusetts, son of William and Sophia (Ladd) Reed. He received his early education in the public schools of his native town as well as those of Newburyport, Massachusetts. Preparing for college at the high school in Cambridge, Massachusetts, he entered Harvard University, receiving his Master of Arts in 1868. Moving to Fall River, Massachusetts, in 1870, he secured a position as editor of the *Fall River Daily Globe*, a popular newspaper. He studied briefly at the law school of his alma mater and was admitted to the Bristol County bar in 1872. That same year, he established a practice in Fall River and purchased, together with his brother, the *Taunton Gazette*, a newspaper in the neighboring city of Taunton, Massachusetts. Both business ventures were successful and occupied him for the remainder of his life. Interested in politics, he served as senator for the Second District of Bristol County in 1880, declining renomination the next year. In 1881 and again in 1882, he ran for the office of mayor of Fall River but was defeated by a small majority. Successful in his bid for office in 1884, he held the mayoralty of that city for one term. Retiring from politics, he devoted his energies to his considerable private practice and newspaper work. Active in Fall River business affairs, he was treasurer of the Seaconnet Mills, president of the People's Cooperative Bank and a trustee of numerous corporations. A member of the Unitarian church, he was superintendent of the Sunday School and served on countless committees. A world traveler, he covered over 150,000 miles in less than five years, visiting both prominent and obscure sites. His travelogue, *A Roving He Would Go*, published in Fall River in 1910, had the distinction of being the best seller of any work by an author from that city. A noted public speaker, he lectured widely on subjects as varied as law, travel and the history of Fall River. He retired from practice in 1930 and spent the rest of his life residing in his adopted city. At the time of his death, he was referred to as the "dean of the Fall River bar." His interest in the Borden case may stem from the fact that Bridget Sullivan was employed as cook in the household of his father, William Reed, circa 1888.

REED, PHILIP GORDON: author of a letter on stationery from the Hotel Kenmore, a leading hostelry in Albany, New York. In his letter to Attorney Hosea M. Knowlton, he professed to be the twenty-five-year-old illegitimate son of Andrew Borden and the perpetrator of the brutal August 4, 1892, crime. Directories for the city of Albany list no one of that name and to date no records have surfaced to validate his existence.

ROBBINS, MRS. M. A.: a resident of Boston, Massachusetts, in 1893. Nothing in the content of this letter indicates the positive identity of the author.

ROBINSON, GEORGE DEXTER 1834 - 1896: see **GLOSSARY A.**

ROTCH, WILLIAM JAMES 1819 - 1893: born in Philadelphia, Pennsylvania, son of Joseph and Anna Ridgway (Smith) Rotch. Educated in the private schools of New Bedford, Massachusetts, he entered Harvard University, receiving his Bachelor of Arts with honors in 1838. Following graduation, he returned to New Bedford and entered into a business partnership with his brother, the New Bedford Cordage Company resulting. Here he laid the foundation for his successful career in business and investing. Diversifying his interests over a period of many years, he had substantial holdings which included investments in real estate, manufacturing, shipping and the railroad. Becoming active politically during the 1840s, he served for two terms as a representative in the Massachusetts legislature. He married Miss Emily Morgan of New Bedford in 1842 and, following her death, wed her sister, Clara, in 1866. He was elected mayor of New Bedford in 1852 and served as a trustee of both the Arnold Fund for the Poor of New Bedford and St. Luke's Hospital, also in that city. Interested in education, he held the positions of treasurer and president of Friend's Academy, a private school built on land donated by his father. He spent his final years actively engaged as president and director of numerous prominent New England corporations. He maintained residences in Boston and New Bedford, as well as at Beverly Farms, Massachusetts, where he died.

RUSSELL, MISS ALICE MANLEY 1852 - 1941: see **GLOSSARY A.**

SAVARY, WILLIAM HENRY 1835 - 1906: born in Savaryville, Groveland, Massachusetts, son of George and Louise (Balch) Savary. He received his early education at Merrimack Academy in his native town and at Oxford Academy in Oxford, Vermont. Entering Yale University, he received his Bachelor of Arts in 1857. Completing his theological studies at Harvard Divinity School three years later, he was ordained a minister in West Newton, Massachusetts, and was subsequently installed as pastor at the Unitarian Church there. In 1862, he married Miss Anna E. Hosmer of Buffalo, New York. Moving to Ellsworth, Maine, in 1867, he was responsible for the organization of the First Unitarian Church and served the needs of that congregation for several years. He later ministered at the Unitarian Church in Canton, Massachusetts, and was appointed circa 1886 to minister at the Unity Church in South Boston, Massachusetts. It was during his residence in South Boston that he penned the communiqué to Attorney General Albert E. Pillsbury, which is included in this volume. His final pastorate was at Green Harbor, Massachusetts, where he ministered until failing health caused his retirement in 1900. He returned to his ancestral home in his native town where he resided for the remainder of his days. Active in the affairs of Groveland, he was a member of the Village Improvement Society, serving for a time as its vice-president. A well-known worker for the temperance movement, he was also a noted lecturer on historical and biographical subjects. A few weeks prior to his death, he gave a lecture entitled "Lives of Two Noble Women: Lydia Maria Child and Lucretia Mott." He died while a patient at Emerson Hospital in Boston, Massachusetts.

SCHULTE, OTTO H. 1854 - 1926: born in Newark, New Jersey. The son of German emigrants, he received his early education in the public schools of his native city as well as the New Jersey Model School in Trenton. He graduated from Williams College in 1876 and immediately became a teacher, being employed in that capacity in both Jersey City, New Jersey, and Massachusetts. Settling with his wife in his native city, he was appointed principal of the Walnut Street School in 1882, retaining that position for two years before taking charge of the Eighteenth Avenue School and, in 1885, the Morton Street School. Despite a movement circa 1903 to have him removed from that office, he was able to retain the post through the support of former pupils and friends. A frequent traveler abroad, he was also active in various recreational sports. Retiring nearly a year before his death, he sent a farewell message shortly before Christmas to the student body at the institution where he was last employed. He died at a private hospital in Orange, New Jersey.

SEGER, J. C.: author of a letter on stationery from Thomas and Seger, a collection agency in DeSoto, Missouri. A partner in this firm with stenographer Harry Thomas, he was likely an attorney as is indicated by that firm's letterhead. The firm of Thomas and Seger was apparently short-lived and does not appear in available directories of the period for DeSoto. No records have to date surfaced to establish his residency there or in the state of Missouri.

SEYMOUR, HENRY HASTINGS 1849 - 1918: born in Mount Morris, New York, son of Norman and Frances (Metcalf) Seymour. Educated in the public schools of his native town, he prepared for college at Mount Morris Academy. Studying at Dartmouth College for one year, he then entered Cornell University, receiving his Bachelor of Science in 1871. While a student there, he received one of the Goldwin Smith prizes, a coveted honor at that university. Following his graduation, he spent a season studying and traveling abroad. Upon his return to the United States, he began to read law in the Mount Morris office of his uncles, Messrs. McNeil, Seymour and George Hastings. Admitted to the bar at Buffalo in 1874, he again traveled abroad, devoting considerable time to sightseeing. In 1876, he returned home and began the practice of law in Buffalo, New York, gaining prominence as an attorney in that community. He served as commissioner of jurors there and held the position of bar examiner for eleven years. Unmarried, he maintained a Buffalo residence as well as a summer home in his native town. He entered the Jordan Health Resort in Dansville, New York, and had been undergoing treatment there for several weeks at the time of his death.

SHERMAN, EDGAR JAY 1834 - 1914: born in Wethersfield, Vermont, son of David and Fanny (Kendall) Sherman. Having received his early education in the public schools of his native town, he also studied at Wesleyan Seminary in Springfield, Vermont. His education completed, he was employed as a teacher in that town until 1853 when he relocated with his family to Lawrence, Massachusetts. He secured a position teaching at Bassettville, Massachusetts, and had many interesting experiences at that time which he later wrote about in *Recollections of a Long Life*, published in 1908. Returning to Lawrence, he began the study of law in the office of George W. Benson, Esq., being admitted to the Essex County bar in 1858. That same year, he married Miss Abbie Louise Sherman, a resident of that city. Entering into a partnership with Daniel Saunders, Esq., he began to practice law. In 1859, he was appointed clerk of the Lawrence police court, serving in that capacity for two years. Following the dissolution of his first partnership, he was associated with several other Lawrence attorneys. At the outbreak of the Civil War, he enlisted as a private in the 48th Massachusetts Volunteer regiment. Promoted to major for gallant service during battle in 1862, he was later breveted colonel of his regiment. Following his discharge, he returned to his legal practice and served as a member of the Massachusetts House of Representatives beginning in 1865. Elected circa 1868 to the office of district attorney for the Eastern District, he served in that capacity until 1882 when he was appointed attorney general. He received an honorary Master of Arts from Dartmouth College in 1884. He resigned as attorney general to accept his appointment by Governor Oliver Ames to a seat on the bench of the superior court in 1887. During his twenty-four years as judge, he presided over several of the most important and difficult cases tried in the Commonwealth, among them the trial of James A. Trefethen. Active in business affairs, he served as director for several Lawrence banking houses. At the time of his death at his country home in Windsor, Vermont, he was considered one of the most famous justices in the country.

SHIPMAN, WILLIAM ROLLIN: 1836 - 1908: born in Granville, Vermont. At the age of two, he moved with his family to Royalton, Vermont, where he obtained his early education in public schools. Working summers on his father's farm, he spent his winter months as a student at Royalton Academy. Teaching school briefly until 1855, he then entered Middlebury College in Middlebury, Vermont, graduating with high honors in 1859. He subsequently accepted the post of principal at an academy in South Woodstock, Vermont, remaining in that position the next four years. Furthering his education at his alma mater, he received his Master of Arts in 1863. He became involved that year in soliciting funds for the establishment of an academy in Barre, Vermont, under the auspices of that state's Universalist denomination. Early in 1864, he was offered, but declined, the Walker special instructorship at Tufts University. He did accept the Goldthwaite chair of rhetoric, logic and English literature at that institution later that same year. Ordained a Universalist minister in 1865, he never accepted a parish but remained affiliated with Tufts for the rest of his life. For twenty years, beginning in 1864, he served as college librarian and was appointed secretary of the College of Letters in 1869, holding that office for four years. In 1870, he accepted the position of president of the board of directors of Goddard Academy in Barre, Vermont, remaining there until his death thirty-eight years later. The recipient of several academic honors, he was awarded the degree of Doctor of Divinity from St. Lawrence University in 1882, the degree of Doctor of Laws from Tufts in 1899 and the same the next year from his alma mater. In 1900, he was made the dean of the College of Letters at Tufts, holding that post until ill health caused his retirement in 1907. He belonged to both the Delta Kappa Epsilon fraternity and the Phi Beta Kappa Society. An active Mason, he had held membership in the Union Lodge of Middlebury since his college days. Called the "Grand Old Man of Tufts," he had visited the college library the day before his death, which occurred at his home in Somerville, Massachusetts.

SLOCUM, EDWARD L.: a clerk in Providence, Rhode Island. Residing in East Providence in 1892, he relocated the following year to the city of his employ. Working at that time at the Rhode Island Time Register Company, he is last listed in Providence in 1894.

SPARROW, WILLIAM EDWARD 1824 - 1899: born in Rochester, Massachusetts, son of Josiah and Minerva Sparrow. Having served as a surgeon during the Civil War, he later established a practice in Mattapoisett, Massachusetts. A prominent physician in that town for over half a century, he was active in community affairs there. He served twice as a member of the school committee, a two-year period beginning in 1857 and, later, a five-year term beginning in 1867. He was on the committee established to supervise the renovation of the Congregational meeting-house necessitated by that structure's being struck by lightning in 1891. He held memberships in various organizations, among them the G.A.R. He was a member of that town's Board of Health at the time of his death.

STILES, WILLIAM CURTIS 1857 - 1911: born in Stoneham, Massachusetts, son of William H. and Martha P. (Hancock) Stiles. A graduate of Tufts Divinity School in 1876, he was ordained a Universalist minister that same year, being appointed to a parish in Orleans, Massachusetts. In Orleans, also in 1876, he married Miss Mary Allen Arey Newcomb of Welfleet, Massachusetts. He maintained a residence at that time in New Bedford, Massachusetts. In 1880, he entered the Congregational ministry in Brooklyn, New York, serving as pastor at the Old East Congregational Church for the next four years. In 1884, he was assigned to a congregation in St. Louis, Missouri, and, two years later, to one in Pittsfield, New Hampshire. In 1893, he accepted the appointment to minister to the First Congregational Church in Jackson, Michigan, where he was to remain only briefly, resigning the next year in a conflict over the proposed reduction of his salary. Among the pastorates which he held throughout his career was one in his native town. A frequent contributor to magazines and religious journals, he was the author of several books with religious themes including *The Upper*

Way and *The Masters Mission*. Following retirement from the ministry, he was employed as an editor on the *Funk and Wagnall's Standard Dictionary*, maintaining an affiliation with that firm until his death.

STORREY, HAMILTON: author of a letter to Attorney Hosea M. Knowlton from New York City. No one by that name appears in that city's directories for the decade beginning in 1890, and nothing in the content of this letter indicates the positive identity of the author.

STRAND, JOHN BURNS 1848 - ? : born in Massachusetts. Marrying in 1882, he settled in Worcester, Massachusetts, with his wife, Lucy. A psychic medium and clairvoyant physician, he appears in that city's directories listed as such until 1891. The following year, his last in Worcester, he maintained an intelligence office. His letter to Attorney Hosea M. Knowlton offered his services as a trance medium to the prosecution in order to "unravel the mystery." He relocated to Gardner, Massachusetts, and was residing there with his wife in 1900.

TOAL, DAVID D.: 1838 - 1904: a veteran of the Civil War. He graduated from the City University of New York, receiving the degree of Doctor of Medicine in 1867. Establishing a successful career in New York City, he also managed a dispensary, assisted by his wife, the former Miss Anna E. Moser. An active member of St. Brigid's Church, he also maintained memberships in the Oriental Club and the G.A.R. He died at his residence in the city of New York.

VAN ELDEREN, J.: a physician. According to his letter to Attorney Hosea M. Knowlton, he was a native of Holland and had been connected with the secret police there. It is likely that he was visiting Newport, Rhode Island, in August of 1892 and it was from there that he wrote Attorney Knowlton. No records have as yet surfaced to establish his residency in that city.

VON KAMEAKE, THEODORE T. 1864 - 1914: born in New York, son of Theodore Fredrick Von Kameake. He made his residence in Milford, Massachusetts, but he relocated in 1887 to Grafton, Massachusetts, with his wife, the former Miss Martha Rose Taft. Employed in the paper and stationery business, he was associated with the National Papaterie Company in Springfield, Massachusetts. Having relocated to Elmira, New York, later in his life, he maintained his association with that firm. He was employed on sales business for that company in Charles City, Iowa, at the time of his death.

WALKER, MRS. GEORGE D.: visiting in Swansea, Massachusetts, the day of the Borden murders. Nothing in the content of this letter indicates the positive identity of the author.

WALKER, MISS MARY EDWARDS 1832 - 1919: born in Oswego, New York, daughter of Alvah and Vesta (Whitcomb) Walker. At the age of sixteen, she was employed in New York City as a public school teacher. Her interest in medicine prompted her to begin studies at Syracuse Medical College, from which she was graduated in 1855. Six years later, she was established in Washington, District of Columbia, as a practicing physician. At the outbreak of the Civil War, she enlisted in the Union Army, entering as an assistant surgeon with the rank of first lieutenant. Never having favored the extremely ornamental women's attire of that era, she dressed at this time as any other army officer. She frequently told the story of how she had the distinction of being recognized as an equal to male soldiers when traded as a prisoner during that war. She continued to wear men's clothing for the remainder of her life, explaining that this was part of her plan for women's rights. After the Civil War, she gained employment on a New York City daily as one of its first female reporters. Tiring of this work, she returned to Washington and resumed her medical practice. While there, she was active in many of the reform movements of the day, among them governmental reform and woman's suffrage. A celebrated lecturer in the last quarter of the nineteenth century, she often appeared for speaking engagements attired in a frock coat. Some of the works she authored include *Hit*, published in 1871, and *Unmasked Or the Science of Immortality*, published seven years later. Ill health caused her to return to her native town and she was subsequently hospitalized at the United States General Hospital at Fort Ontario, Canada. Having recovered sufficiently for release, she returned to Oswego and died at the home of friends.

WEBSTER, PRENTISS 1851 - 1898: born in Lowell, Massachusetts, son of William Prentiss and Susan (Wildreth) Webster. Educated in the public schools of his native city, he then prepared to attend Harvard University. In 1869, he left the United States for Germany with his father, then consul-general to Frankfurt, and entered the University of Heidelberg to study law. He graduated two years later in Strasburg. In 1873, he was appointed consul at Mainz, Germany, retaining that position for four years, at which time he returned to the city of his birth. Resuming his law studies, he read in the offices of John Davis in Lowell and Hon. Henry W. Paine in Boston, Massachusetts. Admitted to the bar in 1880, he practiced for a year in the office of his uncle, Gen. Benjamin F. Butler, Esq. and subsequently entered a partnership with him which lasted until 1892. Active in the affairs of his native city, he served as secretary of the city hall commission there in 1888. Active fraternally, he was also secretary for a time of the Middlesex Chapter of the Sons of the American Revolution. A noted writer on legal subjects, he was writing a treatise on "Citizenship" at the time of his death at his home in Lowell.

WHITE, ALDEN PERLEY 1856 - 1933: born in Danvers, Massachusetts, son of Amos Alden and Harriet Augusta (Perley) White. Educated in the public schools of his native town, he prepared for college at Lawrence Academy in Groton, Massachusetts. Entering Amherst College in 1874, he excelled as a student and was the recipient of several prizes and medals for scholastic achievement. In 1878, he entered Harvard Law School, studying there for only one year. Admitted to the Massachusetts bar in 1880, he established a practice in Salem, Massachusetts, where he made his home. He was married to Miss Mary Howe in Danvers, Massachusetts, in 1885, her death coming only one year later. He was married a second time to Miss Jessie Carter of Springfield, Massachusetts, in 1896. Named to a seat on the bench of the First District Court of Salem in 1890, he remained there until the following year when he was appointed assistant district attorney. Serving under William H. Moody, he was appointed to fill the vacancy created when District Attorney Moody resigned upon election to congress. In that office for a three-year term, he then returned to private practice. Active in the municipal affairs of Salem, he was a member of the Board of Aldermen there. In 1918, he was appointed judge of the probate court of Essex County, serving in this capacity until his death. An authority on the history of Essex County, he published a history of Danvers, Massachusetts, and was a charter member of the Danvers Historical Society. President of the Alumni Association of his alma mater, he was also a trustee of several prominent New England companies and institutions. At the time of his death at his summer residence in Danvers, he was widely known as the "Beloved Magistrate."

WHITEFIELD, EDWIN 1816 - 1892: born in England, son of William Whitefield. A noted English landscape and flower artist, he came to the United States circa 1840, painting views of the Hudson River Valley estates in New York. By 1844, he had settled in New York City where he had successfully established himself as an artist. The next year he illustrated Emma C. Embury's *American Wildflowers in Their Native Haunts*. He issued a series of lithographed views of his paintings in 1847 entitled *North American Scenery*. By 1855, he was living in Canada, employed as a drawing teacher at a female seminary. It was there that he met and married Miss Lillian Stuart, a student at the school. For a three-year period beginning in 1856, he traveled in the state of Minnesota where he established the Wakefield Exploring Company and speculated in real estate and land development. At this time, he produced several watercolor views of that state's scenery, now in the collection of the Minnesota Historical Society in St. Paul. In 1858, he was residing at Kandotta, Minnesota, a town which he was instrumental in developing. Relocating to Chicago, Illinois, two years later, he resided there with his family until 1864, when he moved to the cities of Boston and Reading, Massachusetts. It was there that he published three volumes of *The Homes of Our Forefathers*, depicting views of early New England architecture. In 1888, he considered visiting his native country as part of the research for a book he was preparing on the Bostons of England and Massachusetts, a trip he never was to make. Throughout his career, he lectured widely on the varied topics of art and the settlement of the state of Minnesota. A noted illustrator, his work appeared in numerous periodicals, including *Harpers* and *Frank Leslie's Illustrated Newspaper*. He died at the residence of his daughter in Dedham, Massachusetts, exactly three months from the date that he penned the letter to Attorney Hosea M. Knowlton which is included in this collection.

WHITMORE, JAMES HERMAN: 1838 - 1922: born in Almont, Michigan, son of Samuel S. and Laura A. (Nowlin) Whitmore. Having studied law in New York early in his life, he later attended theological school. Graduating in 1869, he was that year ordained as a Unitarian minister. Assigned to the Unitarian Church in Sterling, Massachusetts, he served there until 1882 when he accepted a pastorate in Stoneham, Massachusetts. Resigning from active pastoral work in 1899, he continued to make his home in Stoneham for the next sixteen years, at which time he relocated with his wife, Laura, to Brookline, Massachusetts. In his lifetime, he traveled extensively, spending a considerable amount of time in the country of Palestine. He died at his home in Brookline.

WHITNEY, JAMES ORNE 1823 - 1895: born in Attleboro, Massachusetts, son of Martin and Mary (Orne) Whitney. He received his early education in the public schools of his native town. In 1835, at the age of twelve, he became afflicted with a diseased hip that was to leave him partially disabled for the rest of his life. Attended to at this time by the Attleboro physician Thaddeus Phelps, he developed an intense interest in the medical profession. He later studied in the office of Dr. Phelps and then attended the Medical Academy in Berkshire, Massachusetts, graduating in 1845. He then moved to Central Falls, Rhode Island, where he established himself in practice. A successful physician, he married Miss Elizabeth Slack Miller of Central Falls in 1850. Shortly thereafter, he moved his residence to Pawtucket, Rhode Island, where he continued his medical practice. Unable to enlist at the outbreak of the Civil War due to his infirmity, he instead served his country as examining physician under the draft act. A founder of the Pawtucket Dispensary, he served as its first physician, being considered one of the best-known practicing in the city at that time. During his lifetime, he was credited with the introduction of a number of new surgical appliances into the profession. A member of both the Rhode Island and Massachusetts Medical Societies, he was a frequent contributor to medical journals. A supporter of Trinity Church in Pawtucket, he served for several years as its vestryman. Active fraternally, he was also a member of the Rhode Island Historical Society. He retired from the medical profession circa 1881 due to illness. He lived the remainder of his days a confirmed invalid and died in his adopted city.

WILLIAMS, A. G.: author of a letter to Attorney Hosea M. Knowlton from Providence, Rhode Island. Nothing in the content of this letter indicates the positive identity of the author.

WILLIAMS, ANNIE L. T.: a resident of Brighton Hill, Massachusetts, in 1893. Nothing in the content of this letter indicates the positive identity of the author.

WILSON, DELIA A. (GIBSON) c.1838 - 1903: born in New York, widow of Jason G. Wilson. In her letter to Attorney Hosea M. Knowlton, she identifies herself as a spiritualist, likely one of the many individuals caught up in that movement as it swept the world during the Victorian period. It was she who suggested that Willis Edwards, a clairvoyant physician, could provide details to Attorney Knowlton regarding the Borden murders. A housekeeper in Lynn, Massachusetts, she died at her residence there.

WILSON, MRS. HENRY, see **WILSON, SARAH A. (BELCHER).**

WILSON, SARAH A. (BELCHER) 1839 - 1910: born in Gibson Township, Pennsylvania, daughter of William Belcher. A teacher by profession, she married Henry Wilson, an attorney, at Factoryville, Pennsylvania, in 1862. She and her husband made their home in Carbondale, Pennsylvania. Shortly after her husband's return from one year's volunteer service during the Civil War, the couple moved to Hazleton, Pennsylvania, and in 1870, to Honesdale, located in that same state, where he became editor of the *Honesdale Union*. His success as an attorney, newspaper editor and, after 1876, as a judge, ensured them a prominent position in Honesdale society. She was an active member of the Presbyterian Church and possessed an avid interest in horticulture. She died at her home in Honesdale.

WINSOR, MISS JOSEPHINE ELIZABETH 1837 - 1904: born in Smithfield, Rhode Island, daughter of Nicholas Steere and Elizabeth S. (Foster) Winsor. An active genealogist, she extensively researched the history of the Winsor family, accumulating a great deal of data pertaining to her ancestors. She died at the family residence in her native town.

WOOD, EDWARD STICKNEY 1846 - 1905: see **GLOSSARY A**.

WOODBURY, JOHN 1856 - 1940: born in Lynn, Massachusetts, son of John Page and Sarah Elizabeth (Silsbee) Woodbury. Receiving part of his early education in Paris, France, he later attended Harvard University, where he was a classmate of Theodore Roosevelt. Receiving his Bachelor of Arts magna cum laude in 1880, he then studied law at Harvard Law School and in the Boston, Massachusetts, office of Messrs. Shattuck and Monroe. Admitted to the Suffolk bar in 1884, he then began to practice law. He married Miss Jennie R. Churchill in Boston in 1885. Appointed secretary of the Metropolitan Park Commission in Boston in 1876, he served in that position until after 1909. Active in the civic affairs of his native city, he served as director and president of the Lynn Board of Trade. Heavily invested in real estate in that city as well as in Boston, he was owner of several commercial properties. A member of the State Board of Publication, he also served as secretary of the trustees of Public Reservations of Massachusetts. He was a member of the Colonial Society of Massachusetts, the Massachusetts Historical Society and the American Antiquarian Society. He also held membership in several social clubs in both New York City and Boston. He was at his residence in the latter city at the time of his death.

WOODWARD, NATHAN ARMSBY: born in Fairfax, Vermont, son of Joseph and Lucy (Wilmarth) Woodward. At the age of fifteen, he moved with his family to western New York state. Preparing for college at Henrietta and Canandaigua Academies, he entered Union College, receiving his Master of Arts in 1845. Following graduation, he taught school at Honeoye Falls, New York, and at Geneseo Academy. He read law in several private offices during this period and was admitted to the bar in 1848. The next three years were spent in Scottsville, New York, where he continued to be employed as a teacher. In 1851, he moved to Batavia, New York, and there he abandoned his former profession and began to practice law. Over the next decade, he formed short-lived partnerships with George Bowen, Esq. and H. F. Tarbox, Esq., after which he resumed his private practice. He married Miss W. Sarah B. Tarbox of Batavia and, following her death in 1861, married Miss Martha Allen. He quickly rose to prominence as an attorney and held a number of public offices. Serving two terms as the superintendent of schools in Batavia, he also held the office of county treasurer. Appointed one of the United States loan commissioners for Genesee County, New York, he served five years and, in 1893, was elected a member of the state constitutional convention. Extremely well-read, he was the author of numerous verses. His 150-page volume of collected poems entitled *Pebbles and Boulders* was published in 1895. An invalid for the last year of his life, he died at his residence in Batavia. At the time of his death, he was the oldest lawyer in Genesee County and was called the "Dean of the County Bar."

WORRALL, MRS. H. F.: author of a letter from "Scotland - Mass - United States" to Attorney Hosea M. Knowlton. Nothing in the content of this letter indicates the positive identity of the author. Attempts to uncover information concerning this individual in the countries of Scotland and England have been unsuccessful. It seems likely that the author was a native of the British Isles who emigrated to the United States. Her statement that she was residing "in this country village near Bridgewater," along with the reference to "Scotland" in the letter's heading, strongly suggests the author was writing from Bridgewater, Massachusetts, a section of which was known as Scotland. No records have surfaced to date to associate her with that town.

WORRELL, ELISHA BACON 1858 - 1943: born in Centreville, Massachusetts, son of James and Hannah (Richardson) Worrell. He resided with his wife, the former Miss Helen F. W. Hill, in Dorchester, Massachusetts. Beginning his career as a lecturer on food and higher food standards circa 1891, he traveled extensively, speaking in many parts of the United States. Reliable and accurate, his lectures were considered beneficial and informative. In 1903, his lecture, "Building the Body," was provided free to the public through the endowment of The Natural Food Company of Niagara Falls, New York. He died at his residence in Dorchester.

WORTHINGTON, ERASTUS 1828 - 1898: born in Dedham, Massachusetts, son of Erastus and Sally (Ellis) Worthington. He was educated in the Dedham public school system, later preparing for college at an academy in Attleboro, Massachusetts. He received his Bachelor of Arts from Brown University in 1850, where he was a classmate of Edward L. Pierce. Inclined toward law, he studied for a year in the Milwaukee, Wisconsin, office of his brother, Ellis Worthington, Esq. Having received his Bachelor of Laws from Harvard Law School, he gained employment as an assistant teacher at Dedham High School, continuing to read law in offices at Dedham, among them that of Hon. Ezra Wilkinson, Esq. Returning to Harvard in 1852, he received the degree of Doctor of Laws from that institution the following year. Admitted to the Norfolk bar in 1854, he formed a short-lived partnership with Hon. David A. Simmons, Esq., with offices in Boston, Massachusetts. In 1856, he was made register of insolvency for Norfolk County, remaining in that office until the next year when the probate and insolvency courts were consolidated. Establishing a practice in his native town, he was soon appointed trial justice by Governor Nathaniel P. Banks, retaining that position for the next eight years. He married Miss Elizabeth Foster Briggs of Boston in 1861. Five years later, he was chosen clerk of courts for Norfolk County, taking office on January 1, 1867 and holding that post until January 1, 1897. That year, he was appointed trial justice for Dedham by Governor Roger Wolcott. Active in municipal affairs, he served his community in various capacities ranging from town moderator to assessor. He also held a seat on the school committee for eight years. An active member of the Dedham Historical Society, he was author of a short history of that town published in 1884 and frequently contributed to the Dedham Historical Register. He was chairman of the board of assessors and vice-president of the historical society's board of curators at the time of his death in his native town.

WRIGHT, WILLIAM BEN 1855 - 1935: born in Toronto, Ontario, Canada. Educated for four years under the supervision of the Order of Christian Brothers beginning in 1863, he was then taken into the home of Rev. John Fletcher at Oakville and Scarboro, Ontario. At the age of fourteen, he moved to Boston, Massachusetts. It was there that Zenas T. Haines, night editor of the *Boston Herald*, took an interest in him and so began his education in the newspaper and publishing business. In 1874, he gained employment at the *Boston Post* as a shorthand reporter, leaving after a time to become secretary to Frank Goodwin, Esq. He became associated with the *Boston Globe* and the *Boston Traveler* in 1880, reporting church sermons and speeches. The following year, he married Miss Antoinette Schlegal. He was employed for three years as editor of the *Fall River Daily Herald* in Fall River, Massachusetts, at the same time maintaining connections with newspapers as distant as New York and Philadelphia. In 1923, he surrendered many of his diversified interests in order to dedicate his services exclusively to the *Boston Globe*. His newspaper work dealt primarily with legal and political topics. An official court reporter with a fine reputation for speed and accuracy, he covered the trial of Sacco and Vanzetti as his final assignment. He died in Medfield, Massachusetts.

WYMAN, ALPHONSO ADELBERT 1862 - 1929: born in West Acton, Massachusetts, son of Oliver C. and Caroline Mitchell (Chandler) Wyman. He prepared for college at Phillips Academy at Exeter, New Hampshire, and entered Harvard University, receiving his Bachelor of Arts magna cum laude in 1883. Following graduation, he began studying law in the Boston, Massachusetts, offices of Henry W. Paine, Esq. and William W. Vaughan, Esq. Admitted to the Suffolk bar in 1885, he opened an office in Boston and began to practice. In 1886, he married Miss Laura Aldrich of Acton, subsequently settling in that town. In 1889 and again in 1893, he served as town moderator there. In addition to his considerable private practice, he was also engaged in revising the United States statutes. Moving his residence to Somerville, Massachusetts, he served as a member of the Board of Aldermen there, circa 1908 to 1909. He was active in business circles, his directorship of the E. L. Patch Chemical Company only one of the several corporate interests he maintained. He died while hospitalized in Newton, Massachusetts, the city where he was residing at the time of his death.

YOUNG, WILLIAM A. 1838 - 1927: born in Danville, Indiana, son of John A. Young. He received his early education in the public schools of his native town. He began his career as a school teacher, moving first to Martinsville, Illinois, in 1859 and later to Charlestown, located in that same state. It was there that he began the study of law, reading in the office of a justice of the peace. In 1862, he enlisted with Company C, 8th Illinois Volunteers, serving a one-year term. As happened in many families during the War Between the States, several of his brothers were commissioned officers in the Confederate Army. Following his military discharge, he relocated to Vermilion County, Illinois, and pursued his legal studies, being admitted to the state bar in 1868. Two years later, he moved to Danville, Illinois, where he practiced law. It was at about this time that he married Miss Elizabeth Maddox, a resident of Danville. Forming a partnership in 1877 with Attorney Penwell, he later practiced in association with Gen. John C. Black, Esq. Interested in Danville political circles, he ran for the mayoralty on the temperance ticket but was defeated. He continued to practice law while also employed as a collector, doing so until his retirement in 1919. He spent his final years attending to his considerable business interests, conducting real estate transactions until days before his death. He expired at his residence in "The Holland" apartments in Danville.

INDEX

Index

Each topic in this index has been given two references, the page number(s) where the item may be found followed by the document number in brackets.

ACCOMPLICES, 40 (HK031); 42 (HK033); 43, 44 (HK035); 51 (HK043); 59 (HK050); 61 (HK054); 68-71 (HK062); 94, 95 (HK093); 99 (HK097); 118 (HK114); 132 (HK129); 139 (HK138); 140 (HK139); 142-144 (HK141); 222 (HK208); 232 (HK214); 239 (HK221); 248 (HK232); 249 (HK234); 266, 267 (HK252); 286 (HK277); 319 (HK313); 332 (HK324)
ADAMS, MELVIN OHIO, 58, 59 (HK049); 59 (HK051); 61 (HK054); 85 (HK075); 96 (HK095); 100 (HK099); 109 (HK107); 161 (HK154); 162 (HK156); 175 (HK171); 195 (HK188); 196 (HK189); 196 (HK190)
ALGER, ISAAC, 214 (HK205)
ALLEN, CHARLES N., 214 (HK205)
ALLEN, GEORGE WILLIAM, 189 (HK184)
ALMY, GENEVRA M. (ALLEN)
  (Mrs. William M. Almy), 102, 105, 106 (HK102)
ALMY, HENRY B., 214 (HK205)
AMES, HOBERT, 214 (HK205)
AMES, OLIVER, II, 214 (HK205)
ASHLEY, MILLARD F., 214 (HK205)
ASSOCIATED PRESS, 202, 203 (HK196); 225 (HK209); 225 (HK210)
ATHERTON, HERBERT L., 214 (HK205)
ATTORNEY COMPENSATION BILL, 155, 156 (HK146)
ATTORNEY MEETINGS, 32 (HK021); 32 (HK022); 35, 36 (HK025); 41, 42 (HK032); 42 (HK034); 83, 84 (HK073); 84, 85 (HK074); 85 (HK075); 89 (HK082); 89 (HK083); 89 (HK084); 90 (HK086); 95 (HK094); 120 (HK118); 121 (HK119); 154 (HK144); 155 (HK145); 156, 157 (HK147); 158 (HK150); 159 (HK151); 160 (HK152);160 (HK153); 160, 161 (HK154); 161 (HK155); 161, 162 (HK156); 162 (HK157); 162 (HK158); 195 (HK187); 196 (HK189); 204, 205 (HK199); 210 (HK201); 211 (HK202); 212, 213 (HK204)
AUTOPSIES
  reports, 10, 11 (HK008); 15, 16 (HK009)
  references, 9 (HK007); 55, 56 (HK047); 205, 206, 209, 210 (HK200); 226, 227 (HK211); 275 (HK262)
  laboratory reports, 30, 31 (HK019)
AVERY, EPHRAIM K. See MURDERS/ CRIMES/ LEGAL CASES, UNRELATED

BAILEY, GEORGE P., 214 (HK205)
BAKER, ANSEL G., 214 (HK205)

BAKER, MR., 33 (HK023)
BARNEY, GEORGE W., 100 (HK098); 100 (HK099)
BARROWS, EUGENE M., 214 (HK205)
BARTLETT, BOURNE S., 214 (HK205)
BATCHELDER, MOULTON, 108 (HK105)
BATES, FRANK M., 214 (HK205)
BENCE, ELI, 185 (HK183); 358 (HK341)
BENNETT, WILLIAM A., 214 (HK205)
BILLINGS, WARREN T., 101 (HK100); 101 (HK101); 107 (HK105)
BLAISDELL, JOSIAH COLEMAN, 80 (HK071); 137 (HK136); 176 (HK172); 348 (HK334)
BLISS, ZEBA F., 214 (HK205)
BLODGETT, CALEB, 164 (HK161); 320 (HK314)
BODMAN, HENRY A., 112 (HK109); 114 (HK110); 116 (HK111)
BOOTH, FRANCIS A., 214 (HK205)
BORDEN, ABBY DURFEE (GRAY)
(Mrs. Andrew Jackson Borden, 2nd wife), 5 (HK001), 7 (HK004); 7, 8 (HK005); 15 (HK009); 22, 23 (HK012); 29 (HK016); 30 (HK019); 33-35 (HK023); 38 (HK029); 40, 41 (HK031); 43 (HK034); 45 (HK037); 56 (HK047); 57 (HK048); 58 (HK049); 60 (HK052); 62, 63 (HK056); 64 (HK059); 65 (HK060); 68, 69 (HK062); 74 (HK067); 79 (HK070); 82, 83 (HK072); 105, (HK102); 113,114(HK110); 115 (HK111); 127-131 (HK126); 132 (HK129); 132, 135 (HK131); 141 (HK140); 141-144 (HK141); 148 (HK142); 199, 200 (HK193); 201, 202 (HK195); 205, 206, 209, 210 (HK200); 211, 212 (HK203); 222 (HK208); 226, 227 (HK211); 227-229 (HK212); 229, 230 (HK213); 230, 231 (HK214); 236 (HK217); 240 (HK222); 241 (HK225); 246 (HK231); 247 (HK232); 248 (HK233); 249 (HK234); 250-252 (HK235); 255, 256 (HK237); 256 (HK238); 258 (HK240); 275 (HK262); 283 (HK272); 286 (HK277); 298 (HK289); 305 (HK298); 312 (HK306); 321, 323 (HK315); 330, 331 (HK323); 333 (HK325); 334 (HK327); 340-345 (HK329); 347 (HK332); 347 (HK333); 351 (HK336); 353-355 (HK339); 356-359 (HK341)
 missing note, 33, 34 (HK023); 45 (HK037); 58 (HK049); 132 (HK131); 199 (HK193); 202 (HK195); 236 (HK217); 240 (HK222); 247 (HK232); 250, 252 (HK235); 286 (HK277); 291 (HK280); 298 (HK289); 313 (HK307); 322 (HK315); 334 (HK327); 340 (HK329); 347 (HK332); 347 (HK333); 354 (HK339); 357, 358 (HK341)
 skull, 15, 16 (HK009); 51 (HK044); 63 (HK058); 176 (HK172)
BORDEN, ALANSON, 80 (HK071)
BORDEN, ALMY, AND COMPANY,
(43 South Main Street, Fall River, Mass.), 99 (HK098)
BORDEN, ANDREW JACKSON, 6, 7 (HK004); 10, 11 (HK008); 22, 23

Index

(HK012); 29 (HK016); 30 (HK019); 33, 34 (HK023); 37 (HK028); 38 (HK029); 40, 41 (HK031); 45 (HK037); 55, 56 (HK047); 57 (HK048); 58, 59 (HK049); 60 (HK052); 63 (HK056); 64 (HK059); 68 (HK062); 74, 75 (HK067); 79 (HK070); 80 (HK071); 81, 82 (HK072); 100 (HK099); 102, 105, 106(HK102);111 (HK109); 116 (HK111); 127-131 (HK126);131 (HK128); 132 (HK129); 132 (HK130); 132, 133 (HK131); 141 (HK140); 141-144 (HK141); 148 (HK142); 158 (HK149); 182 (HK182); 199 (HK193); 201 (HK195); 205, 209, 210 (HK200); 211, 212 (HK203); 226, 227 (HK211); 227, 228 (HK212); 229 (HK213); 230, 231 (HK214); 233, 234 (HK215); 246 (HK231); 247 (HK232); 249 (HK234); 250-252, 255 (HK235); 255 (HK236); 255, 256 (HK237); 258 (HK240); 261 (HK244); 275 (HK262); 283 (HK272); 286 (HK277); 298 (HK289); 305, 306 (HK298); 312 (HK306); 321 (HK315); 330, 331 (HK323); 332 (HK324); 333 (HK325); 333 (HK326); 335 (HK327); 339-345 (HK329); 347 (HK333); 348 (HK335); 351 (HK336); 352 (HK338); 353-355 (HK339); 356-359 (HK341)
    barn, 5 (HK001); 9 (HK006); 24 (HK013); 28 (HK015); 29 (HK016); 37 (HK027); 43 (HK034); 51 (HK043); 52 (HK046); 58, 59 (HK049); 88 (HK080); 131 (HK127); 132 (HK131); 152 (HK142); 235 (HK216); 246 (HK231); 247 (HK232); 251 (HK235); 257 (HK239); 258 (HK240); 344 (HK329); 347 (HK333); 348 (HK335); 353 (HK339); 357 (HK341)
    farmhands employed by, 135 (HK131); 144 (HK141)
    house, 29 (HK016); 42 (HK033); 46 (HK039); 147, 148, 151-153 (HK142)
        burglary (1891), 40 (HK031); 58 (HK049); 61 (HK054); 74, 75 (HK067); 228 (HK212); 334 (HK327)
        doorlocks, 34 (HK023); 131 (HK128); 230 (HK214); 247 (HK232); 249 (HK234); 334 (HK327)
        mutton served, 31 (HK019); 209 (HK200)
    skull, 10, 11 (HK008); 51 (HK044); 56 (HK047); 63 (HK058); 176 (HK172)
    well, 52 (HK046), 237 (HK218)

BORDEN, MISS EMMA LENORA, 8 (HK005); 40 (HK031); 67-71 (HK062); 74 (HK067); 82 (HK072); 118 (HK114); 127-129 (HK126);141 (HK141); 182 (HK182); 185 (HK183); 222 (HK208); 228 (HK212); 231, 232 (HK214); 245 (HK229); 256 (HK238); 261 (HK244); 290, 291 (HK280); 322 (HK315); 325 (HK316); 341, 345 (HK329); 348 (HK333); 354 (HK339); 358 (HK341)

BORDEN FAMILY/RELATIONS, 33-35 (HK023); 45 (HK037); 94 (HK092); 102, 105, 106 (HK102); 182, 183 (HK182); 230, 231 (HK214); 321 (HK315); 334, 335 (HK327)

~ 535 ~

BORDEN, JEROME COOK, 199 (HK193), 202 (HK195)
BORDEN, MISS LIZZIE ANDREW, 5 (HK001); 8 (HK005); 21 (HK010)
  23 (HK012); 33, 34 (HK023); 45 (HK037); 49 (HK040); 68-71
  (HK062); 73 (HK065); 74, 75 (HK067); 85 (HK076); 87
  (HK078); 94 (HK092); 102, 105 (HK102); 118 (HK114); 122
  (HK121); 127-130 (HK126); 131 (HK127); 131 (HK128); 132
  (HK129); 132, 133 (HK131); 141-144 (HK141); 196 (HK189);
  196 (HK190); 197 (HK191); 199, 200 (HK193); 201, 202
  (HK195); 230-232 (HK214); 258 (HK240); 290, 291 (HK280);
  297, 298 (HK289); 321-323 (HK315); 332 (HK324)
    anecdotes, 73 (HK065); 76 (HK069); 136 (HK135); 241
      (HK225); 242 (HK226); 297 (HK289); 321 (HK315); 334,
      335 (HK327); 343, 344 (HK329)
    arraignment, 164 (HK160); 167 (HK161); 168 (HK163);
      174 (HK170)
    as accessory, 43, 44 (HK035); 99 (HK097); 128-131
      (HK126); 159 (HK150)
    bail, 83 (HK073); 85 (HK076)
    church affiliation, 246 (HK232); 258 (HK240); 327
      (HK320)
    clothing, 5 (HK001); 28 (HK016); 45 (HK037); 46 (HK038);
      49 (HK040); 50 (HK042); 79 (HK070); 80 (HK071); 231,
      232 (HK214); 247 (HK232); 250-252, 255 (HK235); 298
      (HK289); 322, 323 (HK315); 346 (HK330)
    dress burned, 27 (HK014); 33 (HK023); 39 (HK031); 58
      (HK049); 83 (HK072); 135 (HK132); 235 (HK216); 247
      (HK232); 248 (HK233); 322, 323 (HK315); 325 (HK316);
      333 (HK325); 334 (HK327); 351 (HK336); 354 (HK339); 355
      (HK340)
    grand tour, 40 (HK031); 142 (HK141); 230, 231 (HK214);
      255 (HK236)
    guilt/innocence. See BORDEN MURDERS, public opinion
    illness/depression, 227 (HK212)
    indictments, 94, 95 (HK093); 96 (HK096); 111, 112
      (HK109);113, 114 (HK110);115, 116 (HK111); 175
      (HK171); 176 (HK172)
    insanity issue, 31 (HK020); 38 (HK029); 39 (HK030); 41
      (HK031); 41 (HK032); 45 (HK037); 69 (HK062); 76
      (HK069); 86 (HK077); 86, 87 (HK078); 95, 96 (HK095); 96
      (HK096); 102, 105, 106 (HK102); 109 (HK107); 130
      (HK126); 138 (HK137); 143 (HK141); 257 (HK239); 283
      (HK272); 305, 306 (HK298)
    laughter, 21 (HK010); 34 (HK023); 40, 41 (HK031); 43
      (HK035); 58 (HK049)
    lies, 199 (HK193); 202 (HK195); 229, 230 (HK213); 356-358
      (HK341)

Index

motive(s), 5 (HK001); 38 (HK029); 83 (HK072); 127, 128 (HK126); 142, 143 (HK141); 247 (HK232); 255 (HK237); 258 (HK240); 261 (HK244); 312 (HK306); 342 (HK329); 346 (HK330); 358 (HK341)
    remark to sister, 70 (HK062)
    whereabouts, 24 (HK013); 33, 34 (HK023); 55 (HK047); 132 (HK131); 158 (HK149); 246 (HK231); 247 (HK232); 250, 251 (HK235); 258 (HK240); 315 (HK310); 331 (HK323); 357-359 (HK341)

BORDEN MURDERS
    blood,
        avoidance,
            apron, 5 (HK001); 39 (HK031); 49 (HK041); 58 (HK049); 82 (HK072)
            frock coat, Mr. Borden's, 250-252 (HK235)
            gossamer/waterproof, 52 (HK045); 60 (HK053); 65 (HK060); 74 (HK067); 92 (HK088); 132 (HK130); 231, 232 (HK214); 247 (HK232); 256 (HK238)
            gloves, 49 (HK040); 128 (HK126); 148, 151, 152 (HK142)
            handkerchief, 325 (HK316)
            long outside garment, 128 (HK126)
            male attire, 262 (HK245); 339-345, (HK329)
            nakedness, 251 (HK235); 259 (HK241); 261 (HK244); 262 (HK245); 351 (HK336)
            newspaper, 127 (HK124); 131 (HK128)
            overdress/wrapper, 43, 44 (HK035); 46 (HK039); 49 (HK040); 51 (HK043); 82 (HK072); 333 (HK326)
            pajamas, 70 (HK062)
            trousers, 339, 344, 345 (HK329)
        stains, 5 (HK001); 43 (HK035); 49 (HK041); 52 (HK045); 63 (HK057); 128, 130 (HK126); 143, 144 (HK141); 148 (HK142); 209 (HK200); 222 (HK208); 227 (HK211); 247 (HK232); 250-252 (HK235); 312 (HK306); 322, 324 (HK315); 325 (HK316); 331 (HK323); 334 (HK326); 346 (HK330); 348 (HK335)
    confessions, 22, 23 (HK012); 36, 37 (HK027)
    evidence, 28, 29 (HK016); 36 (HK026); 46 (HK038); 59 (HK051); 88 (HK080); 257 (HK238); 257 (HK239); 299 (HK291); 300 (HK294); 302 (HK297); 315 (HK310); 329, 330 (HK323)
        search, 5 (HK001); 27 (HK014); 39, 40 (HK031); 46 (HK039); 51 (HK043); 52 (HK046); 57 (HK048); 62 (HK054); 65 (HK060); 72 (HK063); 73 (HK066); 87 (HK079); 88 (HK080); 88 (HK081); 90 (HK085); 91, 92 (HK088); 135 (HK131); 142, 144 (HK141); 237 (HK218); 237 (HK219); 256 (HK238); 339, 341 (HK329); 357, 359

(HK341)
    eyewitness accounts, 147, 148, 151-153 (HK142)
    motives, 42 (HK033); 44 (HK035); 68, 69 (HK062); 135
        (HK131); 140 (HK139); 142,143 (HK141); 354 (HK339)
public opinion, 32 (HK020); 45 (HK037); 46 (HK038); 159
    (HK150); 236 (HK217); 241 (HK224); 265 (HK250); 284
    (HK273); 292 (HK281); 300 (HK294); 309, 310 (HK303); 326
    (HK319); 327 (HK320); 328 (HK322); 329 (HK323)
        on Miss Borden's guilt, 5 (HK001); 8 (HK005); 21
            (HK010); 38 (HK029); 39-41 (HK031); 46 (HK039); 49
            (HK040); 49 (HK041); 50 (HK042); 51 (HK043); 57, 58
            (HK048); 58, 59 (HK049); 63 (HK058); 64 (HK059);
            81-83 (HK072); 87 (HK079); 88 (HK080); 90 (HK085);
            140 (HK139); 141 (HK140); 142-144 (HK141); 158
            (HK149); 198-200 (HK193); 201, 202 (HK195); 229, 230
            (HK213); 230-232 (HK214); 235 (HK216); 237 (HK219);
            238, 239 (HK220); 240 (HK223); 241 (HK224); 241
            (HK225); 245, 246 (HK230); 246-248 (HK232); 249
            (HK234); 250-252, 255 (HK235); 255, 256 (HK237); 256
            (HK238); 258 (HK240); 259 (HK241); 261 (HK244); 262
            (HK245); 293 (HK283); 302, 305 (HK297); 326 (HK318)
            332 (HK324); 333 (HK325); 339-345 (HK329); 346
            (HK330); 348 (HK333); 348 (HK335); 351 (HK336);
            353-355 (HK339); 355 (HK340); 356-359 (HK341); 364
            (HK346)
        on Miss Borden's innocence, 22, 23 (HK012); 23, 24,
            27 (HK013); 29 (HK017); 29, 30 (HK018); 36, 37
            (HK027); 67-71 (HK062); 72 (HK064); 80, 81 (HK071);
            93 (HK091); 107 (HK104); 117 (HK112); 137 (HK136);
            233, 234 (HK215); 239 (HK221); 244 (HK228); 352
            (HK338)
rewards offered, 8 (HK005); 45 (HK037); 143 (HK141)
weapon,
    axe/hatchet, 7 (HK004); 8 (HK005); 21 (HK010); 24
        (HK013); 29 (HK016); 38 (HK029); 40 (HK031); 44
        (HK035); 46 (HK039); 49 (HK041); 50 (HK042); 51
        (HK043); 55 (HK047); 59 (HK051); 62 (HK055); 70
        (HK062); 74 (HK067); 76 (HK069); 80 (HK071); 87
        (HK079); 88 (HK080); 90 (HK085); 93 (HK091); 127
        (HK125); 131 (HK127);131 (HK128); 132 (HK129);
        136 (HK134); 139 (HK138); 140, 141 (HK140); 143, 144
        (HK141); 148, 151-153 (HK142); 199 (HK193); 201
        (HK195); 205 (HK200); 211, 212 (HK203); 222 (HK208);
        226 (HK211); 236 (HK216); 242 (HK226); 244 (HK228);
        245 (HK230); 310 (HK303); 312 (HK306); 322 (HK315);
        325 (HK316); 333, 334 (HK326); 339, 340, 344, 345

(HK329); 354 (HK339); 358 (HK341)
  new axe, 212 (HK203)
chisel, 55 (HK047)
chloroform used with, 79 (HK070), 143 (HK141)
concealment, 5 (HK001); 7 (HK004); 8 (HK005); 23 (HK012); 44 (HK035); 46 (HK039); 50 (HK042); 51 (HK043); 60 (HK053); 63 (HK057); 65 (HK060); 70 (HK062); 72 (HK063); 73 (HK066); 87 (HK079); 88 (HK080); 88 (HK081); 90 (HK085); 91, 92 (HK088); 127 (HK125); 128, 130 (HK126); 131 (HK127); 135 (HK131); 222 (HK208); 232 (HK214); 237 (HK218); 251 (HK235); 257 (HK239); 325 (HK316); 339, 340, 345 (HK329)
flat iron, 21 (HK010); 44 (HK036); 49, 50 (HK041); 55 (HK047); 60 (HK052); 62 (HK055); 63 (HK058); 136 (HK134); 334 (HK326); 351, 352 (HK337)
knife, 8 (HK005); 24 (HK013); 66 (HK061)
sharp instrument, 55, 56 (HK047); 111 (HK109); 113 (HK110); 115, 116 (HK111); 250 (HK235)

BORDEN MURDER TRIAL, 232-234 (HK215); 235 (HK216); 237 (HK219); 245 (HK229); 245 (HK230); 246, 247 (HK232); 248 (HK233); 249 (HK234); 256 (HK238); 257, 258 (HK240); 259, 260 (HK242); 260, 261 (HK244); 262, 263 (HK246); 272, 273 (HK259); 274 (HK261); 277, 278 (HK266); 332 (HK324)
  arrangements, 83, 84 (HK073); 120 (HK118); 122 (HK121); 122 (HK122); 157 (HK147); 158, 159 (HK150); 163 (HK159); 163,164 (HK160); 164, 165 (HK161); 168 (HK162); 168 (HK163); 171 (HK164);171, 172 (HK165); 172 (HK166); 175 (HK171); 177 (HK174); 179 (HK178); 180, 181 (HK180); 181 (HK181); 204 (HK198); 205, 206, 209 (HK200); 212, 213 (HK204)
  court/jury, criticism, 280 (HK270); 283 (HK272); 292 (HK282); 293 (HK284); 294 (HK285); 295, 296 (HK287); 297, 298 (HK289); 300 (HK294); 301 (HK296); 302, 305 (HK297); 308, 309 (HK301); 313 (HK307); 315, 316 (HK310); 319 (HK313); 329-332 (HK323)
  court stenographers, 175 (HK171); 198 (HK192); 200 (HK194); 202, 203 (HK196); 213 (HK204); 225 (HK209); 225 (HK210)
  experts called, 175 (HK171); 176 (HK172); 204 (HK198); 205, 206, 209 (HK200); 210 (HK201); 211 (HK202); 211, 212 (HK203); 221 (HK207)
  jurors, (Fall River, Mass), 164 (HK161)
  jury, 214-217 (HK205); 218-221 (HK206); 291 (HK280); 331 (HK323); 353, 355 (HK339)
  justices, 163 (HK160); 164, 167 (HK161); 171 (HK164)
    response to verdict,

agreed, 273 (HK260); 289 (HK278); 290 (HK280); 299
(HK292); 301 (HK296); 320 (HK314); 363 (HK345)
disagreed, 256 (HK237); 264 (HK248); 265 (HK250);
266, 267 (HK252); 271 (HK256); 271 (HK257); 273
(HK259); 276 (HK264); 278 (HK266); 280 (HK270); 283
(HK272); 284 (HK273); 286 (HK277); 289 (HK279); 291
(HK281); 293 (HK284); 294 (HK285); 295, 296
(HK287); 297, 298 (HK289); 299 (HK291); 300
(HK293); 300 (HK294); 304, 305 (HK297); 305, 306
(HK298); 310 (HK303); 312, 313 (HK307); 314
(HK309); 315, 316 (HK310); 319 (HK313); 324, 325
(HK316); 326 (HK318); 326 (HK319); 327 (HK320); 328
(HK321); 329-332 (HK323); 334, 335 (HK327); 360
(HK343); 363 (HK344)
  witnesses, 181 (HK181); 182-184 (HK182); 199 (HK193);
201, 202 (HK195)
  summoned, 185, 186 (HK183); 189, 190 (HK184); 191,
192 (HK185); 193, 194 (HK186)
BORDEN, SARAH ANTHONY (MORSE)
 (Mrs. Andrew Jackson Borden, 1st wife), 102, 105, 106
(HK102); 233, 234 (HK215)
BORDEN, SIMEON, JR., 112 (HK109); 114 (HK110); 116 (HK111)
BORDEN, THOMAS JAMES, 27 (HK014)
BOULDS, THOMAS, 191 (HK185)
BOWEN, PHOEBE VINCENT (MILLER)
 (Mrs. Seabury Warren Bowen), 50 (HK042); 183 (HK182); 191
(HK185)
BOWEN, SEABURY WARREN, 33, 34 (HK023); 50 (HK042); 117
(HK113); 141 (HK140); 182 (HK182); 193 (HK186); 228
(HK212); 231 (HK214); 237 (HK219); 249 (HK234); 340
(HK329); 354 (HK339)
BRAYTON, JOHN SUMMERFIELD, SR., 105 (HK102)
BRIGGS, CHARLES E., 214 (HK205)
BRIGHAM, DAVID SEWALL, 105 (HK102)
BRIGHTMAN, FRANK W., 74 (HK067)
BROWN, JEREMIAH N., 214 (HK205)
BROWN, THOMAS JOSEPH LEE, 191 (HK185)
BROWNELL, GILBERT K., 214 (HK205)
BUFFINTON HOUSE. See CHURCHILL, ADELAIDE (BUFFINTON),
house
BUNKER, AUGUSTUS, 148 (HK142)
BURRILL, JOHN THOMAS, 189 (HK184)
BURT, ANSEL O., 214 (HK205)
BURT, FRANK HUNT, 175 (HK171); 177 (HK174); 178 (HK176); 178
(HK177); 200 (HK194); 202, 203 (HK196); 225 (HK209); 225
(HK210); 320 (HK314)

Index

BUTLER, MADAME ROSILLA, HAIR GOODS
(131 & 132 Tremont Street, Boston, Mass.), 242 (HK226); 344 (HK329)
BUTLER, WILLIAM F., 214 (HK205)

CAPITAL PUNISHMENT, 38 (HK029); 330 (HK323)
CARPENTER, JOSEPH WILMARTH, JR., 99, 100 (HK098); 100 (HK099); 153, 154 (HK143)
CARR, WILLIAM, 106 (HK102)
CARTER, ROBERT H. 214 (HK205)
CASE, RESCOMB, 105 (HK102)
CATHERWOOD MYSTERY, THE (Southwick), 6 (HK003)
CHAGNON, M. MARTHE, 193 (HK186)
CHAGNON, MARIANNE (GIGAULT) PHANEUF
(Mrs. Wenceslaus Jean Baptiste Chagnon), 69 (HK062); 193 (HK186)
CHAGNON, WENCESLAUS JEAN BAPTISTE
house, 31 Third Street, Fall River, Mass., 75 (HK067)
CHASE, MARK P., 191 (HK185)
CHAUSSE, JOSEPH, 214 (HK205)
CHEEVER, DAVID WILLIAMS, 206 (HK200); 210 (HK201); 211, 212 (HK203)
CHURCH, CHARLES H., 183 (HK182)
CHURCHILL, ADELAIDE (BUFFINTON)
(Mrs. Charles Henry Churchill), 34 (HK023); 59 (HK049); 64 (HK059); 118 (HK114); 182 (HK182); 189 (HK184); 229 (HK213)
house, 90 Second St. Fall River, Mass, 75 (HK067); 152 (HK142)
CLARK, NATHAN, 214 (HK205)
CLARKSON, ALFRED, 193 (HK186)
CLEGG, JONATHAN, 189 (HK184)
CLIFTON, JIREH W., 214 (HK205)
COBB, MR. See COBB, WENDELL HAMLIN
COBB, GEORGE A., 214 (HK205)
COBB, JAMES H., 214 (HK205)
COBB, WENDELL HAMLIN, 38 (HK028)
COGGESHALL, ALEXANDER H., 189 (HK184)
COLE, FRANCIS GRANGER, 214 (HK205), 219 (HK206)
COLLETT, LUCIE, 185 (HK183)
CONE, DWIGHT ELEAZER, 10, 11 (HK008); 15, 16 (HK009); 55 (HK047)
CONNOR, THOMAS J., 151 (HK142)
CONNORS, PATRICK, 191 (HK185)
COOK, CHARLES H., 191 (HK185)

COOK, EVERETT M., 189 (HK184)
COONEY, PATRICK HENRY, 173 (HK168)
COSTELLO, MATTHEW, 214 (HK205)
COUGHLIN, JOHN WILLIAM, 42 (HK034); 182 (HK182); 193 (HK186)
COWLES, EDWARD, 86 (HK077)
CRANSTON, ORVILLE W., 214 (HK205)
CRAPO, MARGARET L. (WALLACE)
    (Mrs. John D. Crapo), 183 (HK182); 189 (HK184)
        servant of, 183 (HK182)
CROSSMAN, OLIVER H., 214 (HK205)
CUNDALL, BENJAMIN T., 214 (HK205)
CUNNEEN, JAMES E., 185 (HK183)
CUNNINGHAM, JOHN J., 185 (HK183)
CURIEN, GEORGE W., 214 (HK205)

DABNEY, LEWIS STACKPOLE, 289 (HK279)
DAMMON, SILAS D., 214 (HK205)
DAVIS, ELIHU M., 214 (HK205)
DAVIS, SELINA ANN (SMITH)
    (Mrs. George W. Davis, Sr.) 148 (HK142)
DAVIS, GEORGE W., 214 (HK205)
DAVOL, EZRA, 214 (HK205)
DEAN, ALBERT E., 214 (HK205)
DEAN, HENRY C., 214 (HK205)
DEAN, WILLIAM FRANCIS, 214 (HK205), 218 (HK206)
DELANO, ALEXANDER JAMES, 289 (HK279)
DESMOND, DENNIS, JR., 74, 75 (HK067); 191 (HK185)
DESROSIERS, JOSEPH, 193 (HK186)
DEVINE, JOHN J., 191 (HK185)
DEWEY, JUSTIN, 164 (HK161)
    post-trial reaction/critical, 274 (HK261); 283 (HK272); 293
        (HK283); 294 (HK285); 301 (HK296); 307 (HK299); 312, 313
        (HK307); 322 (HK315); 324 (HK316)
DIAS, CHARLES H., 215 (HK205)
DINNIE, JOHN, 185 (HK183)
DISCRIMINATION
    anti-Catholic, 61 (HK054); 117 (HK112)
    anti-Irish, 313 (HK307); 352 (HK338)
DIXON, JOHN W., 215 (HK205)
DOHERTY, PATRICK H., 191 (HK185)
DOLAN, WILLIAM ANDREW, 6 (HK002); 9 (HK007); 10, 11 (HK008);
    15, 16 (HK009); 55, 57 (HK047); 61 (HK054); 176 (HK172);
    182 (HK182); 193 (HK186); 199 (HK193); 201 (HK195); 209
    (HK200); 212 (HK203); 250 (HK235)
DONAGHY, THOMAS, JR., 215 (HK205)

Index

DOOLAN, MARY, 185 (HK183)
DOUGLAS, GEORGE L., 191 (HK185)
DOUGLASS, OSCAR R., 215 (HK205)
DOWNS, EDWARD P., 193 (HK186)
DRAPER, FRANK WINTHROP, 6 (HK002); 10 (HK008); 15 (HK009)
    55, 56 (HK047); 61 (HK054); 182 (HK182); 198, 199 (HK193);
    201 (HK195); 204 (HK198); 300 (HK293)
DRISCOLL, DANIEL F., 215 (HK205)
DRISCOLL, PETER M., 99 (HK098); 100 (HK099)
DRISCOLL, TIMOTHY W., 215 (HK205)
DRUG STORE, 199 (HK193), 202 (HK195)
    Smith, David R.,
    (135 South Main Street, Fall River, Mass.), 199 (HK193);
    202 (HK195); 358 (HK341)
DURFEE, MARYA (BENTLEY),
    (Mrs. Joseph Franklin Durfee), 193 (HK186)
DURLING, OLIVER H. PERRY, 191 (HK185)
DWIGHT, THOMAS, 206 (HK200); 210 (HK201)

EAGAN, JOHN J., 184 (HK182)
EARLE, THOMAS B., 215 (HK205)
EDDY, FRANCIS WILMARTH, 193 (HK186)
EDSON, FRANCIS L., 191 (HK185)
EDWARDS, WILLIS, 7 (HK004)

FALL RIVER, MASSACHUSETTS, reputation, 233 (HK215)
FERGUSON (unidentified person), 184 (HK182)
FESSENDEN, SUSAN BREESE (SNOWDEN)
    (Mrs. John Henry Fessenden), 85 (HK076)
FINN, JOHN C., 215 (HK205); 219 (HK206)
FISHER, DAVID, 215 (HK205)
FISK, GEORGE B., 5 (HK001)
FLEET, JOHN, 50 (HK042); 184 (HK182); 189 (HK184); 236
    (HK216); 237 (HK219); 356 (HK341)
FOLGER, CHARLES F., 215 (HK205)
FOREMAN, VICTORIA A. (BANKS)
    (Mrs. William S. Foreman), 154 (HK143)
FORRESTER, CHARLES F., 215 (HK205)
FRANCIS, MISS EDITH A., 184 (HK182)
FRANCIS, EZEKIEL P., 215 (HK205)
FRANCIS, FRANK W., 215 (HK205)

GALE, WILLIAM BOYNTON, 81 (HK071)

GARDNER, ORRIN AUGUSTUS, 193 (HK186)
GAY, GEORGE WASHINGTON, 176 (HK173); 180 (HK179)
GIBBS, SAMUEL WHELPLEY,
    house, 39 Third Street, Fall River, Mass., 75 (HK067)
GIFFORD, HANNAH H. (BORDEN)
    (Mrs. Perry Gifford), 189 (HK184)
GIFFORD, OLIVER E., 215 (HK205)
GLOBE STREET RAILWAY COMPANY
    (Fall River, Mass.), 74 (HK067); 147 (HK142)
GODFREY, GORDON H., 215 (HK205)
GORMLEY, ELIZABETH A. (BYRNE)
(Mrs. John H. Gormley), 189 (HK184)
GRAND JURY, 46 (HK038); 61 (HK054); 82 (HK072); 99 (HK097);
    101 (HK100);101 (HK101); 107 (HK104); 107 (HK105); 108
    (HK106); 109 (HK107); 111, 112 (HK109); 113, 114 (HK110);
    115, 116 (HK111); 118 (HK114); 158, 159 (HK150)
GRAVES, WILLIAM, 215 (HK205)
GRAY, ELIZABETH ANN (HOWARD)
    (Mrs. Nathaniel P. Gray), 102 (HK102)
GRAY, JANE B. (NEGUS)
    (Mrs. Ellery Gray), 189 (HK184)
GRAY, MISS SARAH}, 184 (HK182)
GREENE, CHESTER WASHINGTON, 106 (HK102)
GREENE, OLNEY, 215 (HK205)
GRINNELL, EBEN S., 215 (HK205)
GROSS, HENRY M., 215 (HK205)
GRUNDY JAMES, 215 (HK205)
GUILD, JASON T., 215 (HK205)
GUSHEC, EDWIN, 215 (HK205)
GUSTIN, GEORGE A., 215 (HK205)

HACKING, WILLIAM L., 191 (HK185)
HAGGERTY, TIMOTHY, BOOTS AND SHOES
    (96 Davol Street, Fall River, Mass.), 148 (HK142)
HALL, A. O., 215 (HK205)
HALL, LOUIS L., 189 (HK184)
HAMMETT, JOHN F., 215 (HK205)
HAMMOND, JOHN WILKES, 164 (HK160); 167 (HK161); 168 (HK163)
HANDY, BENJAMIN JONES, 69, 70 (HK062); 193 (HK186); 229
    (HK212)
HARRINGTON, HIRAM C., 183 (HK182); 185 (HK183); 332 (HK323)
HARRINGTON, PHILIP, 184 (HK182); 189 (HK184)
HARRIS, DR., 6 (HK002)
HART, ABRAHAM GIFFORD, 102 (HK102); 182 (HK182); 189 (HK184)
HART, CHARLES SUMNER, 147, 151, 153 (HK142)

Index

HART, FREDERICK BRADFORD, 185 (HK183)
HATCH, JOSEPH W., 215 (HK205)
HATHAWAY, CHARLES F., 215 (HK205)
HATHAWAY, GEORGE E., 215 (HK205)
HATHAWAY, GEORGE W., 193 (HK186)
HATHAWAY, JOSEPH W., 215 (HK205)
HATHAWAY, STEPHEN A., 215 (HK205)
HEARINGS, 28 (HK016); 35 (HK025); 44 (HK035); 45, 46 (HK038);
    50 (HK042); 79-81 (HK071); 137 (HK136); 141 (HK140); 198
    (HK193); 201 (HK195); 250 (HK235); 305 (HK298)
HERVEY, ELIPHALET W., 215 (HK205)
HILL, EDMUND E., 215 (HK205)
HILL, MISS LUCY C., 148 (HK142)
HILLIARD, RUFUS BARTLETT, 28 (HK015); 33 (HK023); 42 (HK034);
    73 (HK065); 74 (HK067); 94 (HK092); 153 (HK142); 184
    (HK182); 185 (HK183); 197 (HK191); 258 (HK240); 334
    (HK327)
HODGES, HENRY A., 215 (HK205)
HODGES, LEWIS BRADFORD, 215 (HK205); 219 (HK206)
HOLLAND, MRS. See HOWLAND, ANNIE HOWARD (GRAY)
HOLMES, CHARLES JARVIS, 96 (HK095)
HOLMES, JOHN HENRY, 107 (HK105)
HOPKINS, HAROLD V., 215 (HK205)
HORTON, DEXTER E., JR., 215 (HK205)
HORTON, GILBERT M., 216 (HK205)
HORTON, JOSIAH T., 216 (HK205)
HOWARD, JOSEPH, 320 (HK314)
HOWE, GEORGE A., 216 (HK205)
HOWLAND, ANNIE HOWARD (GRAY)
    (Mrs. John J. Howland), 102 (HK102)
HOWLAND, GIDEON, 216 (HK205)
HOXIE, HENRY M., 216 (HK205)
HURD. FREDERICK ELLSWORTH, 92, 93 (HK090); 119 (HK116)
HYDE, JOSEPH, 191 (HK185)

INQUEST, 22 (HK011); 42 (HK034); 63 (HK058); 80 (HK071);
    176 (HK172); 195 (HK188); 196 (HK189); 196 (HK190); 277
    (HK266)

JEFFERSON BORDEN, SCHOONER, MUTINY OF, 27 (HK014)
JELLY, GEORGE FREDERICK, 41 (HK032)
JENNEY, HENRY P., 216 (HK205)
JENNINGS, ANDREW JACKSON, 83 (HK073); 84 (HK074); 96 (HK096)
    99 (HK097); 100 (HK099); 120 (HK117); 122 (HK122); 155

(HK145);159 (HK151); 161 (HK154); 162 (HK156); 164
    (HK160); 168 (HK163); 176 (HK172); 180 (HK180); 181
    (HK181); 195 (HK188); 256 (HK237)
JOHNSON, ALFRED C., 193 (HK186)
JOHNSTON, MISS ELIZABETH MURRAY, 185 (HK183)

KELLY (unidentified boy), 151 (HK142)
KELLY, MARY CAROLINE (CANTWELL)
    (Mrs. Michael Kelly), 182 (HK182)
        servant of, 33 (HK023); 183 (HK183)
KELLY, MICHAEL
    house, 96 Second Street, Fall River, Mass., 75, (HK067);
        152 (HK142)
KENYON, HENRY W., 216 (HK205)
KIERAN, THOMAS, 189 (HK184)
KILROY, FRANK H., 191 (HK185)
KING, GEORGE F., 216 (HK205)
KIRBY, ARUBA P. (TRIPP)
    (Mrs. Uriah Kirby), 185 (HK183)
KNIGHT, CHARLES W., 216 (HK205)
KNOWLTON, HOSEA MORRILL
    advice to prosecution, 5 (HK001); 21 (HK010); 39-41
        (HK031); 46 (HK038); 51 (HK044); 52 (HK045); 57, 58,
        (HK048); 60 (HK053); 64 (HK059); 65 (HK060); 67-71
        (HK062); 72 (HK063); 73 (HK066); 87 (HK079); 88 (HK080)
        88 (HK081); 90 (HK085); 91, 92 (HK088); 117 (HK113); 140,
        141 (HK140); 198-200 (HK193); 201, 202 (HK195); 205, 206
        (HK200); 222 (HK208); 237 (HK218); 245 (HK226); 245
        (HK229); 246 (HK231); 249 (HK234); 256, 257 (HK238); 257
        258 (HK240); 261 (HK244); 263 (HK246); 293 (HK284); 351,
        352 (HK337); 352 (HK338)
    circular suggested, 59 (HK051); 61 (HK054)
    family, 118 (HK114); 179 (HK178); 180 (HK179); 196 (HK189);
        260 (HK244); 289 (HK279); 293 (HK283); 311 (HK304); 320
        (HK314)
    letters written by, 28 (HK015); 32 (HK021); 32 (HK022);
        35, 36 (HK025); 42, 43 (HK034); 59 (HK051); 74 (HK067);
        76 (HK069); 89 (HK082); 89 (HK083); 92 (HK089); 96
        (HK096); 99 (HK097); 108 (HK106); 118 (HK114); 120
        (HK118); 123 (HK123); 158, 159 (HK150); 160 (HK152); 161
        (HK155); 174 (HK170); 176 (HK172); 177 (HK174); 178
        (HK177);179 (HK178); 204 (HK198); 210 (HK201)
    post-trial reactions,
        favorable, 263 (HK247); 264 (HK248); 264, 265 (HK249);
            265 (HK250); 266 (HK251); 266, 267 (HK252); 267

Index

(HK253); 267, 268 (HK254); 268 (HK255); 271 (HK256); 271 (HK257); 272 (HK258); 272, 273 (HK259); 273 (HK260); 274 (HK261); 276 (HK263); 276 (HK264); 277 (HK265); 277, 278 (HK266); 278 (HK267); 279 (HK268); 279 (HK269); 280 (HK270); 280 (HK271); 283 (HK272); 284 (HK273); 284, 285 (HK274); 285 (HK275); 285 (HK276); 286 (HK277); 286, 289 (HK278); 289 (HK279); 290, 291 (HK280); 291, 292 (HK281); 292 (HK282); 292, 293 (HK283); 294 (HK285); 294, 295 (HK286); 295, 296 (HK287); 296 (HK288); 297, 298 (HK289); 298, 299 (HK290); 299 (HK291); 299 (HK292); 300 (HK293); 300 (HK294); 301 (HK295); 301, 302 (HK296); 302, 305 (HK297); 305, 306 (HK298); 306, 307 (HK299); 308 (HK300); 308, 309 (HK301); 309 (HK302); 309, 310 (HK303); 310, 311 (HK304); 311 (HK305); 312, 313 (HK307); 313 (HK308); 314 (HK309); 315, 316 (HK310); 316 (HK311); 319 (HK312); 319 (HK313); 322 (HK315); 324,325 (HK316); 325 (HK317); 326 (HK318); 326 (HK319); 327 (HK320); 328 (HK321); 328, 329 (HK322); 329 (HK323); 334, 335 (HK327); 360 (HK343); 363 (HK344)
    critical, 335 (HK328)
  pre-trial opinions,
    favorable, 65 (HK060); 66 (HK061); 71 (HK062); 72 (HK063); 91 (HK088); 107 (HK104); 346 (HK330)
    critical, 23, 24, 27 (HK013); 29, 30 (HK018); 72 (HK064); 137 (HK136); 260 (HK243); 348 (HK334); 360 (HK342)
  reluctance to take case, 158, 159 (HK150)
KNOWLTON, LINCOLN BROWN, 286 (HK277)
KNOWLTON, SYLVIA BASSETT (ALMY)
  (Mrs. Hosea Morrill Knowlton), 289 (HK279); 293 (HK283); 311 (HK304); 360 (HK343)
KNOWLTON, THOMAS, 286 (HK277)

LAMPHIER, CHARLES, 216 (HK205)
LANE, DWIGHT F., 216 (HK205)
LAWTON, FREDERICK E., 216 (HK205)
LEACH, HARRY J, 216 (HK205)
LEAD, 9 (HK006); 21 (HK010); 357 (HK341)
LEARY, JOHN HURLEY, 10 (HK008); 15 (HK009); 55 (HK047)
LEARY, KATE, 189 (HK184) ,
LEONARD, GUSTAVUS D., 216 (HK205)
LEWIS, JAMES A., 216 (HK205)
LINCOLN, HARRISON T., 216 (HK205)
LINCOLN, LLOYD S., 216 (HK205)
LIVERMORE, MARY ASHTON (RICE),

(Mrs. David P. Livermore), 252, 255 (HK235); 255 (HK236)
LONG, JOHN DAVIS, 174 (HK169)
LORRIGAN, PATRICK F., 189 (HK184)
LOVELL, ARTHUR T., 198 (HK192); 200 (HK194)
LUBINSKY, HYMAN, 36 (HK027)
LYNCH, GEORGE, 216 (HK205)

MC CARTHY, JOHN F., 216 (HK205)
MC GOWAN, PATRICK, 189 (HK184)
MC HENRY, EDWIN D., 37 (HK028); 91 (HK087); 92 (HK089); 94
     (HK092); 197 (HK191)
MC HENRY, NELLIE S.
     (Mrs. Edwin D. McHenry), 33-35 (HK023)
MC KEON, THOMAS, 216 (HK205)
MACOMBER, HENRY B., 216 (HK205)
MACOMBER, MARY C., 184 (HK182)
MAGGIE. See SULLIVAN, BRIDGET
MANCHESTER, BERTHA M. See MURDERS/ CRIMES/ LEGAL CASES,
                              UNRELATED
MANLEY, DELIA SUMMERS (MANCHESTER)
(Mrs. Seabury T. Manley), 70 (HK062); 191 (HK185)
MARSTON, MR. See MARSTON, GEORGE
MARSTON, GEORGE, 37, 38 (HK028)
MARTIN, WILLIAM R., 191 (HK185)
MASON, ALBERT, 163 (HK159); 163, 164 (HK160); 168 (HK163);
     171, 172 (HK165); 297 (HK289)
MASSACHUSETTS BAR, 293 (HK283); 308, 309 (HK301); 326 (HK319)
MASSACHUSETTS REFORMATORY, 147, 151, 153 (HK142)
MATHER, JAMES, 189 (HK184)
MEDLEY, WILLIAM H., 28 (HK015); 43 (HK034); 184 (HK182); 186
     (HK183); 189, 190 (HK184); 229 (HK212)
MICHAEL (unidentified person), 184 (HK182)
MILLER, SOUTHARD HARRISON, 102, 105 (HK102)
MILLIKEN, GEORGE H., 216 (HK205)
MILLS, WILLIAM J., 216 (HK205)
MOODY, WILLIAM HENRY, 140 (HK140); 172 (HK166); 173 (HK167);
     174 (HK170); 176 (HK173); 179 (HK178); 195 (HK187); 196
     (HK189); 204 (HK198); 206 (HK200); 210 (HK201); 211
     (HK202); 213 (HK204); 229 (HK212); 232 (HK214); 263
     (HK247); 267, 268 (HK254); 289 (HK278); 307 (HK299); 311
     (HK305); 332 (HK324)
MORSE, ANTHONY, 102, 105 (HK102)
MORSE, ELIJAH ADAMS, 290, 291 (HK280)
MORSE FAMILY, 102, 105, 106 (HK102)
MORSE, JOHN VINNICUM, 7 (HK004); 8 (HK005); 24 (HK013); 33,

34 (HK023); 43 (HK035); 62 (HK056); 68, 70 (HK062); 82 (HK072); 102 (HK102); 119 (HK115); 128-131 (HK126); 131 (HK128); 142 (HK141); 182 (HK182); 185 (HK183); 230 (HK213); 231 (HK214); 249 (HK234); 250, 252 (HK235); 290, 291 (HK280); 332 (HK324); 340-343, 345 (HK329)
MORSE, SARAH ANTHONY. See BORDEN, SARAH ANTHONY (MORSE)
MOSHER, AUGUSTUS M., 216 (HK205)
MULLALY, MICHAEL, 184 (HK182); 191 (HK185); 237 (HK219)
MUNROE, WILLARD B., 216 (HK205)
MURDERS/CRIMES/LEGAL CASES, UNRELATED, 27 (HK014); 38 (HK029); 40 (HK031); 52 (HK046); 65, 66 (HK060); 75 (HK068); 80 (HK071); 81 (HK072); 84 (HK073); 85 (HK075); 93 (HK091); 99 (HK098); 135 (HK131); 135 (HK133); 139 (HK138); 143 (HK141); 167 (HK161); 173 (HK168); 174 (HK169); 212 (HK203); 233, 234 (HK215); 243 (HK227); 255, 256 (HK237); 274 (HK261); 275 (HK262); 279 (HK268); 295 (HK286); 299 (HK291); 306, 307 (HK299); 323 (HK315); 352 (HK338); 335 (HK339)
    Avery, Ephraim Kingsbury, 66 (HK060)
    Manchester, Bertha M., 353 (HK339)
MURPHY, EDWARD M., 216 (HK205)

NEWBURY, AUDERHILL, 32 (HK022); 35 (HK024)
NEWSPAPERS
    Albany Argus, 324 (HK316)
    Boston Globe, 22 (HK011); 76 (HK069); 307 (HK299); 320 320 (HK314); 346 (HK331)
    Boston Herald, 76 (HK069); 100 (HK100); 101 (HK101); 106 106 (HK103); 107 (HK105); 173 (HK168); 174 (HK169); 259 (HK242); 264 (HK249); 273 (HK259); 295 (HK287); 307 (HK299); 320 (HK314)
    Boston Journal, 80 (HK071); 109 (HK107); 137 (HK136); 290 (HK280); 307 (HK299); 313 (HK307); 327 (HK320)
    Boston Record, 91 (HK087); 179 (HK178); 321 (HK315)
    Boston Transcript, 326 (HK319)
    Concord Enterprise, 81 (HK071)
    Fall River Globe, 73 (HK065); 108 (HK106); 257 (HK238)
    Hartford Post, 272 (HK259)
    Herald, 345 (HK329)
    Hingham Journal, 79 (HK071)
    Moosup Journal, 79 (HK071)
    Newburgh Daily News, 324 (HK316)
    News, The, 30, (HK018)
    New York Herald, 76 (HK069)
    New York Post, 315 (HK310)

New York Press, 43 (HK031)
New York Sun, 324 (HK316)
New York Tribune, 229 (HK213); 236 (HK216); 236 (HK217)
Philadelphia Inquirer, 315 (HK310)
Philadelphia Times, 315 (HK310)
Providence Journal, 135 (HK131); 299 (HK291); 324 (HK315)
Providence paper (unspecified), 297 (HK289)
Providence Telegram, 259 (HK242)
Republican, 333 (HK326)
St. Louis Globe Democrat, 31 (HK020)
Standard, 108 (HK106)
NICHOLSON, ROBERT, 189 (HK184)
NYE, GEORGE E., 216 (HK205)

OAK GROVE CEMETERY (Fall River, Mass.), 10 (HK008); 55 (HK047)
OESTING, F. WILLIAM, 216 (HK205)
O'LEARY, JAMES, JR., 216 (HK205)
O'NEIL (unidentified girl), 33 (HK023)

PALMER, LYMAN, 216 (HK205)
PARKER, FREDERICK, 216 (HK205)
PASEL, FRANCIS H., 216 (HK205)
PEARCE, HARRY C., 191 (HK185)
PEASE, JAMES H., 216 (HK205)
PEASE, WALTER, 216 (HK205)
PECKHAM, ANNIE F., 191 (HK185)
PEDDLER. See LUBINSKY, HYMAN
PELTIER, JOSEPH, 216 (HK205)
PERRON, ADELARD, 193 (HK186)
PETTEY, GEORGE AMBROSE, 105 (HK102); 191 (HK185); 353 (HK339)
Phineas Redux (Trollope), 316 (HK310)
PICKERING, FREDERICK A., 189 (HK184)
PILLSBURY, ALBERT ENOCH, 7 (HK005); 9 (HK007); 32 (HK021); 32 (HK022); 35 (HK024); 35 (HK025); 39 (HK030); 42 (HK034); 57 (HK047); 59 (HK051); 74 (HK067); 75 (HK068); 76 (HK069); 84 (HK074); 87 (HK078); 89 (HK082); 89 (HK083); 89 (HK084); 90 (HK086); 92 (HK089); 95 (HK094); 95 (HK095); 96 (HK096); 99 (HK097); 106 (HK103); 107 (HK104); 108 (HK106); 118 (HK114);119 (HK115); 120 (HK118); 121 (HK120); 122 (HK121);123 (HK123);131 (HK127); 136,137 (HK136); 154 (HK144); 155 (HK145); 156 (HK147); 157 (HK149); 158 (HK150); 160 (HK152); 160 (HK154); 161 (HK156); 162 (HK158); 164,167 (HK161); 168 (HK162); 174 (HK170); 176

(HK172); 177 (HK174); 177 (HK175), 178 (HK177); 179 (HK178); 197 (HK191); 201 (HK195); 204 (HK198); 204 (HK199); 210 (HK201); 307 (HK299)
    illness, 123 (HK123); 157 (HK148); 172 (HK166); 176 (HK173); 180 (HK179); 213 (HK204)

PILLSBURY, LOUISE F. (JOHNSON) WHEELER (Mrs. Albert Enoch Pillsbury), 123 (HK123)

POISON
    poison (other than prussic acid), 31 (HK019); 33 (HK023); 40 (HK031); 82 (HK072); 93 (HK091);135 (HK131); 142, 143 (HK141); 228 (HK212); 231 (HK214); 275 (HK262); 339, 345 (HK329); 354 (HK339)
        prussic acid, 30, 31 (HK019); 57, 58 (HK048); 71 (HK062); 76 (HK069); 142, 143 (HK141); 183 (HK182); 199 (HK193); 201, 202 (HK195); 322 (HK315); 332 (HK324); 333 (HK326); 334 (HK327); 341 (HK329); 358 (HK341)

POLICE/DETECTIVES, 23, 24 (HK013); 29 (HK017); 29, 30 (HK018); 37 (HK027); 42 (HK033); 74, 75 (HK067); 137 (HK136); 141 (HK140); 184 (HK182); 222 (HK208); 237 (HK219); 305 (HK297); 307 (HK299); 313 (HK307); 322 (HK315); 346 (HK330)

POOLE, MISS CARRIE, 184 (HK182)

PORTER, EDWIN H., 73 (HK065)

POTTER, GEORGE, 216 (HK205); 220 (HK206)

PRATT, HENRY N., 216 (HK205)

PRESS, 29 (HK017); 41 (HK031); 46 (HK038); 49 (HK040); 49 (HK041); 61 (HK054); 76 (HK069); 82, 83 (HK072); 91 (HK087);101 (HK100); 101 (HK101); 107 (HK105);108 (HK106); 109 (HK107); 109, 110 (HK108); 118 (HK114); 136, 137 (HK136); 138 (HK137); 179 (HK178); 196 (HK189); 200 (HK194); 202, 203 (HK196); 241 (HK224); 257, 258 (HK240); 267 (HK254); 271 (HK256); 274 (HK261); 277 (HK266); 285 (HK276); 292 (HK281); 293 (HK283); 293 (HK284); 294 (HK285); 295 (HK286); 295, 296 (HK287); 301 (HK296); 305 (HK298); 307 (HK299); 309, 310 (HK303); 312, 313 (HK307); 315 (HK310); 319 (HK312); 320 (HK314); 326 (HK318); 326 (HK319); 328 (HK321); 332 (HK324); 347 (HK331)

REAGAN, HANNAH B. (HOWE),
    (Mrs. Quinlan M. Reagan), 185 (HK183); 298 (HK289); 340 (HK329)

RELIGIOUS REFERENCES, 69 (HK062); 81, 82 (HK072); 239 (HK221); 246, 247 (HK232); 255, 256 (HK237); 314 (HK309); 319 (HK313)

RICHARDS, CHARLES I., 216 (HK205); 218 (HK206)

RICHARDSON, MAURICE HOWE, 206 (HK200); 210 (HK201)
RILEY, JOHN, 191 (HK185)
ROBINSON, GEORGE DEXTER, 157 (HK148); 159 (HK151); 160
    (HK153); 162 (HK157); 163 (HK159); 175 (HK171); 206
    (HK200); 235 (HK216); 256 (HK237); 259, 260 (HK242); 263
    (HK246); 274 (HK262); 291 (HK280); 297, 298 (HK289); 332
    (HK324); 364 (HK346)
        post-trial reactions/critical, 263 (HK247); 264 (HK249);
            266, 267 (HK252); 267, 268 (HK254); 271 (HK257); 273
            (HK259); 274 (HK261); 277 (HK266); 278 (HK267); 280
            (HK271); 285 (HK274); 285 (HK276); 293 (HK283); 297,
            298 (HK289); 302 (HK297); 307 (HK299); 308 (HK301); 315
            (HK310); 322 (HK315); 329 (HK323)
ROBINSON, JOHN, CONFECTIONERY
    (112 Second Street, Fall River, Mass.), 147, 148 (HK142)
ROGERS, MR., 177 (HK175)
ROGERS, CARRIE E. BROWN, 185 (HK183)
ROGERS, HENRY MONROE, 242 (HK226)
ROSE, EUGENE F., 216 (HK205)
ROUNSEVILLE, CYRUS COLE, 185 (HK183)
RUSSELL, MISS ALICE MANLEY, 118 (HK114); 182 (HK182); 185
    (HK183); 229 (HK213); 336 (HK216); 251 (HK235); 325
    (HK316); 345 (HK329); 351 (HK337)
RUSSELL, AUGUSTUS S., 216 (HK205)

SARGENT, FRANK E., COMPANY
    (90 North Main Street, Fall River, Mass.), 33 (HK023)
SAWYER, CHARLES S., 182 (HK182); 185 (HK183); 257 (HK238)
SEARLES, MORTIMER, 216 (HK205)
SEAVER, CHARLES L., 216 (HK205)
SHORTSLEEVES, JOSEPH, 182 (HK182); 189 (HK184)
SINKERS, 42 (HK034); 334 (HK327); 347 (HK333); 357 (HK341)
SLOCUM, WALTER C., 217 (HK205)
SMITH, ALFRED A., 147, 148, 151-153 (HK142)
SMITH, ELIJAH, 217 (HK205)
SMITH, GEORGE E., 217 (HK205)
SPRINGER, O. T., 217 (HK205)
STAFFORD, JAMES COGGESHALL, 102 (HK102)
STANTON BROTHERS BOOTS AND SHOES
    (109 South Main Street, Fall River, Mass.), 147, 152 (HK142)
STAPLES, JOHN F., 217 (HK205)
STRANGE MAN, 7 (HK004); 8 (HK005); 24 (HK013); 37 (HK028);
    43, 44 (HK035); 51 (HK043); 58, 59 (HK049); 69, 70 (HK062);
    117 (HK113); 128-130 (HK126); 132 (HK129); 138 (HK137); 139
    (HK138); 142, 143 (HK141); 228 (HK212); 238, 239 (HK220);

Index

239 (HK221); 244 (HK228); 262 (HK245); 330, 331 (HK323); 352 (HK338)
    Chinese man, 59 (HK050)
    Portuguese man, 353 (HK339)
    "Western men," 130 (HK126)
STURDY, H. K, 217 (HK205)
SULLIVAN, BRIDGET ("Maggie"), 5 (HK001); 24 (HK013); 33-35 (HK023); 40, 41 (HK031); 42 (HK033); 43, 44 (HK035); 45 (HK037); 58, 59 (HK049); 61 (HK054); 62, 63 (HK056); 65 (HK060); 68, 69 (HK062); 74 (HK067); 81-83 (HK072); 92 (HK088); 105 (HK102); 117 (HK112); 118 (HK114); 128-130 (HK126); 132 (HK129); 135 (HK131);139(HK138);142,143 (HK141); 155 (HK149);176(HK172);182 (HK182);195 (HK188); 196 (HK189); 196, 197 (HK190); 227, 228 (HK212); 229 (HK213); 230-232(HK214); 246 (HK231); 250-252 (HK235) 298 (HK289); 331, 332 (HK323); 333 (HK326); 346 (HK330); 347 (HK333); 351 (HK337); 352 (HK338); 354 (HK339); 356-359 (HK341)
    previous employers,
        Read, Mrs. Sophia (Ladd), 34 (HK023)
        Remington, Clinton Van Santvoort, 34 (HK023)
SULLIVAN, DENNIS F., 189 (HK184)
SWIFT, AUGUSTUS, 217 (HK205); 218 (HK206)
SWIFT, EZRA J., 217 (HK205)

TABER, EDWARD S., 217 (HK205)
TABER, JOHN H., 217 (HK205)
TAUNTON JAIL
    (Taunton, Mass.), 122 (HK121)
THOMAS, PHILIP, 217 (HK205)
THOMAS, TISH ("Titia"), 242 (HK226); 344 (HK329)
THURSTON, THATCHER THAYER, 73 (HK065)
TINGLEY, LEON H., 217 (HK205)
TINKHAM, DAVID B., 217 (HK205)
TINKHAM, OTIS, 217 (HK205)
"TITIA." See THOMAS, TISH.
"TOBACCO SPOT," 241 (HK224)
TRICKEY, HENRY G., 91 (HK087); 92 (HK089); 92 (HK090); 118 (HK114); 119 (HK116); 121 (HK120)
TUCKER, GEORGE FOX, 37 (HK028)

VISIONARIES/SPIRITUALISTS, 5 (HK001); 6, 7 (HK004); 7, 8 (HK005); 63 (HK057); 239, 240 (HK221); 333 (HK325); 339-345 (HK329)

WADE, JOHN T., 217 (HK205)
WALKER, NATHAN O., 217 (HK205)
WASHBURN, CYRUS, 217 (HK205)
WEAVER, THOMAS H., 217 (HK205)
WESTCOTT, WILLIAM, 217 (HK205); 221 (HK206)
WHALON, DANIEL, 217 (HK205)
WHEELER, GEORGE H., 217 (HK205)
WHEELER, SIMEON A., 217 (HK205)
WHITE, ANNIE M., 183 (HK182)
WHITEHEAD, SARAH BERTHA (GRAY)
    (Mrs. George W. Whitehead), 105 (HK102); 185 (HK183)
WILBAR, FREDERICK C. See WILBUR, FREDERICK COPELAND.
WILBER, LEMUEL K. See WILBUR, LEMUEL KEITH.
WILBUR, FREDERICK COPELAND, 217 (HK205); 220 (HK206)
WILBUR, JOHN, 217 (HK205); 220 (HK206)
WILBUR, LEMUEL KEITH, 217 (HK205); 220 (HK206)
WILCOX, ALBERT M., 217 (HK205)
WILDER, JIM, 344 (HK329)
WILDER, SUSY, 344 (HK329)
WILLIAMS, JOHN T., 217 (HK205)
WILLIS, WILLIAM H., 217 (HK205)
WING, ANJEANETTE (WILBUR)
    (Mrs. Joseph Wing), 191 (HK185)
WINSLOW, GEORGE, 217 (HK205)
WINSLOW, LEANDER A., 184 (HK182)
WIXON, FRANCIS H., 185 (HK183)
WOMEN, REFERENCES TO, 24, 27 (HK013); 29 (HK017); 40 (HK031);
    49 (HK041); 51 (HK044); 64 (HK059); 107 (HK104); 132
    (HK130); 136 (HK134); 139 (HK138); 139, 140 (HK139); 158
    (HK149); 198, 199 (HK193); 201 (HK195); 212 (HK203); 222
    (HK208); 227 (HK211); 240 (HK223); 244 (HK228); 245, 246
    (HK230); 250, 252 (HK235); 301 (HK296); 305 (HK298);
    320-S24 (HK315); 346 (HK330); 354 (HK339)
WOMAN'S CHRISTIAN TEMPERANCE UNION (W.C.T.U.), 85 (HK076)
    323, 324 (HK315)
WOOD, EDWARD STICKNEY, 46 (HK038); 46 (HK039); 58 (HK049);
    59 (HK051); 61 (HK054); 74 (HK067); 80 (HK071); 182
    (HK182); 204 (HK198); 242 (HK226); 322 (HK315)
WOOD, GEORGE A., 217 (HK205)
WORDELL, ALLEN H., 217 (HK205); 219, 220 (HK206)
WORDELL, ISAAC B., 192 (HK185); 194 (HK186)
WRIGHT, MR. See WRIGHT, EDWARD E.
WRIGHT, EDWARD E., 183 (HK182); 358 (HK341)
WRIGHT, MARY JANE (IRVING),
    (Mrs. Andrew Robeson Wright), 122 (HK121)
WYATT, MARY B., 193 (HK186)

www.ingramcontent.com/pod-product-compliance
Lightning Source LLC
Chambersburg PA
CBHW070157240426
43671CB00007B/475